Swimming against the Tide

Swimming against the Tide
TROTSKYISTS IN GERMAN OCCUPIED FRANCE

Yvan Craipeau

translated by David Broder

MERLIN PRESS
in association with
SOCIALIST PLATFORM

Published in 2013 by
Merlin Press Ltd
6 Crane Street Chambers
Crane Street
Pontypool
NP4 6ND
Wales
www.merlinpress.co.uk

in association with
Socialist Platform Ltd
www.revolutionaryhistory.co.uk

First published in French in 1977 by Savelli, Paris as
Contre vents et marées

© Sylvie and Jean-Loup Craipeau

© this translation, David Broder, 2013

ISBN. 978-0-85036-658-7

British Library Cataloguing in Publication Data
is available from the British Library

All rights reserved. No part of this publication may be reproduced, stored in a retrieval system, or transmitted, in any form or by any means, electronic, mechanical, photocopying, recording or otherwise, without the prior permission of the publisher.

Printed in the UK by Imprint Digital, Exeter

CONTENTS

Translator's introduction — 7

Introduction — 23

Chapter 1: Before the war — 27

Chapter 2: The phoney war — 55

Chapter 3: A time of confusion — 82

Chapter 4: Hitler attacks the USSR — 113

Chapter 5: 1943 – The turning point — 172

Chapter 6: Working-class struggles and the armed struggle — 199

Chapter 7: The first cracks in Europe — 231

Chapter 8: Towards 'Liberation' — 257

Afterword: What kind of liberation? — 291

Appendix: The surviving collection of *Arbeiter und Soldat*, and a fragment of *Der Arbeiter* — 293

Notes — 343

Index — 379

TRANSLATOR'S INTRODUCTION

David Broder

Class struggle in the Second World War

Four years after France's capitulation to Nazi Germany, a general strike broke out in Marseille, the country's second city. The Vichy régime of Marshal Philippe Pétain was hated for its collaboration with Hitler, but the spark for the eruption of protest on 24 May 1944 was the cutting of the bread ration to 150 grams a day. Factories went silent; shops did not open; there were no cars on the streets. The movement was so strong that the Wehrmacht troops dared not open fire on the strikers. But things did not go on like this. An American bombing-raid on the morning of 27 May flattened large parts of the city, killing 1,752[1] people and destroying ten thousand homes. The protests ceased.

These events point to the twin political challenges that revolutionaries faced in the Second World War. On the one hand there was the immense human tragedy of war, the blind, senseless killing of millions of working-class people by rival war machines. On the other hand, there was the dilemma of how to fight fascism without simply handing power to Winston Churchill, Charles de Gaulle and Franklin Roosevelt – or Joseph Stalin.

In recent times, the Great Depression had brought poverty for millions; fascists, supported by captains of industry, had come to power and crushed the workers' movement from Berlin to Milan and Barcelona; and a resumption of hostilities between the great powers again dragged the world into conflict, barely twenty years after the First World War, the so-called 'war to end all wars'. However, for many, the only visible alternative to the dominant capitalist system was Stalin's Soviet Union.

Trotskyists, those who opposed both the Stalinists and the British and French colonial empires alike, were, certainly, few in number. They struggled to make themselves heard. But despite their limited numbers, their activity points to oft-ignored aspects of the Second World War. If popular and conventional memory of the conflict largely focuses on revering the generals who changed history and mourning the innocents passively taken to their terrible fate in the camps, some working-class people were more than victims of events, more than mere cannon-fodder. From the February 1941 general strike in Amsterdam to the 1943 Warsaw Ghetto uprising, the French and Belgian workers' strikes against deportations to Germany and the huge workers' movements in northern Italy which helped to bring down Mussolini, hundreds of thousands of people were prepared to take action in spite of severe repression.

These struggles lent some credibility to Trotskyists' hopes that the conclusion of the Second World War would coincide with a revolutionary upheaval as great, or even greater than that which had greeted the end of the 1914-18 conflict. Many of the articles and pamphlets quoted in Craipeau's book may sound incongruously over-optimistic, predicting great feats achieved by mass movements which did not yet exist.

But to condemn them for this would be to ignore their recent history. Twenty-five years previously there had only been tiny pockets of resistance to the outbreak of the First World War, with almost all of Europe's socialist parties supporting their own governments. The historic anti-war congress at Zimmerwald in September 1915 had welcomed only 38 delegates, only some of whom had a revolutionary agenda. Yet within three years, the German masses had forced their government to capitulate, the Russian working class had seized power and soviets (workers' councils) spread like wildfire across Europe. As war resumed in 1939, this experience showed revolutionaries the importance of patient organisation and developing a principled political programme even with small numbers and in what may have seemed a hopeless situation.

Yvan Craipeau's *Contre vents et marées* begins with the preparations for war heralded by the coming to power of Adolf Hitler in 1933. However, English-speaking readers may benefit from understanding the earlier history of the workers' movement and the left in France, which informed their activity in this period.

The early years of the Parti communiste français

France emerged victorious from the First World War, yet with heavy human and material losses. 1,322,000 soldiers were killed and three million wounded in the course of the war; ten eastern *départements*[2] laid waste; and the national debt soared to 175 billion francs, a five-fold increase on 1913.

There were widespread mutinies on the Western Front in summer 1917, involving as many as fifty of France's 113 infantry divisions. However, this rebellion against bloody and fruitless offensives did not translate into the same mass working-class movements against militarism and wartime privations such as emerged in Germany and Russia.

Nonetheless, the war years created a strong pacifist[3] current in society, while millions were also inspired by the revolutionary upheavals elsewhere in Europe. 1918-19 saw a reawakening of the pre-war revolutionary syndicalist current in the trade unions, and in 1920 the mainstream socialist movement split. At the Tours Congress of the SFIO[4], the social-democratic party which had supported the French government during the war, the left-wing and centre factions broke away to form the Parti communiste français (PCF).

Much like the Communist Parties established elsewhere in Europe in this period, the PCF was founded on the 21 conditions of membership of the Communist International (Comintern)[5]. These principles included support for workers' councils and the Leninist 'democratic centralist' means of organisation,[6] as well as opposition to imperialist war. Some leading members of the new party from the old centre faction such as Marcel Cachin and Ludovic-Oscar Frossard had in fact initially been supporters of the war effort[7], but nonetheless joined the PCF having been impressed by Bolshevik successes in Russia. Moreover, the Comintern was keen to avoid a repeat of the split in the German Social Democrats, which had left the Communists in the minority.

Indeed, the French Communists assumed ownership of the SFIO newspaper *L'Humanité* as well as three-quarters of its membership – some 120,000 people – as the party's right-wing were cast aside. However, the PCF's large numbers masked an unstable alliance of Bolsheviks, reformists and pacifists, and syndicalist trade unionists.

These differences soon led to fragmentation. At the 1922 PCF congress the centre faction led by Cachin and Frossard won most votes (1698, as against 1516 for the left and 814 for the right). The centre refused to negotiate with the left, assuming control of all the party's leadership positions. The Comintern condemned this attitude, and further alienated Frossard by proclaiming a ban on freemasons. He resigned from the party on 1st January 1923, protesting Russian interference.

The real blows against political pluralism in the PCF were still to come, as the party was 'Bolshevised' in tandem with the monolithic Soviet Communist Party and the leaders of the left were forced out. First Boris Souvarine was expelled in July 1924 for publishing Leon Trotsky's *New Course*, a polemic against bureaucratisation in the USSR. Three months later he was followed by Alfred Rosmer and Pierre Monatte, after Rosmer circulated Lenin's *Testament*, which criticised Stalin in strong terms[8]. The pair were expelled at an extraordinary party conference in October 1924, accused of 'gross Frossardism, individualist anarchism and barely refined Trotskyism'. They had fallen victim to a bloc between open sympathisers of Stalin and his allies Grigory Zinoviev and Lev Kamenev, and the centrist wing of the party which had a decade previously supported the French war effort. Soon the Zinovievites, including the party's general secretary Albert Treint, were themselves purged, and the Stalinist Maurice Thorez emerged as PCF leader under Moscow's direct command.

Three Periods

At the sixth plenum of the Executive Committee of the Communist International in 1926, the Italian Communist Amadeo Bordiga challenged Stalin face-to-face. He argued that the direct collaboration of the whole International in governing Russian domestic policy was 'absolutely essential', drawing a link between internationalism and the need to resist bureaucratisation.[9] This suggestion was rejected out of hand, but served to highlight the question of whether the Comintern was an international alliance of communists, or merely a conveyor belt for Moscow to pass down policy to the national Communist Parties.

Under the fully Stalinised Comintern, member parties like the PCF had to serve the interests of the 'bastion of socialism', the USSR, and thus change its positions in line with the strategic demands of the Russian state. Indeed, Stalin systematised a theory by which to understand the evolving geo-political situation and thus the strategies which the Communist Parties should follow. It was a series of three distinct historical periods.

The 'First Period' was the revolutionary wave which coincided with the end of the First World War, including the February and October revolutions in the Russian Empire and the creation of workers' councils in Germany, Hungary and northern Italy. Communist Parties were established across Europe as an alternative to the social-democratic parties who had supported their own governments in the First World War and had opposed workers' councils in favour of parliamentarism.

The 'Second Period' was the period of capitalist consolidation, and retreat for the USSR as it was left isolated by the defeat of the revolutions in western and central Europe. This entailed the widespread reintroduction of the capitalist market within the USSR following the 1921 New Economic Policy (NEP); rapprochement with states unhappy with the post-war settlement such as Germany and Turkey; and greater Communist participation in reformist trade unions in the capitalist countries. Moreover, the Communist leadership in the USSR banned opposition parties and factions and emasculated the *soviets* and trade unions, assuming sole power.

However, there were struggles within the party, made all the more acute by Lenin's failing health and ultimate death in 1924. First the *troika* (three-man-committee) of Stalin, Kamenev and Zinoviev warded off the Left Opposition, led by Leon Trotsky, which critiqued the rise of a bureaucratic caste as well as the *kulaks* (wealthy peasantry); with Trotsky marginalised, Stalin then attacked Kamenev and Zinoviev in alliance with Nikolai Bukharin, who had theorised an autarchic 'Socialism in One Country' approach; and finally he rounded on Bukharin, whose continuing support of NEP became unpopular in the party.

Thus by 1928 Stalin had defeated his main rivals in the party and secured a measure of peace and diplomatic recognition. This strengthened position allowed for a more aggressive domestic and international policy: the 'Third Period'. The Soviet leadership suppressed the new bourgeoisie which had emerged under the NEP, with the state taking direct control of almost the entire economy under the 'collectivisation' and 'industrialisation' programmes. Although this in fact represented the fulfilment of aspects of the Left Opposition's programme, it was enforced violently, the mass slaughter of farm animals by dispossessed peasants leading to harsh repression in which Stalin promised to 'liquidate the kulaks as a class'. Meanwhile the onset of the Great Depression in 1929 reinforced the Comintern's belief that capitalism was entering its final collapse. In preparation for revolution the Communist Parties made a sharp break with reformist parties and trade unions in the capitalist countries.

The fascist threat

These orders from Russia forced the PCF to take a more 'revolutionist' stance in line with the 'Third Period' perspective[10], which it implemented by attacking the reformist social democrats as the main obstacle to revolution. They continually denounced the SFIO as 'social fascists', supposedly no better than the actual fascists, if not worse because their true counter-revolutionary character was hidden. The PCF confidently heralded the militancy of the masses and the imminence of revolutionary outcomes from the scattered and defensive strike movements of 1929-30.

The PCF membership, which had already slid in the mid-1920s thanks to the ebbing of the post-war revolutionary wave and the parliamentary advance of the rival SFIO, sank from 50,000-strong in 1928 to 32,000 in 1932. This was in spite of the potentially radicalising effects of the Great Depression. Faced with crisis-era attacks on living standards, the PCF proposed collaboration with rank-and-file social-democratic workers (as opposed to the reformist leaders): but exclusively on the basis of the Communists' own politics and the CGT-U union they effectively controlled. Meanwhile, the far-right Action française had grown to 60,000 members by 1934.

In Germany the bitter fruits of the 'Third Period' policy had also became clear by 1933. The Communists' direct collaboration with Nazi efforts to undermine the Social Democrats[11] paved the way for Hitler's march to power, and a divided left was crushed. Yet the PCF only began to abandon its abstentionist attitude to the rise of fascism after the Paris riots of 6 February 1934. On that day violent demonstrations by far-right and monarchist organisations such as Action française, its youth wing Les Camelots du Roi and the Jeunesses Patriotes forced the resignation of Édouard Daladier's liberal government.

In a joint trade union protest against the fascists on 12 February, rank-and-file SFIO and PCF demonstrators merged their contingents, chanting 'unity, unity!', on the day of a large national strike action. The PCF leadership remained reticent. Thorez wrote in the party newspaper *L'Humanité* on 8 March: 'The Parti communiste will never tolerate a policy of over-arching entente, the politics of retreat and abdication before the social-fascists [i.e. the SFIO].'

But after a meeting with Dmitry Manuilsky in Moscow in April and negotiations with SFIO leaders including Léon Blum, Thorez announced a new programme to the PCF's Ivry congress on 14 June. Now the Communists sought 'unity in action and trade union unity [with the SFIO] at all costs'. The two parties signed a concordat the following month. The CGT-U and the reformist union federation merged into a single CGT. This truce coincided with Stalin's effort to secure greater diplomatic ties with capitalist countries, joining the League of Nations[12] in 1934 and sealing an alliance with the French Prime Minister Pierre Laval[13] in 1935.

The unity tactic reinvigorated the party, its membership rising to 235,000 by 1936. It now far outstripped the SFIO as an activist force. Having decided that Hitler was now the PCF's 'main enemy', the party moved significantly to the right to cut the ground from underneath the liberal Parti radical and SFIO – playing down its previous loud complaints against the Treaty of Versailles[14] and French colonialism. Party demonstrations now featured the French tricolour flag. As early as April 1936, Thorez reached out to forces such as the right-wing Catholic Croix de Feu group in a bid for 'national unity'.

Popular Frontism

The elections held on 26 April and 3 May 1936 handed power to the cross-class Popular Front, with 72 seats won by the Communists, 147 for the SFIO and 167 for the Radicals and other centre-left republicans. The SFIO's Léon Blum became Prime Minister. Although the PCF did not take up any ministerial posts, it was central to the elaboration of the Popular Front's common plan for government.

In the programmatic negotiations with the SFIO and Parti radical, the Communists were constant advocates of moderation, keen to ensure middle-class support for the Popular Front. The PCF argued against the Radicals' plans to nationalise the Bank of France and rail, and like its allies rejected women's suffrage, fearing that, given the chance, women would vote for conservative Catholic parties.[15][16]

However, the euphoria which greeted the election of the Popular Front exceeded the limits of the electoral pact. In May-June 1936 over two million workers participated in a general strike including nine thousand factory occupations. The government hurriedly introduced a raft of legislative measures to appease the strikers, including the 40-hour working week and 15 days' paid holiday, as well as a generalised pay increase of 7-15%.

Far from encouraging the development of the movement in a workplace context, the PCF sought to constrain its aspirations within a parliamentary framework and maintain the unity of the anti-fascist government. The 12 June 1936 issue of *L'Humanité* featured an article conforming to Thorez's slogan 'Comrades, we must know when to end a strike':

> One must even know how to agree to compromises, in order not to lose any strength and, more importantly, not to make the fear and panic campaigns waged by reactionaries any easier. The working class, having imposed wage increases and the right to exercise trade union rights, must protect its unity with middle-class workers, particularly the peasants, by not separating itself from them through more accelerated progress. Thorez reminds us that 'Not everything is possible,' and that the watchword of the party remains 'Everything for the Popular Front! Everything through the Popular Front!'.

Moreover, the PCF had to tolerate the Radicals' apathetic attitude towards the civil war in Spain in order to maintain the Popular Front. Blum refused to send aid to the Spanish Republic (ruled by a similarly-composed government) besieged by General Franco's fascist uprising. Meanwhile Stalin and his supporters in Spain constantly played down – and militarily resisted – the revolutionary forms of government which had emerged amidst the war, focusing exclusively on defending the status quo of the parliamentary Republic.

However, the Popular Front government collapsed in 1938 under the weight of economic recession, a budgetary crisis and growing tension over the Parti radical's conservatism regarding Spain. Throughout the following year the PCF's anti-fascist strategy suffered from the fact that the centre-right French and British governments feared communism as well as fascism: not only did the two powers take a non-interventionist standpoint as Franco crushed the revolution in Spain, but they also acquiesced in Nazi Germany's aggression in central Europe. Indeed in October 1938, it was only the 72 Communists and three other MPs who opposed Prime Minister Daladier's decision to sign the Munich Agreement[17] authorising Hitler to invade the Sudetenland region of Czechoslovakia.

Yet the PCF's patriotism did not flag – they called for an extension of the Popular Front. Although the Parti radical had betrayed their alliance with the PCF and SFIO, Thorez sought yet more conservative partners –he even called on those fascists 'loyal to France' to join a 'French front'. He himself joined the French Army amid much hubbub as war with Germany neared.

But in August 1939 there was a fresh change of direction in Moscow. Stalin had been unable to concretise an anti-fascist alliance with the western democracies, and so instead sought peace with Hitler. On 23 August the Soviet foreign minister Vyacheslav Molotov signed a non-aggression pact with his German counterpart Joachim von Ribbentrop. Hitler had long feared a two-front war such as led to Germany's defeat in 1918, but this pact allowed him to invade Poland safe in the knowledge he would not have to fight the USSR as well as Britain and France. Such an opportunistic deal between the dictators put the Communist Parties of Europe in a difficult position. Even as war began on 3 September, the PCF at first maintained a verbal allegiance to national unity: but supporting the Allies became untenable when Stalin invaded eastern Poland in concert with Hitler.

The early French Trotskyists

Early supporters of the Russian Left Opposition in France included Boris Souvarine, Raymond Molinier, Marguerite and Alfred Rosmer,[18] the ex-Surrealist Pierre Naville[19] and Pierre Frank.

Many activists who fell victim to Stalinist purges in the PCF retreated into the SFIO or everyday trade unionism, or else abandoned politics altogether. However the expulsions also sparked the creation of a series of critical Marxist publications and discussion circles including *La révolution prolétarienne*, Le Cercle Marxiste-Léniniste and its *Bulletin communiste, La Lutte de Classe*, Maurice Paz's *Contre le Courant*, and Albert Treint's *L'Unité Léniniste* (later, *Redressement Communiste*).

These dissident communist groups in France were not ideologically homogenous and 'Bolshevik-Leninism' – or 'Trotskyism'[20] – did not unite all oppositionists under its banner. Trotsky was unable to sustain his attempted collaboration with the Italian left communists exiled from Benito Mussolini's Italy; by 1927 Souvarine had diverged with the Trotskyists with his assertion that the USSR was a 'state-capitalist' society and not a workers' state[21]; Treint, initially a Zinovievite hostile to Trotskyism, moved sharply to the left and became a council communist; Paz broke away and pursued the publication of the short-lived *Le Libérateur*.

The abstract debates between dissident communists reflected the fact that they were organised as intellectual discussion circles without roots in the working class and with little organisation outside of Paris. Recalling Karl Marx's 1875 dictum that 'Every step of real movement is worth more than a dozen programmes', Trotsky encouraged these diverse groups to engage in joint mass activity.

> 'You should start by producing a weekly newspaper. That is already a step forward: on the condition, of course, that you do not stop there and press on determinedly towards a daily'. The weekly should bring together 'all the healthy, red-blooded and truly revolutionary elements of the Left Opposition', rejecting 'the mentality of a discussion circle and mediocre concerns and objectives'.[22]

This newspaper, *La Vérité*,[23] was launched in August 1929. With this practical collaboration in producing a newspaper, militants soon decided they needed a structured organisation.

In April 1930 they founded the Ligue communiste de France, the first formal organisation of the Left Opposition in the country. They considered themselves an external faction of the PCF, from which they had been unjustly expelled.

Therefore at first the Ligue only admitted PCF members and ex-members, and attempted to organise a tendency within the party. The organisation was tiny relative to the PCF, however, with at most a hundred activists, the majority of them in Paris. A disproportionate number were intellectuals; almost all of the industrial workers in the group in the capital were immigrants, forced to flee their own countries by repression[24]. But the Ligue worked on trying to relate to Communist workers. Its members sold

La Vérité at PCF meetings and demonstrations, in spite of physical assaults by Stalinists.

The Trotskyists' opposition to the totalitarian Soviet régime was a perilous endeavour, and the Stalinists' attacks soon became deadly. In February 1938 Trotsky's son Leon Sedov was murdered in his Paris hospital bed; that September the decapitated body of Rudolf Klement, administrative secretary of the Fourth International,[25] was dredged out of the River Seine. Following these Soviet secret police actions, the French Stalinists exploited the wartime breakdown of order to silence their Trotskyist opponents, assassinating Mathieu Buchholz[26] and Pietro Tresso.[27]

The united front and left unity

The Ligue communiste de France, along with Leon Trotsky, argued for a united front of working-class parties, most importantly the PCF and SFIO. Their intention was to help bring together the mass of the working class to take action to defend its basic interests – including the struggle against fascism – whilst at the same time maintaining full freedom of criticism of the reformist and Stalinist parties. Thus the revolutionary minority in the movement would be able to win wider layers of workers to its own politics, at the same time as advancing the unity and power of the class as a whole.

To this end Trotskyists opposed the Stalinists' denunciations of the SFIO as 'social-fascist', which the Ligue blamed for sowing division in the workers' movement; and from 1934 they criticised the PCF's sudden turn to embrace the French political establishment in the name of unity against the fascists[28].

While the Trotskyists had a common understanding of the malign role of the Stalinists in the struggle against fascism in Spain, the Popular Front and June 1936 general strike and their accommodation to French nationalism, they themselves faced internal disagreements over how they should amplify their voice and sink roots among the masses. While initially an external faction of the PCF, the Trotskyists gave up hope of reforming the Comintern and its member parties following the 1933 coming-to-power of Hitler: they blamed the sectarian Stalinist policy for leaving the working class divided and defenceless against the Nazi threat.[29]

In furtherance of their goal of a cross-party workers' front, and aware of their own small numbers, in August 1934 the Trotskyists joined the SFIO – which afforded more space for open policy debates than the PCF – and attempted to build a revolutionary tendency within its ranks. The energetic Trotskyists began to assume a number of leadership roles in local branches and in the SFIO's youth organisation, the Jeunesses socialistes (JS), their influence far exceeding their meagre numbers.

But at the same time, the PCF was also turning to the SFIO, having abandoned its characterisation of that party as 'social fascist'. Léon Blum stated at the SFIO's June 1935 Mulhouse congress that he was far keener on unity with the Communists than dealing with the Trotskyist 'groupuscule', which although small was able to trouble the SFIO leadership. The political space open in the party to the Trotskyist-animated Groupe bolchévique-léniniste (GBL) was soon closed down. In July the JS dissolved the GBL tendency and expelled its leaders: a campaign against the expulsions followed, but by November the Trotskyists had been forced out of the SFIO.

Trotsky argued that the expulsions – together with a high pitch of labour militancy, heralded by major strikes in Brest and Toulon that August – highlighted the need for an independent party. However, a faction led by Raymond Molinier and Pierre Frank persisted with SFIO 'entryism', attempting in vain to re-join the party as individuals. Molinier and Frank were thus excluded from the 'official' Trotskyist current in December 1935. They established the Parti communiste internationaliste (PCI), which published *La Commune* and initiated politically loose local Groupes d'action révolutionnaire (GAR).

The majority led by Pierre Naville founded the Parti ouvrier révolutionnaire (POR) in April 1936. The POR also included the young revolutionaries who had been expelled from the JS and formed the autonomous Jeunesses socialistes révolutionnaires (JSR). In May-June, at the same time as the election of the Popular Front and the massive strike wave, the POR briefly reunited with the PCI. In July, however, Molinier and Frank were again excluded and resumed publication of *La Commune*. This left the majority to proceed with the building of a new party comprising of the ex-POR and the JSR. It is very much from the standpoint of this organisation, the Parti ouvrier internationaliste (POI), that Craipeau writes his history of the Second World War.

A note on the author

Yvan Craipeau was born in 1911 in La Roche-sur-Yon, a small town in the western *département* of Vendée.

While still a *lycée* (grammar school) student in his hometown he set up an independent 'Marxist group' with a dozen fellow students. He was however expelled from the school after refusing to stand for the national anthem during a prize-giving ceremony, and had to move to another *lycée* in Poitiers.

Although too young to have experienced the Stalin-Trotsky split and its echoes in the Parti communiste français at first hand, by age 17 Craipeau considered himself a Trotskyist. However, he had no knowledge of the small oppositionist circles in faraway Paris. After briefly liaising with the Le Libertaire group in 1928, he and his young comrades decided against joining this anarchist current.

Upon moving to Paris in 1929 Craipeau met with the militants who published La Vérité. In 1930 they founded the Ligue communiste: still a very young man, he was at first not allowed to become a member of this group since he had never been a member of the PCF. He attempted to join the Communists in order to be able to fulfil this condition, but was refused on account of his Trotskyist reputation. However, the Ligue accepted him as a full member the following year.

The Ligue's executive committee entrusted Craipeau with youth work. The International Left Opposition still hoped to reform the existing Communist Parties, and thus on returning to the Vendée over summer 1930 he founded a local branch of the Jeunesse communiste, the youth wing of the PCF. The Trotskyists tried to unite with the young Communists and Socialists, with Craipeau chairing a meeting of 1,500 such young people at Paris's Boxing Hall on 12 January 1933. However, he was expelled from the Jeunesse communiste in 1934 for his 'fractional activity' for the Trotskyists: indeed, in 1933 he had even served as Trotsky's personal secretary.

Very critical of the Stalinist response to the rise of Hitler and looking for an urgent response to the 6 February 1934 fascist riots in Paris, Leon Trotsky advocated that his French comrades should establish a revolutionary tendency in the SFIO. Craipeau supported this orientation, since he was keen to break the Trotskyists' isolation: accordingly, he helped to establish the GBL fraction of the SFIO's youth section, the Jeunesses socialistes. He was elected to the regional JS leadership in Seine-et-Oise.

Following the 1935 expulsions from the SFIO, Craipeau at first stood aloof from the split between the Naville majority and Molinier-Frank. He and other young 'Bolshevik-Leninists' such as Fred Zeller and Jean Rous were active in the formation of the autonomous Jeunesses socialistes révolutionnaires, publishing the newspaper Révolution. The JSR also included non-Trotskyists who had broken to the left of the PCF. In April 1936 the JSR joined the POR, which became the POI that June.

1936 also saw the publication of Leon Trotsky's The Revolution Betrayed, which comprised not only a withering attack on Stalin and the Soviet bureaucracy, but also a systemisation of the theory of the 'degenerated workers' state'. This conception maintained that even if the bureaucratic elite had expropriated the political power of the working class, it did not own the economy as would a ruling class: the fact that the economy was almost entirely nationalised – as a result of the October 1917 revolution – represented continuing working-class economic power. Trotsky's book characterised this contradiction as a source of instability, predicting that either the working class would overthrow the bureaucracy and reassume full power, or else the bureaucracy would lead the USSR to collapse and capitalist restoration.

In 1937, having studied *The Revolution Betrayed*, Craipeau began to question the Trotskyists' understanding of the USSR. He argued that the bureaucracy had in fact assumed the role of a new and historically unique ruling class, and termed Soviet society 'bureaucratic collectivist': it was not capitalist, but neither did state ownership of the economy necessarily imply working-class rule, if the working class did not control the state. At the founding conference of the Fourth International on 3rd September 1938 Craipeau was the only delegate to vote in favour of his thesis[30] questioning the 'workers' state' theory, although this view had substantial support within the POI itself.[31] [32]

Craipeau was the first person within the Trotskyist movement to adopt the 'bureaucratic collectivist' position:[33] [34] his role is often ignored, sinceced the theory is commonly associated with the malign politics of others who also embraced it. First was Bruno Rizzi, an Italian who called on the totalitarian régimes of Italy, Germany and the USSR to make common cause and who published an eccentric version of this idea in his 1939 book *La Bureaucratisation du monde*,[35] to which Trotsky made several public replies.[36] Moreover its best-known Trotskyist advocates, the Americans Max Shachtman and James Burnham, developed conservative and anti-communist politics on the basis of the theory, believing democratic capitalism to be more progressive than bureaucratic collectivist societies.

A further reason why Craipeau played a relatively minor role in the debate over the character of the Soviet Union was that he did not see a position on this question as sufficient basis for a distinct political programme or activity in France. In *Contre vents et marées*, which includes a number of polemical passages on other matters, he refers little to this debate and passes over references to the Soviet 'workers' state' without comment. Throughout his activist life he placed great importance on unity with other tendencies, and in 1938-39 was a keen advocate of unity with the Parti socialiste ouvrier et paysan (PSOP), a left-social-democratic group led by Marceau Pivert; similarly in 1944 he was a leading architect of Trotskyist unity, in spite of his unremitting criticisms of the Comité communiste internationaliste (CCI) group.

The advent of war in 1939 shattered the PSOP and the Trotskyists were left isolated. The heavy repression of the entire left under the occupation was married with the distancing of the Trotskyists from what remained of the mainstream Communists and socialists. They were unable to participate in the French Resistance given its pro-imperialist and French chauvinist politics, and were also subject to deadly attacks by Stalinist agents. These difficult conditions left Craipeau personally responsible for various functions in the POI, particularly insofar as he had the good fortune to be determined unfit for military service. Evading pursuit by the French Gestapo, he was responsible for the continued clandestine publication of *La Vérité* (together with Marcel Hic) and, from 1943, the party's military organisation and finances. He also had a continuing interest in the Youth Hostel movement, whose Paris organisation was controlled by the Trotskyists during the war.

Three of the four Trotskyist groups in France merged into the Parti communiste internationaliste (PCI) in 1944, and were soon able to resume somewhat more open organisation thanks to the end of the occupation, although their newspaper did not secure legal status until April 1946. That year Craipeau was elected the party's general secretary as well as a delegate to the International Secretariat of the Fourth International.

At the 1946 PCI congress the perspectives of the 'broad' faction, led by Craipeau and other prominent ex-POI cadres such as Roland Filiâtre and Albert Demazière won out. These tempered the Fourth International's confident predictions of capitalist stagnation and revolutionary crisis: indeed, the next three decades would see the longest capitalist boom in history. The PCI developed increasing influence over the Jeunesses socialistes and the left of the SFIO, and merger discussions began. At the same time, the tiny Union communiste[37] group, and to some extent the PCI, played an important role in sparking and spreading an April-May 1947 strike at the massive Renault plant at Boulogne-Billancourt. This was the first major post-war strike movement in France: it broke out against the wishes of the PCF, who had been keen to maintain a common front with their Gaullist and SFIO coalition government partners.[38] It seemed as though the Trotskyists' voice was growing.

However, this progress did not last. At the November 1947 PCI congress, the former CCI leader Pierre Frank and Marcel Bleibtreu gained control of the organisation. The new leadership insisted on the correctness of the Fourth International's predictions of imminent capitalist collapse and thus defended the need for organisational tightness, abandoning the policy of convergence with the JS and the left of the SFIO. The 'broad' faction believed that the PCI was not willing to take the initiative in uniting the anti-Stalinist left: most of them either split away or were expelled, many joining the short-lived Rassemblement démocratique révolutionnaire (RDR) established by Jean-Paul Sartre, Georges Altman and David Rousset. The *Socialisme ou Barbarie* tendency, who had developed the position that the USSR was a state-capitalist society and the PCF a ruling class in embryo, also broke away from the PCI in 1948.

Craipeau was similarly disillusioned with the PCI. He had played a leading role in the wartime activities of the POI and the 1944 Trotskyist unification, but now believed the party had taken a sectarian course with no hope of organisational development or engagement with wider layers of the working class. He took a sabbatical from politics. In 1951 he moved to Guadeloupe, a French territory in the Caribbean: there too he was an active trade unionist, becoming secretary of the teachers' union on the island.

Returning to France in 1954, Craipeau participated in the creation of the Nouvelle Gauche, one of a number of anti-Stalinist groups which ultimately merged into the Parti socialiste unifié (PSU) in 1960. The PSU was ideologically heterodox, uniting reformists and revolutionaries, but placed a strong focus on workers' management of industry as an alternative to state control. Craipeau remained a PSU member for many years, serving as its secretary in the Alpes-Maritimes *département*.

This political life was rather more sedate than the rigours of the war years, and Craipeau took the time to write a number of historical works, including *Le mouvement trotskyste en France*, *Contre vents et marées*, *La Libération confisquée*, *Ces pays que l'on dit socialistes...* and the autobiographical *Mémoires d'un dinosaure trotskiste*.

He died aged 90 in 2001.

A note on references

All footnotes and brackets are Craipeau's, except where I have added '- DB'.

Craipeau's references are almost entirely without page numbers or year of publication. Where he quotes documents translated from English-language originals or otherwise widely available in English, I have substituted this for the French reference.

INTRODUCTION

According to bourgeois ideology, the national interest is the same thing as our common well-being: in peacetime political differences and the conflicts between different classes and social groups may lead one interest or another to prevail, but when the nation is under threat, its citizens must close ranks, forget their secondary squabbles and build national unity behind the state. In wartime, when faced with the foreign enemy, all of France, except a few traitors, stands shoulder to shoulder to defend the homeland and its honour. As they said in 1914, the French people constitute a 'union sacrée'.[39]

What does this mean in reality though? The union sacrée was created by the reformist organisations who promote nationalist mythology. In doing so, they swim with the current. Abruptly plunged into the cauldron of war, the masses side with nationalism: not only because they are beaten over the head with propaganda, or because of censorship and the repression which silences its opponents, but above all because of a spontaneous desire to defend the nation against enemy forces.

That is how in the First World War, in every belligerent country, nationalists were able to get socialists, syndicalists and even anarchists to support their own bourgeoisies. Alfred Rosmer has described how in France only a tiny minority stood up against chauvinist ideology. Even this opposition was mostly in the name of pacifism.

At the international socialist conference in Zimmerwald – and even that at Kienthal[40] – only a minority of this minority followed Lenin 'against the current' in his radical critique of the union sacrée, namely that the war displayed the contradictions of capitalism in the imperialist epoch at their most intense; social-patriotism was a treason against socialism; and revolutionaries had to take advantage of the weakening of their own bourgeoisies in order to prepare the social revolution, calling on the workers mobilised for war to turn their guns against their own rulers. This was the 'revolutionary defeatist' agenda which Lenin stuck by even after the fall of Tsarism and the proclamation of a 'democratic republic' in Russia. It was by resisting the treason of the social-patriots that the revolutionaries broke with the reformists and established the Communist International.

With a strong state borne of the October Revolution and Communist Parties in every country, one might have imagined that if imperialism plunged into the unknown of a Second World War, this time the balance of forces would be massively shifted in favour of the socialist revolution. But the opposite happened. Only the vocabulary changed. They talked of a 'national union', a 'national front' and a 'French front'. But again the workers' movement was treading in the footsteps of the union sacrée.

That was nothing surprising from the social democrats, who were staying loyal to their programme. But the Communist Parties? They did not, in fact, simply identify their interests with those of their own bourgeoisies. This was made clear in September 1939 when Stalin sealed his alliance with Hitler: in the name of revolutionary defeatism the Parti communiste français agitated in support of the German-Soviet pact.[41] For the PCF, internationalism meant supporting the strategy of the USSR. But the USSR of 1939 was not the USSR of Lenin's day. Its strategy had nothing to do with the world revolution. It used the Communist Parties and the masses in the interests of its own state. It was the same after the break with Germany. The Communist movement was placed at the service of the Allies and everywhere played the game of national unity alongside the bourgeoisies fighting against Germany.

Even then, the PCF pursued its own aim: its own coming to power. But how could the PCF hope to achieve that while tailing the plans of the French ruling class, abandoning its own ideology and exalting chauvinism and bourgeois values? Because, for the PCF, socialism does not mean smashing the bourgeois state, overthrowing the social order and supporting the masses taking power for themselves. As was clarified in 1945 in the writings of Fajon,[42] socialism for them means the nationalisation of the means of production and the coming to power of the 'party of the working class'. In this view, where state socialism is identified with state capitalism, they just need to get their hands on the economy as it is, on the state as it is and on society as it is. The Party will later be responsible for the necessary changes.

The masses' only role is to help the PCF take power. The Party is happy with capturing their discontent and stirring up their anger and their hatred. It hardly matters if they do not really know who the real enemy is, as long as they trust in the Party. It uses them like a sailboat uses the currents and the strength of the wind. Rarely does it find itself against the current as it was in 1939-40, when it relied on friends of the German-Soviet pact to achieve its goals. Sometimes also it happens, as in 1947, that the workers, finding it hard to bear the consequences of the union sacrée, stop carrying the Party: as sailors say, the sails start to flag. But the Party changes course to catch the wind behind its sails again.

It is not surprising that in these conditions the Party is more or less able to keep the wind in its sails. Neither is it surprising that its various manoeuvres do not bring socialism any nearer. Ultimately the only beneficiary is the bourgeois order, re-established with the help of this turbulent ally.

This being so, historians can tell the story of the war years according to the myth of national unity. In this version of events, the class struggle disappears. The French population is divided into two camps: those who collaborate with the German authorities, and the majority who fight for, or at least put their hopes in, the Allies. They furthermore have to show that most of the collaborators were really just working to preserve the state in readiness for later revenge. They say that, as opposed to during the First World War, there was not any revolutionary opposition hostile to the union sacrée and which sought to transform the imperialist war into a civil war.

This is a dishonest over-simplification. The policy of union sacrée was resisted in various ways: at points even within the PCF itself, as well as by many activists including left-wing socialists and 'ultra-lefts' as well as those loyal to the Fourth International, who led the most coherent opposition. These internationalists produced and distributed a relatively significant amount of propaganda, yet it receives no mention in the official history. In the course of the struggle they led, many of them lost their freedom or their lives, which in and of itself would be sufficient reason to record their history.

But there are other reasons too. We must understand why they remained isolated in small groups which, with a few rare exceptions, did not really manage to have a bearing on the course of events. We must understand why, despite having engendered fascism and war, capitalism was able to stave off social revolution in Western Europe. We must try to understand this more clearly by retracing the history of the French workers' movement during the war, above all that of the internationalist groups.

This work is totally different from the various histories of the French Resistance. The historians of the Resistance, including those of the PCF, primarily recount tales of battles, sabotage, the exploits of spies and the spectacular adventures of war on the underground. They reduce to nothingness, or near nothingness, the political motivations of those who participated. In their eyes, the objectives of all the combatants seem obvious, namely working with the Allies to restore an independent French state. We, on the other hand, ignore everything to do with anecdote and the spectacular. We do not want to add another book to the list of Resistance adventure novels.

What matters to us is to understand: what were people's aims and motivations? What analysis did this or that tendency make of the situation? What were their tactics and their strategies? What were the results?

To us it seemed that the texts themselves would supply the best answers to these questions. We have cited a significant quantity of the working-class press, above all the internationalist texts, which in many people's eyes are too little-read. The events of the war, in particular social struggles, are therefore for the most part seen through the lenses of the internationalists. Readers will be able to discern their objectivity and their lucidity as well as their weaknesses, their mistakes and perhaps the reasons for their weakness. They will understand their failings as well as their successes.

The first volume *Contre vents et marées*[43] tells the story of the internationalists during the 'phoney war' and the German occupation: we have devoted the first chapter to the period immediately before the war, without which it would be impossible to understand the development of parties and groups.

The second volume, *La liberation confisquée*[44] retraces the events of the Liberation and the story of workers' movement until the end of the war. The last chapter is devoted to the period immediately after the war: the union sacrée remained in force until the beginning of 1947 and this period displayed the consequences of that policy.

One final word on the difficulties we faced in putting together the pieces of this history. Aside from a few superficial articles and some pamphlets more concerned with propaganda than historical accuracy, we have to hand no prior study on which to base ourselves. Many archives are still inaccessible. Most of the many dozens of internationalist publications have been lost. What remains of them has been collected with great difficulty thanks to the Centre d'Études Socialistes and the devotion of Jean Risacher. In any case, the illegal press cannot sufficiently portray the deeds of the internationalists. We have to rely on those who witnessed them. Besides, most of those who took part in these actions are dead. And even among those who have not broken from our movement, the survivors are split into rival groups who distrust one another. Many displayed little desire to take part in compiling a history the conclusions of which they were unable to determine. We were able to make use of barely fifty testimonies, whose authors we thank.

Above we have written of the limitations of this history. All the same, we hope that it will help people to understand the struggle of revolutionaries during the war. We dedicate this history to them, particularly those who lost their lives in the fight for socialist revolution, such as Bodenez, Marc Bourhis, Buchholz, Cruchandeau, Pierre Gueguen, Marcel Hic, Henri Kunstlinger, Henri Molinier, Sadek, Henri Souzin and Pietro Tresso.

Chapter I

BEFORE THE WAR

The Parti communiste against the imperialist war

In 1929 the Communist International, whose leader Bukharin had been replaced by Stalin's ally Molotov, proclaimed that war was imminent. According to their rationale, capitalist society had entered the 'Third Period' of its existence: that of its final collapse. It had to rely on terror to continue to survive. Therefore, in their eyes all bourgeois parties became fascists, including social-democrat parties. On the other hand, the masses around the world were quickly becoming radicalised and were on the road to revolution. No longer could there be any reformist or economic struggles. Every struggle became a struggle for soviet power. Imperialism could not survive except by striking at the heart of the proletariat, with a generalised war against the Soviet Union. There was a race on between the rising revolutionary tide and the war being planned against the USSR. The Communist International thus launched a call for the radicalised masses to show their power to resist war on 1st August.

In the end, the 1st August 1929 demonstrations were a fiasco. The theory of the 'Third Period' and the idea of 'social-fascism'[45] which stemmed from it led to defeat and the isolation of the Communists. They would soon guarantee the victory of Hitler. Their objective was not to take account of reality but instead to justify the violence of the civil war ('the third revolution') which the Soviet bureaucracy had unleashed against the peasantry, the emergency powers which it took to rule over the working class and the violent repression which it exercised, including against tens of thousands of communists.

The Communist International was not wrong, however, to point to the inevitability of war. The economic crisis of 1929 would aggravate inter-imperialist tensions. But contrary to the simplistic schema of the 'Third Period', it would exacerbate above all the tensions between the biggest imperialist powers and the newer imperialisms, hungry for breathing space for their suffocated industries. Inevitably, this put into question the division of the world by the powers victorious in the First World War.

The Treaty of Versailles had divided Europe to their liking. It had broken Germany under the weight of reparations, cut the country in two with the 'Danzig corridor' and handed German-populated areas to Czechoslovakia. It had cut down the outlets for German industry and placed it under the guardianship of American finance. This peace arrived at by the conquering 'imperialist bandits', imposed by force on the conquered bandits, carried within it the seeds of revenge.

The economic crisis which hit America in 1929 had dramatic repercussions on Germany. Wanting for a revolutionary response, the masses brought to power the Nazis, who promised to tear up the Treaty of Versailles and to forcibly open up 'living space' for the German economy.

At the start of 1933, war was on the cards. During the six years that followed, all of the Great Powers feverishly prepared for war: each of them intensified arms production, developed up-to-date weaponry, sought to seal alliances and worked to force their people to make their leaders' cause their own and to consent to the sacrifices being imposed on them.

Of course, at the same time they made proposals for peace and threats of war. Aside from his two shock manoeuvres and two military interventions, Hitler was keen to make offers of peace. From 1933 he had proposed disarmament, and the French government led by Daladier replied that they would see if, in four years' time, they could count on the good faith of the Germans. Germany won back its freedom and left the League of Nations. *L'Humanité* commented on 16 November 1933: 'It is the policy of Versailles and the policy of imperialist security which are today producing their bitter fruits. The French workers must never forget that.'

The diplomatic efforts of the Soviet Union

It was therefore clear to Communists that the USSR, the world's 'first workers' state' could not line up with either imperialist camp. After the Austrian Social Democrats (Austro-Marxists) had suggested that the Soviet Union should align itself to the 'democracies' to fight the fascist powers, on 1st June 1933 *L'Internationale communiste*, organ of the Third International, replied sharply: '… The world's first workers' state's task is not to prop up the continuation and entrenchment of the division of the world decided at Versailles.'

In fact, the orientation of Soviet diplomacy was quite the opposite. Ignoring the warnings of Trotsky – who in 1928 explained that Hitler would be the super-Wrangel[46] of capitalist Europe and sought to launch a war to destroy the Soviet Union – instead it looked to establish ties with Nazi Germany. The day after Hitler came to power, *Pravda*[47], covering the event in a few lines, asserted the USSR's desire to pursue with the 'new government' the good relations with Germany it had enjoyed since the Treaty of Rapallo.[48] However, they quickly had to face reality: the crusade against the USSR was Hitler's primary objective and the cement of the alliances he sought to arrange.

This being so, Stalin began to align himself to the 'democratic' powers. The USSR joined the League of Nations, which had become a tool of Britain and France. Its diplomats attempted to lash up an alliance of all of the rivals of Germany, including Piłsudski's Poland[49], in the name of 'collective security'. It negotiated this alliance in terms of military and territorial guarantees. Like all the other powers, it gave these secret negotiations an ideological veneer: the solidarity of the democracies against fascism.

At the same time as the USSR adopted 'the most democratic constitution in the world', Stalin unleashed terror. In order to have a free hand to do as he pleased, he wiped out the old leaders of the revolution, then the cadre of the party and the army (even Stalinists) who he thought might one day constitute a pole of resistance to his rule. At the same time, he multiplied his assurances to the imperialist powers in order to prove that alliance with Russia meant a guarantee against revolution. Such was the character of his May 1935 declaration to Laval, approving the French government's re-armament policy. Across the world, Communists had to put off any idea of revolution and convert themselves into 'democrats' and 'patriots'. In Spain, their task was to hold back the revolutionary torrent and defend republican legality. All means at hand were used to maintain social order, from diplomatic pressure to the actions of the GPU.[50]

The Munich agreement marked a serious defeat for Stalin. On 7 October 1938 Trotsky predicted: 'We must now expect with certainty a Soviet diplomatic initiative to build links with Hitler at the cost of further retreats and new capitulations.'[51]

This was the new turn Stalin announced to the Soviet Communist Party congress at the same time as he sought military negotiations with the 'democracies'. While international opinion was blinded by these negotiations, and would see in the German-Soviet pact six months later a piece of theatre, in March 1939 Trotsky had foreseen Stalin's negotiations with Hitler:

> The abandonment of the policy of *alliance with the democracies* will soon result in a humiliating capitulation at the feet of Hitler and being forced

to lick his boots – such is Stalin.

What a lesson! For the last three years Stalin has claimed that all of the comrades of Lenin are agents and allies of Hitler. He has wiped out the flower of the General Staff and shot, made destitute and deported around 30,000 officers, accusing each of them of having been agents and allies of Hitler. Having dismantled the party and beheaded the army, now Stalin openly displays his credentials to play the role … of Hitler's leading agent.[52]

The negotiations were played out even more cynically than ever on the basis of territorial deals. They were explained away with an ill-fitting new ideological coat, this time from the fascist wardrobe: 'the solidarity of proletarian nations against the wealthy imperialists'.

Trotsky warned that the drive to war would reach its climax in 1939:

The only obstacle on the road to war is the fear of the ruling classes faced with revolution … Stalin has definitively freed the hand of Hitler, as well as his rivals, and pushed Europe to the brink of war.

The Parti communiste's turn to the union sacrée

In 1934 the Parti communiste finally seemed to have learned the lessons of the tragic impasse to which the theory of social-fascism had led. Of course, several months of procrastination had followed the unity demonstration of 12 February.[53] At the end of July, a pact of unity in action brought together the Parti communiste and the Parti socialiste. But for the PCF, this was just the start of the 'turn'. In October it reached out to the Radicals, proposing a broad alliance of 'all democrats'. It began to build a movement which had as its goal not socialism but the electoral victory of a 'left-wing' coalition: the Popular Front.

In truth, the Party was carrying out a turn decided upon by the Communist International, that is to say, the Soviet government: the point was to form a government committed to alliance with the USSR. As soon as Stalin's declaration was made known, the Parti communiste was covering the walls with the poster 'Stalin is right'. The Parti communiste became the Parti communiste français. It now availed itself of the tricolour flag, the *Marseillaise,* and all sorts of chauvinist colorations. In December 1935 it held a large meeting for 'French reconciliation' which would offer a preview of the later efforts to turn the Popular Front into a 'French Front' including the nationalist right. Indeed, during the January 1936 negotiations over the programme of the Popular Front, the PCF was remarkable for its extreme moderation: it rejected anything which might worry the bourgeoisie.

These were Moscow's orders. Speaking to young socialists oriented to the Communist International, the leaders of the Youth International said, without beating about the bush, that preparing for revolution in a country allied to the USSR was treason.[54] Maurice Thorez's moves to put an end to the June 1936 strikes were cut from the same cloth. It had nothing to do with gauging the balance of forces, and everything to do with the international strategy the USSR had embarked upon.

Its orientation to world politics was of central importance. The Parti communiste now led a campaign for 'collective security', what *L'Humanité* had in 1933 called 'imperialist security'. When it campaigned for intervention in Spain, it was not in order to support the Spanish Revolution (the PCF only knew of 'republicans' in Spain) but to cement the alliance of democratic powers in the Iberian peninsula, and defend a bastion for this alliance against the Axis powers.

In the face of widespread pacifist sentiment, the Party again disguised the meaning of this alliance, claiming that the opponents of Germany constituted a 'Front for peace'. But the Communist press pushed more and more overtly for war. In September 1938 *L'Humanité* and *Ce soir* poisoned public opinion by pretending that the Americans were getting involved, and calling for 'firmness'. As Gabriel Péri wrote in *L'Humanité* of 13 September:

> A Front for peace has been built around the world. A basic force for collective security has been outlined … The Front for peace has declared its veto [against war]. This veto must be made real in the widest possible sense.

The Parti communiste was soon deeply involved in the union sacrée. Jean Carasso, trade union secretary for the Paris region, declared in *Ce soir*: 'We want to put our arms and our minds to work in the service of our country'. Henri Reynaud, another union official, claimed that 'the Union des syndicats has had to try and spare the working class from the shame inflicted on our country by the policy of surrender'.

A good example of the union sacrée in practice was given by Arrachard, secretary of the building workers' federation. Before the Munich agreement the government ordered him to put an end to the builders' strike. *Syndicats*[55] summarised his speech to the builders' representatives, the majority of whom decided to end the strike:

Arrachard then said that the word 'war' must not frighten us, and that it is necessary because this is a war against fascism: he insisted on the point that the goal of the war is a United States of Europe guaranteed by the Soviet Union. As for the builders' strike, perhaps it will be necessary to tell the workers to stop it in order to take up the cudgels against fascism.

As we see, the implementation of the union sacrée requires all sorts of ideological covers.

The SFIO and the pacifists

In 1932 the Parti socialiste SFIO had 137,000 members, as against fewer than 30,000 for the Parti communiste; and it won almost two million votes, as against barely 800,000 for the PCF.

Politically it was a patchwork. At its thirtieth congress in 1933 its far-right 'neo-socialist' wing made markedly fascistic noises: 'The birth of fascism', declared the socialist Montagnon, 'and the strength of fascism emerge from the evident necessity for a strong State, a powerful State and a new State'. Marquet's new slogans were 'Order, authority, nation'. Leon Blum interrupted him, saying, 'I am horrified'. Condemned by the congress, the 'neos' broke from the SFIO to create the Parti socialiste de France (with Déat, Ramadier and Renaudel) which would, as it happens, support the Popular Front before giving birth to a pro-Nazi party, the Rassemblement national populaire (RNP) under the German occupation. In the meantime they were partisans of a compromise with Hitler, Déat's *L'Oeuvre* arguing for this policy under the cover of pacifism.

Many MPs sympathetic to the 'neos' stayed in the SFIO, and a significant wing of the majority supported their politics. Their leader was the party secretary Paul Faure. Vehemently anti-communist and hostile to the Soviet alliance, he sought the path of compromise and 'appeasement'. He used all of his influence to prevent any French intervention on the side of the Spanish Republic when it was attacked by the Francoites with the backing of Mussolini and Hitler. He welcomed the Munich agreement with enthusiasm. In 1940 Faure's MPs would vote through dictatorial powers for Marshal Pétain.

The left, united until 1935 in demanding unity in action and an aggressive stance against fascism, was divided over the question of national defence. The leader of *Bataille socialiste*, Jean Zyromski, followed in the footsteps of the Parti communiste: it was necessary to fight fire with fire. Therefore Hitler's armies could only be fought with the 'democratic' armies. The Axis could only be combated with the democratic powers' 'collective security', cemented by the Soviet alliance. And even if collective security was unable to guarantee peace by forcing the aggressor to back down, at least it would make it possible to win the war.

In the centre, Léon Blum wavered. When Stalin signed his deal with Laval in 1935, restoring his prestige, Blum was shocked by the turn of events but delighted in seeing the Parti communiste return to the patriotic fold. All the same, these new-found patriots were soon worrying him with their chauvinism and jingoism. However much he supported collective security, he feared that France would in any case be dragged into war. As Prime Minister he declared his solidarity with his friends the Spanish republicans, yet he arranged a policy of non-intervention which meant handing them over to Hitler. He tried to overcome British reticence at the Soviet alliance, but when the Munich agreement was sealed he declared himself 'hugely relieved':

> The report of the meeting […] has aroused a widespread feeling of confidence and hope. We would be committing a serious mistake if we were to counter any of this hope and this confidence, since they in themselves represent a force for peace and a guarantee of peace.

At the Royan congress in June 1938 he voted along with Paul Faure for a motion opposing Zyromski: 'Socialists want peace, even with totalitarian imperialists, but we are not ready to submit to all of their schemes'. But in December the extraordinary congress was strongly opposed to Blum and Faure. The Aude MP's motion declared 'If the Nation was forced to choose between slavery and war [the party] would not recommend that it choose slavery'.[56]

In fact, all of these positions had one trait in common: they relied on imperialist armies and diplomatic intrigues, whether to co-exist with fascism or to stop it. All of them took for granted a union sacrée led by the bourgeoisie, its diplomacy and its army. The pacifist Paul Faure took in hand the nationalisation of the weapons industry, whose output had proven insufficient. Blum's rearmament plan devoted 14 billion francs worth of credits for national defence. The right wing, for its part, said that it voted through 'all the credits the army had asked for'.

The ultra-pacifist tendency appeared to position itself rather differently. Even the title of its weekly *La Patrie humaine* ['The homeland of humanity'] suggested that it refused to accept the system of national borders. In the name of humanism it made an appeal to universalism 'against all wars' and against all recourse to violence to resolve disputes.

This tendency found support from a significant section of the petty bourgeoisie. It was also dominant in several union organisations, for example in teaching, publishing and the post.

However, it remained ill-defined, including both the bourgeois and petty-bourgeois readers of *L'Oeuvre*, ready to tolerate fascism in order to avoid war as well as anarchists who looked for a wave of pacifism which would lead to social revolution.

As the threats of war became more acute, the ultra-pacifists would descend from their humanist clouds. Plans for peace came one after the other, all of them vague, suggesting to French diplomats various means of avoiding war. The pacifists placed their confidence in diplomatic games to find terms acceptable to their own country's imperialism. They disagreed with the means of the jingoist bourgeoisie but not with their objectives. Nothing distinguished their discussions from those which took place within the reformist party: indeed they were intended for the same audience.

When war broke out, they would have nothing more to say. Some abandoned their pacifism and rallied around the union sacrée. Others, through their pacifism, went down the road of accommodation to Hitlerite imperialism, while some like Giono collaborated with the Nazi occupiers.

The opponents of the union sacrée

Opponents of the union sacrée were in a tiny minority among the workers' movement.

The anarchists, above all those grouped around the weekly newspaper *Le Libertaire*, still had a certain influence. But they identified themselves with the pacifist tendency, who they tried to give a revolutionary echo.

Some small far-left groups declared themselves loyal to proletarian internationalism, like that of the Third International in its early days. These included the 'council communists' grouped around the Revolutionärer Kommunisten Deutschlands (RKD), a splinter of the short-lived Kommunistische Arbeiter-Partei Deutschlands (KAPD),[57] and the Union communiste, which arose in 1933 from a split in the Trotskyist movement. The latter group followed Bordiga's position. Its newspaper *L'Internationale* ceased publication in 1938, and the photocopied bulletin which followed it only survived for a few months. It would have no activity during the war.

In 1935, as the Parti communiste made its 'turn', the great majority of the opponents of the union sacrée could be found in the Parti socialiste. Since 1933 the old far-left tendency l'Action socialiste and its newspaper *L'Étincelle* had all but disappeared: its leaders had been expelled for having signed up to the Amsterdam Movement against War, organised by Henri Barbusse on behalf of the Parti communiste. The Comité d'action socialiste révolutionnaire (CASR) which followed it, under the leadership of the enlightened Claude Just, found barely any support.[58]

On the other hand, two tendencies in the SFIO declared themselves to be opposed to the union sacrée, The first, around Marceau Pivert, broke with Zyromski's *Bataille socialiste* and claimed the tradition of Karl Liebknecht and Rosa Luxemburg. This constituted the Gauche révolutionnaire, which in 1938 won 16 percent of conference votes. The second was that of Trotsky's partisans, who constituted the Bolshevik-Leninist tendency.

After the German Communist Party was defeated by Hitler without a fight, the [Bolshevik-Leninists] ceased to believe in the possibility of reforming the Communist International. However, they argued that new revolutionary parties could not arise from their own small propaganda groups, but that in France, for example, there would need to be a change in consciousness among the left wing of the Parti socialiste. Therefore in 1934 they decided to join the SFIO.

For them, the struggle was not between fascist states and democratic states, but between fascism and revolution. Smashed without having put up a fight in Germany, in Austria the working class waged a desperate struggle against Dollfuss's reactionary forces.[59] In October 1934, the workers of Asturias rose up with the slogan of working-class unity. The lessons had to be learnt. In France and Spain it would be possible to hound out the fascists if there was a proletarian revolution, which would require the unity of workers' parties and a break with the bourgeois ones.

If the working class did not take power, war was inevitable. It would pit the rival imperialist powers against one another. French and British imperialism would take to war not to defend freedom but to safeguard their markets and their colonies. In the event of war the workers would therefore have to fight for the overthrow of the bourgeoisie by taking advantage of its weakness, as Lenin's revolutionary defeatist theses had argued. This position won a certain level of support. In June 1935 at the regional congresses in preparation for the congress at Mulhouse, the Bolshevik-Leninists won 20 percent of votes in the Seine region and 15 percent in the Rhône. *Le temps* was worried by their success. At the congress, as it happens, Marceau Pivert adopted some of their key arguments: 'The best means of fighting Hitlerite fascism is to fight our own imperialism and to incite the German proletariat to do the same.'

In August, Marceau Pivert argued that:

A growing number of socialist workers are in agreement with the Bolshevik-Leninists' ideas, such as workers' militias, revolutionary defeatism, the insurrectionary general strike, a working-class seizure of power and the dictatorship of the proletariat.

But when the Popular Front with the Radicals was sealed, the reformist leaders could no longer tolerate in their ranks a militant far left opposed to alliance with the bourgeoisie and national defence.

On 10 June 1935, in a letter not known at the time to the Bolshevik-Leninist leaders, Trotsky wrote:

> The struggle of various tendencies against us corresponds almost exactly to the ideological preparation ... for a fresh imperialist war. Opposition to the war must, more and more, coincide with sympathy for the Fourth International. The condition for success is an unflinching struggle against the slightest concession to the idea of national defence. The inevitable coming together [of people with such ideas] in various workers' organisations (the Communist Party, the trade unions etc.) offers for us an opening to the working-class masses. We must orient to this with all the necessary independence. Given a certain amount of time this regroupment may result in the creation of a revolutionary party.[60]

As Trotsky wrote, the SFIO national majority's campaign against the Paris region Jeunesses socialistes had already begun. Of course, it would justify this offensive by invoking the youth's lack of diplomacy and the ardour of their newspaper *Révolution*. But these were just pretexts. During negotiations with the expelled leaders of the Jeunesses socialistes, Léon Blum offered this deal: 'Stop propagandising for revolutionary defeatism and you will be reinstated'.

But the JS leaders refused and their organisations backed them.

A wave of expulsions from the party followed, dispensing with all of the Bolshevik-Leninist representatives. Trotsky commented: 'The expulsion of the revolutionary internationalists amounts to a manoeuvre by the "patriotic police" with the goal of promoting national unity in readiness for war.'[61]

In an open letter to the young Socialists, Marceau Pivert appeared to express the same idea:

> We understand that we will need more vigour in fighting those tendencies who may well want to hound us out of the Socialist community and who will, perhaps, drag the proletariat into a new 1914.[62]

Throughout he uses the future tense and the conditional. For the moment he supported the demand to re-admit the Bolshevik-Leninists and the youth; but at the same time he criticised them: they too held some of the blame, given their lack of subtlety and diplomacy. With more diplomacy they could have remained in the party with the same politics. Keen to avoid a significant split in the run-up to the elections, the SFIO allowed the Gauche révolutionnaire to stay.

Several leading Bolshevik-Leninists shared Marceau Pivert's basic analysis. Raymond Molinier and Pierre Frank sought a compromise, then tried to find a middle-of-the-road position: to organise around a minimum programme 'revolutionary action groups' in which the activists of the traditional parties could participate. On this basis, breaking with the discipline of the Bolshevik-Leninist group, they launched a 'mass' weekly newspaper, *La Commune*; then, faced with the failure of their efforts, they established their own party: the Parti communiste internationaliste (PCI).

A final effort at conciliation allowed the creation on 2 June 1936 of a joint Parti ouvrier internationaliste (POI) and Jeunesses socialistes révolutionnaires (JSR). But when the international executive committee refused to readmit Molinier, his four comrades launched a fresh split. The POI retained the majority of activists and almost all of the young socialists. Including the youth it had around a thousand supporters; its activists now had a certain understanding of mass action. But it had barely any roots in industry and in the unions. Its election results (around 0.2 percent) underlined its isolation.

However, it was born into a revolutionary movement which confirmed its perspectives. Looking for the invisible 'ringleader' of the revolutionary actions rising from deep in the belly of the working class, the Blum government denounced Trotskyism and seized the first two issues of *La Lutte Ouvrière*. In fact, the Trotskyists played a role here or there but nowhere led the vanguard of the working class. This vanguard in fact let itself be held back by 'republican legality' and served to strengthen the ranks of the Parti communiste. The Trotskyists remained isolated.

By 1938 the situation was becoming more and more dangerous. Having the previous year crushed the Barcelona revolutionaries[63], the Republican forces in Spain were falling back on every front. In March, Hitler annexed Austria. Following the interlude of the second Blum administration, Daladier became the head of government. In the interests of national defence he demanded all sorts of sacrifices from the working class, got rid of the forty-hour week in industries related to war, governed by decrees and engaged in classically reactionary policies.

The PCF did not mobilise the working class against these policies until the point when Daladier concluded the Munich agreement with Hitler and Chamberlain.[64] The general strike called by the CGT for 30 November 1938 was however sabotaged by the reformist unions in the name of pacifism. Heavily repressed by Daladier's police, the strike was a failure. The Radicals renounced the Popular Front. Now, the Parliament elected under the banner of the Popular Front was engaged in the worst police repression.

The Trotskyist movement's critique of unnatural alliances with bourgeois parties was thus vindicated. However, in this period of general defeat, it was unable to profit from this. Its activists found it difficult to bear their impotence.

In the middle of 1938 came another important event: the Gauche révolutionnaire broke with the SFIO and created a new party which called itself revolutionary.

The foundation of the Parti socialiste ouvrier et paysan (PSOP)

Since its creation, the Gauche révolutionnaire had found itself beset with irresolvable contradictions. In June 1936, Marceau Pivert had written a radical article in *Le Populaire*: 'Everything is possible'. It argued that it was necessary to build action leading to the victory of the revolution. He was vehemently attacked as a Trotskyist adventurist by Maurice Thorez, who replied 'We must know when to end a strike'.

However, at the same time, Marceau Pivert accepted a minor role in the Blum government as Secretary for Information (in the leadership committee of the Gauche révolutionnaire only Daniel Guérin was opposed to this). Therefore tied up with the authorities, the Gauche révolutionnaire was not able to play any independent role in the course of events. Moreover, promoted to the rank of director in chief of state propaganda, Marceau Pivert applied himself to the task of brainwashing the masses by popularising the myth of Léon Blum.

These compromises were not however sufficient for the Gauche révolutionnaire to remain in the SFIO. Its opposition to the policy of non-intervention in Spain had already seen it dissolved as a tendency in April 1937. As much as the leadership of the Parti socialiste made clear their counter-revolutionary politics, the Pivertists pushed on. As leaders of the Seine region they tried in April 1938 to mobilise the workers against the reactionary Senate which had provoked the downfall of the second Blum government. They organised a demonstration, in which the Trotskyists took part, which brought together 25,000 people – a PCF leaflet denounced it as a 'Trotskyist provocation'. But the Parti socialiste had not the slightest interest in stepping outside the bounds of republican legality. The Socialist Minister of the Interior, Marx Dormoy, protected the Senate House with the police, against those who demonstrated with the slogan 'Vive Blum!'.

It was against the left of his own party that Léon Blum took action. The invasion of Austria led the SFIO to take another step on the road of national unity: 'The great seriousness of foreign events', declared Blum to the national council, 'demands that the nation rally around the Popular Front'. At the same national council, Marceau Pivert declared himself an opponent of the union sacrée. His statement was censored. The Seine region thus addressed an appeal to the whole party: 'Yes or no, will the party support the national union?'. The reply was immediate: on 13 April the SFIO leadership dissolved the Seine region branch, just as it had dissolved the youth section three years before. Like the Trotskyists in 1935, the Pivertists ramped up their efforts at conciliation. It was in vain. Daniel Guérin, at that time a Gauche révolutionnaire leader, explained why:

> Our unflinching opposition to the national union has finally made keeping the Gauche révolutionnaire in the SFIO impossible, since the political incompatibility between our revolutionary conceptions and the party's collapse into social-patriotism has become intractable ....[65]

Three years later, the same causes produced the same results. The matter was even clearer in 1938. Daladier's reactionary policies profited from Socialist support. Social-democratic politics had given their bitter fruits, both in France where the bosses were on the offensive and in Spain where the Axis forces and the Francoites were wiping out the resistance of Republicans deprived of weapons. Disappointed left-wing activists redoubled their criticisms of the party, but the majority fought back with a campaign of dissolutions and expulsions.

In June 1938 the SFIO congress in Royan ratified their expulsion. At the same time, the Parti socialiste ouvrier et paysan held their founding conference. If one believes the voting figures, the expelled tendency represented 30,000 SFIO members, but in reality the new party was only 5,000 to 6,000 in number. It did however have a significant working-class base, above all in the Seine region.

The Trotskyists could not be indifferent to the efforts of these thousands of activists who had broken with the SFIO through hostility to social-patriotism and who wanted to build a revolutionary party. They could not just ignore them and continue with their routine work.

Reduced to around a hundred members, the 'dissident' group which produced *La Commune* suffered the most from isolation. Before the end of 1938 it decided to join the new party. However, the PSOP leadership blocked the membership of its two leaders Molinier and Frank, invoking against them the grievances of the international Trotskyist movement which had excluded them.

In the Parti ouvrier internationaliste, a minority of the Central Committee led by J. Rous and Y. Craipeau proposed merger with the PSOP. They were strongly supported by Trotsky and the international leadership.

In September 1938, faced with an immediate threat of war, eleven organisations proclaimed the Fourth International. But this could not take shape unless it was built from representative sections. Trotsky pressed the French comrades to devote every effort into trying to transform the PSOP into a revolutionary party before the outbreak of war. Neither he nor the POI minority had any illusions in the PSOP membership, nor its political maturity. But neither did they idealise the POI itself: if the organisation was not capable of winning to revolutionary politics the few thousands of activists who had been through the experience of the Popular Front, what kind of mass work could they hope to carry out in wartime? 'We must decide,' wrote Trotsky, 'that our section should enter the PSOP. It has several thousand members. For a revolution, the difference is not enormous, but for the work of preparing the vanguard, it is considerable.'

The majority of the Parti ouvrier internationaliste was hesitant. The adult organisation only had a few hundred members, but most of them satisfied themselves with routinism, in particular in their unions. As regards the youth, the JSR, they had a certain activist dynamism. They had taken brave anti-militarist actions, which earnt many of their leaders harsh jail sentences (in 1939 Stève, Rigaudias[66] and Schmidt were condemned to ten years in a high-security prison). Wanting for larger openings, they had begun to get involved in the Youth Hostel movement. For their part, the PSOP had little to bring to the youth. The majority of the JSR stuck by their independence: there were many anti-Trotskyist prejudices in the PSOP and the leadership (CAP[67]) declared a merger to be 'inopportune'. The December national council ratified this position but suggested that POI members could join the PSOP as individuals.

In January 1939 the POI conference decided against entering the PSOP.[68] In agreement with the international secretariat and Trotsky the minority decided to join anyway: the merger was complete in February. In June 1939 the executive committee of the Fourth International invited French militants to join, commenting: 'The Fourth International does not have responsibility for the POI and does not recognise it as a section.'

But the majority of the activists who followed these directives came over to the PSOP too late to participate in its activity.

A fraction of the POI Central Committee (around the brothers Bardi and Lhuillier) decided to maintain an independent organisation. *La Lutte ouvrière* re-appeared in July, as the organ of the POI. It included a 'Declaration of the Central Committee', dated 20 June, protesting against the executive committee's decision. In reality, it would not be long before the group broke up.[69]

The test of September 1938[70]

Would it be possible to make the PSOP into a revolutionary organisation sufficiently grounded to meet the difficult challenges of wartime? The question did not even occur to Marceau Pivert and the leaders of the PSOP.

'Born in the fight against the union sacrée', the PSOP was proud of the intransigence of its internationalism. A November 1938 pamphlet reminded the reader that it was 'in the vanguard of the struggle against war'. It wholeheartedly denounced the imperialist character of the coming war:

> Fascism only serves to exacerbate the danger of war, it does not create it […] For us there is no question of supporting any defence of the nation identified with 'revolutionary defencism', something which would suppose that political and economic power in this country had passed into the hands of the working classes […]
>
> If war nevertheless breaks out before revolution, the task of the workers will be to take advantage of the situation to, sooner or later, seize power […]
>
> We believe in the value of revolutionary contagion. It is only in pursuing the class struggle and the struggle for power in our own country that we can give the workers in fascist countries self-confidence and encourage them to rise up against their dictators ….

But would this theory find any practical application in day-to-day activism? The test of September 1938 seems decisive for the PSOP leaders. When the mobilisation for war began and war seemed inevitable, the party did not back down.

'The PSOP has passed through its rites of passage with success,' declared Marceau Pivert. Its activists displayed courage in the face of an outbreak of chauvinism. But could it be deduced from this that the PSOP would confront a real situation of war in the same way? Trotsky wrote to Daniel Guérin:

I wish with all my heart that this prophecy is accurate. But now it seems rather too quick for me. There has been no war. The masses have not been faced with a *fait accompli*. The fear of war dominates the thinking of the working class and petty bourgeoisie. Your party has given expression to these pre-war sentiments in its abstract internationalist slogans. But do not forget that in 1914 the German Social Democracy and the Parti socialiste in France remained very internationalist and very 'intransigent' right up to the point when the first shots were fired… of course, I must salute your party's refusal in September to go down the path of chauvinism. But this is only of merit in a negative sense. To affirm that your party has passed the internationalist test would be to content oneself with too little, and would mean not being aware of the offensive which will come with war, including its social-patriot and communo-chauvinist wings. To prepare the party for such a challenge you must at once seek to refine and re-refine its consciousness, harden its intransigence, get to the bottom of your ideas and offer no quarter to your treacherous 'friends'. For a start, you must break with the freemasons (who are patriots to a man) and the pacifists of the ilk of Maxton, and turn towards the Fourth International.[71]

Against pacifist illusions

This letter by Trotsky summarised well enough the manner of the Trotskyist intervention in the PSOP. They had no secret plan to break up the party or to win over a fraction and split it from the organisation. The task was to harden the party for the coming tests.

It should be noted that Trotsky was essentially talking about what political stances to take. But another important defect of the PSOP was that it had not broken with the organisational practice of social democracy: there was a constant division between words and deeds and a lack of consistent work in industry and the mass organisations of the class. The 'hardening' of the party also required a transformation of these organisational attitudes. The Trotskyists wanted to help the PSOP convert itself into a revolutionary party, which meant helping it to organise effectively and to grow roots in unions and workplaces. They tried and sometimes succeeded, for example in the Mantes region.[72] But all in all they hardly had any opportunity to engage in mass action. They were principally concerned with winning a 'parliamentary' majority within the party. Firstly there was an urgent need to wage a struggle for political clarification, against bourgeois pacifism.

This was no easy task. Revolutionaries necessarily related somewhat to the pacifism of the masses and their fear of war. It was a lever in the struggle against capitalism. That is why they sought to coordinate their action with anarchists and revolutionary syndicalists in the Centre d'action syndicale contre la guerre (CASCG).[73]

But the pacifism of the masses was not in itself revolutionary. It would never be so unless their hatred of war was mobilised against the bourgeoisie. The pacifists, after all, were ready to bloc with the most reactionary sections of the bourgeoisie in order to preserve peace.

This was clearly seen during the Munich crisis. In *Front populaire, revolution manqué*, Daniel Guérin recalled the pacifist writer Giono's telegram to Daladier and Chamberlain, imploring them to form '[…] a close union of the British and French governments to arrange a just settlement to protect peace'.

The pacifist trade unionists like Emery in teaching and Chazof, the anarchist proofreaders' union activist, had no problem in meeting reactionary leaders like Flandin whose pacifism was an attribute of their complicity with Hitler's régime. Mathé, in post, declared without beating about the bush: 'Rather slavery than war!'.

On 25 September 1938 the CASCG put their name to a joint leaflet, calling for 'peaceful negotiations'. The POI refused to take part, but the PSOP joined in. At the national council of the PSOP in December 1938 this agreement was approved by 229 votes to 43. This showed the influence the ultra-pacifists enjoyed in the party. Along with petty-bourgeois movements like those led by Valois and Bergery,[74] they led the PSOP into a union sacrée of capitulators, a mirror image of the union sacrée which was readying for war.

From its first appearance in April 1939, *La Voie de Lénine*, the journal of Trotskyists in the PSOP, laid into bourgeois pacifism and those in the revolutionary movement who echoed it.[75] At the PSOP national conference the ultra-pacifists backed Modiano's motion which had the theme 'Only peace is revolutionary'. The PSOP had to affirm: '[…] its irreconcilable opposition to war [which constitutes] the only means for capitalism, whether democratic or fascist, to seek temporary resolution to its contradictions.'

From that they deduced the necessity of collaborating 'with all political and economic groups who reject the union sacrée and the drive to war'. If war broke out, the defeat for the revolutionary cause would be such that it was not worth thinking about what would happen. However, forced to express some opinion on what it would be necessary to do in that eventuality, Krestler and Modiano made an addition to their motion:

If despite all our efforts war breaks out, the PSOP would have to stick to the slogan 'Immediate and unconditional peace', which would be the only way of directing mass discontent towards a revolutionary seizure of power.[76]

The debate on revolutionary defeatism

The other motions proposed to the members of the PSOP looked to decide what action the party should take during the coming war. These seemed only to be different in terms of nuance. For example that of Hérard and Blaise: '[...] denounces as a lie the suggestion that the democracies can show revolution the door with a military victory over the fascist countries'.

The party was not put off the belief that 'the main enemy is in our own country' by the consideration that mass revolutionary action in time of war would contribute to military defeat. Accepting the possibility of capitalist military defeat did not mean wanting the victory of fascism. The motion gave the party the objective of turning 'the imperialist war into a revolutionary war'. But Hérard and his friends were not ready to accept all of the consequences of this, particularly that of having to organise a very disciplined illegal revolutionary party. In reality, the members who voted for this motion wanted to show their formal loyalty to Leninist ideas but refused to engage with them practically. Lucien Hérard himself quit the PSOP – and political activity altogether – a few weeks later.

In common with the left (Lucien Wietz and Daniel Guérin) Jean Rous proposed a motion taking an unequivocally revolutionary defeatist position.

> Faced with ever more dangerous threats of war, the PSOP, loyal to the revolutionary tradition of the left of the Second International before 1914 (the Stuttgart motion) and the Third International at the time of its creation, declares:
>
> If, in spite of the actions of the working class to try and prevent the outbreak of war, this occurs nonetheless, the task of the party will be to turn the imperialist war into a civil war, with the goal of the revolutionary seizure of power by the proletariat, the smashing of the bourgeois state and the installment of the dictatorship of the proletariat.
>
> The party will not be put off the belief that the main enemy is in our own country by the possibility that mass revolutionary agitation in time of war may contribute to the military defeat of our country. Accepting this possibility does not mean encouraging or wanting victory for Hitler, but on the contrary will encourage the total defeat of Hitler and worldwide fascism.

Indeed:

1. Revolutionary agitation led by workers in our country will exercise a powerful contagious influence on workers in the fascist countries; will provoke the break up of the rival capitalist armies, fraternisation between soldiers of both sides and the collapse of the dictatorships; and will light the flame of world revolution, the only means of defeating war and fascism, across the globe.

2. Besides, a revolutionary seizure of power by the working class in our country will turn the imperialist war into a civil war and create the conditions for meaningful national defence: only a proletariat in control of its own destiny and defending a socialist order will be able to mount an invincible resistance to fascism abroad....

The motion was unambiguous. But it was rather abstract. It was based on the understanding that the differences between the belligerent powers were no greater than they were during the First World War and that the balance of forces at the front, as in 1914-1918, would allow a slow development of social conflict in the rear. But what would happen if Europe was rapidly taken over by Axis troops? Czechoslovakia gave an example of such an occupation, but no-one tried to analyse it.

The fourth motion, authored by Marceau Pivert and Collinet, only seemed to be distinguished from the third by half-shades, but it made no specific reference to the idea of revolutionary defeatism. However, during the discussion Collinet engaged with the real debate, advancing several objections to revolutionary defeatism worthy of some reflection.[77]

The attitude of Marxists towards the war has always made use of a concrete analysis of the conflict and the character of the antagonists. They are not content with dismissing them as all the same, even if some are capitalist and imperialist. Lenin himself approved of Jules Guesde and Huysmans's support for Japan during the Russo-Japanese war. It was only in the First World War that he recommended taking a defeatist stance in each country. During this war he attacked internationalists like Rosa Luxemburg, Karl Liebknecht and Trotsky as 'opportunists' for raising the slogan 'Neither victory nor defeat!'.

For him, it was not enough to hope for the military defeat of your own bourgeoisie, but also to contribute to bringing it about. For Lenin, defeatism was based on three concepts: 1. The war was reactionary; 2. Revolution was possible everywhere; 3. In every country there was a revolutionary movement fighting the same cause and able to help one another.

Here, Collinet saw proof that revolutionary defeatism could not be applied to the coming war. Even if this war was also imperialist, like that of 1914, there was a fundamental difference: both sides were imperialist, but Hitler and Mussolini ranked above their rivals as 'the champions of counter-revolution against socialism'. 'The Spanish workers had the experience' of the fact that there was a difference between fascist imperialists and democratic imperialists.

> The proletariat therefore has today two enemies: a domestic enemy, the bourgeoisie of its own country, and a foreign enemy, Hitlero-Mussolinite fascism.
>
> May we add that there is, within the proletariat's own ranks, a third enemy which is no less dangerous, Stalinism, an agent of demoralisation and destruction of working-class forces with its mendacious revolutionary myths. These contradictions are not the same as those of 1914.

In these circumstances, [Collinet maintained] there were two mistakes to avoid: only seeing the foreign enemy, in the manner of the partisans of the union sacrée such as Blum, Zyromski and Jouhaux, as well as the Stalinists; or only seeing the domestic enemy, in the manner of the revolutionary defeatists.

However reactionary it was, the Daladier régime could hardly be described as fascist. On the other hand, the destruction of all revolutionary organisations in Germany and Italy made any revolutionary uprising unlikely.

> No-one can promise that the inevitable result of military defeat would be revolution. Defeat may well, on the contrary, strengthen nationalist sentiment among the conquered people. [...] Far from uniting the continent and therefore preparing the way for international brotherhood, annexations will almost inevitable provoke a reactionary nationalist resistance by the conquered people. [...] Unification à la Hitler would be a return to the Europe of a hundred years ago, where national disputes appear as life-or-death, the class struggle is attenuated and reactionary forces are strengthened.

It was thus wrong to confuse the patriotism of the masses with that of the bourgeoisie. Collinet quoted Rosa Luxemburg:

> For the classes struggling for freedom, the most acute class struggle possible has always proven to be the best weapon in the face of invaders. […] It is merciless class struggle which, building courage for sacrifice and the power of the masses, constitutes the best protection for the country against foreign enemies.

He took from this that in the war the proletariat could not use the same tactics against both sides. Trotsky himself made a distinction between the attitude of German workers, who had to fight for the military defeat of their own state, and workers in other countries, who had to continue to build a revolutionary struggle *even* if that meant undermining their own national defence.

Finally, said Collinet, revolutionary contagion relied on long time periods and could not develop unless the belligerent powers were all equally exhausted. A revolution which broke out in the democratic countries first would find itself in mortal danger and could hardly count on fraternisation.

These were real problems. But the Collinet-Pivert motion had no solutions to them.

The Saint-Ouen PSOP congress

At the Saint-Ouen congress in June 1939 the pacifists were able to ensure that the discussion on anti-war action in the immediate was separate from that concerning what it would be necessary to do 'if war broke out anyway'. The minority who criticised pacifism and the endorsement of the CASCG poster only won 53 votes against 120 (Jean Roger's 'revolutionary pacifists' received 15).

On the second point the pacifist motion won 20 votes, Hérard's took 45 and the other two motions (Collinet and Pivert's as well as Rous and Weitz's) each had 59.

No-one left the congress with a majority, even in relative terms. These votes sowed disarray in the leadership, but in the *Juin-36* editorial Marceau Pivert consoled himself by remarking on the similarity of the positions, all of which counterposed internationalism and class struggle to social-chauvinism and national-communism. 'But in this vein,' he wrote 'the positions reflect certain hesitations and contradictions, which the revolutionary vanguard would only lose at the cost of authoritarian dogmatism: something we absolutely reject.'

The congress attempted to mask its inauspicious impotence by adopting unanimously an appeal which tried to use ardour to compensate for a lack of precision:

If despite everything our efforts are in vain, if the clashes between the imperialists must result in war, we will remain implacable opponents of the enemy living in our own country. Whatever the difficulties and risks of this attitude, we shall not either in times of war or peace cease our struggle for the revolutionary seizure of power by the workers and peasants....

On the issue of international relations the PSOP left suffered a defeat at the conference. Faced with imminent war, it believed the building of a revolutionary organisation to be the 'principal historical task'.[78] That was the reason why the Fourth International had been declared, in spite of the very weak forces represented at its founding conference.

At around the same time, organisations not belonging to any international held a meeting. Some of them were relatively significant, for example the Independent Labour Party (ILP) in Britain, Henk Sneevliet's Revolutionair Socialistische Arbeidspartij (RSAP) in Holland and the PSOP in France. Some almost only existed in exile, such as the Partido Obrero de Unificación Marxista (POUM) in Spain and the Sozialistische Arbeiterpartei Deutschlands (SAP) in Germany.

These parties were heterogeneous: the RSAP had a long revolutionary tradition, but had fallen into industrial routinism with its 'red' union; the POUM had shifted to the right under the leadership of Gorkin; the SAP was sliding towards Stalinism; and the ILP was mixed up in a vague pacifist movement.

The rest of the organisations represented were small propaganda groups, dissidents from Trotskyism (in Belgium and Greece) or had come from the right wing of the Communist International (e.g. the German 'Brandlerites' and Lovestone's group in the USA).

Unwilling to make any decisions about the International, the PSOP proposed a Front ouvrier international (FOI) whose sole task would be international solidarity: the FOI was moreover, in its manifesto, pledged to a revolutionary defeatist position. The left of the PSOP wanted to bring together a revolutionary wing of the FOI (with the RSAP and the left of the POUM).

But the anti-Trotskyist wing of the FOI was keen to build an organisation which could compete with the Fourth International: the International Revolutionary Marxist Centre. Daniel Guérin has demonstrated that Jay Lovestone – later unmasked as a CIA operative working in the American labour movement to corrupt the international workers' movement – was at the centre of this move. Indeed, he acted to try and make Europe's revolutionary organisations join the camp of the union sacrée beside the democracies'[79]

The Saint-Ouen congress voted to join the International Revolutionary Marxist Centre.

One last debate, dealing with freemasonry, brought to a head the anti-Trotskyist fervour in the PSOP. A powerful force under the Third Republic, freemasonry meant long-term collaboration between bourgeois and socialist leaders. The Parti communiste had been unable to overcome reformism before it decided on the incompatibility of party membership and freemasonry. Trotsky, who had advised the left of the PCF in this fight, argued during his stay in France that it remained a problem.

The majority of the PSOP leadership, with Marceau Pivert at the head of them, were freemasons. How could the PSOP hope to break with the union sacrée when its leaders were Masonic officials? They claimed that their freemasonry was limited to philosophical study, but the following year their conference spokesperson Suzanne Nicolitch would show that the opposite was the case.

Some branches realised the danger of all this, particularly Morocco: in the Protectorate, freemasons were the agents of colonialism and reaction. But in most branches, attacks against freemasonry met with hostility. It clashed with the liberal attitudes inherited from social democracy. And were the Trotskyists not just trying to discredit the most popular leaders?

Although winning very strong support over this issue, the left of the party became isolated because of the angry feelings which it unleashed. At the start of the congress a 'preliminary motion' was presented which threatened with exclusion all those carrying out 'Trotskyist factional activity', and was voted through without discussion 'three votes short of unanimously'. Sanctions were taken against many of those close to Molinier. Marceau Pivert wrote a threatening editorial for *Juin-36*. However, he still played a conciliatory role. His departure at the beginning of the war would cut the last tie between the Trotskyists and anti-Trotskyists. Not only was the PSOP unready to face the test of war, but the atmosphere of suspicion which reigned within it would make fighting together on the underground almost impossible.

Le Réveil syndicaliste

The role certain trade unions, such as Merrheim's engineering workers' union, played in fighting against the first imperialist war is well-known. But were there any trade unions which played the same role during the Second World War?

This time the situation was clearer in some ways, but more confused in others. It was clearer because in 1914 the CGT's rallying to the union sacrée was a crude change of position, in contradiction with its long-held stance, voted through its conferences, proclaiming its anti-militarism and warning that the workers would wage a general strike to oppose war, while in the case of 1938-39, the CGT leadership had already taken a position in favour of national defence against fascism. Following the Parti communiste and the majority of the Parti socialiste, it openly took part in the union sacrée. A cause of confusion was that the opposition to this 'jingoist' position was led by the reformist tendency grouped around *Syndicats*; this tendency, which was vociferously anti-communist, had little to do with class struggle. Rather, it believed that concessions to Hitler were preferable to war. It strongly approved of the Munich agreement. In November 1938, denouncing the general strike as a Communist manoeuvre against the Munich agreement, it welcomed strike-breaking.

Government procrastination over foreign affairs led the majority of the CGT leadership to oppose Daladier's reactionary policies on the domestic front. But it was no less committed to the union sacrée. Just as the authorities justified their reactionary measures by invoking the demands of national defence, the CGT leadership which accepted the logic of 'sacrifice' found itself tied up in knots. Workers abandoned the impotent and tattered unions.

Only one tendency in the unions rejected this logic: the Cercles syndicalistes lutte de classe, who from 1938 published a bimonthly journal *Le Réveil syndicaliste*. They brought together Trotskyists, anarcho-syndicalists and the majority of PSOP activists. In the CGT they were only in the majority in the technicians' federation; but they were also a significant minority in the teachers' federation, since the former majority of the federation who were grouped around the *L'École émancipée* journal had joined the Cercles in late 1938. In every other federation they were a tiny minority.

At the December 1938 national conference 53 Cercles were represented: 28 from the Paris region, 10 from the rest of France and 15 from *L'École émancipée*. They refused to bloc with the pacifist minority and defined their approach as 'struggle against Stalinists and reformists'.

> During the Austrian crisis in March our Cercles called for working-class action against war, and in so doing differentiated themselves from jingoist currents in the workers' movement as well as sentimental pacifists.
>
> This argument was made even more strongly when disputes over Czechoslovakia threatened war – first in May then again in September – by linking the anti-capitalist struggle to the struggle against war.[80]

The Cercles participated in the November general strike while denouncing 'its shoddy preparation, the negotiations which preceded it'. They disavowed the Rhône teachers' union, led by *L'École émancipée*, which refused to support it. They emphasised the fact that the failure of the strike, in sowing disarray among the unions, had also undermined 'class-struggle' circles in industry. Their conference, as it happened, renounced the tactic of building such circles in industry for fear that the CGT leadership would use it as a pretext to expel their activists.

Despite the repression meted out against them (two of their officials, Jourdain and Duvernet, were sentenced to eighteen months, imprisonment for 'fomenting sedition among the troops'), the Cercles stepped up the pace of their activity in 1939.

In April 1939 the Central Committee of the Cercles addressed the debates which had taken place at the highest levels of the CGT. Under the title 'Homeland against the working class', *Le Réveil syndicaliste* commented:[81]

> The union leaderships are shifting. As we write, the National Central Committee is meeting, like many federations' national councils before it.
>
> A huge contradiction dominates their discussions: they say they want to defend the working class against being 'put on a war footing' under emergency powers and rule by decree, but above all, they are assuring the government of their ardent desire to strengthen national security and increase production in the interests of national defence.
>
> They want well-being and freedom in the shadow of the cannons, an idyll in a *blockhaus*, a loving kiss in a gas mask, a pat of butter in the barrel of a howitzer; they want to be soldiers but remain human beings. They will the end, not the means.
>
> The national council of the engineering workers' union has openly discussed this contradiction, which screamed out from the pages of the motions it adopted. Comrade Marcel Roy – the same man who wrote in *Syndicats* that 'war must not happen!' – debated Mr. Pomaret in *Le Peuple* of 5 April and with much intricacy tried to persuade him that it was possible to increase production in the war industries by means other than speed-ups [...] Roy would be angry if he realised it, but he used the same language as Timbaud, who also suggested in *Le Peuple* of 1st April that workers' productivity could be improved by lowering their workload (an April fool!). He wanted to assure the country that production would be increased by making the factories work 24 hours a day, and he made great play of the idea that some businesses, such as the Compteurs de Montrouge, were still not working in the interests of national defence [...].

The Central Committee of the trade union Cercles did not try and square the circle of reconciling the interests of the reactionary and bellicose bourgeois homeland with those of the working class. Instead it talked about the lessons of the past and the gulf which separated these interest groups: it realised the massive contradictions between them.

To defend one would be to sabotage the other. Organising resistance, whether secret or overt, to the rule-by-decree of slavery and war meant fighting so that the workers would not exhaust themselves in trying to achieve a superhuman task; so that their wages would not be spirited away; so that they should not be gassed like beasts in their workplaces: this meant undermining the imperialist war effort and refusing to take part in the union sacrée both in words and in deeds.

Keen not to slow down production, the CGT decided against calling a strike on 1st May. Despite the orders of the unions, *Le Réveil syndicaliste* called a strike 'against the 60 hour week and emergency powers':

The strong France of 1939 has triumphed over the strong proletariat of 1936, and it could not be otherwise, since the strength of bourgeois France is fundamentally rooted in the weakness of its proletariat [...] Following in the tradition of the engineering workers' federation which on 1st May 1915, in the middle of the war, defended its honour in defiance of the bureaucrats (among them Jouhaux) we want to make clear to our rulers that some of the working class, revolting against the union sacrée, will resign themselves neither to capitalist slavery nor to dying for the imperialist cause.

In truth this call to action found little support, and *Le Réveil* could only cite the example of a strike by the 350 workers at a building site in Poissy. The Lille tramworkers' union was expelled from the CGT for having called a strike.

On 31 July 1939 *Le Réveil syndicaliste* underlined the imminence of the danger of war 'in the coming weeks'.[82]

But in France the summer holidays are sacred, even for revolutionaries. Having predicted imminent war, the editors of *Le Réveil* announced its suspension until September. In September, war came. *Le Réveil* would not appear again.

Trade union opposition to the union sacrée

Some might be surprised by the fact that the technicians' union was only federation where the ideas of the class struggle Cercles were dominant.

Without doubt, the reason for this was that the field had only recently been unionised. Before the 1936 strikes, only a small minority of workers had joined the union, and those who had did so for ideological reasons. In the union leadership could be found members of all the far-left groups (including Trotskyists, members of the Union communiste and opponents of the Parti communiste). This leadership was in place until 1936, when the union membership suddenly went up to 75,000.

Here also, the failure of the 30 November 1938 general strike was damaging. Four hundred technicians were laid off. Léon Bardin estimates that only 25,000 people remained in the union.

However, the 21-22 January 1939 congress voted by 2,611 votes to 233 to maintain the same orientation, with 246 abstaining, mostly Stalinists. The reformists made concessions and equivocated, but all the same, the Lutte de classe tendency won 1,991 votes, as against 741 for the Amis des syndicats and 338 for the Stalinists. But in the other federations the opponents of the union sacrée were in the minority. *Le Réveil syndicaliste* could only point to a few other examples of workers sharing their positions, for example post workers in the Bouches du Rhône at their 23 March conference; or Lille food workers on 7 May. The only significant minority they had in any federation was that in the teachers' union. At the July 1939 congress, the *École émancipée* tendency proposed:

> [...] Faced with this drive to war, the congress declares without hesitation that the national, religious, political and racial ideas being put forward are nothing but lies designed to deceive the masses into taking part in a struggle which is not their own; that in reality the rival imperialist groups are simply fighting over raw materials and the world market; and that, as a result, in this struggle inherent to the laws of capitalist development workers do not have to any take side except taking sides against imperialism itself [...] At the same time the congress denounces the fascists who are building their forces in France as they are abroad: the reactionary wave which the world is experiencing as the consequence of economic crisis is strengthened with plans for war.
>
> [...] Fascism and war are products of the same system. We cannot save ourselves from one by accepting the other. We cannot defend ourselves from either except by fighting the system which creates both.

The tendency was divided. The Rhône groups rallied to the pacifist majority led by Haguenauer. The motion only won 194 votes, as against 763 for the reformists and 148 for the motion put forward by the Stalinist teachers.

The publishing union, led by anarcho-syndicalists, also held its fifteenth congress at the end of July (the previous one had been held … five years before, in 1934!). *Le Libertaire* reported on the event enthusiastically:

> Liochon (the federation leader) spoke fittingly on behalf of everyone when he said: 'It is not war that will restore freedom to those who have lost it. We must be pacifists, since we do not believe in the virtues of war. But if war came, trade union activism would be finished. We would not want it to be at all possible for them to rely on trade union organisations to make decisions about the war, assist in the conduct of hostilities or prepare conditions for peace. I refuse to take any section of the union movement to war'.[83]

Thus the bravery of the anarcho-syndicalist leaders would be over as soon as the declaration of war came: they did not even plan to pursue their pacifist propaganda.

> Charbit, of the Paris typists, put forward a motion on war which the congress voted through unanimously. The resolution declared the hostility of publishing workers to any war, even one waged under ideological pretexts. All the same I could not help but have a little doubt about the passage which referred to 'the policy of peace necessary to satisfy, in a spirit of equality, the legitimate demands of all peoples'. In truth, it is too idealistic and too generous … too generous, like all utopias. That makes us regret all the more the fact that not a single voice was raised at the congress in support of the only tactic which can save us from catastrophe: proletarian violence. Imperialist war? We can only avoid it with another war: the war against the State and against Capital ….

Having unanimously voted for a motion which said next to nothing, as is so common in the typographic community, the congress was rounded off with sloganeering and singing. *Le Libertaire* concluded: 'May we be broad, may we be forthright, and may we consider the fifteenth congress of the publishing federation to be a strong display of unity.'

This was not much to get excited about.

Chapter 2

THE PHONEY WAR

The last days of peace

After the annexation of Czechoslovakia in March 1939, there were no longer any doubts as to the imminence of war. Franco's decisive victory in Spain had bolstered the Rome-Berlin Axis. Hitler now threatened Poland, demanding Danzig and the corridor which divided Germany in two. For their part Britain and France had built a close alliance with Colonel Beck's Poland and had pledged to safeguard its territory. But their negotiations with the USSR went nowhere.

In France, reaction was strengthening its grip. In August 1939 the government banned *La Jeune garde*, organ of the Jeunesses socialistes ouvrières et paysannes (JSOP). In *Ce soir*, Louis Aragon welcomed this measure, but soon he was himself charged after writing about two journalists' relations with a German official: the government had banned all comment about the money the big dailies received from the Nazis. At his tribunal Aragon made a touching speech in favour of the freedom of the press.

The Communist press was remarkable for its chauvinism and energetically pressed for intervention on the side of Poland. *L'Humanité* had the headline: 'Will Poland be betrayed? Beware! They will again betray France by sacrificing Poland'.

And when Magnien titled his editorial 'We must stop this infamous plan!' he was talking about resisting the efforts of those who would abandon the colonels' Poland.

But on 23 August came quite a spectacle: the signing of a pact between Germany and the USSR was announced. Its secret terms planned the carving up of Poland. Now Hitler had a free hand. He knew that on the ground the French and British guarantees to Poland meant little. On 1 September, a date set by his General Staff long before, he invaded Poland. On 3 September France and Britain declared war.

When the German-Russian pact was announced, the Communist

press made an about-turn. *L'Humanité* welcomed it as an 'important contribution to peace'. The government immediately suspended the two Communist dailies in Paris. Despite this, the title of the banned 26 August *L'Humanité* proclaimed across eight columns 'Unity of the French nation against Hitlerite aggression'.

The PCF produced a leaflet in response to the ban:

Defend the country, defend peace! The German-Soviet non-aggression pact is a victory for the Soviet Union and a victory for peace. The fact that Hitler's ambassador was forced to go to Moscow is far from proof of fascism's strength. It was a blow against the anti-Comintern pact. It has weakened international fascism and thus served the cause of peace. The fascists are furious.

The leaflet continued by blending enthusiasm for the Hitler-Stalin pact with pursuit of the union sacrée:

Why have they suspended *L'Humanité* and *Ce soir*? Is it because the Parti communiste has declared that it shall do its duty in defending the homeland, democracy and peace? [...] If despite our wishes war breaks out, the Communists will do their duty in the defence of the country and democracy against fascist barbarism.

All of the media poured scorn on the 'treachery' of the USSR and the Parti communiste. On 24 August the Seine region SFIO launched a patriotic manifesto 'Faced with treachery!' The PCF itself was torn apart. The next day Gitton, the national secretary of the PCF, along with 22 of its 74 MPs, broke with the PCF in order to remain faithful to the nationalist policy. Confusion was widespread. The leaders who stayed with the PCF did not themselves want to break from the union sacrée. On 27 August Marcel Cachin wrote to Blum:

Comrade Blum, we are not renegades. At this time of great difficulty, the Parti communiste will clearly and loyally state that if Hitler declares war, he will find before him a French people united to defend the country, with the Communists in the front line. Nothing could lead the hundreds of thousands of French workers behind us to abandon that attitude.

These declarations of loyalty did not stop the repression. On 28 August all of the Communist newspapers were suspended, without the slightest sign of disquiet from the masses. But the PCF's parliamentary group was no less loyal to the union sacrée. Cogniot informed the Finance Commission that:

> He would vote through [military] credits in the same spirit with which he had applauded the Prime Minister's speech, and hoped for the unity of the whole nation with all of its loyal and fighting forces, as well as hoping for the reestablishment of equal rights for the whole press.

Indeed, on 2 September the Communist parliamentary group voted through the military credits. Daniel Lizou, the historian of the SFIO, recounts this memorable occasion:

> Parliament was convened on 2 September, not to declare war but to vote for a special credit of 75 billion francs destined to help France fulfil its obligations, after Daladier had affirmed in a well-received speech that the country would stand by its alliance with Poland. Like in 1914, every party turned down the opportunity to argue against this, in order to demonstrate the unity of France to the world. Parliament then closed until 30 November.

He added to this commentary:

> The SFIO played no particular role in this episode. We made war without remorse but also without enthusiasm. We had confidence in the decision taken; had General Weygand not stated that the French army was invincible? The Party was just about totally united.[84]

The anarchists' last stand

The only false notes in the union sacrée concert came from *Le Libertaire* and *Juin-36*. But the anarchists' attitude was not lacking in equivocation.

On 3 August the anarchist weekly described the passivity of the masses and denounced the chauvinism of the PCF. It announced the future revolution which would be the work of the most exploited workers:

> So here we are, twenty-five years on. This time, there are no demonstrations against the crime as it is prepared. The [labour movement] leaders have not waited for the treachery of the masses before themselves committing treachery: they have led the way. The Communists, at the behest of Moscow, have cried the clarion call of Déroulède.[85] They are the most to blame for the defeat of the working class now taking place. Bolshevism

has brought us to war.

Our rulers would be wrong, however, to think that they have won a decisive victory. Already among the proletariat there exist the ideas which tomorrow shall show it to be a young and growing force on the offensive against the old capitalist system. During its ascent the proletariat shall first off cast asunder the political parties which pretend to promote its well-being but which in truth represent the labour aristocracy, a class as rotten as the bourgeoisie itself. That is the first task of the proletariat on the road to emancipation.

Yet on 24 August, when the German-Soviet pact was announced, it joined in chorus with the rest of the press: 'Hitler and Stalin go hand in hand in their treachery! The proletariat must open its eyes to the Russian lie exposed.'

It concluded: 'After the Stalinist blow the proletariat must finish with Bolshevik duplicity and hound the agents of Stalin and Hitler out of the labour movement.'

Like the reformists and the bourgeois press, it called for splits in the unions. It did however maintain an anti-war stance:

But it would be an act of blindness on the part of [the proletariat] to accept being sent to be massacred for the capitalist and imperialist cause without having lifted a finger in defence of its own interests.

The anarchist weekly did appear on 31 August, but the censor left it with large blank patches. Of course, it did leave in an article with the title 'The time has come to sort out the labour movement by kicking out all of the Bolsheviks'. The anarchists thought they could 'sort out' the labour movement during wartime in tandem with the union sacrée reformists!

Le Libertaire planned to continue appearing legally. Under the title '*Le Libertaire* goes on' it declared:

Because of the difficult times we are living through and the reintroduction of censorship, our newspaper is going to find more and more difficulty in maintaining its already precarious existence. We have a choice: either to suspend publication, say nothing and wait for better times, or to try and continue appearing all the same [...] The censor will be there to stop us saying what we think. But you can be sure that we will never say what we do not think. *Le Libertaire* will therefore try and continue publication. *Le Libertaire* will remain the link between our comrades as we wait for things to settle down.

As we have seen, its revolutionary ambitions were modest. It added 'However we can, whatever they say, we shall continue publishing!', which suggested the possibility of illegal publication. But this issue would be the last. During the war, or rather, during the occupation, the anarchists would devote themselves to producing a few issues of an internal bulletin, *Lien*, of which the sole objective was to maintain communication between anarchist activists.

Le Libertaire would not appear again until 24 December 1944, five and a half years later, when things started to 'settle down'.

The end of the PSOP

On 23 August there appeared the last issue of *Juin-36* before the outbreak of war. It loudly proclaimed its internationalist positions: the German-Russian pact displayed the falsehood of the PCF's 'patriotic' arguments; the only cause worth fighting to the death for was proletarian revolution.

But would the PSOP be able to build an organisation capable of fighting for this revolution under the conditions of illegality imposed by the war? Would it be able to maintain unity with the left? Between 23 August and 3 September the PSOP fought for its existence: and it lost.

On 2 August Marceau Pivert left for the United States, where he was to give a series of meetings for the Lovestone group.

Before his departure an improvised meeting of the National Bureau took place, which no-one from the left attended. According to the administrative secretary Maurice Jaquier, Pivert had given it the instruction to create a clandestine organisation based at Poiraudeau in the Vendée, which would be constituted of Marceau Pivert, Daniel Guérin, Maurice Jaquier and Lucien Weitz. A strange leadership, given that Pivert was in the USA and Lucien Weitz was imprisoned in the Santé jail. As for Daniel Guérin, when war broke out he was mandated to establish an international secretariat for the FOI in Oslo; he left for Norway on the 25, and knew no more of his role in the 'illegal' leadership than Weitz did.

In fact the Permanent Administrative Commission (CAP) was the group's only leading body. On 31 August it held a dramatic meeting, where Jean Rous and Yvan Craipeau were in the minority. They demanded that the party and its press immediately turn to clandestinity, that the party constitute itself in tight cells in order to cope with repression and that a clandestine leadership including one Trotskyist representative be created.

Some of the majority leaders (Jaquier, Rouaix, Barré, Chapelain and Lefeuvre) also saw the need for a clandestine organisation. But they wanted it to replicate the legal organisation, and to stay based at the party headquarters 'where many comrades from Paris and the provinces as well as mobilised comrades visit'.

Hostile to the Trotskyists, they voted against their proposals. The majority of the CAP (D. and S. Nicolitch, L. Vaillant, Goldschild, Spinetta, D. Haas) refused outright any turn to clandestinity: the party and its press would remain legal; peacetime structures would be kept in place; and the leadership would be entirely composed of supporters of the majority.

The consequences of this were obvious: the propaganda of a legal party would have to be within the limits set down by the authorities; if it went outside these limits, the legal structures of the party would be transformed into police booby-traps. On 1 September the CAP met without the left and the JSOP majority. The left had to do what was necessary. In the absence of D. Guérin and L. Weitz the comrades responsible for the journal *La Voie de Lénine* met in the Jardin du Luxembourg. They decided to create a new autonomous clandestine movement based on the programme of the Fourth International. In order to respect the views of comrades who did not recognise it, it took the name Comités pour la IVe Internationale ['Committees for the Fourth International']. The leadership committee was composed of three comrades who were not suitable for conscription: Y. Craipeau, H. Kunstlinger and Marcoux.[86] The 'Comités' had not formally broken with the PSOP, but their communication with it became ever more scarce. The PSOP began to break up and its political trajectory now had little to do with its positions before the war. *Juin-36* resurfaced on 8 October in small format, much of it censored. 'The Party goes on, we remain loyal to socialism' declared the editorial. In fact, under S. Nicolitch's leadership the newspaper expressed little more than a vague pacifism. Its denunciation of jingoism was largely directed against the USSR, as the censor had blanked the rest. Stalin was portrayed as a sort of Machiavellian Lenin who had plunged the world into war in order to hasten the march of revolution.

The following issue, which appeared across four pages on 11 November, was even more confused. This time the censor hardly had to cut anything, except penciling out some of a pacifist statement by the British ILP. The main article, 'a better world', was primarily devoted to arguing against the illusion that the war could result in revolution.

An article titled 'Our Marx and our Rosa' did indeed reproduce an extract of Rosa Luxemburg ... but it was a polemic against the Bolsheviks' slogans on collectivising land.

The 20 December 1939 issue of *Juin-36*[87] was subject to greater censorship. Except for a page on the crisis in the trade union movement, almost nothing was left apart from an article on the rise of Napoleon III and a one-page warning against 'Trotskyist activities'.

The PSOP leadership, meeting on 1 September, only took one decision: to properly integrate the youth who had been afflicted by Trotskyism. Jaquier, disheartened, left Paris. However, Rouaix, Barré and Chapelain told him to come back and help organise the clandestine struggle, in spite of the leadership's opposition. They too tried to create a clandestine organisation at the edges of the official organisation:

> Some comrades have through their own initiative organised clandestine cells of two to five members in Aubervilliers, Bondy, Bagneux, Plessis-Robinson and in the eighteenth *arrondissement*.[88] Wanting for materials and money, they have gathered together the last few texts published by the party before the war. They have made episodic contact with other activists in Yonne, Cher, Vendée, Ain, Gard, Pyrenées-orientales, Somme, Loire, etc.[89]

20 November saw the last leadership meeting in which Trotskyists would participate. They attacked the PSOP's new trajectory and demanded autonomy in action for the Comités de la IVe Internationale. The majority for their part demanded that they accept a resolution which declared:

> No leaflet, circular or newspaper shall be distributed unless it has been submitted to the Party Bureau in advance and unless it has met with the approval of the Party Bureau or the CAP ....[90]

The representatives of the minority refused, and the CAP thus decided to expel them.

However, Jaquier and Rouaix and their allies decided to create their own organising centre. To this effect, Rouaix rented a local office on the grounds that 'the rue Rochechouard office has become a trap'. Letters were sent in small packets to comrades mobilised on the Maginot Line, particularly to the town of Longwy. This attempt at clandestine organisation quickly resulted in catastrophe. They could not help themselves from seeking out contacts in the 'trap'. In early December they were met there by police. Jaquier, Rouaix, Chapelain, Preiss from the eighteenth *arrondissement* and four JSOP activists were charged with re-creating the illegal Parti communiste (!) and publishing leaflets opposed to the interests of boosting morale in the army and among the population. On 1 March 1940 they were sentenced: the first four received five years' imprisonment; one of the youths three years;

and the others a one-year suspended sentence.[91] Later Jaquier and Rouaix would receive even harsher sentences for their pre-war activism. By the time the third issue appeared, announcing the expulsion of the 'Trotskyists', the PSOP had ceased to exist as an organisation.

However, a fourth issue was produced legally in January-February by what remained of the right wing. In May 1940 another issue appeared, this time illegal. It published an 'Appeal from the PSOP' with a profoundly different tone:

> We have told the proletariat a hundred times: either you stride on towards socialism or you will succumb to fascist dictatorship; if you do not hasten the proletarian revolution you will be thrown into imperialist war. And now? Who would dare claim that we were wrong? We must suffer *at the same time* imperialist war and fascist dictatorship. Who saw that coming?
>
> Stalin on one hand and Léon Blum on the other broke the mass movement in France in June 1936. [...] Some individuals have sadly capitulated in the face of the enemy's formidable pressure. Too bad for them! The demoralised and the primadonnas, the fatigued and the defeated have no place in our ranks. Those who doubt in the working class because they have seen it divided and disoriented by betrayal do not deserve the name 'socialist'. Such a situation as this demands quite the opposite: that the vanguard should multiply its numbers and build people's spirits, re-animate their hope, rally the forces of the working class and lead them into struggle.

Sadly, this appeal could only have been written by Marceau Pivert in America, unaware of what was really going on. It was not 'a few individuals' who had given in, but the party itself.

Was this a situation particular to France? The experience of the Oslo Bureau shows that it was nothing of the sort. Daniel Guérin has recounted in detail the way in which the PSOP right wing, at the last moment, mounted a series of manoeuvres to try and stop him going to Oslo and the post which had been granted to him by the Front ouvrier international [FOI].[92]

Along with Modiano, who joined him there, he tried to maintain contact with comrades and succeeded in publishing a few issues of the planned *Bulletin du liaison* in French. But the difficulties he faced were considerable. The young Norwegian socialists were slow to help him, both for political reasons (they themselves were a mixed bag) and for fear of being expelled from their organisation. The Swedish anarcho-syndicalists followed 'a reprehensible course'.[93] The British ILP kept in touch but was immersed in pacifism.

The Bureau only received a few letters – of little note – from the PSOP. They only maintained contact with the 'leftist' Moroccan branch and the Comités pour la IVe Internationale. The split in France provoked an exchange of bittersweet letters between Marceau Pivert and Daniel Guérin: Daniel Guérin held back from playing a double game with the FOI and the Fourth International. He thought that the left had split prematurely. But he warned Marceau Pivert that if he was taken up in the anti-Trotskyist hysteria, he would himself leave. A last letter from Daniel Guérin to Marceau Pivert in December 1940 welcomed his break with the Lovestone group. The Front ouvrier international broke up in several directions and none of the surviving groups remained linked. The FOI had no real existence beyond the PSOP.

It might seem surprising that although the Trotskyist movement was organised in the Comités it did not try and coordinate its activity with PSOP groups also involved in illegal activity. This was because it refused to use the legal channels with which these activists continued to engage with, since it considered them dangerous.

For its part, the new 'left' did not keep in touch. Thirty years later, Maurice Jaquier explained why:

> Why did we not maintain contact with you? For you it was a question of safety … and you were right. For us? It was more complicated: your departure gave us a certain measure of relief. Of course, tactically your positions were not that far from ours: but you know what they said about you, both in the SFIO and PSOP, that you were like an elephant in a china shop. When we should have broken with the right wing, when we should have been harder, we were too afraid of finding ourselves seeing eye-to-eye with you![94]

Would the revolutionaries be ready to face war?

The collapse of the PSOP was evidently no historical accident. Maurice Jaquier wrote:

> The PSOP was not ready to fight in the shadows. The first preparations did not come until July. They were insubstantial, aiming to disguise us all using nicknames and designating a less well known comrade as a secret messenger.
>
> Neither the organisation nor its members could cope with voluntary clandestinity, even less so because of the battles to come. The heterogeneity of their former political sympathies hardly lent itself to taking the type of

action necessary under the circumstances.

The PSOP came too late. It did not have the opportunity to harden, nor the means to transform itself. It wahs not a revolutionary party.

Several weeks before the war, Trotskyist activists knew that they could not rely on the PSOP's preparations for clandestinity. They had decided to make their own plans to cope with illegality. But their plans were hardly any better than those of the PSOP.

The members of the *La Commune* group, however, organised with some care. Copying the classic (Russian) rules of illegal activity before 1914, they decided to send Raymond Molinier and Pierre Frank out of France in order to maintain a leadership abroad. But the conditions of war rendered international relations precarious. As for the group itself, it was armed with secret material for propagandising among the army: an anti-militarist pamphlet with an anodyne title *Petites histoires de studio*. But such an item written before the war was so abstract that it was hardly of much use.

The members of the *La Voie de Lénine* group did not trouble themselves with any 'leadership abroad'. They were happy to recognise the International as their leadership. They furthermore communicated with the secretariat in Oslo. But for them also, such liaisons were so difficult that they were essentially left to their own devices.

When war broke out the Trotskyist movement was confronted with terrible circumstances. Not only had it proven impossible to transform the PSOP, but it was itself more divided and less powerful than ever. All that was left of *La Commune* was a small and isolated group. Of the activists who had refused to join the PSOP some had already given up on all activity, while the others, after publishing one issue of *La Lutte ouvrière*, either dispersed or joined the Union communiste group, which did not raise its head during the war. Some others were in prison (like Rigal, Stève and Schmidt). Of those who had joined the PSOP on the orders of the International, only a few (like Beaufrère) joined *La Voie de Lénine*; most of them (like Hic and Rousset) were not linked to it.

Should we therefore condemn the strategy of joining the PSOP? That would be to confuse cause and effect. This course became necessary precisely because the experience of the masses during the Popular Front period took place outside the Trotskyist movement. The latter, torn between activism and mere discussion, had proven unable to sink roots in the working class. It had shown itself unable to organise its forces as a vanguard. This powerlessness continued to show itself during the few months that the Trotskyists worked within the PSOP.

Some saw the decapitation of the movement on the eve of war as the work of Stalin's GPU.[95] Undoubtedly, the GPU did what it could: in France it assassinated Trotsky's son Sedov and Rudolf Klement, a German activist from the international secretariat; in Spain Held,[96] one of the leaders of the international movement, as well as the POUM leader Andreu Nin;[97] and soon it would murder Trotsky himself in Mexico. But the steamroller of working-class defeat was even more of a force.

In April 1939, in an interview with the black American comrade CLR James about the problems of the French movement, Trotsky said that its weakness was primarily a result of having been developed during a period of heavy defeats for the working class, as well as the degeneration of the Communist International and the USSR after the crushing defeat and extermination of the Left Opposition. Those who went against the current were:

> [...] always more or less outsiders from the general current of the workers' movement. Their value inevitably has its negative side. He who swims against the current is not connected to the masses. The social composition of every revolutionary movement in the beginning is not primarily of workers.
>
> [...] Insofar as it concerns France it is a long tradition of the French movement connected with the social composition of the country. Especially in the past the petty-bourgeois mentality – individualism on the one side, and on the other hand a tremendous capacity for improvising.
>
> [...] Our organisation suffers from the same illness, the traditional French sickness. The incapacity to organization and at the same time lack of conditions for improvisation. Even so far as we now had a tide in France, it was connected with the Popular Front. In this situation the defeat of the People's Front was the proof of the correctness of our conceptions just as was the extermination of the Chinese workers. But the defeat was a defeat and it is directed against revolutionary tendencies until a new tide on a higher level will appear in the new time.

Trotsky concluded:

> [...] history has its own laws which are very powerful, more powerful than our theoretical conceptions of history. Now you have in Europe a catastrophe, the decline of Europe, the extermination of countries. It has a tremendous influence on the workers when they observe these movements of the diplomacy, of the armies and so on, and on the other

side a small group with a small paper which makes explanations. But it is a question of his being mobilized tomorrow and of his children being killed. There is a terrible disproportion between the tasks and the means. If the war begins now, and it seems that it will begin, then in the first month we will lose two-thirds of what we now have in France. They will be dispersed. They are young and will be mobilized. Subjectively many will remain true to our movement. Those who will not be arrested and who will remain there may be three or five. I do not know how many, but they will be absolutely isolated.[98]

The Parti communiste français during the war

Over the first few weeks of the war the Parti communiste français found itself caught in a paradox. Because of its support for the Hitler-Stalin pact and the stance of the USSR it was subject to violent repression. Its official press was banned.[99] But at the same time the PCF declared its support for the union sacrée. What was left of its press joined in chorus with the nationalist press. The first sign of reservations appeared in *L'Humanité* on 7 September (published in leaflet form):

> But the French people do not confuse, and will never confuse, the people of Germany with these hangmen who, unable to give the workers and peasants bread, want to send them to die on the battlefields. The France of the Popular Front does not confuse the Germany of Beethoven, Goethe, Kant and Schiller [the leaflet oddly omits to mention Marx and Engels], which it admires and loves, with the Germany of concentration camps and Nazism.

This contradiction could not hold for long. The Allies had proven unable to help the Polish army. Hitler smashed it within 26 days. Conforming to the German-Soviet agreement, the Red Army itself invaded Poland on 17 September and 'liberated' the east of the country. On 28 September von Ribbentrop and Molotov signed a joint statement:

> The Reich government and the government of the Soviet Union, having decisively resolved the questions raised by the dissolution of the Polish state with an agreement signed today, and thus having laid the foundations for lasting peace in eastern Europe, together express the opinion that it would suit the true interests of all nations to put an end to the state of war which exists between Germany and France and Britain.
> The two governments will therefore engage in a common effort to

work with other friendly governments to reach this goal as soon as possible.

If the efforts if the two governments are nonetheless unsuccessful, then it shall be clear that it is Britain and France who are at fault for the continuation of the war.

The Parti communiste, banned on 26 September, took a new turn. On 1 October 1939, in the name of the party's greatly depleted parliamentary group, Florimont Bonte wrote a letter to Herriot in support of this German-Soviet 'peace offensive' (no more would be heard of this apart from in Hitler's 6 October speech to the Reichstag.)

France has again and again been given offers of peace. The mere thought that peace may soon be possible has raised great hope among the people of our country, who are terrified by the prospect of a long and cruel war … But barely had we heard of the new proposals for peace which have come thanks to the efforts of the USSR, and immediately the press responded in chorus 'No!'

Could it be that peace proposals are being rejected before they are even made known and before the representatives of the nation have been consulted?

On 4 October the Belgian weekly *Le Monde* published André Marty's[100] letter to Léon Blum, 'My lord, councillor of State' in which he vehemently denounced the treachery of the social-patriots and the lie of the union sacrée:

The current war in Europe is a war provoked by two imperialist camps, each of which wants to dispossess the other; as a result, workers and peasants have nothing to do with this affair.

This being the case, the Parti communiste decided to take the road of defeatism. A leaflet from early October declared:

No union sacrée!
The Communists have always fought, and shall always fight, against the big capitalists like Wendel and Schneider and other weapons-dealers for whom the war is excellent business. The union sacrée with these people, the union sacrée with their agents, with the La Rocques, the Maurras and the other fascists?

'Never! Never!' reply the people of France, leaving to the Socialists like Léon Blum and Paul Faure the unhappy privilege of being pulled along in their anti-Communist campaign, awaiting the spoils given to lackeys, rewarded by being beaten over the head….

The issue of *Cahiers du bolchévisme* which appeared in January 1940 sought to rearm the party politically. It included an analysis of Lenin's positions on the First World War and then critiqued the PCF's pre-October position:

Turning the imperialist war into a civil war. Favouring the defeat of his own government in the imperialist war.
That means that it is necessary to vote against war credits, create revolutionary organisations in the army, encourage fraternisation between the soldiers on the frontline and organise workers' and peasants' action against war and turn this action into insurrection against their imperialist government.

The *Cahiers* published A. Marty's letter and an October 1939 appeal by the executive committee of the Communist International. In fact, as against Marty, this appeal established a hierarchy of blame between the two camps and did not say a word about fascism and Hitlerism. Dimitrov commented:

At first Italy, Germany and Japan were very much the aggressors … Today the British and French imperialists have taken the offensive; they have thrown their people into a war against Germany […] This difference between *aggressors and those threatened* has disappeared. Moreover, it is the British and French imperialists who have shown themselves to be the most zealous in propagating the fire of war.

The camp of peace … was now with Hitler! Molotov affirmed this view without beating about the bush at the fifth session of the Supreme Soviet of the USSR on 31 October 1939:

When we talk today of the Great Powers of Europe, Germany now finds itself in the situation of a state which hopes to see peace and the quickest possible end to the war, while Britain and France are in favour of the continuation of the war and are against peace being concluded.
In addition to this, in Britain, just like in France, the war party have declared something of an ideological war against Germany, which brings

to mind the old wars of religion … it is foolish, criminal even, to lead such a war to destroy Hitlerism while draping oneself in the flag of 'democracy'. Today our relations with the German state are based on friendship, our support for Germany's plans for peace and, at the same time, our desire to contribute by all means to the development of Soviet-German economic relations in the interest of both countries.

These were the texts which, as A. Lecoeur later testified,[101] served as the Bible for the French Communists. Little by little, all of the attacks against Hitler disappeared from Communist propaganda. For example, in February 1940 a leaflet by the PCF's Paris region had as its title 'Daladier-Chamberlain-Mussolini-Franco and Pius XII'. It seems that Hitler was no longer among their enemies. The leaflet called for sabotage:

Workers, do not be accomplices of your worst enemies, those who are fighting against the triumph of socialism over a sixth of the globe in the Soviet Union. By all appropriate means – by putting to use all of your wits and all of your technical skills – stop, slow down and render useless the machinery of war.

Some sabotage really did take place. At the Farman works the young Communist Roger Rambaud and five workers provoked an explosion while stealing some equipment: four of them were condemned to death and three were executed in Bordeaux. Revolutionary defeatism turned into defeatism pure and simple.

However, PCF activists thought they were renewing Leninist internationalism and fighting for the revolution. At the start of June 1940 Leon Trotsky paid homage to their courage:

In France the Stalinists have proved their bravery in fighting their government. They are still inspired by October. They are a group of revolutionary forces under the thumb of Moscow, but are nonetheless honest.

The PCF distributed a relatively significant amount of propaganda in the army, including *L'Humanité du soldat, la Liaison* (223rd Infantry Regiment), *Soldats de France* (Mayenne), *Ceux du 31e* (Le Havre), *l'Étoile rouge* (Metz), *Cherbourg naval.* It called on soldiers to mutiny and to fraternise with enemy troops.

Workers … soldiers sent into the massacre for Swedish iron or Romanian oil are not afraid of death! They would rather risk their lives fighting for the end of the capitalist system of war and poverty than die for business interests.[102]

In fact, this propaganda had little effect. The press had already widely reported Stalin's December 1939 telegram to Ribbentrop: 'The friendship of the Soviet and German people, *cemented in blood*, has every hope of being stable and lasting.'

When Hitler occupied Denmark and landed in Norway, Molotov declared: 'The Soviet government can well understand the measures that Germany has been forced to take. We wish Germany complete success in its defensive operations.'

In this vein the masses did not see the PCF as the vanguard of the revolution, but as a satellite of Hitler. That was why the Parti communiste was cut off from its former popular support.

The PCF was considerably weakened. Its organisation shaken by repression and the departure of 22 of its MPs, it was abandoned by the majority of its members. It only had a few thousand activists left. Its material resources were severely reduced. It could no longer rely on its municipalities, trade unions and legal apparatus.

However, it had not disappeared 'as an organisation of the working class' as the Trotskyists believed. Its structures had not collapsed. For its activists, the USSR remained the *deus ex machina* which would strike in the service of revolution. They kept listening to Radio-Moscow (and also, no doubt, the clandestine station 'Radio-Humanité' which would later be denounced as Hitlerite). They remained hopeful that the situation would soon change.[103]

Socialists for national unity

No one in the SFIO argued against the policy of 'national defence'. Whether they were left-wing pacifists like Zoretti, right-wingers like P. Faure, devoted partisans of war like Zyromski or, like Léon Blum, more hesitant, all accepted the principle of national unity. In this union sacrée the SFIO Socialists would play a secondary role. They let Parliament meekly give up its power to declare war. The Daladier government led a reactionary police-dictatorship, but the SFIO was happy with whingeing about the lack of parliamentary control.

On 5 September its parliamentary group took a critical stance for the first time in public. Its motion, with 115 votes for, 10 against and 7 abstentions, called for support for Chamberlain's proposals to seek a compromise with Hitler by sincerely looking into German-Russian peace offers. A summary motion began by recalling that:

France only entered into the war in order to meet its obligations to a free people who fell victim to a despicable attack, thus satisfying the most powerful demand of human solidarity.

But how then could they negotiate on the basis of German-Russian proposals, whose first demand was recognition of the division of Poland? This problem was why the motion demanded 'that the government makes known to the world the economic and political demands which, for the French, are conditions of peace'.[104]

There was little room for manoeuvre.

The Socialists had no political initiative. They devoted themselves to assuring the government of the passivity of the working class and joining in the campaign against the Communists. Albeit with some reservations, the SFIO supported anti-Communist repression. On 27 September Léon Blum wrote in response to the banning of the Parti communiste: 'Without being acclamatory, the majority of the Party sees this as legitimate and only natural.' But, he added: 'I think that the ban is a mistake. The PCF has been stricken by unthinking errors, but now will take those ideas on to another plane. The ban will not hasten its collapse, but rather, abate it.'[105]

The Ligue des Droits de l'Homme took to action against the repression, but Le Populaire censored its press release. After the USSR's invasion of Finland in November, the SFIO hardened its positions. Its parliamentary group voted in December to cancel the Communist MPs' parliamentary immunity, and in January, to expel them. In the Senate, the SFIO representative Bachelet was keen to make an exception for Marcel Cachin, given his patriotic record: but Marx Dormoy vehemently argued in favour of his expulsion.

In Parliament the Socialist Barthélemy said on 20 February 1940: 'Thorez, Catelas and many others should not be put in front of a firing squad – that would give them too much dignity – but instead they should feel the blade of a guillotine.'

The Socialist Serol, who had become Minister of Justice, announced on 10 April that 'propagandists for the policies of the Third International' would receive the death penalty.

The repression went on to threaten the Socialists themselves. Le Populaire complained about the partiality of the censor and its de facto banning. In January 1940 some SFIO activists were arrested for 'anti-French activities'. The conference of regional secretaries held in February protested against 'government and police abuse, trying to tar Socialists and Communists with the same brush'. It decided to 'hold the government responsible for the difficulties our branches and fractions face in organising meetings'.[106]

These branches often pushed the logic of the union sacrée as far as it would go: their own disappearance. The SFIO historian wrote without irony: 'Some branches with an admirable desire for national unity decided to cease activity completely. However, the SFIO leadership tried to keep in touch with its members.'

Like the PCF, the SFIO was a mere shadow of its former self.

In the unions, the reformists also jumped at the opportunity to expel the Communists, to unseat their officials and to seize their power bases.

They made use of the repression to expel their own rivals. The national technicians' federation could hardly be charged with complicity with Moscow: it had condemned the German-Russian pact as well as the British-French-Polish alliance. But its leadership affirmed its desire to stick by its class-struggle politics. The CGT leadership dissolved the federation on the ridiculous charge of late payment of dues.

The unions no longer met. Their numbers collapsed. The engineering workers' federation, which had almost 800,000 members in 1937, now had barely 30,000.[107]

Although its 10 November 1939 decree dispensed with all elections and replaced them with officials 'chosen by the most representative legal workers' organisations', in fact the CGT only managed to find representatives for 200 'national defence' businesses out of a total of 10,000.

In January 1940 one of the new CGT leaders, Belin, was forced to admit their failings, and further remarked two months later: 'Trade union action has been pared down to the minimum: it yields nothing; it is missing its basic tenet, i.e. expressing the views of the working class.'

That is to say that the workers, even if they did not trust in the Parti communiste, felt even less represented by the reformists. That did not stop the latter, now the only official spokesmen of the working class, from shamelessly kowtowing to the government and the bosses in its name. Just like during the First World War, they said they had taken this line in the interests of 'national defence', but this time around they made clear that they had been doing the same thing as far back as 1936.

A good illustration of this policy was given by the Hotel Majestic agreement, signed at the beginning of October by CGT and business representatives, under the watchful eye of the Minister of Armaments. All of the media rejoiced in this. *Le Temps* (the ruling class in newspaper form) set the tone:

> We have had good news this morning, although it was unsurprising. Under the auspices of the Minister of Armaments, employers and workers

have made an agreement to supply the armies of the Republic with the means necessary for victory with the least suffering for all concerned. They have just signed a joint statement which is worthy of spirit and rich in human feeling and patriotism.

Charles Maurras, leader of the monarchist Action française party, congratulated the trade union and employers' representatives for their 'excellent statement'.

Le Populaire was no less full of enthusiasm. Léon Blum was teary-eyed: the Majestic agreement reminded him of Matignon in 1936. As for the 'left-wing Socialist' Zyromski, he wrote in an article with the title 'The working class in the life of the nation':

It is worth emphasising the statement made by Messrs. Lambert, Ribot and Lente and our comrades Jouhaux and Chevalme, acting on their own account but keeping in mind the need to express the views of those whom they represent. We have repeatedly stressed our desire to see the trade unions and the public authorities collaborate closely in all matters concerning war production and the economic life of the country [...] We note today's declaration with satisfaction [...] We do so all the more keenly because this declaration displays the close links between national defence and human and social progress.

Opposition to the policy of union sacrée remained weak. The class struggle Cercles' *Réveil syndicaliste* stopped appearing in July. Only the teachers' union minority expressed opposition, through *L'École émancipée* (in number 3 of 1939), but it published no further issues. The technicians' federation produced a statement in protest against the national union: the reformist CGT leadership, as we have seen, disbanded this federation in December 1939.

A new opposition was in the works. In November appeared *Notre Syndicalisme*, a newsletter published by syndicalists like Guénec, Tidone, Galli and Gourdin. Its headline read '*L'Humanité* being wrong isn't the reason that *Syndicats* is right'. Its manifesto finished:

Trade unionism as we see it [...] must be less abstract, less theoretical and less academic than the pen-pushers would have it, but it must also pose sharply the problem which the victors of 1918 could not resolve: that of the proletariat. It rejects the Russian régime – which has edified the proletariat all the better to subjugate it – as well as all dictatorships' 'proletarian' demagogy. *It wants neither Bolshevism nor corporatism.* It says that the Europe of the future shall never be human and just unless all countries take action together. The first action must be … the abolition of wage-labour.

All of this was vague enough. The syndicalists hardly had any opportunity to demonstrate their opposition in action. The working class was demoralised and paralysed. This demoralisation was a result of the behaviour of the two parties who claimed to represent it. But the political situation also explained the lack of any action. War was here, but Hitler had not ceased trying to find some arrangement with Britain. Mobilisation for war in France had also had its effect. The French army, after a brief incursion at Sarre, stuck to its positions. The Allies were relying on a campaign of exhaustion and naval blockade to force Germany to give in.

For several months the war on the Western Front was limited to patrol missions, with a few skirmishes between the Rhine and the Mosel. This 'phoney war' was reminiscent of the 'phoney peace' which had preceded it. Gas-masks were just somewhere to keep snacks.

The population was not beset with any patriotic fever. It was reassured to be placed under a régime of police repression much more bearable than that which it had feared. Workers saw their working day get longer, their standard of living fall and their rights swept away: but they hardly protested at all, for fear of being mobilised.

The Communist and Trotskyist press could only refer to a few incidents: At the 'Petites voitures d'Aubervilliers' the workers went home at 6pm rather than the 7pm clocking-off time which the bosses were trying to force on them. Workers at an aircraft plant refused to work extra hours. At the Compteurs de Montrouge they walked out for twenty minutes in response to a 15 percent pay cut.

The Comités pour la IV Internationale

Even more than the repression, this social climate paralysed the activities of the internationalists. In the face of the power of the military machines, every struggle seemed rather derisory. When war was declared there were few signs of revolutionaries. We are only aware of two events in the country: 30,000 leaflets were given out in Marseille (where the PSOP was Trotskyist) and a few hundred posters were put up in Nantes by the JSOP.[108]

Trotsky had been pessimistic in predicting that only three or four people would stay loyal to the cause. However the situation was hardly brilliant. A few did still take action, such as J. Rous in Paris and R. Filiâtre in Nantes.

But most were practically cut off from the organisation; the rest were only engaged in piecemeal activity. Strict regulations prevented any direct contact with imprisoned activists. The organisation had few workers in the national defence industries: it was largely based on young people who could not be mobilised and women. In the Nantes region, for example, the PSOP went with the Comités, but it was reduced to a small core.

The repression contributed to these organisational problems. Sometimes, as in the Paris region, the authorities struck out against the activities of the Comités. Often previous activity was punished: in Paris, Marcel Beaufrère was arrested at the news meeting the PSOP dared to stage on the same day as the announcement of general mobilisation; in Brittany the Concarneau organiser Marc Bourrhis was interned at the Châteaubriand camp along with the Communist mayor Pierre Gueguen, who had joined the Fourth International. Foreigners were taken to internment camps, among them POUM members and a member of the Comités' leadership trio, Marcoux, who was replaced by Marcel Gibelin.

The movement suffered above all from its reliance on improvisation. Activists actually had only clandestine contacts with the west of France. It was only several months later that contact was established with Bordeaux, Lyon and Marseille. Its practical means were poor. The *Bulletin de la IVe Internationale* carrying the date of 20 September appeared late. Their agitational bulletin *L'Étincelle* was only produced – copied across four pages – three times, in November, December and January. Comrades outside Paris sometimes had to copy it out by hand.[109] Only a few nation-wide leaflets were produced in the early months of 1940.

Divided into three branches, the Paris region[110] functioned reasonably well. But in October it lost contact with the East Paris branch when the organiser there decided to leave[111] after telling her comrades that the national organisation had collapsed; she published three issues of a clandestine newspaper, *l'Ouvrier*, before being arrested at the start of 1940. Most of the branch's activists resumed contact with the Comités after the arrival of German troops.

Initially international contacts were maintained. The *Bulletin mensuel d'informations internationals* was sent from Oslo. The Americans kept up contact. The *Bulletin de la IVe Internationale* published Trotsky's statement on the German-Russian pact, the interview Marceau Pivert gave to *Workers' Age* on the same subject, an appeal by the South African Trotskyists, an except from the Danish newspaper *Politiken* on the appearance of leaflets titled 'Down with Hitler and Stalin! Long live Trotsky!' in Berlin. New York was contacted from Paris with the help of the American journalist and poet Mangan. But soon contact was reduced to exchanging letters under the cover of personal correspondence: a primitive means of secrecy which resulted in indecipherable dialogue. The international news in *L'Étincelle* became suspect, for example its announcement of a strike on the Siegfried line.

The small group of Comités activists in France was isolated. However *L'Étincelle* featured news from a fair few Parisian factories (Chausson, SIFA, la Lorraine, les Mureaux and Gnome et Rhône) and from the front (Daladier being jeered; the refusal of the 31st Infantry Regiment in Kairouan in Tunisia to obey orders). *L'Etincelle* reported on the anti-union sacrée resolutions of the teachers' federation minority and the technicians' union.[112] Along with the *Bulletin de la IVe Internationale* it attacked splitters in the unions. The second issue denounced the Law on Suspects, the internment of revolutionaries and Communists in camps, unemployment, the reformist politics of the unions and the ban on the technicians' federation. But wanting for a base among the working masses, its propaganda tended to be rather abstract.

However, the *Bulletin de la IVe Internationale* stuck by its principles. On 18 September Gilbert (an alias of Yvan Craipeau) tried to respond to the arguments of the media and the concerns of the working class:

The Second World War had not even started when the protagonists unleashed, via radio and mass leafleting, an enormous campaign of brainwashing to place all the blame for the war on their enemy. Hitler, as he would have it, only wanted to defend peace against the provocations of the Polish militarists and British encirclement. As for the British-French-Polish allies, they would only make war to 'consolidate' a peace threatened by one man alone, Hitler.

The article attacked the 'manoeuvres of the treasuries' and showed that the war was imperialist, seeking to re-divide the world's markets. Hitler had been brought to power by international capitalism. It explained that in reality the war had begun with the invasion of Ethiopia.

The article analysed 'the errors of pacifists' who believed that war was a special phenomenon caused by the activities of 'jingoists'. Under the capitalist system peace could only mean cease-fire. If Hitler managed to secure peace, which seemed highly unlikely, national questions – far from being resolved – would be even more sharply posed, as the Czech crisis had already proven.

After taking to task the 1939 version of the union sacrée – in which the

PCF was again trying to participate – the article showed that the war was neither a struggle against any one aggressor nor a war for freedom and democracy against fascism.

> Faced with the reality of conflict, there has not been a single instance of slogans calling for soldiers to disobey orders, sabotage or insurrection against the war. As we had predicted, a wave of chauvinism has broken out. But the situation is not the same as 1914. Nationalists have been forced to restrain themselves somewhat.

They could not expect big workers' struggles in the coming months. Rancour would initially be directed against investors and war profiteers. Propaganda had to spread among the masses this idea: 'we are waging war in the interests of capitalist dividends'.

They had no doubt that 'the rising tide of the working class faced with shortages, bombing raids and bloody massacres' would lead to a proletarian revolution.

> Typical are the words that the intelligent bourgeois weekly *Match* puts in the mouth of Coulondre, French ambassador to Germany: 'Coulondre led Hitler to believe that the real winner will not be Stalin, but Trotsky'.

It was still necessary to build a revolutionary party. The PSOP had shown itself to be inadequate. If it persisted in sticking to 'the maintenance of social-democratic ideology and organisational practices […] it would disappear'.

The powerless London bureau was incapable of leading a revolution. They had to build the Fourth International, the world party of socialist revolution. The article finished with an optimistic quote from Trotsky: 'Despite its extreme weakness, the situation of the revolutionary vanguard is incomparably more favourable than it was 25 years ago.'[113]

For the moment revolutionaries could not find an echo. They had to wait for that. The article had as its title 'Against the current'. They expected a long war of attrition to mature the revolutionary situation both on and behind the front line.

The Western Front collapses

In early 1940 the situation seemed stable. The American ambassador Sumner Wells toured the European capitals in search of a compromise. He failed. However, the French bourgeoisie was not keen to engage in combat with Hitler. In March, it was rather more concerned with the threat of war with the USSR, which had just forced Finland to make territorial concessions. It planned to use Turkey as the base from which to attack. It was projects such as this, as well as putting the Communist MPs on trial, that Parliament discussed in its secret sessions.

For the first time, the Socialists took the initiative politically by uniting with the right to overthrow Daladier, who had not kept his promise to help Finland. When Parliament met there were only 256 votes in his support: 283 Socialist and reactionary MPs abstained, and he had to resign. The nationalist Paul Reynaud took charge of a new government including six SFIO ministers. As Reynaud himself noted, the Socialists were his most devoted followers.[114]

In April, Hitler occupied Denmark and marched into Norway. The French government responded by sending an expeditionary corps to Narvik. 'We have halted the juggernaut' announced Paul Reynaud, who received the unanimous backing of Parliament. But the expedition did not last long. Hitler occupied the whole of Norway and installed a puppet government under Quisling. The British were only able to hold on in Iceland. On 9 May Paul Reynaud brought the far right into his Cabinet.

On 10 May Hitler abruptly unleashed Blitzkrieg on the West. The 'phoney war' was over. He occupied the Netherlands in five days, and Belgium in ten. The British army managed with some difficulty to evacuate Dunkirk along with some French troops.

The impotence of the General Staff was obvious. Paris was threatened. Disorganisation screamed out from every level of command. This time around, defeat was a certainty.

On 12 May the SFIO National Council affirmed:

> The party's desire to wholeheartedly support the French forces assembled to resist aggression, protect the nation's territory, guarantee the independence of peoples and to achieve the just aims of France everlasting.[115]

On 19 and 20 May Paul Reynaud totally reshuffled his Cabinet. On the 20th, when Pétain became Minister of State and vice-president of the Council, Blum wrote that the reshuffle 'could only serve to maximise the country's wartime potential.'

Total disaster ensued. Between 5 and 9 June the new front collapsed. The tide of refugees spread towards the south. On the 10th, G. Mandel decided to evacuate the prisons: certain activists, including Jaquier, took the opportunity to escape.

A Comités pour la IVe Internationale leaflet called on soldiers to take power over their units and try and defend the capital against Hitler themselves. In taking power from the army, they would incite the workers to overthrow the teetering authority of the bourgeois: the character of the war would change. But this small group of Trotskyists had no means by which to make themselves heard in the ranks. Here and there soldiers replaced incompetent officers; but the great mass of them were only thinking about how to get out of the army. They did not give the Communists any more of a hearing.

Paris was declared an open city[116] and the government fled to Bordeaux. Radio Comintern advised the Communists: 'Whatever happens, do not leave Paris; make sure *L'Humanité* appears legally as soon as the German troops arrive, in order that they will face a fait accompli.'

However, just like Parliament, the PCF's secret command was moved to Bordeaux. It was on standby, ready for its eventual coming to power. A PCF leaflet called for the Reynaud government to be replaced by a government which, taking up Herriot's ideas, would be able to make peace in tandem with the Soviet Union. Given the USSR's support, the Communists hoped that defeat would make way for a Maurice Thorez government. In April the party leader proclaimed:

> Our country deserves better than being cited as an example of reaction and as a British dominion. The country does not want a government of Pitts and Coburgs. It wants a government of peace supported by the mass of the people, giving guarantees against reaction and working with the Soviet Union to re-establish general peace. Only a government like this can guarantee the independence of our country, freeing it from the control of the agents of French and British capital.[117]

We might note that he makes no allusion to the control of German capitalism nor of Hitler. But when Hitler took to the offensive, *L'Humanité* changed its tone. You could not expect an uprising by the population and the army except by making use of their anger against government weakness and the power of anti-fascist sentiment. On 17 May 1940 *L'Humanité* headlined 'Save our country and our people from poverty, ruin and death'. Denouncing the capitalists aided by the treachery of the social-democrat leaders and the CGT traitors, it argued:

> Through class egotism they have strengthened international fascism. To crush the Popular Front in Spain they helped Hitler and Mussolini to

crush the Spanish Republic. At Munich they sacrificed Czechoslovakia, handing 1,500 planes over to Hitler's Germany [...]

For many years the politicians who are now in the machinery of government have constantly flirted with Hitler, thinking of him as a gendarme defending capitalism against the workers' movement [...]

All of these people planned war, but they hoped it would break out between Germany and the USSR. That is why they did everything they could to prevent an agreement with the Soviet Union which could, for a time at least, have prevented war [...]

The Fifth Column of the agents of capitalism and fascism remains intact in our country.

Some people reckoned on a popular uprising. A leaflet in Bordeaux declared: 'Workers, organise popular militias and disarm the reactionary bands.'

L'Humanité of 20 June proclaimed 'Long live peace, for the revolution!'. In fact, no popular movement arose in answer to these proclamations.

In Paris, around 18 June some still believed that the front might hold on the Loire. Therefore there was the chance that the south would ferment with revolutionary culture.

In deserted Paris, there was a meeting between representatives of the Comités and the old *La Commune* group: the latter[118] suggested taking advantage of the disorder by taking over a radio station and symbolically declaring a revolutionary government. This was unreal. More prosaically, the Comités comrades got their hands on a copier and a typewriter, which they took to their new base in Nantes. There they found a strange situation, with the Nantes organisation enthusiastic in the belief that the revolution would soon follow the defeat.[119] A copier and typewriter, which were oddly hidden within some trees, served to produce leaflets calling on German soldiers to turn their fire against Hitler. The organisers doused false hopes and put an end to agitation which was just as useless as it was dangerous.

It was not surprising that the comrades were disconcerted by events. So too were the Allied governments. The British tried in vain to keep France in the war. Churchill made an extraordinary proposal to the French government on behalf of Great Britain: to unite the two countries under a common government and parliament. On 18 June an almost unknown general made a radio appeal from London, calling for the continuation of the war. Few people heard it.

But the chips were down. On 16 June Pétain replaced Reynaud. He brought two SFIO ministers into his government. Under the pressure of

General Weygand, the majority of the Socialists abandoned any idea of resistance. On 22 June the Pétain government signed the armistice. A new period began: the Occupation.

Chapter 3

A TIME OF CONFUSION

The attitude of Socialists and Communists after Hitler's victory

The working class did not use defeat as an opportunity to take power. It was atomised, demoralised and, moreover, its vanguard had completely lost its political compass. It was a time of great confusion.

The majority of Socialist SFIO MPs voted for Pétain. On 10 July, along with the majority of what had once been the Parliament of the Popular Front, they handed over all power to the new régime based at Vichy: they themselves put an end to the republican order. A significant section of the CGT reformists, after muzzling the working class, gave their backing to the new régime of collaboration with Hitler on the pretext of serving the wartime needs of the union sacrée. With Belin in the lead, these people devoted themselves to replacing trade unions with corporatism.

It was not until October (after the failure of the German project to invade Great Britain) that we saw the first leaflet by Socialists 'in resistance'. Lebas and Augustin Laurent produced *L'Homme libre* in the North at the same time as the first Gaullist publications (such as *Pantagruel, Notre droit* and *En captivité*) appeared, and it was indistinguishable from them.[120]

As for the Parti communiste, it still dreamt of a Maurice Thorez government. On 17 June Molotov addressed the German ambassador von Schulenburg with 'the Soviet government's most enthusiastic congratulations for the magnificent success of the German army'.

On the same day the clandestine *L'Humanité* appeared, with the slogan 'Workers of the world, unite!' in French and German. It demanded a break with Britain and a popular government to secure peace.[121]

> Will the City of London manage to continue the massacre of our brothers and our sons?... Or shall the will of the people of France carry the day? The answer will depend on the people themselves. Our action must guarantee peace and security, using all the means available to a government based

on the mass of the people, working with the USSR to re-establish general peace across the world.

The formula was the same as before the collapse, although 'taking measures against reaction' and the demand for independence had been dropped. On the same day two party organisers, Denise Ginollin and Maurice Tréand, held negotiations with the German authorities over the legal publication of *L'Humanité*.

The party envoys were arrested by the French police, but the Gestapo freed them and negotiations resumed on 25 June. The PCF's letter to the Propaganda-Staffel – which, according to Auguste Lacoeur, was written by Jacques Duclos[122] – described what the politics of a legalised *L'Humanité* would be:

> Our newspaper *L'Humanité* would dedicate itself to denouncing the work of the agents of British imperialism who want to drag the French colonies into the war, and to call on the colonial peoples to struggle against their imperialist oppressors for independence.
>
> Our newspaper *L'Humanité* would dedicate itself to arguing for a policy of European peace and for a French-Soviet friendship pact, which would complement the German-Soviet pace and so create the conditions for a lasting peace.[123]

The 25 June 'Appeal to the people of Paris' took up the same themes:

> In vain do the agents of British imperialism now try to persuade the people of France that they must continue the war in the interests of the City of London financiers [...]
>
> The government the country is waiting for and which events demand is a popular and democratic government, supported by the people, inspiring confidence in them, giving them reason to work and hope: a government of struggle against the plutocrats.[124]

In the course of the negotiations over the legal appearance of the Communist press, difficulties arose concerning the title and the party's logo. The PCF hoped to get around this by publishing *Ce soir* instead of *L'Humanité*. In the meantime, it altered its language and made noises as to display its goodwill.[125]

Through the month of July it called on Parisians to send 'petitions and individual letters' to the occupation-controlled council which had replaced the municipal council. *L'Humanité* attacked Pétain and Laval, reproaching them for not being able to 'put France back to work' as the occupier – wanting to use the country's resources for its war effort – had demanded.

Thus the 7 July edition under the title 'Down with the rotten government' it commented:

> The plutocrats, after driving France into war and defeat, are now planning to reduce it to slavery ... They talk a lot about putting France back to work, but they're not making progress; the Vichy government with its attitudes is not going to give the necessary impetus [...] France does not need a government of the 'rotten' but ... a government which will grab the plutocrats by the throat and give work and bread to all.

At the same time it encouraged workers to fraternise with German soldiers:

> It is particularly comforting in these unhappy times to see many Parisian workers getting on well with German soldiers, whether that be on the street or in the bistro. Bravo, comrades, and continue even if it does not please certain bourgeois who are as stupid as they are nefarious. The brotherhood of peoples is no longer just a hope: it is becoming a living reality.[126]

We might note that this fraternisation had nothing to do with calling on German soldiers to stand up to Hitler, but instead securing the 'brotherhood of peoples' with Hitler's army.

L'Humanité may well have attacked the Vichy government, but for many months it did not write a single word criticising Hitler. It was not until 4 January 1941 that it dared to write 'the chatter of Messrs. Occupiers simply serves to hide the sad reality of capitalism'.

In a country occupied and crushed by Hitler's army, *L'Humanité* amazingly managed not to mention words like Hitler, Nazis or Hitlerism even once. It did not break with this line until 18 May 1941 when it described a demonstration 'against Brinon[127] and Hitler'.

The PCF attempted to pursue legality. It ordered its elected representatives to hold their surgeries openly. The result: they were arrested. *L'Humanité* of 2 August 1940 protested: 'They arrested Grandel, the general councilor from the Seine who was meeting with constituents; the comrade Dumont; five councilors from Montreuil....'

This did not stop them from – the same day – celebrating the fact that their instructions for delegations to the Vichy representative had been obeyed.

In January 1941, still, we saw the Villejuif Communists consulting with the Gestapo to find out if Communists pursued by the French police might take refuge in the Kommandantur. After the Liberation, the Communist leader Tillon criticised this tactic:

> Concretely speaking, it was a mistake that in the Parisian region we let several comrades come out of clandestinity and hand themselves over to police surveillance, as if Communists could have legal status under fascist occupation.[128]

After the Liberation PCF historians focused attention on a manifesto written by Maurice Thorez and Jacques Duclos, dated 10 July 1940 and which included the proud statement 'Never will a great people like our own be enslaved'. This appeal apparently 'played a decisive role in the birth and organisation of the resistance'[129]. Some have claimed that the document refers to events that happened after 10 July. In any case, no issue of *L'Humanité* made any reference to such a statement and the arguments made in their main newspaper were very different indeed, at least until February-March 1941.

Marceau Pivert offers De Gaulle his 'revolutionary dynamite'

The PSOP barely existed apart from its 'representatives abroad', namely Daniel Guérin on his own in Oslo – he would soon return to France – and Marceau Pivert in the USA. But Marceau Pivert did distinguish himself with one significant move. On 25 June, answering General de Gaulle's call [for continued resistance to occupation], he offered him his collaboration:

> Without doubt your methods of struggle are very different to those we would advise: your specialism is military force and you have powerful material resources. But you yourself have realised that force will not be enough unless it is in the service of a clearly defined cause.

But Marceau Pivert had means at hand which were not available to De Gaulle: 'a few packages of political dynamite which he thought could be effective.'[130] Concretely he meant using Allied planes to drop leaflets on Germany with the text (in French and German) of the 'Front ouvrier international's appeal against war'.

Thus could develop a movement of revolutionary fraternisation, which we think possible due to the suffering the war doles out to all workers, whether conquered or conquerors.[131]

Marceau Pivert admitted not being certain that his proposal would be accepted: 'I am aware of the possibility that this message might be misunderstood ... I am aware of the powerful interests at play which might mean that this letter is in vain.'

But he appealed to the 'realism' of his correspondent. De Gaulle's response was interesting:

> Although we are obviously not following the same path, and you and I have different means of combating the enemy, I keenly note your desire to fight Hitler and Mussolini, who have enjoyed a temporary success.

The head of 'Free France' understood that the collaboration of 'revolutionary' socialists would entail their rallying, pure and simple, to the aims and objectives of the French ruling class he represented.

On 18 August 1940, Marceau Pivert replied to De Gaulle: 'I was greatly pleased to receive a reply to my previous letter but I was dismayed that there was no specific answer to the plan I suggested to you....'[132]

He gave De Gaulle a lesson in socialist politics to show him that he was wrong to dismiss his proposal. He further added:

> The leadership of my party[133] assures me that nothing is lost for good. The men who stand by the idea of salvation (sic) are not weak or powerless except in that they lack the material resources and the arms available to you. Would you rather abandon these masses of workers and peasants, betrayed but not defeated, to the propaganda of the Stalinists, the Doriotites,[134] or Mr. Déat, who have at hand powerful propaganda machines?

He suggested a meeting with [Fenner] Brockway, leader of the Independent Labour Party.

Marceau Pivert said that De Gaulle had met with the ILP secretary John Macnair, but had not been favourable to the distribution of the appeal. However, the BBC broadcast sections of it.[135]

In France, where the PSOP had disappeared, the direct influence of this correspondence was zero. It only fed discussion in the USA. But it represented the confusion which reigned even among those who benefited from a certain degree of distance. Gaullist pressure would soon be felt very strongly among former PSOP activists. Indeed many of them rallied, pure and simple, to Gaullism, like Weill-Curiel in May 1940.

In 1941 we saw Suzanne Nicolitch and the Lyon freemasons send a message to 'brother' Franklin Roosevelt, calling on him to intervene in the war.

The Mouvement national révolutionnaire

Neither was the small Trotskyist and revolutionary socialist vanguard safe from confusion. This was initially demonstrated by a curious group which from late June linked PSOP activists (M. Jaquier, L. Weitz, H. Barré, M. Lissansky and Ladmiral) with working-class militants like Miasnikov from the Russian Workers' Opposition,[136] Consani, the Italian Maximalists,[137] the Bergeryists (Rebeyrolles, Puderoux, Hytte and Pérez) and a few Trotskyists (Claire and F. Zeller). Inspiring the project was J. Rous. For him, Hitler's victory was now secure. It was not a happy occurrence, but, it represented a real transformation of the shape of capitalist society, albeit with a barbarous twist. This necessitated a total re-working of socialist perspectives and programme. Using of the 'draft theory for the French national revolution' published in the first issue of *la Révolution française*, these ideas could be summarised as follows:

> The defeat of the classical proletarian revolution does not mean as a result [...] that we have seen the victory of the proletariat's natural enemy, international financial capital. The end of capitalism is not only a part of Marxist or Leninist perspectives. It is a part of hard reality. Rather than real, universal socialism, this is another kind of society, which overcoming classical capitalism will itself express in its own way the demands of social and economic development. That is the only meaningful explanation of the anti-capitalism embodied in the so-called 'totalitarian' phenomena in Europe. They were of course at first supported by the capitalists who hoped thus to guard their rule over society. But they did not hesitate in overcoming capitalism themselves in the form of a system where the state and the party substitute for the functions of classic financial capitalism, all the while tolerating and even supporting certain forms of capitalism, with nepotism and exploitation incomparably greater than nascent socialism and taking a progressive form of economic management – drawn from the arsenal of socialism – in the framework of an economy taking a backward step in relation to advanced capitalism.
>
> In this new society there exist traits of capitalism trying to survive its collapse as well as traits of socialism in development. Furthermore, as

regards national interests, this economy inevitably engenders the national oppression of other peoples. It must be based on social development, or it will produce nothing other than pure and simple barbarism. In conclusion, this reality, this demand of society today, powerfully imposes as the biggest and first task the creation of a conscious national group or party of revolutionaries, drawn from among the people, in particular the youth, who must take in hand not only the destiny of one class, but of society and the whole nation... the leadership of such a movement, given the defeat of the bourgeoisie and in spite of the relative weakness of the proletariat, can by definition only be 'socialist' and proletarian, for this is the essential need of society. But this development concerns the interests of the whole of a society which continues to be divided into classes... The national and social re-arrangement of France must be understood as the work of a whole generation, with the aim of creating from a great nation a Europe renewed by dispensing with national oppression.[138]

Such was the essential basis for the Mouvement national révolutionnaire. It adopted as its motto 'Collaborate? Yes, but not under the jackboot'. 'Neither Vichy nor London, nor Berlin nor Moscow!'. On this basis it sought allies and partisans: it won over a group of Bergeryists who opposed Bergery's support for Pétain, but it was in vain that it tried to get them to give it money. Contacts were made with Marcel Giton, Paul Faure, and even Loustanau-Lacau and a group of colonels. According to *Le Mémorial de L'Insurgé*, contacts were made 'in the name of the PSOP' with Vichy. Maurice Jaquier denied this. In any case, if they did take place, they proved as pointless as Pivert's contact with De Gaulle.

The group established relations with SFIO Socialists (Tanguy-Pigent and H. Sellier, mayor of Suresnes), the Youth Hostels, the High Commission of Struggle Against Unemployment (R Guillou and Jarry), military figures (colonel Lhermitte and later Armée secrète officers) and trade unionists (Le Bourre and Poulet). It pursued its secret activity under the disguise of 'Friends of Music'.[139]

The MNR bulletin *La Révolution française* appeared clandestinely in July, August and September 1940. In March it produced a new bulletin *le Combat national révolutionnaire*, 'to be circulated hidden in your coat', which lasted for three months. Its last issue was dated June 1941.

How could socialist and communist revolutionaries, who were obviously honest and sincere, have come out with such a theory? They were not of course the only people in the workers' movement who thought Hitler's victory was decisive. It was the view of most Europeans. The Parti communiste also based its strategy on this assumption. As for the solidarity between the Soviet system and Hitler's dictatorship, we need only look at the proclamations of the Soviet leaders[140], even if we do not have to take them at face value any more than their statements of solidarity with the democracies before 1939 and after 1941. Before the war the Italian Bruno Rizzi had already produced a whole theory on the growth of bureaucratic systems, which threatened to become the evolutionary path of human society. At the same time as the MNR was taking shape the American Burnham was plagiarising Rizzi while claiming that this development was not only inevitable but also desireable: Léon Blum wrote a glowing preface to the French translation of his work *The Managerial Revolution* when it was published after the war. People like Rous, Claire and Zeller had always defended Trotskyist orthodoxy that Russia was a 'workers' state' against theories of 'bureaucratic collectivism'[141]. But in 1940 the facts seemed to show that Stalinism was no mere accident of history and that fascism was a variant of the same trend, rendered inevitable by the inability of capitalism to survive and the inability of socialist revolution to overcome it.

Therefore they sought to face up to the new situation, as did the PCF, who, without such theorising, hoped to use it to take power.

Hitler's attack on the USSR cast their theories into the dust. They crossed over to the Gaullist resistance where some of them distinguished themselves with their bravery.[142]

The Trotskyists try and find their place

The Trotskyists from the start denounced those of their number who took part in the MNR adventure. For them, Hitler's victory was just one episode in a war which would be long and would culminate in socialist revolution. It was necessary to build the revolutionary organisation by adapting their strategy to the new conditions. The first stage in this was to overcome the splits which happened when they entered the PSOP.

Activists who had opposed entering the PSOP met in Paris at the end of June.[143] They remained skeptical of the *L'Étincelle* group, which they accused of having 'liquidated' the party and whose agenda they found suspect. They adopted as their platform a 'Letter to the British workers'[144] written by Marcel Hic. Its main ideas can be summarised as follows: the Nazis, temporarily victorious in Europe, would not content themselves with getting rid of democratic freedoms and workers' rights and throwing the people into poverty; to achieve their aims they would enslave or break up nations; the tasks of democratic and national liberation could not be separated from the struggle for socialist revolution; the French and European proletariat had to take charge of these struggles; it would find allies in the petty bourgeoisie and the national bourgeoisie, that is to say, the section of the bourgeoisie which would be forced to ally with it.

From early July there was a discussion between these activists (Hic, Beaufrère and Parisot) and representatives of the Comités pour la IVe Internationale (Craipeau, Gibelin and Souzin). The latter had serious reservations about these theses, which had been proposed to them as the basis for an eventual merger. They agreed on the essential points: the pillage of industry and agricultural produce which threatened the poor with famine, the two million prisoners in the stalags, the annexation and re-division of territory by Hitler, the deindustrialisation of non-German Europe and its reduction to the role of agricultural land, the Nazi diktats imposing their own laws and currency, along with the puppet role to which it reduced the French government (soon going as far as to force it to resume the war, fighting against its own allies) all gave fresh value to democratic and national demands, inseparable in this situation from social demands and revolutionary struggle.

This had already been the view of the Communist International in relation to Germany when it was crushed by the diktat Treaty of Versailles. Indeed, the dangers of such a position had been made clear when the Communist Party held this 'national' policy in 1923 under Radek's leadership.[145] [146] It risked sliding towards nationalism and blurring class lines. The *L'Étincelle* comrades were adamantly opposed to any suggestion of allying with a section of the so-called 'national' bourgeoisie.

Despite the significance of these differences, merger came in August 1940. It was made necessary by the demands of taking action: in July Trotskyists had come to blows with fascists in the Paris Youth Hostels. A relatively significant number of young people engaged in this struggle joined, and breathed life into the organisation. In such circumstances, differences could be overcome in action.

The Hostellers against the fascists

The Centre laïque des auberges de la jeunesse[147] (CLAJ) was created as a leisure organisation during the Popular Front period. Looking for a field of activity, the Jeunesses socialistes révolutionnaires got involved in order to transform it into a revolutionary organisation dealing with young workers' problems with regard to free time. They won a certain degree of influence, combating the paternalist adult leaders who merely wanted to establish a network of budget hostels for young people and who supported the 'pure' so-called 'apolitical' Hostellers led by Marc Augier, who was in truth a close friend of the Nazi youth leader von Schirach.

In early July the ex-JSR Trotskyists decided that the 'apolitical' Youth Hostels could serve as a cover for their propaganda fight. M. Beaufrère, who had recently left prison, was designated as the organiser. The Youth Hostel activists got rid of the old social-democrat leaders and decided that the customers would now lead the movement. They did elect some activists to the leadership who were not known as Trotskyists, including Lucienne Abraham and Maurice Laval. But they were a strong element. Marc Augier tried in vain to remove Beaufrère by offering him a journalist job at *La France au travail*,[148] before looking for support among various fascist groups. These groups wanted to take over the movement. The Hostellers denied them membership and forcibly rebuffed their attacks against the Rue de Valois office… right in the middle of Paris occupied by German troops.

They transformed this office into an arsenal; under the command of a telephone technician they sealed the cables with lead. They went on a counter-attack against people selling the anti-Semitic newspaper *Le Pilori*. A well-organised commando of three young men and three young women marked them out and hospitalised them.

However, at the end of July Marc Augier took advantage of their absence and occupied the headquarters. The Hostellers took it back by force. They wanted to snatch the archives and destroy the address lists, which included many Jewish names. Amusingly, one night the Prefect who so admired these young 'patriots' sent a group of police to oversee the snatching of the archives and allow them to burn the files.

The fights with the fascists continued. The Trotskyist press did not mention it: they did not want to attract the Nazis' attention to the links between the CLAJ and their own organisation. In contrast the 18 July issue of *L'Humanité*, reported under the title of 'Thugs against the Youth Hostels' a fresh assault by Doriotite gangs against the Rue de Valois office: another assault rebuffed.

This office was a curious spectacle, a sanctuary in the middle of an occupied Paris bristling with German soldiers. Young people hustled and bustled there, with Communists, anarchists and Trotskyists engaging in open and passionate discussions. Notably, the comrades reported on a violent altercation they had with the PCF's Pierre Daix, who argued 'Your struggle against the Germans is like fighting the sea with a sword; we must concentrate our efforts on fighting Vichy'. But the youth followed the Trotskyists. They recruited and trained remarkable cadre like Lubra, Pouly, de Sède, Guikovaty and a young engineering worker with the surname Pierre. Very few of them survived the war.

In the Southern Zone, the Trotskyists tried to organise the Hostellers and expelled the leaders who collaborated with the occupiers.[149] The Youth Hostels were reconstituted in an autonomous organisation 'Les Compagnons de route' who would later play an important role in organising the maquis.

The Comités de la IVe Internationale

The new activists who had come from the Youth Hostel movement needed the support of a united movement and were impatient to take action on a wider terrain. That is why the *L'Étincelle* and Hic group organisers decided to hold a conference of all the groups in the Paris region. They convened this conference around mid-August in a cave near Aubergenville; it would be known in the movement under the name of 'the harvest mite[150] conference' because of the bites suffered from these insects. It united the national organisers of the two groups with the representatives of thirty-odd secret groups in the Paris region. Several incidents suffered by delegates trying to get there showed the dangers that existed. But it was the only way of putting an end to political division and allowing the organisation to exist.

The main debate centred around political orientation and Marcel Hic's theses. These were critiqued by Yvan Craipeau, and more vehemently so by M. Gibelin. It was decided that the Central Committee would decide on a defining text. As well as the plan for action in the Youth Hostels, the conference adopted new structures: the movement did however keep the name of Comités pour la IVe Internationale. The theoretical organ remained as *Bulletin de la IVe Internationale*, while the propaganda newspaper took its old name of *La Verité*.

A political bureau was elected – it designated itself as the Central Committee – including three members of the *L'Étincelle* group (Craipeau, Gibelin and Souzin), three members of the Hic group (Beaufrère, Hic and Rigaudias) and a young Hostellers' organiser, Guikovaty. That meant that the new recruits from the Youth Hostels would be the kingmakers. Hic was put in charge of *La Vérité*.

The first issue of *La Verité* appeared, duplicated, on 30 August 1940. At this time, apart from the ambiguous case of *La Révolution française*, the only clandestine newspaper was *L'Humanité*. Unlike these two newspapers, *La Vérité* did not of course ask the occupation authorities for permission. The banner headline read 'Neither Pétain nor Hitler: for a workers' government' and it raised the slogan 'Workers of the world, unite'. Faced with chaos and the crimes of the French and German bourgeoisies, this was an abstract propaganda slogan. But its plan of action attempted to get to grips with the situation more concretely. The newspaper called for the organisation of groups of self-defence against fascists and anti-Semites. It attacked the

Stalinist press, which did not contain any criticism of the Nazi occupiers.

Some former *L'Étincelle* activists had significant political concerns: *La Vérité* was not officially linked to the Comités, which in their eyes appeared to suggest that the editors of the newspaper would develop their own political agenda. That is why some activists published a fourth – final – issue of *L'Étincelle* on 15 September as 'the organ of the Comités de la IVe Internationale'.[151] In fact, this issue's politics were no different from those of *La Vérité*. The masthead read 'We want a free France in a Europe freed from capitalism'. Like the issue of *La Vérité* appearing at the same time, it emphasised the importance of 'housewives' committees': underlining the fact that sixty percent of the grain harvest had headed for Germany, it also called for resistance to milk requisitions.

The national question

Most of the criticism of *La Vérité*'s positions – both during the war and thirty years later – came from activists who, in the name of internationalism, denied even the existence of the national question and the need for revolutionaries to get a grip on it.

But for the Fourth International this was obviously necessary. In June 1940 Trotsky wrote:

> In the wake of a number of other and smaller European states, France is being transformed into an oppressed nation. German imperialism has risen to unprecedented military heights, with all the consequent opportunities for world plunder.... In the defeated countries the position of the masses will immediately become worsened in the extreme. Added to social oppression is national oppression, the main burden of which is likewise borne by the workers. Of all the forms of dictatorship, the totalitarian dictatorship of a foreign conqueror is the most intolerable.[152][153]

In November 1940 the Executive Committee of the Fourth International meeting in New York declared:

> Hitler has reduced Europe to a vast concentration camp of nations. The struggle for the unity of all Germans has been followed by that for the unity of non-Germans under the Nazi boot. But history is a sure guarantee that there has never been national oppression without national struggles.
>
> The big bourgeoisie has already succeeded in arriving at an understanding with Hitler. National resistance is concentrated in the poor sections of the population: the urban petty bourgeoisie, peasants

and workers. But it is the latter which give the most resolute character to the struggle and will know how to connect it with the struggle against French capitalism and the Petain government.

In the face of oppression and dictatorship the workers will not abandon the struggle for democratic liberties (freedom of the press, freedom of assembly, etc.) but they must understand that this struggle cannot revive the decaying bourgeois democracy which has engendered this very oppression and dictatorship. The only democracy now possible in Europe is proletarian democracy, the system of soviets, the lected organs of the working people …

In a Europe which is the prey of national and social oppression, revolts are inevitable. But the essential condition for success is the existence of a revolutionary leadership.

The authors of this resolution were, it seems, unaware of the discussions which had taken place in Europe. Their text was not published there until much later. However, the fundamental ideas were the same in both Paris and New York, similar to the draft action programme.

In September 1940 the discussions on the national question resulted in the Central Committee voting for a set of 'Theses on the national question'. This document could be summarised as follows: Hitler's re-organisation of Europe showed the need to get rid of national borders, but it was effected in barbarous conditions and marked a significant regression not only of workers' and democratic rights but also of the continent's economy. The peoples of Europe (not only those in the conquered countries, but also in Germany and Italy) had to struggle to free themselves from fascism as well as the capitalism which engendered it by mounting a proletarian revolution. Revolutionaries had to try and unite the mass of the people, starting with immediate objectives related to the oppressions they were subject to: social (against capitalist super-exploitation), democratic (winning back their freedoms) and national (for the right to the self-determination of peoples, against the political and economic domination of Hitlerite imperialism). In this struggle, the working class would have to make an alliance with the petty-bourgeois masses and even a section of the bourgeoisie. The first phase of struggle would seek to organise passive resistance against fascism. This struggle would have to be organised across Europe, linking the insurrection of the oppressed peoples to the German and Italian peoples' struggle against fascism.

The most important disagreement in the Comités pour la IVe Internationale was over the idea of allying with a section of the bourgeoisie which refused to kowtow to London and Berlin and would decide to 'throw itself into the arms of the revolution' whether this was 'in good heart' or not. The *L'Étincelle* comrades believed that this change of principles paved the way to class collaboration. But at the same time they thought the terms of debate were false. The big bourgeoisie was behind Pétain and collaborated with the occupier. The small minority which wanted to defend national independence backed De Gaulle. There was no section of the bourgeoisie hostile to both collaboration and Anglo-American imperialism, meaning that there was no section of the bourgeoisie susceptible to 'tactically' rallying to the revolutionary camp.

The theses had determined against any union sacrée with the bourgeoisie, whether collaborationist or Gaullist, but taking this position seemed utopian rather than perilous.

The same went for its practical application. The theses called for the building of Comités de vigilance nationale, 'formed, wherever concrete action demands it, by representatives of all organisations who want to call on the masses to fight for specific goals'.

The minority thought that such committees would be extremely dangerous if they entailed working with nationalist and bourgeois organisations. These people would use the working class for their own ends. But given the conditions prescribed by the document, the committees had no chance of ever existing. In the archives of *La Vérité* there is only one mention of the idea: on the occasion of the 11 November 1940 demonstrations, whose slogans it criticised as bourgeois. There were no further proposals for alliance with sections of the bourgeoisie.

These considerations eventually led the minority to vote for a compromise text, despite its 'excessively nationalistic tone', since it seemed to give sufficient guarantees for the internationalist perspectives of the movement. But the debates would remain very bitter.

Barta's critique

Only Barta and Louise[154] publicly critiqued the 'Theses of the Committee for the Fourth International'. As it happened, they were not members of the organisation, but they emphasised that their disagreements were much more to do with organisational methods than political orientation.

Their tiny group published a duplicated pamphlet, *La Lutte contre la Deuxième Guerre mondiale*, which would remain practically unknown, even to the Trotskyists. But its quality means that it is worthy of study. In terms of principles, its author stopped himself short of questioning the need to struggle against national oppression:

The Fourth International fights against the class and national oppressions which have beset Europe, the violence whose bastion is German and Italian imperialism. The defeat of Hitler and Mussolini, that is to say, their defeat at the hands of the exploited, is the goal the Fourth International sets out for the workers of Europe. This goal can only be achieved with class struggle. The workers' and poor peasants' struggle against the pillage of the country by German imperialism as well as their struggle against the French bourgeoisie when it clashes with German militarism – and it will – will inevitably provoke unrest in Hitler's army.

Barta attacked the 'tactical' slogan of Comités de vigilance in alliance with the 'national bourgeoisie', writing that 'You may as well make an appeal to the inhabitants of the planet Mars'. Failure to understand class relations had now led *La Vérité* into a nationalist deviation. For example, on 1st January 1941 it commented:

All non-working-class forces who fight against the oppressor must understand that working-class support is vitally important to the success of the national liberation struggle. Therefore they must guarantee them rights at work which will give them an interest in national renaissance and defending the nation of which they are the lifeblood.

Here the working class appears as an essential supporting cast who 'national' bosses must know how to look after! In the same newspaper, reporting on the 500,000-strong British engineering workers' strike, the editor similarly wrote: 'By satisfying this just demand, the British government can begin to build real national unity against German imperialism'.

We can find several such formulations here and there in the press of the time. But they do not correspond to *La Vérité*'s general perspectives. For example, look at its coverage of workers' struggles in the United States:

The National Maritime Union, the most militant dockers' union in the United States with a leadership influenced by revolutionary communists, has taken the lead in fighting Roosevelt's imperialist agenda. It organised an enormous workers' and unemployed workers' march on Washington opposing US intervention in the war – whether direct or indirect – and responding to the Smith Project's attacks on the right to strike. The French workers waging a struggle against French and German imperialism enthusiastically salute their American brothers' fight against Yankee imperialism.

Raising slogans for national liberation

Aside from the ambiguous or unMarxist formulations of certain articles, the goal of the Trotskyists was to mobilise the masses against the oppression inflicted by the occupying imperialists, who were crushing them with the aid of the French ruling class and the puppet government.

For example, with the complicity of Vichy the Nazis stole cereal products to fill their war stocks, threatening the workers of France with famine. On 15 September 1940 *La Vérité* commented:

> Down with the looters, down with those who make us starve! The Ministry of Food says that sixty percent of the French harvest will be taken by Germany. Yet the French government does nothing. Is it that it agrees with Hitler's plan to make the French starve? Brother peasant, meet the requisitions with passive resistance; only sell your grain if it will be used to make bread for the women and children of France.

When the occupation began the Nazis took machinery from factories, brutally carrying out their policy of deindustrialising Europe (the demands of war would later force them to leave these machines in place for a while and make use of French manpower). The Theses sought to mobilise workers to defend their workplaces.[155]

The Nazis bought what they wanted with an occupation mark, which was not worth the paper it was printed on given that no reciprocal purchase of German goods was allowed. *La Vérité* argued: 'Down with German currency! The French people want their work to create real wealth, not to be thrown into poverty and inflation'.[156]

The masses' main concern was food. The Trotskyists tried to incite housewives to take charge of goods:

> The housewives should, house by house, send delegates to a neighbourhood committee which will ration goods, work with the small shopkeepers to divide the population by shop [...], take over food stocks, police the queues and hunt down thieves. Only housewives' action and unity can bring a little order to the current chaos and allow a less harsh winter for poor people, big families and the mothers and children of France.[157]

These slogans were just for propaganda however: only a few embryonic committees ever existed.

The Chantiers de jeunesse

However, thanks to their influence in the Youth Hostels, the Trotskyists managed an effective intervention among the youth. In doing this they profited from the particular conditions the Vichy government faced in carrying out its agenda of youth training. General de la Porte du Theil was in charge of this project from July onwards. Unable to mobilise the class of 1940, he founded the Chantiers de jeunesse to regiment the youth and brainwash them with nationalist ideology and the principles of the Vichy régime. In the [non-occupied, Vichy-ruled] 'free zone' this task fell upon the officers and sub-officers: the Chantiers de jeunesse would serve as one of the foundations of the new régime. However, in the occupied zone this type of paramilitary organisation was impossible. Vichy proposed to the two remaining legal organisations tolerated by the Germans, namely the JOC and CLAJ, that they take charge of organising Chantiers de jeunesse.

From the start *La Vérité* attacked the Chantiers de jeunesse : 'Although the essential problem is the need to train a specialised (qualified) youth, they want to introduce France's young people to the joys of gardening'.[158]

The Central Committee devoted a resolution to a theoretical analysis of the Chantiers de jeunesse, denouncing the reactionary character of the project and counterposing to it a plan for economic reconstruction (flexible working hours, financing public works by expropriating war profiteers, nationalising key industries, workers' control over production, etc.). It also stressed the demands of the young people in the Chantiers.

Nevertheless it decided that the CLAJ should accept the Vichy régime's offer and should use the organisation of youth to exploit the weaknesses of the government. Lucien Schmidt was put in charge of the operation. The Chantiers would serve as cover for revolutionary propaganda. In the disused castles put at the use of the CLAJ there was an active system of propaganda and training for young workers. In the stations each departure would be heralded with the sound of revolutionary anthems: only the best known songs like the *Internationale* were excluded from their repertoire, although they could be heard in the Chantiers themselves.

Rejecting the doctrine of 'back to the land', activists put in place effective centres of professional training, but not for one moment did they neglect political training. Some of these were still running as late as 1944.

This paradoxical situation could not of course last forever. In January 1941 the Nazis arrested the leaders of the CLAJ (including L. Abraham) and of the JOC. The fact that these were arrested at the same time shows that they were unaware of what was really going on in the CLAJ-run Centres. They only knew that there was some critical propaganda.

The Trotskyists had already left all the Chantiers, apart from the professional training centres where they played a technical role as teachers. But they had reinforced their implantation among working-class youth. In October 1942 *La Vérité* gave an epilogue:

The debacle of the youth secretariat: They have closed down the Chantiers de jeunesse. For a long time the centres in towns and cities have been converted into centres for training for bosses. Now the Comités des Forges[159] have taken over most of those left. Faced with collapse Pellerson hopes to build 'national teams' based on community work and leisure … with the goal of creating another fascist SA. But who will back this project? Certainly not the Chantiers de jeunesse, in any case!

He held a meeting in the salle Pleyel. But alas! He managed to unite his audience: but they were united against him, against Vichy, against collaborationism and against the 'national revolution'. He was barely able to finish his speech, noting his sadness that the 'national revolution' had not won over hearts and mind …. the secretariat was overwhelmed with resignations.

Trade union and workplace action

A significant number of businesses were shut down in July 1940. Although two million people were being kept in stalags, there were 700,000 unemployed in the Paris region alone (according to *La Vérité* of 15 October). The Trotskyists tried, without success, to organise them to demand the re-opening of the factories in the form of workers' co-operatives. They drew up a plan to reorganise industry under workers' control.[160] But although four-fifths of the working class were not working, their over-riding concern was individual survival.

The workers did not have any autonomous organisations of their own. The first issue of *La Vérité* attacked Belin, the former 'pacifist' CGT leader who now supported the New Order:

He has fought to destroy what is left of the CGT […] now, after getting rid of his former master and accomplice Léon Jouhaux, he wants to convert the remaining union structures into the cornerstone of the fascist corporations.

But Mr Belin will only be able to do this if the workers let him: without the CGT's member unions, his corporations plan is doomed to failure. For this reason, through organising the CGT on the basis of class-struggle politics, workers can prevent the establishment of a 'compulsory union'.

At the same time, workers must take the initiative in creating committees in every factory – bringing together unionised and non-unionised workers – which will fight for workers' rights.[161]

The two courses of action proposed were firstly to prevent the establishment of fascist corporations and secondly to bring together workers in each workplace to fight together in spite of any differences they might have.

The Central Committee charged Henri Souzin with the task of organising this work. He was a young building worker, a member of the leadership of the Paris region decorators' federation and very much linked to Louis Saillant in his union activism. The 'trade union commission' was composed of three organisers – Jean Aubré (electricity workers), Louis Bonnel (engineering workers) and Pierre Pradalès (clerical staff) – before being broken up in late 1942.

It produced six issues of a duplicated bulletin, known as *Bulletin ouvrier* in 1941 and as *Informations ouvrières* in 1942. No doubt unbeknownst to its authors, *La Vie ouvrière*[162] commented on it favourably and made comradely overtures...

Activists tried to link their opposition in the unions to the organisation of workplace struggles. But the struggles which began to flare up again were all wildcat actions with no relation to the remnants of the unions.

Internationalism

La Vérité tried to link the struggle of French workers to that of workers in other countries. At its most basic level, this involved reporting: but its editors had little information to go by.

La Vérité stressed its solidarity with colonised peoples. On 3 November there were uprisings in southern Vietnam under the leadership of the Trotskyist group La Lutte (whose leader was Ta Thu Tau) and the Vietnamese Communist Party. In its 1 December issue *La Vérité* hailed the struggle of Indochinese revolutionaries. There were radio reports of a communist uprising in Saigon which had left 6,000 dead. On 15 December *La Vérité* covered the events, commenting:

> French workers must know that the Indochinese workers' and peasants' revolutionary movement is a very powerful one, that it is a conscious struggle for socialist revolution and that it seeks close unity with the French movement. At its head, our comrades in the La Lutte group are organising resistance against both Japanese and French oppression.

In close union with the masses in Indochina, the French workers will bring their struggle to its victorious conclusion, liberating all peoples by establishing a Socialist United States of the World.[163]

La Vérité spread news of the Belgian workers' resistance to Nazism and the Amsterdam general strike[164] as well as strikes in Britain and America. It interpreted Italian reverse in Albania not as proof of military weakness or the incompetence of Italian soldiers but as evidence of Italian workers' opposition to Mussolini's wars. It published news (from British sources) of riots in northern Italy being attacked by Stuka dive-bombers. It stressed the importance of fraternisation between French workers and German soldiers. For example, one comrade related the following incident:

> A soldier who escaped from the Abbeville camp reported: 'Told that we were soon to depart for Germany, forty of us managed to escape along with four German guards who managed to get hold of civilian clothes." The newspaper concluded: 'Here is evidence of common action against the common oppressor'.[165]

Fraternisation did not mean, as the PCF would have it, telling the German soldiers that their army and the French workers were engaged in the same struggle against plutocracy. On the contrary, it meant winning them to a common struggle against Hitlerism: 'We are friends of the German people, which is why we fight Hitlerism'.[166]

The 15 September 1941 headline emphasised the German police's fear of such fraternisation:

> The Gestapo against fraternisation: a German police edict dating from February means that anyone who tries to establish relations with prisoners of war by speech, sign or any other means will face a 500 Mark fine or imprisonment for up to six weeks. But the German police will not be able to stop fraternisation between German workers and French prisoners.

La Vérité and the Communists

The propaganda of *La Vérité* had nothing in common with that of *L'Humanité*. Never had there been such vehement opposition to the Stalinists. The first issue of *La Vérité* displayed this with its homage to the murdered Leon Trotsky.

We must cast as much light as possible on the crime, who was directly responsible and who was behind it. For now at least we can say this: Stalin is the greatest culprit; Stalin who had already made thirty-eight attempts on Trotsky's life; Stalin who executed Trotsky's two sons Serge and Leon Sedov and killed his two daughters Nathalie and Zéla Bronstein; Stalin who had two of his secretaries, Rudolf Klement and Erwin Wolf, assassinated; Stalin who, after staging a sinister judicial farce, wiped out all of the Bolshevik Old Guard: Zinoviev, Kamenev, Bukharin and Rykov.[167]

As we have seen, at the time on Stalin's orders the Communists accommodated to the Nazi régime and only criticised Vichy. Thirty years later, Charles Tillon, a PCF leader at this point, recalled the International's directives '… which did not call for struggle against the Nazis but instead advocated keeping quiet and tolerating them'.

La Vérité commented on this approach in a 'Letter to a Communist comrade':[168]

> The Parti communiste is helping Hitler. Comrade, again read over the literature you distribute: can you see any attacks against Hitler in it? Can you find a single line against the German occupation? Do you believe that your leaders, by dint of meeting Mr. Abetz,[169] have forgotten about it? Yes, I know, you'll tell me that it's just a tactic, saying nothing and waiting for that happy day when both Germany and Britain are exhausted.
>
> But then tell me why Stalin has delivered more than ten million francs' worth of goods to Germany in the last eight months, including many tons of valuable oil, without which Hitler would have had to surrender.

That did not stop *La Vérité* from protesting against the repression suffered by Communist militants.

La Vérité was also well aware of the opposition to the policies of the PCF leadership which arose in several regions.[170] In a second 'Letter to a Communist' on 1 January 1941 it wrote:

> Entire regions cut off from the leadership are reconsidering and looking for political direction. Many Communists, both organisers and ordinary activists, are totally disconcerted by the policies of the USSR. For several months activists in the Toulouse region have discussed the direction of the party, criticising the content of *L'Humanité* and printing leaflets whose content meets the real needs of communist workers. In Brittany the party is in similar turmoil….

Indeed, in Toulouse one branch (whose secretary was André Barjonet) met with the Trotskyists to discuss and carry out joint activity. There were similar comradely relations in some towns in Brittany. Roger Pannequin, a former PCF leader, clarified the events thirty years later:

> The attitude of the Communists who first mounted resistance against the occupier, at a time when the leadership was calling for fraternisation, was by no means patriotic, nationalist or anti-German. [...] In reality the first Communist resistance fighters were first and foremost anti-Nazis and anti-fascists. Most of them were Jeunesses communistes men who had been recruited and educated by former International Brigades fighters. The former International Brigades fighters offered real leadership to the JC at the end of 1940. But many of these young men were themselves escaped prisoners, fighters from the collapsed front line or men too young to have been mobilised. For the men of the International Brigades there was no question of 'timing' – they had to fight the fascists. The JC in the first sabotage groups were fighting for revolution. And what were they singing in the prison cells when they were locked up? *La Jeune Garde* and the *Anthem of the Comintern*.[171]

But even if these Communist activists' revolutionary ambitions were beyond doubt, the limits of their internationalism would soon become clear. But in April 1941 the PCF seemed to be responding to their concerns and starting to turn. As was usually the case for the PCF, this turn corresponded to two totally different considerations: on the one hand there was pressure from its activists, itself an expression of pressure from the masses for whom the Nazi occupation was more and more intolerable, and so it became impossible to keep silent. On the other hand, relations between the USSR and Nazi Germany were deteriorating. Molotov's November 1940 visit to Berlin had shown the existence of insurmountable differences over the divvying-up of the war booty. In spite of the German-Russian treaty's re-drawing of the borders, by December relations between the two powers were increasingly tense. The Soviet government had not changed its approach: in February 1941 Litvinov, who had represented the USSR in negotiations with the 'western democracies', was kicked off the Central Committee. In March, Stalin's meeting with the Japanese Prime Minister Matsuoka set the foundations for a Soviet-Japanese alliance. But the German army's invasion of Bulgaria and – even more so – its invasion and carve-up of Yugoslavia represented heavy blows against the USSR. The division of spheres of influence in the Balkans was repeatedly put into question by German forces.

In May, Stalin put himself in charge of the Council, replacing Molotov.

The deterioration of German-Soviet relations was reflected little by little in the content of *L'Humanité*. On 8 February 1941, the PCF newspaper dared to write that the USSR was the only country without plutocrats, which might lead people to believe that they still existed in Germany... On 12 April it spoke more openly of the 'crimes of Pétain and the occupier'. At the same time, the PCF organised women's demonstrations to demand the return of prisoners, not only making demands on the 'French ambassador' Scapini but also on the German Embassy in Paris.

L'Humanité of 1st May 1941 did not differentiate between the Allied and Axis imperialist powers:

> The rival imperialisms are driven by the same desire to destroy freedom, and when the British propagandists present the Gaullist movement as a democratic movement, they are shamefacedly lying. What this aristocratic general wants is not freedom for our country, but rather the triumph of the imperialist interests with whom he has thrown in his lot.

This is pretty much what *La Vérité* was saying. But soon enough the PCF was taking up the nationalist cause again. On 11 May, on the anniversary of the Battle of Valmy, it organised a demonstration in Paris in commemoration of Joan of Arc. It looked to build a 'National Front'.

The miners' strike

The 26 May 1941 miners' strikes in the North and Pas-de-Calais were very significant. They showed the combativity of the working class, their opposition to Nazi oppression and also nationalist deformities resulting from decades of Stalinist and reformist propaganda.

Auguste Lecoeur, at that time at the head of the North and Pas-de-Calais section of the Parti communiste, described the PCF's activity in the mines:

> An unrelenting struggle was waged against the mining companies, the collaorators and the occupier. It was therefore possible to create a strong illegal organisation there and to educate activists in clandestine work.[172]

The Communists in the North made the first of May 'a day of struggle against the double yoke of capitalist oppression and foreign oppression' (*L'Enchaîné*). Lecoeur explained:

The miners were called to stage a day of unity and action against the capitalist exploiters, the collaborators and the *Boches*. In the North and Pas-de-Calais, the occupier has always been referred to as such.[173]

This 'anti-Boche' chauvinism was hardly conducive to helping miners understand the class character and the fascist character of German oppression, nor for that matter the class character of Gaullism. Indeed, according to Lecoeur the PCF's national manifesto for 1 May was not distributed because it contained attacks against De Gaulle.

On 26 April a general strike broke out in the mines. It is interesting to see how the Communist Madeleine Riffaud describes the growth of this movement – remember, she was writing after the Liberation when the PCF wanted to emphasise the patriotic character of its wartime activity:

The strike started over small grievances – a little more soap, a little more bread and a little more money. It was the clandestine Parti communiste leadership and in particular Auguste Lecoeur who led the way. It first broke out at Pit 7 in Dourges-Dahomey. The people resisted the occupier – which was as always hand-in-hand with the bosses – with its old class weapon: the strike! From the start the strike was patriotic and called for reform. At one pit in Bruay, when an engineer addressed the assembled workers, 'You have asked for soap – you can have it! You have asked for bread – you can have it! … What more do you want?', a miner shouted 'We want guns!'….[174]

In an article by Julien Hapiot *L'Enchaîné du Nord* portrayed the strike thus:

The occupier has seen what the young workers and the working masses think of the 'Collaboration'. They have realised that our youth will never submit to national oppression, and on the issue of the independence of our country, there is but one attitude: wanting to get rid of foreign domination as quickly as possible.

This suggested that the miners' struggle was merely a 'national' struggle. At the time, *L'Humanité* feared that the movement would be ensnared by Gaullism. On 20 June 1941, in an 'Address to the miners', it commented: 'Miners, who have fought side by side, you must all stay united and understand that our common desires cannot be satisfied by the victory of one imperialism over the other'.

But *La Vérité* was only interested in one essential aspect of the miners' struggle: for the first time the working class had taken action *en masse*, using the strike as its weapon. Rigaudias wrote a twenty-page pamphlet *Only the working class can free France from the Nazis* to spread news of the strikes in the North. The Trotskyists believed that this re-awakening could only develop into a large-scale struggle on two conditions: the proletariat had to achieve unity in action and a new revolutionary leadership had to be forged.

The 1 May 1941 issue of *La Vérité* tried to link these two questions:

> Several workers' groups have been created across France. In these places Communists, Trotskyists and Socialists have formed joint organisations. Elsewhere, they meet separately in the old fashion. How can we bring them together? In the immediate, with 'workers' groups'. Scant news, difficulties in meeting and an irregular illegal press: all these problems must be looked after by the workers' group; it must build united fronts everywhere, even for limited campaigns. It is from common action by these groups – which must be created everywhere – that the new revolutionary party will arise.

In reality there were very few examples of such groups building unity in action, especially among those who were meant to be organising the new revolutionary party.

The organisation of the Comités pour la IVe Internationale

The Trotskyist groups were the most likely to be isolated. Their political discussions were lively, but the organisation was largely oriented to taking action, for example distributing newspapers and leaflets or trying to build workers' groups and housewives' committees. Starting in October their activists (they were not the only ones) organised demonstrations against the news reports shown in working-class cinemas. These demonstrations became so widespread that the German authorities threatened to close the cinemas.

Their basic organisational unit was a cell of three to five comrades, which was cloistered and had no 'horizontal' contact with other cells. Organised according to industry and region, their main task was to make propaganda in the workplace and, above all, in the local area.

Initially there were also technical cells copying *La Vérité* (it was copied until September 1941, producing nineteen issues of four pages), the theoretical journal, bulletins and leaflets and also forging official papers and transport permits.

At the start of 1941 they started running a print office: but it was a difficult job. The print office, which belonged to a comrade, was sealed shut, so they broke down the door and loaded the machines into a van. Would the police watch them going out into the street? No, instead they asked if they wanted help carrying! The machines were taken across Paris. Everywhere there were police checkpoints, both French and German, examining all vehicles in order to stop Jews from putting their furniture in safe-houses. Of course, they had to rent a villa in the rich suburbs; furnish it elegantly; arrange convincing fake identities for the printers; and make them look like wealthy bourgeois types (the people in question were the Tixier brothers – two young print workers from Nantes – and the partner of the elder brother, who was entrusted a child in order to make her look more respectable). Then the equipment was put in a cellar, which they also had to soundproof. All that was left to do was find ink and paper: not so easy! Finally, they organised distribution networks. These tasks would take several months. The first printed issue of *La Vérité* appeared on 15 September 1941. The Gestapo never discovered this print office, nor that of the International, set up at Rueil in 1942. The print workers doggedly stuck to their work. Along with constant, nervous tension, their main problem was isolation.

One of the greatest practical successes was news-gathering. In 1941 David Rousset put together a remarkable information network, with all of the wires of the Vichy government and a special wire-tapping service at hand, as well as the documents of the fascist parties of Déat (RNP) and Doriot (PPF), news from the Gaullist Resistance and foreign newspapers delivered as contraband. One organisational weakness was the lack of special military networks, which would only appear later and in embryonic form.

Militants would only be admitted to the organisation after three months of education. This education did not have the aim of teaching sympathisers catechisms, but rather to avoid amateurism and maintain safety standards. The organisation was run along democratic-centralist lines as far as that was possible under illegality: centralism predominated over democracy, and organisers were chosen 'from above' except in the case of basic branches. The political bureau's composition changed during the war due to co-option, incidents and new elections.[175]

The political direction taken by the political bureau and enacted by the whole party was however periodically subject to discussion and reconfigured either by national conferences where the Central Committee met with regional organisers, or by congresses of delegates elected by the whole party. During four years of occupation the movement held many conferences and two congresses.

A national conference in April 1942 decided to change the movement's name to Comités de la IVe Internationale and ratified the creation of a European secretariat. Another conference in June 1943 saw the group take the name Parti ouvrier internationaliste, in line with the tradition of 1936. The congress held in Saint-Germain-la-Poterie in January 1944 in order to launch a Parti communiste internationaliste insisted on maintaining a democratic structure, in contrast to all other movements.

There were however a few cases of indiscipline. We have seen the editorial team flirting with nationalism (this led to Swann's removal from the political bureau); equally, in March 1941 the western region newspaper *Front rouge* described itself as 'the newspaper of the Parti communiste révolutionnaire' although the Central Committee had only gone as far as changing the subtitle of *La Vérité* to read 'revolutionary communist newspaper', which it kept from 1st April until 1 August 1941.

More serious were violations of the secrecy rules, almost inevitable given that many groups held their meetings in Youth Hostels.

What was surprising was that, before 1942, there were so few arrests, and on each occasion they were small-scale, except for those of October 1943. Arrested comrades never gave evidence under torture. No secret agent or wrecker ever infiltrated the organisation (except for the Gestapo in the German soldiers' organisation in 1943). Perhaps that is why bonds of friendship complemented political ties.

It is true that the organisation was tight: it was composed of three or four hundred activists, almost all young people between 18 and 25 years old, one hundred of whom were arrested (mostly during 1943)[176]. Outside the Paris region it was strongest in western France; but also in the regions around Marseille, Lyon, Toulouse and Bordeaux, along with small groups in Valence, Albi, Limoges, Castres, Pau and Nice. It had no base in the North or East.

Later we shall look at this activism in the regions: but there is hardly any trace of their material from before 1942 and even less from 1943. But perhaps we can understand their difficulties by following the activities of Beaufrère, who was sent to the non-occupied zone in 1940. After finding a 'smuggler' in Orthez and crossing the border (not without much difficulty) he reached Toulouse where he met with young activists. Then he went to Marseille, where he made contact with the 'le Croquefruit' co-operative recently set up by Marcel and René Bleibtreu, Guy d'Hauterive, Sylvain Itkine and Georgette and Elio Gabey, who were soon joined by Jean Rougeul. This business, which found considerable commercial success before its collapse due to the cutting-off of raw materials from North Africa after the British-

American landings there, was a refuge for a very significant number of revolutionaries and anti-fascists from France and central Europe.[177] [178]

Activists in Marseille were divided into four branches under the leadership of Albert Demazière, and were very active, notably in the collieries and in the camps where Indochinese workers lived. All but one of the organisers were hostile to the platform outlined in Marcel Hic's 'Letter to the British workers'. To them, Beaufrère seemed more like a representative of that tendency than of the movement as a whole, and he would move on to Clermont-Ferrand (where Laurent Schwartz was the organiser) and Lyon (where the organisers were Colliard and the blue-collar worker Sadek).

Notre révolution

On 1 January 1941 a new newspaper calling itself revolutionary socialist appeared in Paris: *Notre révolution*. It explained its title:

> Nowadays everybody talks of 'revolution'. But listening to these 'revolutionary' gentlemen, whether they are from Vichy or Paris, offers sufficient proof that their 'revolution' really means a reactionary struggle against freedom, particularly against the freedom of the working class [...]
>
> However, revolution is the way ahead for History: a revolution which must overthrow the capitalist system – whether free-marketeer or statist – and build a collectivist society atop its ruins. A revolution which must abolish borders and unite all peoples in one World Republic. This revolution will not be made by noble gentlemen or corrupt politicians. It will not be made by some mysterious saviour from East or West. No! Our revolution will be the work of the people itself. The proletariat will be its soul and its guiding force: united with the poor peasants and the poor in the cities it will smash the chains which hold the world prisoner, strike down the reactionaries and build a world where freedom and social equality reign.

Notre révolution was printed, since the small group which published it was mostly composed of people who worked in publishing, particularly proofreaders. Among them were Rimbert, Berthier, Fourrier, Jean Lejeune and Meichler. They belonged to the PSOP and the *Lutte de Classe* group, but they never alluded to their involvement in these organisations.

Their activity was of a purely propagandist character, publishing and distributing their newspaper. They did this like clockwork: by July 1944 they had published 43 issues, one each and every month. They were normally four pages long but sometimes six. The newspaper changed its title twice, becoming *Nos Combats* then, from May 1942, *Libertés*. In 1944 the group revealed that the title changes were motivated by safety concerns at a time when repression was being redoubled. As we shall see, they also had a strong correlation to changes in political direction.

The group did not try and organise workers who agreed with its positions. It did not seek to become a force for action: even in April 1942 *Nos Combats* emphasised that it was a time for distributing propaganda, not one for building a centralised organisation or a party. Unlike *L'Insurgé*, its homologue in the unoccupied zone, it only called on activists to ready themselves for action, for example by marking out 'collaborators'.

Despite the working-class orientation it claimed and the group's composition, the newspaper was not concerned with working-class grievances, the situation of the unions nor strikes and struggles. When the first issue of *Libertés* in May 1942 analysed the international situation, it was only interested in the military balance of forces among the great powers.

Notre révolution was primarily of interest for the positions it took, which were in tune with the politics Collinet had argued for at the first congress of the PSOP:

1. The war was defined as an imperialist war. The historic task of the proletariat was still the same as that set down by the Stuttgart congress in 1907: 'Take advantage of the social crisis provoked by the war to take power'.

2. *However* there was a significant difference between 1914 and the current war: while there was an organised workers' movement in both camps in 1914, in 1939 there was no workers' movement in the Axis powers, which were, besides, based on all that was reactionary in the world.

3. In these conditions the workers could not be neutral. 'The defeat of the Axis is not only in the interests of the peoples it has conquered, but also in the interests of the workers in the countries which constitute it'.

4. As for Britain, it would tomorrow be the enemy of any revolutionary movement arising in Europe (to the extent that its proletariat would let the government do so). But insofar as it was currently in struggle with the greatest enemy of the working class, it had for now become their 'temporary' ally.

5. The workers had to oppose a peace based on indemnities or a new Treaty of Versailles, and to put forward their own solution: 'The collectivisation of the means of production and the abolition of borders with the creation of a new federation of free peoples'.

6. National independence was the primary objective of the struggle of the French proletariat, since social emancipation is impossible in a

country which lacks national independence. 'But every country must be independent, including the colonies and Germany itself'.

7. As for the Gaullist movement: 'The proletariat must not get mixed up in this movement, and must defend its class independence, since General de Gaulle's movement is essentially bourgeois: his struggle is not against fascism, but against Germany and the German people, on whom he wants to impose a new Treaty of Versailles…'

But because he was fighting for national liberation 'and for that reason alone' it was necessary to support his struggle. On the other hand, it was necessary to combat the collaborators 'who have only one aim, to crush the workers' movement'.

In January 1941, therefore, they had a position different from any other current in the workers' movement: different from the Socialists, who (except for the MPs who went over to Pétain) were part of the Gaullist, anti-German and nationalist movement, in spite of their political reservations about the general; different from the PCF leadership who continued to avoid criticism of Hitlerism but denounced the City of London and its agent De Gaulle; different from the *La Vérité* Trotskyists, who opposed any alliance with imperialism or Gaullism and for whom raising national demands was simply one of several means of promoting revolutionary action; and different from the *Lutte de Classe* Trotskyists who considered support for these demands as a nationalist deviation; not to mention the MNR, who considered the victory of fascism an inevitable development to which they had to adapt their activity to.

On the contrary, it offered some sort of theoretical basis for the behaviour of the significant number of Communist activists who disobeyed the orders of *L'Humanité* (but *Notre révolution* did not have the antennae necessary to have become aware of this, and it did not make reference to them).

Although it did not explicitly claim to stand in the internationalist tradition (which without doubt it did, albeit by chance) it stuck to the main ideas of this tradition: the imperialist character of the war, the need to turn it into a revolutionary war, the leading role of the proletariat and the need for class independence; the right of peoples to self-determination, the liberation of the colonies, a European socialist federation, etc.

Not once did the newspaper give in to the prevalent anti-German (or 'anti-Boche') hysteria. And when it came to strategy for taking advantage of the contradictions between the rival imperialisms, it looked to the Marxist tradition. Its statement of principles alluded to the policy of Marx and Engels who in the nineteenth century saw Tsarist Russia as the greatest enemy of the European working class. It furthermore made reference to the 'defencist' policy of the Paris Commune of 1871,[179] which, supported by Marx and the First International, defended the French Republic against Bismarck.

However, their statement was confused in several ways:

1. It began by denouncing the war as imperialist; but later wrote that the war although 'including imperialist elements is in reality a huge social crisis which puts in doubt the survival of the capitalist system itself'.

2. It relied on the military force of the Allies to defeat fascism. To put it another way, it was the 'temporary ally' which would bring an end to the war as suited its own objectives.

3. In these conditions the defeat of German imperialism would not help the German workers by weakening the power of the state which oppressed them and thus letting them overthrow it, but instead would mean the installation of a liberal bourgeois régime (which explains why the statement neither called for fraternisation nor international solidarity).

4. The slogan 'no to an unworkable peace' alluded to revolutionaries' hostility to the Treaty of Versailles, but its real meaning was 'no to a peace based on indemnities'.

5. Similarly, the call for a 'federation of free peoples' was initially presented as a socialist slogan presupposing the collectivisation of the means of production. But later the words were used in a vaguer sense, all the more worrying since the Allies presented themselves as the camp of the 'free peoples'. Finally, its leaders supported the bourgeois call for European federation.

We must conclude that these slogans had two faces, serving either as revolutionary demands or as a turn towards the politics of pragmatism… and indeed, Gaullism.

The demands *Notre révolution* raised were exclusively concerned with the national question. Since it put forward no plans for independent working-class organisation, this could only mean support for Gaullism. This support was in fact the only concrete idea put forward in their statement. Given these conditions, political criticism of the general had no more weight that the 'reservations' Daniel Mayer and his friends had about the general: some of them would, inevitably, join the Gaullist movement itself, hardly the way towards 'the seizure of power by the proletariat'.

Chapter 4

HITLER ATTACKS THE USSR

How Hitler caught Stalin by surprise

On 26 May 1940 the 'Emergency appeal' of the Fourth International warned:

> Hitler's friendship with Stalin will not last forever, nor even for a long time. It is possible that Kremlin foreign policy may take another turn before our call reaches the masses. If this is the case the character of the Comintern's propaganda will change too. If the Kremlin sides with the democracies, the Comintern will again dig up its fallback black book of Nazi crimes. But that does not mean that its propaganda would take on a revolutionary character. Despite changing its course, it will remain as servile as ever.[180]

This prophetic warning overestimated Stalin's strategic acumen. In fact, he had taken no such initiative and had spent the last year giving military reinforcement to his main enemy.

In November 1940 Barta commented on this policy:

> What is it that has allowed Hitler to break his capitalist enemies *first* with Stalin's assistance? The fact that the German-Russian agreement destroyed the last workers' movement in Europe: *anti-fascism*. Hitler's decision to shy away from attacking the USSR for now was achieved by the *political destruction of the French proletariat*. The foreign policy of the bureaucracy has facilitated *the crushing of the proletariat by their own imperialist rulers*. If Stalin can now claim mastery over a Soviet Union expanded by 23 million new inhabitants, Hitler can claim mastery over the whole of Europe. The result is a decisive defeat for the USSR. The world proletariat has collapsed, yet the bureaucrats are building socialism over one sixth of the globe! […]
>
> But what are the real relations between imperialist Germany and the

Soviet Union? A few days before Molotov went to Berlin, on 8 November 1940, Hitler claimed that he was an unwilling participant in the war: 'Right up until the last moment, even a few days before war broke out, I tried to realise my *longstanding* foreign policy plans'. *Forced* into war against Britain, does Hitler still want to realise his 'longstanding plans' – destroying the planned economy of the USSR and re-establishing capitalism – if not by taking arms against the Soviet Union, then through the capitulation of Stalin and Molotov? Stalin does not dare to remember those 'longstanding plans'; his spokesman Molotov speaks of nothing other than his 'commitment' to the policy of peace. And so he goes to Berlin with an entourage of experts to guarantee Hitler's 'rear-guard': in fact, Stalin has transformed the Soviet Union into a supply depot for the anti-Comintern Axis.

But the Axis powers will want more and more control over this 'depot'; they demand that the plan is changed to suit their needs; in view of a long and lasting 'friendship' with the Soviet Union the Axis imperialists will hijack the plan *in their own interests* and, unbalancing it, they will re-establish capitalism. That is the price Stalin, or indeed his successor, will pay to guarantee a lasting accord with Hitler. But if one day Stalin decides to stand up to those pushing him towards the abyss, then Molotov's sermons about 'commitment' to peace will not stop Hitler from carrying out his 'longstanding plans' with arms. The tool for their intervention? The 'three-way' pact which the Soviet press has welcomed so enthusiastically and which Molotov's diplomatic antics have strengthened.[181]

Indeed, by 12 December 1940 Hitler had committed himself to war against the USSR and ordered his General Staff to prepare the invasion plan: Operation Barbarossa. From early 1941 the Comités pour la IVe Internationale expected an imminent attack, but as it happened the invasion was delayed by a month because of unexpected levels of resistance in Yugoslavia.

Stalin alone refused to see it coming, so keen was he to maintain his alliance with Hitler. This fact was confirmed by Khrushchev's secret speech at the Twentieth Congress of the Communist Party of the Soviet Union.[182]

The internationalists and defence of the USSR

Even if it entered into battle unwillingly, the USSR's involvement in the war changed everything, particularly for the peoples living in countries occupied by Hitler. The apparent stability of Hitler's empire had been rocked. The fascist nightmare could be brought to an end. The oppressed peoples regained confidence.

Trotskyist militants reacted immediately. The *Lutte de classe* group distributed a leaflet on 30 June 1941: 'The communist strategy must be to link up the struggle of the Red Army with the class struggle in the capitalist countries'.

La Vérité came up with the same idea soon after Hitler's attack, as shown in the two issues it produced in July.

Two pamphlets were published. There are no extant copies; but their content was summarised in the June 1942 *Quatrième Internationale* journal:

> One copied pamphlet produced at the start of the German-Soviet war forewarned the disasters the Red Army would suffer and called for workers to defend the endangered workers' state; the other pamphlet, which was printed, offered clarity after these disasters had happened and showed the way forward – Lenin's way – an appeal to the workers of the world and the German workers in particular.

The editorial of the 1st August issue of *La Vérité* expressed these ideas in an agitational form:

> We must defend the USSR. Why?
> 1. Because the pillage of more raw materials and the exploitation of more manpower would strengthen Hitler, allowing him to prolong the war.
> 2. Because Hitler's need to throw all the Nazi forces onto the Eastern Front will force him to neglect western Europe (he has no more than 200,000 men for the occupied areas) and will furthermore create more favourable conditions for the struggle, which the Soviet resistance will reinforce.
> 3. Because Hitler wants to take advantage of the dangerous situation created for the USSR *by the treachery of the Stalinist bureaucracy* to destroy the workers' state, planned economy and collective ownership and make the USSR into a raw materials and manpower market and an outlet for the products of capitalist industry. Because Hitler could then breathe new life into dying capitalism, make a deal with his imperialist rivals and drown in blood any possibility of workers' struggle for years to come.

Almost all Trotskyist activists agreed with these basic ideas, even those who did not characterise the USSR as a workers' state: only a small minority were in opposition in 1942. Whatever one's view of the USSR, its transformation into a German colony would surely represent a huge setback, and it would be a major coup for Hitler's régime; furthermore, given the traditions of the October revolution, Russia's entry into armed struggle (against the will of the ruling bureaucracy) could reawaken the oppressed classes in fascist Europe: indeed, this did happen in Yugoslavia. It did not seem an opportune moment to resuscitate the theoretical debate of 1937-38.

La Vérité explained 'how to defend the USSR' as follows:

> The workers of our country are in an excited state of mind. They can understand what is going on without much need for explanation….
>
> Napoleon could not conquer Russia because he had to devote so much of his army to keeping down the insurgent Spanish people. Hitler shall also meet his Spain. Thanks to us he will be unable to defeat the Red Army before winter. In spring we the workers of Europe and the USSR shall taste victory, carrying out a proletarian revolution.
>
> Hitler cannot conquer the USSR without the support of French industry. The French capitalists are united with Hitler, both when they war-profiteer and when they fight against the revolutionary threat. To their reactionary class solidarity we counterpose revolutionary class solidarity. We must smash the weapon of French industry which lies in Hitler's hands, using all appropriate and effective means.
>
> Only success for the European workers' movement will allow the Soviet peoples to hold out until the revolutionary crisis breaks. Every demand raised, every strike and every act of resistance represents direct solidarity with the Soviet peoples.
>
> In order that the struggle to defend the USSR and free ourselves (these are one and the same struggle) might find success, we need unity. To secure unity we must build 'workers' resistance committees'. These committees must bring together workers from all tendencies who want a revolution to bring down Hitler.

We should make clear that this appeal was launched at a decisive moment: the German advance was breathtaking; five weeks after the start of the offensive it seemed invincible. The question asked anxiously was: will the USSR hold out until winter? No-one thought the victory of the revolution would take place in the coming months: the 'revolutionary springtime' was clearly a symbolic idea.

Disasters for the Red Army and the Communists' turn

From early on in the war it was easy to see the flaws of Stalin's nationalist war of conquest, even from a military point of view. With Hitler's consent he had captured Poland and the Baltic states with no concern for those peoples' right to self-determination. But in just a few days the Red Army was driven out of these territories. By 27 June Hitler had taken Kaunas, Vilnius and Riga. The USSR signed a treaty with Poland's government in exile on 20 July recognising that 'the conquests of 1939 are null and void' but in reality it had already lost hold of the conquered territories several weeks beforehand. Minsk, Smolensk and Kiev fell in August and September. On 22 November 1941 von Kleist occupied the Caucasus port of Rostov, and the Germans were also just twenty kilometres from Moscow. It was not until December that the Soviets evacuated Moscow and established a stable front.

Red Army units were decimated, encircled or captured. On 15 November *La Vérité* commented:

> The Soviet High Command has shown itself to be completely incompetent. The 1923-28 elimination of Trotsky's collaborators – the organisers of the Red Army – including the executions of Tukhachevsky, Yakir, Gamarnik and all the career officers who had displayed their talent in the Civil War, as well as the purges in the wake of the disastrous Finnish campaign and all the attacks on the General Staff, have led to the appointment of the most mediocre of leaders.

These arguments earnt the wrath of the PCF, who made violent attacks against the Trotskyists.[183] But Khrushchev showed that they were true in his speech at the Twentieth Congress:

> Stalin's annihilation of numerous military leaders and party workers between 1937 and 1941 had very serious consequences, particularly at the start of the war… The policy of repression directed against the military hierarchy also threatened to sow indiscipline in the army, since over a period of several years officers of every rank, as well as soldiers who were members of the Party or the Komsomol, were encouraged to 'unmask' their superiors as hidden enemies.

La Vérité also spoke of dissenting voices in the highest levels of the Soviet bureaucracy (including Malenkov and Timoshenko). Khrushchev's silence on the matter at the Twentieth Congress does not prove that such dissent did not exist. But the news did suit the Trotskyists' expectations of developments in the USSR: the division of the bureaucracy into two camps, with one ready to side with counter-revolution and the other realising that defence of the USSR required a return to soviet democracy and the preparation of an international revolution. This theme was reiterated by *La Vérité* as well as *La Lutte de classe* throughout the war, and indeed on 15 October *La Vérité* argued that the General Staff 'have proven themselves unable to elaborate any strategy for the international civil war'.

In reality this was the least of concerns for the Soviet government. On 2 July Stalin called for a 'national struggle'. Soon afterwards he replaced *the Internationale* with a Russian anthem. Germans, or 'the Boche' were now the enemy. On the international plane, Stalin voiced support for Roosevelt's war aims. Far from working towards revolution he told the people to abandon their revolutionary objectives – even more bluntly than he had done before the German-Soviet pact – and called on them to support their 'democratic' governments. Stalin ordered the Communist Parties in occupied countries to join the bourgeois resistance movements.

La Vérité commented on 1 August 1941 :

> Not only does Moscow proclaim 'Follow De Gaulle, he shows the way forward!', but the British [Communist Party] has declared its intention to support all the work of the life-long anti-communist Churchill. Moscow has gone as far as saying that the Red Army is not fighting for the overthrow of world capitalism – the task set for it in the decree which marked its foundation – but for 'honour, law and freedom' (as Molotov said). This is the meaning of the Stalinists' new unconditional alliance with imperialism, which comes at the expense of the Soviet workers and the world proletarian revolution.

The Gaullist Resistance to Vichy

But in 1941-42 what was the character of this Gaullist Resistance which the USSR's entry into the war bolstered and which Moscow had told its supporters to follow?

It was very diverse. We have discussed the politics of the Mouvement national révolutionnaire (which joined the Resistance in 1941): the Resistance historian Henri Noguères counts its newspaper *La Révolution Française* as a Resistance newspaper as early as 1940, from the point when it adopted the slogan 'Collaborate, yes, but not under the jackboot'.[184] Even that was a position taken to suit the demands of the time, and reflected the ideological disarray of the Socialists. Other movements involved were not that different ideologically from the Nazis, but they were vehemently anti-

German. For example, the ideology of the Organisation civile et militaire (OCM), largely composed of the far right and nationalists, was anti-Semitic, fascistic and technocratic. Indeed, in the *Cahiers de l'OCM* Blocq Massart wrote of the 'disastrous experience' of Léon Blum's rule: 'It showed that this Jew only had Jewish friends and only trusted Jews'. Noguères recounts the furore caused by an article '…which could well have been printed in [the pro-German anti-Semitic newspapers] *La Gerbe, Le Pilori* or *Je suis partout* too'.[185]

The lines between this organisation and the fascistic Vichy reaction were very much blurred. It was not only illegal newspapers like *Défense de la France* that refused to condemn Vichy. De Gaulle himself did not hide his sympathy for the reactionary anti-working class policies of the Vichy régime, and only criticised Marshal Pétain for compromising his agenda by capitulating to the Germans:

> In the financial and economic sphere these technocrats showed themselves to be very competent, despite all the problems faced, and furthermore the social doctrine of the 'National Revolution' – corporatism, a labour charter and benefits for families – was not without charm. But the fact that this project was mixed up with capitulation could only lead the masses to look for something else.[186]

It was not surprising, therefore, that throughout London kept up relations with Vichy. Heurteaux was in permanent contact with Pétain's Deuxième Bureau[187]. The Gaullist colonel Groussard collaborated with the Minister of War, Huntziger. Noguères writes:

> Groussard, after returning from Britain via Lisbon and Madrid, had several meetings with General Huntziger, whom he informed about his double-agent dealings with the British and the Free French.

But among the Vichy vipers' nest was the Minister of the Interior Pucheu, who was keen to be seen in a good light by Berlin. On 15 July 1941 he had colonel Groussard arrested. Similarly, Loustanau-Lacau, head of the 'Alliance' network was arrested on 18 July: in indignation at such a lack of *fair-play*[188] he wrote in 1948:

> I provide these details so that the reader can understand the behaviour of these commissars, who now hold high office. There was nothing forcing them to arrest me: my activities were entirely clandestine.[189]

The Croix de Feu leader Colonel de la Rocque, a leading propagandist for the Vichy régime, himself belonged to the *Alibi* network, which worked with the Intelligence Service.[190]

The 'anti-French campaigns' office was charged with hunting down revolutionaries and anti-fascists, but it was itself part of the Resistance. Henri Noguères commented:

> It is always regrettable to have to take sides like this, even more so when freedoms and lives are lost and above all when political and ideological principles are in dispute.[191]

Or, to put these euphemisms in plain English: these people 'took sides' by sacrificing revolutionaries and Communists to the Nazis, which also suited their ideology. All this was 'regrettable' but allowed them to serve the Allies in patriotic fashion – which also suited their ideology.

The main Resistance movement in the Southern Zone, the Mouvement de libération nationale, was no more clearly delineated from the far right. This group, led by Frenay, fused with the Christian Democrats who published *Libertés* (de Menthon and colonel Boudet) in 1941, and published *Combat*. In February 1942 Frenay had several meetings with Pucheu, the same minister who a few months previously had worked with the Nazis to draw up the list of fifty hostages to be shot at Châteaubriant.[192]

According to Passy, the *Combat* movement declared itself absolutely ready 'to stop attacking the person of Marshal Pétain and make fewer attacks against his ministers in its clandestine newspaper, in the interests of reconciliation'. But the negotiations collapsed when Pucheu informed his police chiefs about them.

This imbroglio becomes even more unbelievable when Frenay's leading lieutenant Chevance tells us who financed the movement:

> The first big donation we received was given by the director of Lemaigre Dubreuilh's newspaper *Le Jour*. This was pretty much tied to *La Cagoule*, which in the North said that it supported the Germans but in the South encouraged an Allied victory.[193]

So we see that the 'anti-fascist' Resistance was subsidised by *La Cagoule*, the clandestine fascist movement which opportunistically sided with Hitler and the Allies all at once! Here was a union of pro-German fascists, ultra-reactionary supporters of the Vichy régime, fascists and reactionaries who hoped for an Allied victory, and also 'democrats' who backed the Allies.

In 1942 most of the 'democrats' in the Southern Zone were participants in D'Astier de La Vigerie's *Libération* movement. Jean Moulin, tasked with bringing together the various Resistance groups, faced reticence from their quarter: they had not yet taken in Frenay's negotiations with Pucheu. But they agreed to join De Gaulle 'symbolically'. And they were not themselves untainted by compromise with the far-right. They had, for example, had contact with a *La Cagoule* representative … who would later head up the Deuxième Bureau of Pétain's Milice. And when they created their 'paramilitary' armed wing, the weapons were supplied by officers from the Vichy Army.

The Socialists and De Gaulle

Forty percent of the *Libération* movement's forces came from the SFIO and, after a deal with Léon Jouhaux, CGT reformists. The Socialists took some time to account for their parliamentary group's decision to vote through dictatorial powers for Pétain. Those among them who had not capitulated to Pétain began to re-organise under the leadership of Léon Blum's spokesman Daniel Mayer. In 1941 the Centre d'action socialiste tried to bring these activists together, and the first illegal issue of *Le Populaire* appeared in June 1941. It was published by *Libération*, thanks to an agreement that the Socialists would participate in that movement's activities. Socialists unhappy with their limited role in the *Libération* leadership (their sole representative was Vienôt) and the significant number of Parti communiste members around D'Astier created autonomous Resistance groups (*Veni*) in Marseille and Toulouse. But most activists continued to work alongside *Libération*.

In the occupied zone, on the other hand, they led their own *Libération Nord* movement, whose first clandestine newspaper appeared in December 1940 (this group also involved Louis Saillant who was simultaneously a member of the Comités de la IVe Internationale's trade union commission).

The Parti socialiste had learned nothing from 1936 and 1940. Its propaganda reported on the statements of Léon Blum and Le Troquer at the Riom trials (which began in February 1942) which displayed the courage of those on trial, but also the true character of their politics.

Like his co-accused, the Parti socialiste leader defended his politics so courageously that it came to look like a trial of the accusers, and with Hitler growing unhappy the tribunal decided in April to break off the trial and send the accused back to their cells. Léon Blum's defence speeches were the expression of his real thoughts, and nothing else.

Indeed, Léon Blum explained to the tribunal that his role in June 1936 was to prevent revolution, in league with the bosses:

No doubt, I could have put forward something like the Matignon accords myself. But to be fair I must admit that it was the employers who first took the initiative. Messieurs Lambert-Ribot, Duchemin and Dellouze, former Presidents of the Paris Chamber of Commerce, visited me and together we arranged negotiations with the CGT, as the employers had already instigated... No-one [among the bourgeoisie] was opposed to this ... There was only one demand placed on the Chamber of Commerce: act quickly and vote to put an end to this dangerous situation: I did not characterise the situation as revolutionary, but it was much like a revolutionary situation. [He added:] The bourgeoisie, particularly the employers, thought, waited and hoped for me to be their saviour.

[...] On 6 June, after five days in power, the government was clearly out of sorts. It hoped to put an end to a movement whose revolutionary potential grew day by day by meeting with one fell swoop all of the basic grievances under which the movement sheltered.

The Socialists distributed thousands of copies of this text in March 1942 under the title 'The republic accuses'. In doing so they openly admitted their June 1936 support for the bourgeoisie. Nor did they plan to change this policy in the middle of the war: of course, they were in the camp of the 'national resistance' and supported its leader De Gaulle.

This support did cause them some problems, however. In December 1941 the Southern Zone Parti socialiste committee asked the Free French envoy Morandat a series of questions about De Gaulle:

They asked me questions about General de Gaulle, his aims and his thoughts on various topics for two hours', [Morandat reports,] ... it was of course a very wide-ranging discussion, taking an overview of the situation: naturally we discussed the question of the Republic as well as democracy, trade unionism, what would happen after the war, schools ....

'Whatever Morandat now says', Henri Noguères adds, 'his interviewers – as they told us – did not actually ask him very many questions that day, since they just had a few worries... they only wanted some reassurances.'[194] That seems all the more likely when it is considered that *Le Populaire* was financed by Morandat.

Many of them later went to London: Philip, Tixier, Pineau (of *Libération-Nord*) and Félix Gouin (who was sent by Blum and the leadership).

Philip did not ask anything indiscreet. He was taken by Passy and got a safe-passage from the London government: soon he would be welcoming with open arms the PSF (Croix de Feu) MP C. Vallin, who shared the blame for the inculpation of Blum and his co-defendants: but the indignation in London was such that he had to give up on plans to hand him a ministry. Christian Pineau still felt some concern; 'don't ask anything about the Resistance', he explained. 'I replied that, like Passy, [De Gaulle] knew almost nothing about the Resistance and had a purely military understanding of France.'[195]

Tixier and Pineau asked the leader of Free France to affirm his loyalty to the Republic and to democratic freedoms.

'It matters which ones!' interrupted De Gaulle. 'There must be no more taking liberties like there was before the war. I want to get rid of the order of things which led us where we are now.'

He eventually agreed to write a message in terms which touched base with the Socialists.

He [De Gaulle] objected to any additions, particularly ones relating to economic questions.

Finally, when I asked him if he had anything to say to trade unionists, he said with a smile a sentence which took me by surprise 'Just tell those brave people [sic] that I will not betray them'.

However, the *Libération-Nord* representative was somewhat reassured by the final version of the message De Gaulle sent him:

The criticism of Vichy was strengthened, and the description changed to: 'Another [régime] borne of criminal capitulation is glorifying dictatorial power'. But why, for the sake of balance, did he have to change the passage about the Third Republic too?: 'A moral, social and political system collapsed in defeat after being paralysed by taking liberties'.

Pineau was above all pleased on account of his success as regards the following passage which, he said, 'alludes to economic problems':

At the same time, making plans for a powerful renovation of the nation and the empire, we want the French ideals of freedom, equality and brotherhood to be put into practice at home.

Armed with this support the *Libération-Nord* envoy returned to France … where the trade unionists (C. Laurent, Neumeyer, Saillant, Tessier and Bouladoux) welcomed him 'with some reservations, if not coldness'. Still, Noguères adds, Christian Pineau held back from telling these 'brave people' that his special mission meant he was now an agent of Passy's BCRA.[196] [197]

De Gaulle's declaration was warmly received by most people. 'The Communists said it was 'republican in spirit' and reassuring for democratic organisations.'[198]

It seemed that only the Socialists were not yet convinced. But to guarantee the unity of the Resistance they pretended that they were.

> Some think that the manifesto denouncing the 'moral, social, political and economic' system which collapsed in defeat after paralyzing itself by taking liberties is worthy of some examination' commented *Le Populaire*. It continued: 'If we are to believe the official commentaries, General de Gaulle attacked errors including high unemployment figures, burning grain and destroying stocks at the point when the population was most in need and it could have shared out the riches of the world. This critique of the bourgeois system is the best tribute you could pay us.[199]

Daniel Mayer, the author of the article, had quite a sense of humour, but only the initiated few could understand it.

The Socialists' representative in London had no illusions about the real nature of Gaullism. Arriving in August 1942, Félix Gouin was even more amazed than his predecessors about the welcome he received:

> I came to London not just as some hack but to officially represent the Comité d'action socialiste there. It was with this title and this status that I joined la France combattante. So my role was to liaise between la France combattante and the party which, from 1941, had fought with the dual aim of liberating France and re-establishing democracy. On my arrival here the thing that surprised me was that they had hardly any time for organised parties: I said that the point was to have very clear and worked-out policies.

Alluding to a polemical article by the former Socialist Pierre Brossolette in *la Marseillaise* he continued:

> Parties, Brossolette tells us, don't exist any more. There is no point reviving them. Only one thing matters: the Resistance, the only framework for uniting all anti-Vichy and anti-Hitler forces.
>
> A few days after this article there was a meeting of the Jean Jaurès group during which I made quite clear that I did not at all agree with such ideas, firstly because it runs counter to reality and secondly because

there can be no democracy without organised parties.

My position was thus one of the most clear-cut and I did not doubt that from this moment onwards I would be considered as a subversive type or, at least, as a naïf person wrong to take seriously, very seriously, the democratic façade which had little by little replaced the semi-fascist set-up that existed until 1941.[200]

But the Parti socialiste had other bitter pills to swallow. Its only aim was to restore the *status quo ante*: the parliamentary republic, the empire, secularism and the trade unions. In this struggle the Anglo-American imperialists were the only possible allies: the working class could only support – continue to support – the section of the bourgeois state and the bourgeoisie which maintained their alliance with them. De Gaulle was an uncertain character who, if the balance of forces allowed it, would establish another type of authoritarian state. But they had no choice. The Socialists continued to participate in the Gaullist Resistance.

La Vérité polemicises against André Philip

Emboldened by the general's declaration, André Philip talked about it on radio and called on the French to build a single party, the party of the Resistance, following the ideas of De Gaulle and Brossolette. The Trotskyists took advantage of this and engaged in discussion with Socialist workers, trying to get their message across to them. An article (by Yvan Craipeau) appeared in *La Vérité* no. 37 of 15 September 1942 under the title 'When a monarchist general defends the traditions of 1789':

> Concluding a series of speeches he has made since arriving in Britain, the Socialist MP André Philip spoke on Monday 31st August to the listeners of London radio. In this speech, summarised for the British public, he outlined the essentials of the political programme of 'la France combattante'. The three main themes of his explanation were:
>
> 1. 'La France combattante' fights for freedom and human dignity. Workers and bosses, socialists and conservatives are united in this struggle.
>
> 2. Freedom and human dignity are gains of 1789: 'la France combattante' defends the tradition of 1789.
>
> 3. The tradition of 1789 is the tradition of the Republic, France's legal government. The Comité national in London is by law the French government – De Gaulle being the only member of the government who wanted to, and could, continue the struggle the legal government had

been determined to fight to the finish.

This legalistic and moralising prattle is amazing, coming from the mouth of a socialist who claims to know what the masses think. A working-class representative like André Philip should have made these three points:

1. Under the capitalist system the great mass of workers has only one freedom: the freedom to be exploited by the bosses; and the individual has no fate other than being killed in war or ground down by the machine. Only socialism can offer freedom and human dignity. So how can bosses and workers, conservatives and socialists unite around a socialist programme?

Does this demagogy not remind you of the empty chatter of the Radicals?

2. The working class wants to defend the tradition of 1789, the real and revolutionary tradition of seizing power from the feudalists. That is why a monarchist general like Mr Charles De Gaulle does not seem particularly qualified for standing up for the tradition of 1789.

3. General de Gaulle has continued the war; but let's not forget that the war he has continued, the war of Daladier and Reynaud, the French capitalists' war, is one the French people did not want to fight. If they do want to fight a war today, it is the war against reaction and oppression and for socialism. That is why the working class of France wants a people's government of workers and peasants to fight the war, not a government of bourgeois order.

We understand well enough André Philip's aims: he wants to unite all those who want to fight against Hitler's oppression. But you cannot maintain unity forever if it is based on empty banalities. Unity can be built today in struggles over wages and food and against deportations to Germany. But it cannot and must not be built on a programme which once again subordinates the working class to the bourgeoisie. It must on the contrary open the way for a working-class struggle for power. The task is not to repeat 1789 and the Third Estate, but rather to make a new revolution, that of the Fourth Estate: the proletariat.

The Communists' nationalist turn

The Parti communiste français's turn began at a time when relations between the USSR and Germany were increasingly tense, but before the Nazi attack took place. It was in April 1941[201] – when *L'Humanité* began to talk of the 'crimes of the occupiers' – that Marrane started to make inquiries with a view to creating a broad Front national[202]. On 13 May 1941 the PCF officially launched a call 'for the formation of a Front national to fight for the independence of France'.

Rol Tanguy defined its aims – for the benefit of historians of the Resistance – thus:

> This Front national set out [...] to unite all sorts of people under its banner, from men of the Church to workers and politicians, etc. Its ambition was [...] to act as an important rallying-point for patriots from all sections of society, and this created a powerful base for the Resistance across the country.

Therefore they again took up the idea of a Front of the French, as Thorez had advocated before the war, to 'broaden' the Popular Front. The difference was that it sought to serve the masses' hope for liberation from Nazi oppression.

However, this 'national' movement kept its distance from De Gaulle and counterposed itself to him. On 13 May 1941 *L'Humanité* argued:

> Some French men and women, suffering when they see our country oppressed by the invader, have wrongly placed all their hopes in De Gaulle's movement. We tell these compatriots that it is not with such a movement of colonialist and reactionary inspiration, in the image of British imperialism, that we can build the unity of the French nation for national liberation.

On 20 June, on the eve of the Nazi attack against the USSR, *L'Humanité* could still lead with:

> The miners in the North and Pas-de-Calais, by taking strike action, have shown the way forward for the struggles of the workers of France, who all demand increased salaries and better food supplies. Pétain has admitted how afraid he is of communism. The Vichy traitors are leading Frenchmen to their deaths in Syria for the Germans, while De Gaulle and Catroux are leading others to their deaths for Britain.
> Down with the imperialist war!
> Long live the freedom and independence of the colonial peoples!
> Long live the Front national and the independence of France!

Such an orientation was very different from De Gaulle's. We have noted the condescending tone with which he made a few words in tribute to the 'brave people' who led the reformist trade unions. He had nothing in common with the striking miners.

'We search in vain', Noguères writes, 'for an allusion to the May-June 1941 strikes in the *Mémoires de guerre* of the leader of Free France. It was not until 7 March 1943 that the miners were congratulated on their strike, by Fernand Grenier on the BBC.'[203]

But when he did so Grenier made out that the strike was part of the Resistance effort, pure and simple. But looking back the historian of the Resistance must ask himself if this was a Resistance action. If conceived of as nationalist and an act of diversion, then possibly so; but if it was a working-class action making demands about pay and conditions, then clearly not:

> We may therefore objectively ask ourselves to what extent such a movement can be considered, properly speaking, as a Resistance action. It seems that in London, in any case, they quickly – perhaps too quickly – gave a negative answer to this question, if they even thought about it.[204]

That makes clear that the bourgeois and military-led Resistance had nothing in common with working-class resistance.

But after the Radio-Moscow appeal ('Follow General de Gaulle, he shows you the way forward') the PCF changed tack. First off, the war stopped being 'imperialist' and there was no more talk of imperialism nor of De Gaulle. *L'Humanité* declared on 2 July 1941: 'The liberation of France depends on the victory of the USSR: we must do everything to hasten this victory. Fascism is the enemy we must defeat'.

The summer 1941 issue of the PCF theoretical journal *Les Cahiers du bolchévisme* completed the turn: 'The French salute De Gaulle's soldiers as fighters in a noble cause, fighters against Hitler'.[205]

Recalling the line in *L'Humanité* of 13 May, *La Vérité* mocked 'A noble cause… a reactionary and colonialist one'.[206]

But it was not the reactionary and colonialist character of the leader of Free France that worried the nationalists grouped around the Communists in the Front national leadership. We only need remember who these men were. Charles Tillon cites Langevin and Joliot Curie. He forgets some others though: for example Bidault (also a *Combat* activist and later the Organisation de l'armée secrète leader during the Algerian war), Louis Marin and J. Debu-Bridel. Let us look at how the latter explained his decision to join the Front national:

> A collaborator of Louis Marin, André Tardieu and Emile Buré, I am a longstanding nationalist. Why would I now disown Déroulède? We

wanted to make war, not politics. That was the central idea. Strengthened by Louis Marin's assistance we looked for the most effective means of fighting. Given that the USSR was in the war there was no doubt that the pre-existing secret organisation of the PCF was the strongest force in France, except for movements of direct foreign inspiration like the organisations of the Intelligence Service.[207]

The Front national could only satisfy J. Debu-Bridel and Louis Marin. Militarily speaking it was remarkably effective. Sabotages, which had been taking place for several months, had considerably increased in number since the USSR's entry into the war; demonstrations were guarded by armed teams, arms depots were raided, machines were put out of use, depots and factories torched, fuel stocks exploded, collaborators executed and Wehrmacht trains derailed. Soon, the FTP [Francs-tireurs et Partisans, led by the PCF] would start making attacks on German officers, placing bombs at army meeting-points, then going on to attack troop detachments, convoys and trains.

Politically speaking, the chauvinism of PCF and Front national literature surpassed that of *Combat* and even the OCM. It used the language of Déroulède. There was no question of distinguishing between German capitalists and German workers, Nazis and anti-Nazis: all Germans were 'boches', like in the good old days of the 1914-18 war and *Le Matin*'s campaigns.

Contrary to what Lecoeur claims, this chauvinist tone had not been used in Communist propaganda during the strike in the North in 1941: the extracts of *L'Enchaîné* he reproduced are proof enough of this. But it is true that it was commonplace among the population, particularly in the areas devastated by the two wars and where, as a result, socialism in the Guesdist tradition was deeply coloured by nationalism. This type of hatred evoked the chauvinist themes of the 1914 war and hostile sentiments arising from Nazi oppression. Using the power of nationalist hatred in its crudest form soon brought dividends.

The two camps were presented in a simplistic manner: on one side were the Nazis, the 'boches' and their agents, and on the other side were the anti-Nazis of all classes and all political stripes, supported by the Soviet and Anglo-American allies. This simplification allowed them to avoid answering difficult questions ('after liberation, we'll see what happens...') and instead to advance to taking action.

The Communists took advantage of all this. Firstly, they benefited on a 'moral' level: they were welcomed back into 'national' society, which regarded them with admiration as much as with concern. 'In 1942', declared Colonel Rémy, 'the FTP represented the sole armed underground organisation waging an effective struggle against the Germans'.

This compliment is significant if we remember that colonel Rémy at the same time held a secret admiration for Pétain, which he revealed after the war in the reactionary *Carrefour*.

The Communists also made material gains. In October 1942 they agreed to set up an information network for the BRCA (the Fana network). This relied on Passy's representative Rémy supplying them with 1.5 million francs a week to help them encourage waverers to join the maquis.

However, British radio hardly made any propaganda about them. The 'Free French' did not give them many weapons. But their role as the activist wing of nationalism gave them a stark political advantage: as repression stepped up they won new recruits to the struggle: spilt blood was replaced with fresh blood.

Now, the Communists were swimming with the current and encouraged it along with the massive means available to them.

In August 1941 they decided to start armed attacks on German officers: on 23 August Fabien killed a leading officer at the Barbès métro station. This triggered a terrible wave of attacks and hostage executions.

In October 1942 in their newspaper *France d'abord* ['France First'] – a title which summarised its programme – the FTP high command launched the call 'Everyone kill a Kraut'.[208] Reproducing this statement Charles Tillon leapt to its defence:

> Some otherwise well-meaning types are confusing things when they pompously write that Marx would have been sick if he heard the slogan 'Everyone kill a Kraut'. But isn't this neo-internationalism – expressed fifteen years after the event, when the task of every Frenchman was to engage in the liberation struggle against the limited number of Germans who held the country in terror – at odds with a war like that the Germans were waging in the occupied countries? Without doubt. The word 'boche' today bothers those who of their own volition forget that V. Feldmann shouted to the Germans who were about to shoot him, 'Imbeciles, I'm dying for you!'
>
> He fought alongside those whose guerrilla slogan was 'Everyone kill a Kraut'. The real meaning of Feldmann's cry was the armed struggle of the soldiers without uniform. The freedom of the German people relied on the 'boches' not occupying our territory.

You could hardly 'confuse things' more than Tillon does.

For sure many Communists who cried 'Everyone kill a Kraut' nonetheless thought of themselves as internationalists, in the sense that, like Feldmann, they were also keen to win the freedom of other peoples, including the German people. The front line of the FTP had long been composed of Communist émigrés from various countries, the Main d'oeuvre immigré (MOI) for whom the slogan 'France First' could obviously only be of tactical use.

The question which concerned Tillon was the armed struggle against the Nazis. Was it necessary to engage in combat? When? How? With whom? These were tactical as well as strategic questions. We can admit that his answers to these tactical questions were fair enough. But the fact remains that a tactic can only have meaning in the context of a given objective. Here, the objective itself was determined by chauvinism and alliance with the nationalist big bourgeoisie: this could only mean restoration of the capitalist state and its colonial empire. The workers who hoped that driving out the Nazis and liberating the country would bring social liberation were cut down by the PCF: 'the liberation' would mean a return to exploitation by French capitalism. Far from 'transforming the imperialist war into a civil war' the PCF joined one of the imperialist camps and co-opted the workers' struggle into the imperialist war. The armed struggle of the FTP became a part of this war.

The chauvinist propaganda of the PCF would indeed have 'sickened' Marx and Lenin, not through any linguistic purism on their part but because it ran contrary to their objective: the emancipation of the workers, which can only be achieved by the international unity of the working class against their 'own' bourgeoisies.

Individual terrorism

When in August 1941 the PCF turned to individual attacks on German officers and soldiers, it was not without some ripples of discontent among its ranks.

Opposition was firstly on the theoretical plane: Leninism had always condemned individual attacks, to which it counterposed mass organisation. J. Duclos recalled these ideological concerns at the 31st August 1944 Central Committee meeting:

> At that time, certain elements amongst our ranks attempted to combat our policy 'theoretically' and spoke of 'individual actions': in truth they were shrinking from the fight. What they called 'individual' and terrorist acts were the starting point, albeit timid and hesistant, for the armed struggle of the whole of our people.

It is significant that this opposition first arose in the MOI, where the communists who had migrated to France were to be found, most often because of the victory of fascism or of reaction in their own countries. They had supplied the leading cadres of the International Brigades during the Spanish civil war. Fiercely anti-fascist, experienced in warfare, they were driven to contemplate the action on a military level. They were the first to engage in combat – notably the Czechs – and were in the forefront of the fight against fascism at the same time that Duclos was putting it to one side. Artur London[209] explains how the opposition developed:

> The actions taken at first led to a certain reticence. Certain comrades, grouped according to their language, counterposed ideological considerations to the orders given, equating armed struggle against the occupier with individual terrorism as advocated by anarchists and condemned by Marxists.[210]

The 15 March 1942 *La Vérité* argued the same point, quoting Lenin:

> So many attacks, so many pointless gestures. Lenin, polemicising against a terrorist organisation, explained himself thus:
> 'The Svoboda advocates terrorism as a means of 'provoking' the workers' movement and giving it a powerful shock. It is difficult to imagine an argument more evidently self-defeating. Are there so few abuses in Russia that it is necessary to invent special provocations? Similarly, it is clear that those who have not been provoked and are not susceptible to being provoked by the tyrant who reigns in Russia, will equally turn their noses up at the duel between a handful of terrorists and the government.'
> Today if we substitute 'occupied Europe' for 'Russia', Lenin's text seems marvellously relevant for today.
> Yes, like Lenin we always unflinchingly prefer organising the masses, and condemn individual terrorism, a bottomless pit into which desperate, directionless revolutionaries throw themselves', [Noguères wrote.]

Soon the opposition took on a practical character:

'Others' within the MOI, London adds, 'foreseeing hostage executions, questioned the correctness and the effectiveness of armed struggle'.

Tillon also added 'that soon after the execution of a German officer in Nantes, an organiser in the region had written in his report to the Central

Committee that the man who shot the officer should give himself up in order to prevent the killing of the hostages'. He comments:

'At the same time, very close to Nantes, there was no such idea in the heads of the prisoners at Châteaubriant, who were going to die as hostages because a Communist had recently killed a German officer.'[211]

London's argument is specious. These activists (two of whom were Trotskyists) did indeed go to their deaths with courage, but none of them had been consulted on the strategy of the PCF.

A Communist leader Joseph (Beaufils) supplies us with a more realistic argument – Rémy asks him: 'Do you find it worth the shooting of five or ten of your men in exchange for the capture of a revolver or a karabiner?'

'Certainly', Joseph replies, 'since when it is made known that five or ten of our men have been killed, we will sign up another fifty or a hundred new recruits to the FTP.'[212]

Rémy, in the 1945 edition of his *Mémoires*, concludes: 'Joseph's response, which might appear cynical, is very much the truth'. He explains: 'I will be even more cynical than Joseph: I only needed to track the executions in order to sign up new recruits'.

But this arithmetic is not only 'cynicism'. It has a political meaning. The hostages shot were working-class militants: Joseph and Rémy's recruits were nationalist fighters.

The most interesting opposition was sharply internationalist. We see, for example, how Albert Ouzoulias recounts a 15 August 1941 discussion among the cadres of the Jeunesses communistes, who Fabien wanted to convince to carry out attacks. He could not dispel qualms about this except by getting involved himself:

> The comrades refused to execute a German soldier who may well have been a communist from Hamburg or a worker from Berlin. An officer could have been an anti-Nazi professor. At best they accepted the idea of shooting at Gestapo officers. But our comrades still did not understand that the best way to defend our country in a time of war is to kill the maximum number of German officers. This would hasten the end of the war and bring an end to the pain which a great number of peoples – including the German people – were suffering. Internationalism, at this moment, meant killing the greatest possible number of Nazis.[213]

The confusion lay in the fact that the Jeunesses communistes were challenging the very objectives of the struggle. They agreed with 'taking down' Gestapo officers. But they believed that solidarity with anti-Nazi

Germans, German communists and the German working class was necessary for the proletarian revolution.

In reality they were being offered a different objective: 'Defending our country in this time of war'. 'Internationalism' thus became a collection of various countries' national struggles against German oppression. Here they looked to re-establish the 'democratic' bourgeois states (later including Germany too), at the expense of the working class's common objectives (socialist revolution, the Socialist United States of Europe).

La Vérité's campaign against individual terrorism in 1941-42 was obviously rooted in the assumption that the aim was international revolution. The necessary violence was the violence of the masses, for which the ground had to be prepared. Individual attacks on the German army lacked military effect ('for each officer killed, Hitler has thousands more'). As for attacks on soldiers, they ran contrary to any revolutionary goal: 'Terrorist acts drive a wedge between French workers and German soldiers, preventing the unity without which a victorious revolution is impossible'.[214]

Indeed, an orientation towards terrorism weakened the working-class mobilisation 'for bread and freedoms', both because of the brutal re-enforcement of repression and because of the hostility it sowed among the population. The disagreement was not about the necessity of armed struggle, but over its character, and also about its timing. What was necessary was sabotage to 'threaten the whole economic machine' and which would be a training ground for the working class, never separate 'from the workers' struggles for more bread and freedoms'.

La Vérité did not understand one thing: the ambiguity of the PCF's policy not only represented 'a bottomless pit into which desperate, directionless revolutionaries threw themselves'. It was also, as Duclos suggests above, part of the still-hesitant shift towards generalised armed struggle. Artur London, although confirming the unpopularity of this policy, comments:

> These difficulties did not only affect us, but the whole Resistance. The terror unleashed by the Germans – curfews, raids, searches, arrests and shootings of hostages – at first left certain sections of the population indisposed and hostile to armed struggle. This state of mind was exploited not only by the Germans but also by fence-sitters and even some Resistance groups who had a different outlook to our own and who could only see short-term results, not understanding that before a mass struggle arose the armed struggle would necessarily pass through this stage.[215]

Individual terrorism would indeed lead to mass struggle (thanks to the forced labour the Nazis imposed). But this mass struggle would not be a revolutionary struggle. Each strategy has its own internal logic.

It is interesting to see why De Gaulle stated his opposition to the PCF's strategy. On 23 October 1941 he expressed himself thus on the BBC:

> It is absolutely normal and absolutely justified for Frenchmen to kill Germans. If the Germans do not want to die at our hands, they only have to go back home... Since they have not managed to crush us all, they are all sure to become either prisoners or corpses. But there are tactics in warfare. The war effort must be led by those in charge... At this moment in time, I order people not to (openly) kill Germans in the occupied territory. There is just one reason for this: it is still too easy for the enemy to respond with massacres of our temporarily unarmed soldiers. However, when we are ready to go on the offensive, the desired orders will be given.[216]

So, at root De Gaulle was very much in agreement with the PCF (on the necessity of killing Germans, without discrimination). He diverged on the military worth of such attacks at that given moment; in relation to the costs; on the character of the war to be fought (it had to be led by military leaders according to their own strategy and tied to landings by the Anglo-American Allies); and by consequence on the short-term role of the Resistance (it had to give priority to building a military organisation capable of intervening in D Day, and above all in terms of 'giving information', that is to say spying, for the Allies).

For the Communists, on the contrary, it was necessary to threaten the rear of the Eastern Front in France: 'Today Hitler needs a secure rearguard, at all costs, and all the more so in that he is going to have to draw on his reserves constantly.'[217]

At the same time, they wanted to organise armed groups capable of cohering into an autonomous national force which the Allies could count on: Communist influence on this national force would allow it to exercise pressure on the restored national government. This objective could not be realised without integrating themselves into the bourgeois Resistance, while maintaining organisational autonomy and playing on nationalist hatred against the occupier.

Between the two factions of the Resistance there was therefore a tactical disagreement which hid a political difference (which political force would gain predominance?). But both had a fundamental common aim: supporting the victory of the Allies and restoring bourgeois democracy.

The internationalist strategy

The strategy of the PCF and of the Resistance was simple: the Anglo-American and Russian Allies would militarily crush Germany and thus allow the liberation of the occupied territories, with the help of the oppressed peoples, whose only task was to facilitate this victory. Retrospectively, it may seem that this perspective was the only realistic one, and the whole population viewed the situation like this. But this is a mistaken view, even if it is true that the Allies – the Soviets as well as the Anglo-Americans – did everything they could, with the help of bourgeois, reformist, and Communist parties, to make sure that this was the only course of action left open.

But in 1941 another perspective was possible, and part of the population believed it to be the most plausible one. For example, see how in July 1941 the Andelys sub-prefect informed the Eure prefect of the state of mind of those hostile to the régime – whom, he added, were '– alas! – legion': 'In truth, in the minds of many layers of the population hoping for Russian and British success, these successes will provoke a revolutionary movement in Germany and the fall of the National Socialist régime. Following this, the oppressed peoples will in turn rise up and kick out the invaders.'[218]

This was, at a basic and very simplified level, at the centre of the internationalists' strategy. With the qualification, of course, that the oppressed peoples' struggles would accelerate the defeat of the Nazis' armies and the fall of Hitler's régime at the same time as paving the way for a working-class seizure of power in each country.

At the end of 1941 – that is to say, at the moment when Hitler's army was at the peak of its powers – their analysis of the military situation led them to relatively optimistic conclusion: the superiority of Hitler's army continued to be a reality, but it was starting to fade. Not only was it suffering enormous losses, but it was not finding any support among the Soviet population. Goebbels had to admit that he no longer knew when the war would end, and made known his determination not to let a revolutionary movement raise its head in Germany.

This did not mean that an Allied military victory was close. The USSR would take time to get out of its critical situation. As for the Anglo-American imperialists, although they would not bee too upset 'to see the USSR collapse, suffering decisive blows' they were in no position to choose. Marcel Hic even wrote: 'Nazism cannot be defeated by an opposing army. It can only be defeated by a revolution in Germany and in the occupied countries'.

The working class in the occupied countries had to lead the masses to fight oppression and poverty. The fight for liberation therefore had to bring together the struggle for freedoms (workers' rights, democratic rights, national freedom) and the struggle against capitalist exploitation, which was aggravated by the fascists' support for the bosses.

The working class had to set up, on a local level, *people's liberation committees* organising this struggle, following revolutionary objectives. The perspective was the building of a revolutionary movement of the masses like in Yugoslavia – but also hoping to find support among the ranks of German soldiers. This would not be possible unless the working class was organised in advance, or if the struggle was diverted towards national unity and nationalism.

The immediate task was to reconstitute the working class *as a class* with its own objectives and its own organisations. Therefore its main weapon was mass struggle and strikes. Sabotage could not be disassociated from working-class and revolutionary objectives. At the outset this required clandestine *workers' groups*, united or acting in unison, and which could promote such actions and begin to organise the working class. Individual terrorism ran counter to this perspective.

Revolution required the joining-together of the revolutionary movements in the oppressed countries with the revolutionary movements in Italy and – above all – Germany. An essential task was to assist the development of a revolutionary movement in Germany, particularly in the ranks of the German army, which would play a decisive role; thus the urgency of engaging in fraternisation work, looking to organise revolutionary nuclei in the German army.

Revolutionary organisation capable of sparking and co-ordinating struggles would be forged in action. It also had to be international: the European conference of the Fourth International hoped to create the embryo of such an organisation.

Such was the strategy that the *La Vérité* group attempted to put into effect. We will later see that the two other small Trotskyist groups diverged on numerous points. They believed that war had now become the modus operandi of the capitalist system. They had to start from scratch and try and train cadres – the former group privileged theory, the *Lutte de classe* group privileged organising. The former believed hopes of national freedom to be counter-revolutionary; the later considered them to be a secondary matter.

Communist agitation in the Wehrmacht

In what ways were the Communists' and Trotskyists' strategies counterposed? We can see this clearly through the differences in their work in the German army.

It would be wrong to imagine that the PCF neglected to make propaganda amongst the German troops. Let us recall that when German troops arrived in Paris and throughout the early period of the occupation, *L'Humanité* called for fraternisation under the slogan 'Let's learn to understand each other'. Such a policy was at this stage dictated by the Russian-German alliance and hopes for the legalisation of the party. The Communist history of the Resistance is quiet on this subject: Charles Tillon's book does not make the slightest allusion to it, although Artur London's account makes reference to the FTP's involvement in this activity.

From September 1941 onwards the PCF devoted themselves to such work with relatively considerable means: significant numbers, a printed (remarkably!) newspaper called *Soldat im Westen*, taking on the headings *Zeitung der Armee* then later *Organ den soldaten komitee im Frankreich*.

Artur London explains:

> The people taking part in German army work were French Resistance members who spoke German, supplied by the PCF or the FTP, and German-speaking immigrants who had been designated for this work by their MOI language groups… Contacts and liaisons with German troops were mostly assured by women or young Austrian Jewish girls, or those of other nationalities who could speak fluent German …
>
> Our anti-Nazi propaganda among the occupying troops was rendered more effective when it was adapted to suit the state of mind, living standards and preoccupations of German soldiers. We informed ourselves about these questions with the help of the information we managed to receive via our contacts. At first the distribution of our materials only came from the outside: that is to say, newspapers and leaflets were thrown over barrack walls or left in theatres, cinemas, parade grounds, streets, cafés and restaurants. More substantial actions where documents were distributed by the hundred were protected by FTP detachments.
>
> Later, in many cases, distribution was carried out just as much on the inside, thanks to the efforts of our anti-fascist services. The greatest difficulty we faced flowed from the rotation of occupation units, which became more regular due to the reverses suffered by the Nazi armies on the Russian front. Among the better organised German anti-fascist groups, I would mention among others that of the Marine Ministry in Paris, the units stationed in Saint-Germain-en-Laye and the submarine base in Bordeaux.[219]

This propaganda was not without its successes, at a certain level:

Thanks to the anti-fascists' activity, in some units we managed to foment sharp discontent with living standards and the behaviour of their officers. Thus in Saint-Germain-en-Laye, in summer 1942, a significant protest movement broke out, stimulated by the standard of food and the bad treatment of soldiers by officers.

Because of anti-fascist soldiers parting the way for us, we were able to get anti-Nazi propaganda to Germany and Austria.[220]

Some passages in *Soldat im Westen* had an internationalist tenor:

The murderers are the Laval types who walk along hand-in-hand with Hitler's clique. The German and French workers must do the same. Laval is not the same as France, Hitler is not the same as Germany.

What do we want? What do the French want? The same thing: calm and peace in our homeland.

The French people's fight is our fight. Their victory will be our victory. Let us help the French today so that they will help us tomorrow, after the fall of the Hitlerite clique, in building a free new Germany.[221]

Soldat im Westen even claimed to be a resumption of the soldiers' committees which existed during the 1918 revolution. But its articles never called on soldiers to be conscious of their strength and to prepare the revolution. They wanted to show that the defeat of the Wehrmacht was certain and so these men ought to capitulate.

London shows the real aim of this propaganda: 'The defeatist propaganda we made led many soldiers to desert when they were posted to the Eastern Front'.

He explains how safe-conducts were given to German soldiers heading for the Russian front, with which they could hand themselves over to the Soviets. Radio Moscow announced that soldiers with such safe-conducts were to become prisoners of war.

London stressed himself that it was essentially an effort to demoralise the opposing army: indeed the agitation was referred to as 'anti-German work'. It was the sort of propaganda which supported all the general-staffs against the enemy: it looked to break the troops' morale, and sow panic among their ranks. At best, it wanted them to surrender. The Nazis themselves exploited it; the RAF too. It had nothing to do with revolutionary agitation among the troops.

This does not mean that the activists engaged in this work, which was nonetheless dangerous, were not motivated by an internationalist spirit. The foreign militants of the MOI – including Germans and Austrians – could not enthuse themselves with French chauvinism. But for them internationalism meant, first and foremost, support for the Red Army. Its hopes were tied up in the progress of the Soviet armies, not the building of a revolutionary movement.

The German Communists' 'defeatism' brought to mind the 'defeatism' of the French Communists after the Russian-German pact. Of course, it was allied to the PCF's nationalism by 1942.

The Trotskyists' work in the German army

Trotskyist propaganda had a totally different character. It aimed at helping the German proletariat overcome its 1933 defeat, give fresh confidence to revolutionaries in the Wehrmacht, and help them organise revolutionary propaganda in the army and in their country. For this reason they had to stress, over and above the national divisions cultivated by the imperialists, the solidarity of the oppressed peoples with the German people against Nazism.

That was why in January 1942 *La Vérité* commented, with some optimism, under the title 'No to chauvinism in the working class':

All the information reaching us from Germany attests to a significant collapse in morale already being felt there. It is certain that the defeats suffered on the Eastern Front, the mounting number of dead and wounded [...] and the starving of the living are now weighing on the German people's state of mind.

The grievances German soldiers are voicing against Hitler's régime have been reported to us by freed prisoners. French workers and prisoners, upon returning from Germany, have confirmed to us that disturbances (particularly housewives' demonstrations) have take place in Nuremburg and in Berlin in particular. The February 1941 decree banning the German people from communicating with French prisoners has not stopped their sympathy for these prisoners, and they often fraternise with them.

So at a time when the German masses are aroused by a spirit of rebellion (some German regiments have refused to march to the Eastern Front); at a time when Hitler's régime is in trouble; when it is time to propagate across Europe the slogans of fraternisation between workers and the socialist liberation of Europe and the world: the Parti communiste has chosen to raise the stupid, ignoble slogan: 'All united against the Boches'.

Thus renouncing the very principles of proletarian internationalism, renouncing Lenin's theses on the imperialist character of the world war (the war is not the work of 'the Boches' but the result of the antagonisms between rival imperialisms) the Parti communiste has once again betrayed the interests of the international working class – to unite and organise all workers, without exceptions. French workers will fight for their liberation. They will unite against Hitlerite despotism and Vichyist reaction. They know that their struggle is a just one, but not that of Churchill and Roosevelt.

They will rise up with force against chauvinism, which leads to impasse and defeat.

Just like the population of Palinges (Sâone et Loire) who fraternised with soldiers who had been jailed for rebellion and indiscipline, they will unite their struggle with that of their German brothers in uniform.

The Nazi régime must be overthrown by socialist revolution. All together, Germans and French, against the Nazi régime! All together against the chauvinists of all stripes, the worst enemies of the working class.

Swann, the author of this article, recounts a significant incident which he witnessed in early January 1942:

We were returning from Belgium in a train packed with Germans, both soldiers and workers. In the corridor there was a young Jewish girl and her little brother. At the border there was a Gestapo checkpoint. The Jewish kids hid in the compartment, and a German woman who took them under her wing pretended that they were her children. None of the Germans present betrayed them, even though [Swann adds] all of them exposed themselves to considerable risk.[222]

La Vérité published all the stories that hinted at the first signs of an awakening among the German workers and soldiers, without always checking them. For example, it published this report from some comrades in Brest:

On 3 December 1941 a large German submarine with two torpedo-tubes headed from a base at Brest out into the ocean. Soon afterwards, workers in Brest saw the submarine returning to the base. The dynamos had blown. The workers learned that there had been a mutiny on board the submarine and the crew had sabotaged the machinery. But we are yet to hear any more news on the mutineer crew. A fairly large number of workers in Brest saw this, and it made a deep impression on them. It showed them that even within the German army, among so-called élite troops, there are a large number of allies they can count on.

After seeing riots in Milan, Turin and Palermo, the 20 May 1942 editorial commented on these signs of insubordination among the German troops:

> The French proletariat knows that during the Amsterdam general strike, German troops refused to shoot at the crowds and they had to call in the SS to crush the movement. It knows that thanks to Hitler's talk, disobedience and 'nervous collapses' have taken place on the Eastern Front. It knows that the mutinies in Moulins, Palinges, Poitiers, Lille and Brest herald the lightning-bolt reawakening of the revolutionary movement across the Rhine.

An optimist take on things, for sure. But the proliferation of such evidence could indeed be seen as a warning-signal.

In France and Belgium Trotskyists had already distributed German-language leaflets to soldiers during the attack on the USSR, at a point when the German army was not susceptible to revolutionary agitation. They believed that the situation had ripened and agitation within the Wehrmacht was indispensible.

In June 1941 a 28-year-old German activist, Widelin, was elected to the Central Committee of the Belgian section. The European conference, at the end of the year, decided to install him in Paris with the task of re-organising German activists as to engage in systematic agitation in the Wehrmacht.

Under the pseudonym 'Victor' he set himself up in the house of a Swiss comrade (Laroche[223]) who did not belong to the Fourth International and who had organised a group opposed to the defence of the USSR. He established a working relationship with this group, which had a large number of *émigrés*, in particular Germans. At first it was in this house that they copied the newspaper used for army work, *Arbeiter und Soldat*,[224] a dozen issues of which were produced.

'It was at my house', says Laroche, 'that *Arbeiter und Soldat* and many German-language leaflets were produced. Widelin often received letters from soldiers, particularly from Brittany, and the comrades published these. Our collaboration lasted for more than a year.'[225]

Even before *Arbeiter und Soldat* – and then parallel to it – German soldiers in Brittany produced their own organ, *Der Arbeiter*.[226] [227] Later on, *Unser Wort*,[228] the newspaper of the German Trotskyists, resurfaced.

From 1942 German army work was carried out under the leadership of Widelin, Abosch (alias Béno), two German soldiers (Hans and Willie) and a cell of three French comrades.

The electrician Roland Filiâtre was one of those responsible for this work, working under the pseudonym Dupont. He recalls:

> The French comrades initiated discussions with German soldiers and got them talking and giving hints of their past politics. Once they had shown themselves trustworthy, after screening they were put in touch with the German soldiers who produced *Der Arbeiter* and then taken care of by their organisation. The Paris region was organised as two branches. But the heart of the organisation was in Brittany, both around Nantes and in particular around Brest where the soldiers provided the party with *Ausweis* [identity cards] and weapons. In Brest the organisation had about fifty soldiers on average despite some people being posted elsewhere. Contacts were established in Toulon, Valence, La Rochelle and at Conches aerodrome. There was also an organisation in Belgium. Links were established with the German Trotskyist organisation, most importantly in the port of Hamburg, in Lübeck and in Rostock. Victor was responsible for these contacts. *Arbeiter und Soldat* was also distributed in garrisons in Italy.[229]

Repatriated to France on account of his serious illness, Filiâtre spent most of the time at Val-de-Grâce, where he had set up his headquarters:

> They had given me a room in the appartment of Colonel Benoît, a doctor. Mrs de Lichtenberg (who was part of a Resistance network, and who was later arrested and shot) helped make contacts and introduced German soldiers to me. I also received reports from organisers and organised actions. Widelin was informed of the significant contacts made. Later Pradalès became responsible for our materials, and Yvonne Filiâtre for transportation.

Based on three-person cells, for a long time the organisation appeared to be sheltered from the Gestapo.

Working-class struggles

Every issue of *La Vérité* – or almost all of them – spread news about working-class struggles. By 1942 they had started to become widespread.

Montceau-les-Mines, the miners in Gard and Saint-Etienne, the engineering workers of Fives-Lille, Kuhlmann, Heinkel in Nantes, Deveaux in La Chapelle-sur-Erdre, etc.

Large demonstrations marked 1st May in the free zone: in Lyon, Nice, Toulouse, Saint-Etienne, Sète, Clermont-Ferrand, Chambéry and in particular in Marseille, where there were 100,000 demonstrators. The initiative for this came from the Mouvement ouvrier français, a group of pro-Resistance trade unionists. The MOF declared:

> The Mouvement ouvrier français, which took the initiative for the trade union and democratic demonstration of 1 May, joyfully welcomes the complete success of its efforts: everywhere, particularly in the major population centres, the working class, faithful to its traditions of freedom, has proven with its disciplined mass marches its desire to win back trade union independence and democratic freedoms, and to carry out the liberation of the country.

But the MOF had definitively renounced its independence. Enthused by the reporting of its slogans on the BBC, it continued,

> We thank General de Gaulle, today the incarnation of Free France, for having thrown his weight behind the trade union movement's call in his radio message, and for having sincerely declared that the workers, today the main weapon of France's liberation, will tomorrow have their place, respecting working-class tradition, in the building of a new France ....

Having been integrated into the movement for the re-establishment of capitalist society – thanks to its ambitions for power – the workers' movement lined up behind the Gaullist banner.

Trotskyist activists tried to preserve the class character of the workers' movement. In some cases they succeeded, despite all the dangers faced. See, for example, the report of a Trotskyist worker who played an essential role in the Chenard et Walcker (Chausson trust) strike at Gennevilliers. Here we can see the mood of working-class struggles in 1942:

> The third winter of the Nazi occupation was coming. The workers were almost on starvation wages; they worked eleven or twelve hours a day,

six days a week. The lack of goods (food, clothes, coal) as well as the development of a black market, made their lives more and more difficult. It was faced with these circumstances that in early November 1942 a significant strike broke out at Chenard et Walcker.

For several months the staff had been getting a bonus of 400 francs (26 to 32 hours' work) on top of their monthly salary, which was enough to buy a sack of coal, ten kilos of bread or a kilo of butter on the black market. Suddenly management announced, without any explanation, that they were to stop paying this bonus.

Fury exploded. Spontaneously the men walked off the job. The gearwheel workshop and heat treatment were completely at a halt. The foremen, shocked, tried to get work going again. One comrade suggested a meeting with management. A few minutes later the director arrived at a foreman's office and received a delegation of twelve representatives of the workers.

Three workers expressed the workers' discontent: they would not accept this pay cut. The director: 'First of all, let me say that I am happy we have this sort of relationship. It is healthy to discuss our problems and common difficulties together. We are all living in difficult conditions. We are suffering privations. I have been wearing this self-same suit since the evacuations happened. We are all suffering the effects of the war. That is why I understand where you're coming from. But we are not the only people making the decisions. We are tributaries of our clients (the Nazis) and they, inspecting our accounts, have decided that you are over-paid. We will discuss this with them and we hope to re-establish the bonus. But for the moment, it is not possible. I advise you to return to work and place your trust in us'.

Having said this, the director discussed with everyone then set about returning to his work.

Most of the workers' representatives were inexperienced. The old employee reps, members and sympathisers of the PCF, did not want to take part in the delegation, for fear – and with some justification – that they would be found out. But the delegation included a POI activist and a former member of the left wing of the Jeunesses socialistes. They saw that there was the risk of a return to work before the workers' demands were satisfied. They posed the question on a class footing:

'You have spoken with us in a friendly manner. But you have not resolved any of our problems. You have told us about our common troubles. Let us tell you that ours are not of the same character. For us it's not just about having to replace an old suit, but a question of survival.

We cannot accept the pay cut you want to force on us. We will inform our comrades of your rebuttal'.

The whole delegation approved this.

The director: 'We are living under a military occupation régime. By not advising a return to work, you are taking on a heavy responsibility. This affair could end very badly'.

A worker: 'The managers of the factory will hold the responsiblity for the consequences'.

The director declared that he could not continue negotiating under these conditions and left.

The reps went back to the workshops. They had not had time to finish speaking when shouts went up on all sides: 'Continue! They must give in!'.

The gear-wheel and heat-treatment workers spread out across the factory.

Everywhere workers stopped working, staying at their machines.

On the second day, management left the movement to rot away.

On the third day, the Nazi army inspectors realised that the workers were not working, and that everywhere groups of workers were discussing. They made this known to management. The foremen implored the workers to go back to work. The management and foremen were more frightened than the workers.

On the fourth day, under their pressure, there was the onset of a return to work. But striking workers were still very much in the majority. The director went back to the workshops to negotiate, to no avail. In late afternoon the reps were summoned to the owner, who repeated the director's arguments. But no-one was about to give in. Suddenly the telephone rang. The owner picked up the receiver – 'Yes, I'm with them right now. I'll pass you over'.

'Hello, this is General von Stüpnagel, commandant of Greater Paris. I have heard that you have stopped work. I warn you that if you do not go back tomorrow morning, my soldiers will intervene and force you back'.

This phone call – authentic or not – sent a chill through the room. But the reps said that a number of workers would not go back to work, and that management would be responsible for the violence.

On the fifth day, returning to the factory, the workers found a poster on the noticeboard: the bonus would be paid the next day. They would be paid for the strike days.[230]

The struggle against deportations

In the second half of 1942 the working class was confronted with fresh problems.

Given the increasing demands of war mobilisation, Hitler needed to replace German workers with foreign workers. Obeying the orders of the Gauleiter Sauckel, the Laval government committed to supplying 350,000 workers in one year. At first there was talk of 'volunteers'.

Soon enough, realising that he would not be able to meet this target, Laval decided to 'supply' 150,000 North African workers as part of this number. The press had to keep quiet about the columns of Algerian workers forced to head for Germany. On 3 September 1942 Laval abandoned the myth of volunteering and instituted 'obligatory national labour service', the same measure as had been taken in Belgium.

La Vérité had already warned of the imminent implementation of such measures in its 15 March 1942 editorial, titled '*Razzia*[231] of slaves in occupied Europe'. After analysing the re-organisation and the intensification of German war production, Marcel Hic explained:

> This new push by German imperialism has from the start come up against one of the most serious of obstacles: the growing lack of manpower in Germany … In this situation, there is only one solution left to the German magnates: ramp up the recruitment of foreign workers. Occupied Europe is being subjected to a terrible blackmail. They give no – or hardly any – raw materials to the factories; salary rises have been banned and sometimes wages have even been cut. The worker, haunted by the spectre of poverty and unemployment, thus hands himself over to German capitalism, setting off to forge his own chains.
>
> The German press and its French representatives Déat and Luchaire have informed us of even more severe measures to come if 'voluntary' recruitment does not totally satisfy our 'new masters'.

Quoting the *Kölnische Zeitung*, Marcel Hic wrote:

> It would be nothing other than the military requisition of workers and supervisory staff, in France and Belgium particularly, and sending them across the Rhine, where they would be employed in work 'more useful' for the new Europe.
>
> We are informed, indeed, of some limited number of requisitions that have already taken place. Now this is practice is to be stepped up and to become commonplace.

It is 'new' indeed, this Nazified Europe. Well, yes, the 'new masters' want to abolish wage-labour. But only in order to replace it with *slavery and arbitrary rule!* The worker will be chained to the factory, at the whim of our 'socialist' masters from the Third Reich. We already knew that much of this was the case for the German worker. We already knew such monstrosities during the war in 1939-40. But, this time, it is about taking the worker away from his loved ones, seizing him from what gives him joy and is his reason for living. It means strictly regimenting him in the war against his Soviet brothers.

But this *razzia* of slaves in occupied Europe will be costly for the Nazis and their masters, the German financial and industrial magnates. The most formidable breeding ground for revolution will be created within Germany itself.

French workers heading for the German factories, never forget that your interests are the same as those of your Belgian, Dutch, Polish, Russian, Yugoslav, Spanish and Italian brothers.

French workers, you will be in contact with German workers. Open their eyes to the fine vistas of the Nazi occupation of Europe. Show them that when they fight against their exploiters, they will not be alone, and that when they ask for it they will have the support of the whole European proletariat.

French workers who are going to work making weapons for Nazism to use against the Soviet Union, do what you can so that they are useless and as few as possible reach the enemies of the workers' state.

No, not one worker will accept slavery with joy in his heart. All must unite in Germany itself. All must unite to strike a wholehearted fatal blow against German imperialism.

On 15 September, under the title 'French workers will not be the slaves of fascism', *La Vérité* called on workers to organise resistance to *razzias* of slaves. Here, Henri Souzin took up the above themes, displaying the aggravation of workers' situation (for example the 54-hour week). But he called for the organisation of working-class resistance:

In the immediate, the occupiers should be met with a generalised resistance to the execution of their project. The police deployment they would then be forced to make would make such measures worthwhile.

In October *La Vérité* distributed two special issues opposing the deportations, the main slogan being 'Refuse to sign! Resistance!' It reported on walk-outs at the majority of the major factories in the Paris region in the first days of the month. It related what was happening outside the capital too, like in Nantes where workers struck for up to twenty-four hours, and when forced by the police to leave, departed from the station to chants of the *Internationale*, stopping the trains every three hundred metres by pulling the alarm cord.[232]

In its first issue on 15 October 1941, *Lutte de classe* gave the same analysis and elaborated the same politics. Its slogans, however, were less brash (it limited itself to calling for a refusal to sign) and it refused to accept what was left of the unions as a substitute for struggles.[233]

The action proposed by the Trotskyists was two-fold: refusing to leave and sabotaging the draft; but also making use of the revolutionary potential existing in Germany itself, as represented by workers arriving there from across Europe.[234]

On the first point, they were of course in agreement with the whole 'Resistance'. On 2 October the organisations linked to the Parti communiste launched a manifesto 'Not one man for Germany!' On 10 October, with the participation of the PCF, they called for nationwide strikes against deportations.

But, as we have seen, this activity remained on the terrain of nationalism. It did not seek to develop class solidarity among workers, still less international solidarity. There was no question of organising a struggle in Germany. He who deserted the soil of the homeland, even if forced to do so, was a traitor[235]. Except in concentration camps, activism stopped at the border.

It is true that the Trotskyists had a tendency to over-estimate the re-awakening of the German proletariat at a time when the Nazis sent to the front all those who they suspected of being able to resist them. However, *La Vérité*, from 1943, reported on a certain number of examples of such resistance. The major workers' parties did nothing to escalate or organise it.

Repression against the Trotskyists

In 1941-42 the Trotskyists did not suffer as badly from repression as PCF activists. Not only because they were only a few hundred in number, but also because they were not engaged in any type of military action and, above all, because they were politically experienced and knew never to let on anyone's name. With the exception of a raid in Marseille, there were few arrests.

However, they also paid a heavy price for engaging in armed struggle. One of the most long-standing activists in the movement, Jean Meichler, was shot on 10 September 1941, one of the Gestapo's first three hostages.[236]

La Vérité commented:

On 10 September the first three hostages were shot in Paris. Among them was our comrade Jean Meichler (Meiche), a former member of the Central Committee of the Ligue communiste, then on many subsequent occasions, the leading bodies of our organisations. Meiche was well known for his dedication, principally in the thirteenth *arrondissement* where he was active (he was the secretary of Red Aid in the thirteenth *arrondissement*). He was in charge of *Unser Wort*, newspaper of the German Trotskyist *émigrés*.

In late October news broke of the Châteaubriant massacre. Following the murder of a German lieutenant-colonel in a Nantes street on 20 October, Stüpnagel responded with the execution of forty-eight hostages from the Châteaubriant camp. The ignoble trading of a list of names had taken place between the Nazis and the Vichy Interior Minister Pucheu, who himself supplied the list of people to be shot.

The Châteaubriant sub-prefect explained: 'The Interior Minister today made contact with General Stüpnagel to designate the most dangerous among the Communists currently interned at Châteaubriant.'

Pucheu defended himself: 'I could not have, I would not have let forty good Frenchmen be shot'.

There can be no better proof that Vichy's collaboration with Berlin was out of class solidarity.

Not all those shot were from the PCF. Among them were a Socialist, Fourny, as well as the mayor of Nantes and two Trotskyists, Marc Bourhis and Pierre Gueguen.

Marc Bourhis, a teacher at Trégunc (Finistère) had joined the POI in 1936. Secretary of the Trotskyist group in Concarneau, he was arrested by the French police on 2 July 1941. Pierre Gueguen had joined the Parti communiste upon its foundation. Mayor of Concarneau, he had broken with the PCF after the German-Russian pact. He then rallied to the programme of the Fourth International.

Arrested in 1939 and placed under quarantine by the PCF, every night he and Bourhis had to stay awake keeping watch as to evade Stalinist attack. This did not stop the PCF from annexing the pair to their list of martyrs.

La Vérité ran the headline 'The repression is coming together, the fightback must come together': 'Hitler and Stüpnagel, uniting Nazism's enemies in death, have shown what we must build: unity in struggle for the anti-imperialist liberation of Europe'.

In 1941-42 many dozens of activists fell while engaged in day-to-day activity. We shall make note of some of them.

In the Paris region, it was mostly those responsible for liaison work, such as Pauline Kargeman, who died in March 1942: she was twenty years old and died after being deported. In April the regional organiser Braslavsky, a Youth Hostel activist aged 24, also in charge of forged papers; and J. Joffe (Pouly) a 25-year-old student: both died during deportation, as well as the electrician Lebrun (21 years old) and Bella Lempert (23 years old). In August, Pierre Barthelemy, a young engineering worker, responsible for technical equipment, and Simone Ferlinger, a 21 year old typist, were both killed. Letellier was thrown into a concentration camp in France but managed to escape in late 1943. In November Régine Felsenschwalbe, 22, died during deportation. In late 1942, Henri Souzin, former regional treasurer of the Jeunesses communistes, decorating worker and member of the building workers' executive commission. Souzin was a member of the political bureau and was organiser of the trade union commission: he did not come back from the camps.

In Brittany, the regional organiser, the artisan Alain Le Dem, was arrested in September 1942: he managed to escape from Chartres prison in 1943. In Lyon, the repression struck against two regional organisers, Robert Colliard, who was linked to the 'Libération' network and died in a concentration camp, the young grocer Sadek, imprisoned in late 1942, as well as a young activist, Gerard, sentenced to 20 years' forced labour. G. Bloch, from Clermont-Ferrand, was arrested and deported.[237]

But it was in Marseille that the organisation suffered the heaviest blow. In 1941 it consisted of four branches, with somewhat serious roots despite the political crisis caused by two of its organisers' departure for the nationalist Resistance. The regional organiser was Albert Demazière, member of the Southern Zone committee. It was Marseille that organised, together with sailors who were members of the American Socialist Workers' Party, communications with the Fourth International executive committee in New York. In April, one of their letters, concealed in several small bars of soap, was intercepted by the police. The ensuing police operation led to the arrests of A. Demazière, the sugar refinery worker Reboul, who organised one of the group's cells, the teacher Marguerite Usclat, Pierre Delmotte and Pietro Tresso (alias Blasco), a former Red Trade Union International representative, former deputy secretary of the Communist Party of Italy and a long-time leader of French Trotskyist organisations, responsible for international contacts.

The 'American Aid Centre' run by Daniel Benedite (himself also affected) helped people suspected by the authorities, particularly Jews, to reach America. The police pretended to have uncovered a plan for armed insurrection in the non-occupied zone, a plan which had in fact been placed there by an *agent provocateur*. Bravely and unselfishly, young lawyers (Deferre, a future minister and mayor of Marseille, Gaston Monnerville, a future president of the Senate, and Mrs Poinso-Chapuis, an MRP[238] parliamentarian after the Liberation) agreed to defend them before the special courts of the 15th Military Region, which accused them of propaganda 'directly or indirectly taking up the slogans of the Third International'.

All of them received harsh sentences: lifetime forced labour for Demazière, ten years for Tresso and five years imprisonment for M. Usclat etc.

Most of them were imprisoned, after Marseille, in Lodève, Mozec, then in Puy prison, where they met Pierre Salini (alias Ségal), a CCI activist who had already been arrested and sentenced.[239]

International relations

Until Blasco's arrest, the executive committee of the Fourth International (now seated in New York) maintained links with the French and European sections. We have seen how, under its control, the French exile group in the USA published *La Vérité* from April 1941 onwards. The paper was written in order to be read in France and Europe, so had to cross borders, reaching the two zones of France, Switzerland, Belgium and the colonies.

The first issue included a manifesto by the executive committee ('France under Hitler and Pétain'); the second, a text by Marc Lorris (Van Heijenoort) which the Paris *La Vérité* printed ('European perspectives') and Nathalia Trotsky's commentary on the assassination of the Fourth International's leader. The third issue, in September 1941, made public the Fourth International manifesto 'For the defence of the USSR' (this appears not to have reached France, since it received no mention there) and an article by Trotsky ('The class, the party and leadership') where he polemicised against the POUM. In October, the New York *La Vérité* polemicised with those who sided with Britain and with the 'centrists'. In December, it was entirely devoted to a vehement denunciation of the Nazis' so-called 'socialism'.

It stopped appearing in 1942, both because it barely fulfilled its objective (only weak numbers reached Europe) and because the French and Belgians now had sufficient means for producing propaganda.

Moreover, the International's executive committee's discussions on strategy for the occupied countries were lively. In October 1941 the (émigré) leaders of the German section – the IKD – Johre and Ludwig, explained their position in 'Three theses', provoking a stormy debate.

Having reported on the disappearance of any organised working-class force in Germany (and even any bourgeois opposition), the IKD argued:

There is no more pressing question in Europe than the national liberation of the countries enslaved by Germany: and its resolution, with the help of and in the name of international socialism, is important and indispensible for two reasons. Firstly, it is one of the democratic demands which must be fought for always and everywhere, without which socialism cannot triumph. Second, socialism cannot find the necessary allies in the towns and countryside to carry out the revolution, it cannot mobilise the masses for the final struggle and it cannot win their sympathies if it does not declare itself a determined fighter for their demands over a sufficiently long period of time, and if it has not thus earnt the leadership of their struggles. In the last analysis, only revolutionary socialism is able to carry out the democratic programme and give goals and direction to the movement [...] Transition from fascism to socialism is a utopia unless there is an intermediate stage, basically equivalent to a democratic revolution.

The American Socialist Workers' Party expressed their agreement with these theses on the first point that 'there exists a real national oppression in the occupied countries'. They also agreed 'as to the fact that national oppression now exists in Europe on an unprecedented scale, requiring of us an attentive and sensitive understanding of what is "new" in the European situation as well as what is similar to the First World War':

Our differences center around the relationship between the slogan on national liberation and the slogan of the Socialist United States of Europe. We insist that these slogans must go together, for otherwise the slogan of national liberation degenerates into bourgeois nationalism pure and simple, in the service of one of the imperialist camps.[240]

The Americans criticised the notion of a democratic stage which, in the first instance, sought to re-establish the Third Republic and the Weimar Republic.

What is really new in the occupied countries is that the national sentiment of the workers and peasants is sharpening their class bitterness against the collaborating bourgeoisie. National oppression has given a new edge to the class struggle.[241]

This was exactly the same position as the French and Belgian Trotskyists. But the latter were unaware of this whole debate. Communications with the International were guaranteed thanks to several comrades (Katel, the Czech Karel, Rigal, and a few other French comrades who managed to reach the USA). But hardly any communications went in the opposite direction, except the New York *La Vérité*. From April 1942 onwards, contact became more and more difficult.

Activists in France itself had hardly any contacts except with the Indochinese in the camps. The 20 January 1942 *La Vérité* commented, under the title 'Repatriate the Indochinese victims of French imperialism':

> The public is largely unaware of the unfortunate fate imposed by French imperialism on the 40,000 Indochinese mobilised and 'imported' to France at the beginning of the war. 20,000 of them were sent to the front, where 10,000 were made prisoners and the others killed or disappeared. The remaining 20,000 were employed in gunpowder factories, where there was deplorable hygiene and working conditions, on the unbelievable salary of 4.5 francs a day for the men and 6.5 francs for the interpreters.
>
> Once the armistice was signed, these military workers were put to excavation work (for the same princely salary!), waiting to be sent home 'soon'. They are still now in non-occupied France, mostly homed in stables at barracks, warmed by the air outside, dressed in work overalls, and insufficiently nourished because of thieving by the military intendants who are meant to feed them.
>
> But the Indochinese workers, prisoners of the French military machine, have mounted courageous resistance to their oppressors. Certain units, influenced by Fourth International militants, went on strike despite the officers' threats, and ultimately won double rations ....
>
> All French workers must fight to free the Annamite workers from French imperialism, just as they fight to free imprisoned French workers from Hitlerite imperialism.

The Indochinese similarly found communications with Asia very difficult. This was the reason for the fantasy of news stories published in *La Vérité*, such as the report that Mao had adhered to the Fourth International.

In occupied Europe the Trotskyists sought to establish an international leadership. But the circumstances were hardly ideal. In Germany all the activists of the IKD had either been murdered, been sent to concentration camps, or emigrated to America. There was an active group in Austria, many of whose leaders were sentenced to death by the Nazis, but there was no contact with it. The Polish section had been 'almost totally destroyed'. Contact had also been lost with the Czechs, who 'lost a dozen cadres'[242]; with the small Dutch group – not to mention the decimated RSAP, all of whose leadership had been shot at the same time as Henk Sneevliet; with the Danish 'Class Struggle' group, who worked with the Norwegians but whose existence was otherwise only known to New York; as well as with the Italians. Combative groups were engaged in struggle in Greece, but communication was episodic. As for the Spaniards, ties with the POUM had broken off and only a few émigrés supported the Fourth International. All contact had been lost with the handful of Swiss Trotskyists, who could have been very useful.

The only country with which contact was continuous was Belgium, where there were two Trotskyist groups. Firstly, Vereeken's group, which had broken with the Fourth International: it was opposed to unconditional defence of the USSR ('red imperialism'). His small group 'Contre le courant' was affiliated to the Front ouvrier international. For quite some time it had been tied to the French *La Commune* group (the future CCI). Only in mid-1942 did it produce a duplicated bulletin, *Idées et Documents*. In reality, each of these bulletins (of 24 or 36 pages) consisted of only one article, by Vereeken, devoted in the main to critiquing the positions of the Parti communiste révolutionnaire.

The PCR was the Fourth International's section there. From the start of the occupation it published a printed newspaper, *La Voie de Lénine*, as well as a theoretical journal and some pamphlets. It suffered heavy losses when engaged in action. Several of its leaders were arrested: Lesoil, Nopère and Léon de Lee, who died in a concentration camp; Teunynkx was killed during a mission. The political line of the PCR was close to that of *La Vérité* in 1942.

Relations between the French and Belgians were re-established in late 1940 or early 1941. In January 1942 a first European conference took place at Saint-Hubert in the Ardennes. It brought together fifteen comrades, including Hic, Swann and Craipeau (from France), Widelin (from Germany), Raptis (from Greece), Sem and Léon (from Belgium). The discussion focused on their attitude to national struggles (Léon taking the same positions as Hic), the general orientation of the movement and the creation of a European organisation. A provisional secretariat was elected, with the headquarters based in Paris. It included Raptis, Hic and Widelin. Raptis was responsible for international contacts. The journal *IVe Internationale* would become the organ of this secretariat, and the print-shop where it would be produced was put at its disposal by the French section.

In fact, this initial secretariat hardly had any activity, except in regard to the German army. The first issue of *IVe International*, appearing in June 1942, still carried the sub-title 'Theoretical journal of the Fourth International committees'[243]: Marcel Hic hesitated in giving political responsibility to a still fragile body.

The Union communiste internationaliste

Up until 1942 the *La Vérité* group was the only internationalist group to organise clandestine actions and propaganda, except for a few publications by activists grouped around Barta. By 1942, many other small groups were involved in clandestine activity.

The Union communiste internationaliste[244] united activists considered 'ultra-left' by the Trotskyists and who saw 'Trotskyism' as an appendage of Stalinism. In 1941 French, German émigré, Italian, Hungarian and Spanish activists grouped around Laroche, opposed to the Trotskyist position of defence of the USSR and largely organised in the name of council communism (like the German RKD). For them, the Soviet Union was an imperialist state like any other, and it was a dangerous illusion to entertain any hope that this imperialism might aid the revolution, even involuntarily.

'Politically', wrote Laroche, 'we shared none of the other groups' illusions: the situation was not revolutionary; Stalinism had killed off any internationalist spirit; the Communist movement was totally nationalist; besides, talking about taking power in the presence of imperialist armies was pure folly'.[245]

He added:

> Our group was established in 1942, under the name Union communiste internationaliste, operating in secrecy. We published French and German language leaflets, which we distributed in small groups (unfortunately these leaflets have been lost). Because of this work, Trotskyist comrades who disagreed with the official line got in touch with me. They wanted to know our opinion on the USSR. At this point a real Trotskyist minority was constituted. With them I organised conferences on the workers' movement and the German and Russian revolutions. We often found ourselves in the forests of the Chevreuse valley, at the Villeterte plateau, in youth hostels, etc.

As we have seen, a working relationship was also established between these comrades and the Fourth International for German army work.

Wehrmacht work was under the control of the European provisional executive committee, which had recently been established. The executive committee could not allow Laroche to take part in leading this work until he agreed to recognise the conference resolutions. At a meeting with Hic and Daniel Guérin he refused to do so.

Besides, the French organisation was concerned by the clandestine meetings organised by the Union communiste, less for political reasons (many activists had since 1938 disagreed with the official line on the character of the Soviet state) but rather for reasons of security. Laroche wrote:

> The Fourth International leadership sent two commissars to me, with an ultimatum – very much in the best Bolshevik style – either my conferences would be controlled by them, or they should stop happening. I refused. Our relations with the Fourth International ended there.

It should be made clear that the Trotskyist organisation did not have the power to stop them doing this, but could only demand that its activists either respect group discipline or leave.

In 1943 this minority organised a conference to decide what political line to take. After stormy debates our group's (the Union communiste's) positions were in the majority. The opposition was split: some comrades came over to us, others set up small groups, like Kaspar (Raymond Hirzel) and the Scheuer group.

The 'Lutte de classe' group

The 'Lutte de classe' group was Trotskyist in its outlook. It was little more than a small group of militants around Barta. Later it gave rise to the '*Voie ouvrière* [sic][246]' group, which became *Lutte ouvrière*.

Barta summarises the activities of the group he founded thus:

> After the 1940 collapse and the evacuations, we returned to Paris in September 1940 and published the pamphlet *La Lutte contre la Deuxième Guerre mondiale* in November. Between then and the October 1942 publication of the newspaper *Lutte de classe* we worked building contacts and training the youth, including Mathieu Buchhotz [sic][247], thanks to which our work (by Barta and Louise) could proceed from solid foundations. Our only publication was a leaflet upon the attack on the USSR by Hitler.
>
> Throughout the length of the occupation our activity was therefore

limited to the publication of the newspaper and training up youth cadre on the organisational bases defined in our July 1943 document which, along with the 1940 pamphlet, were the central pillars of our activity under the occupation. Two *Cahiers du militant*, critiquing the attitudes of the Parti ouvrier internationaliste towards the 'national movement' were produced in December 1942 and February 1944.

But although political differences were apparent from the start, it was not on political grounds but rather on organisational grounds that we were fundamentally at odds with the other Trotskyist groups. The real political differences, *in action*, became clear upon Liberation, particularly as regards orienting towards the PCF and CGT.

Under the occupation our activity took place in very difficult conditions and so was very limited. It represented a period of preparation and when the time was right we were effectively ready for it, despite the loss of Mathieu Bucholtz [sic], a leading comrade, murdered by PCF members in September 1944.[248]

The first issue of the newspaper *La Lutte de classe* came out on 1st October 1942. Twenty-two issues copied recto-verso had been published by 31st December 1943.

Contrary to *La Vérité*, which was above all an agitational tool, *La Lutte de classe* was conceived of as a means of political education. Each issue consisted of just one article:

> 'Defeat the imperialist draft' (13 October 1942); 'The illusion of the Second Front' (22 October); 'Commemoration of October 1917' (7 November); 'Occupation of North Africa by the USA' (15 November); 'From the "democratic" war to the war for the liberation of peoples' (30 November); 'Permanent revolution, not permanent war' (12 December).

This point is largely attributable to a difference in outlook. All Trotskyist activists had from the start of the war warned that it would be long. In 1940 they repeated this, as against those who thought Hitler's Germany had practically won the war and that a long period of totalitarian power was beginning. They said it again in 1942 after the Allied landings in North Africa, as against those who thought that the Anglo-Americans would bring the war to a close within a few months.

But so far as *La Vérité* was concerned there were only a few years which had to be made use of to launch an insurrection: action was the test-bed for revolutionaries. This was not the perspective of the *Lutte de classe* group.

'At the beginning', Barta wrote, 'our understanding was that there was a 'permanent war', until we saw the events in Italy'.

The 12 December 1942 *Lutte de classe* commented:

> The belief that only a second Allied front can bring an end to the nightmare of war, giving Hitler a fatal blow, proves to be a glaring illusion loudly promoted by the capitalist Allies (the United States and Britain) in order to hold the masses – exploited and oppressed by Hitler – in tow to their military operations, and to use them, passive and unawares, for their war policy ....
>
> The strategic position of Germany in the Second World War is incomparably stronger than in the First. All of Europe is under its control and Japan and Italy are on its side.
>
> But even in the event of the collapse of all the Axis powers, the war will not be over for the Allied camp: the USSR and China, militarily indispensable in the current war, will imminently be the source of military conflicts, and these conflicts may well not only break out *after* the collapse of the Axis – we only have to think of the central antagonisms which make peace an impossibility in an era of imperialist capitalism, the first workers' state and wars of national liberation in India, China etc. In reality, the imperialist fear of a new 1918 means the prolongation of this war and the collapse of civilisation [...] There is only one perspective we can counterpose to permanent war, that of permanent revolution.

Therefore it would be necessary to wait through an indeterminate and very long period of fascism and war which could only be ended by proletarian revolution. The task was to patiently train up cadres for this objective.

This slow and systematic work was also the only way of training working-class militants and breaking with the petty-bourgeois amateurism from which the Trotskyist organisation suffered before the war. We will see this more clearly in the organisational report drawn up by this group in July 1945.

La Seule Voie

Until 1942 members of the old *La Commune* group were content with maintaining contacts with one another. The only allusion made to links with the Comités pour la IVe came in a note in *La Vérité* on 15 December 1940:

We have been sent this communication:

> Please note that the clandestine newspaper *La Vérité* has nothing to do with the journal *La Vérité* published by the Parti communiste internationaliste before the war. Duly noted.

The first public activity of this group came in March 1942 with the publication of a copied bulletin, *La Seule Voie*.

The bulletin came with the sub-heading 'Bolshevik-Leninists for the reconstruction of the Fourth International'. It appeared in March, June, July and November 1942. Four issues were published in 1943.

In reality it only had a semi-public distribution. Each copy was numbered. The first page made clear: '*La Seule Voie* must not be distributed except to steadfast comrades. Each activist must be responsible for the comrade he gives it to and must refer him to his organisation'.

The header of *La Seule Voie* carried the words 'The crisis of humanity is the crisis of revolutionary leadership'. For them, building this revolutionary leadership would not be achieved – as the *La Vérité* group had it – by trying to prove themselves in the masses' struggle, but rather by meticulous theoretical education of cadres, which took place in an atmosphere of repression.

> The Bolshevik-Leninists cannot currently reach a juncture with the masses and so must prepare the way for their high-minded goal by training cadres for the party ....
>
> The Bolshevik-Leninists know that Stalin's war cannot end in victory. Their task is not to align themselves with temporary shifts determined by the unfolding of the war, but to explain to those who they can reach that the USSR's defeat is inevitable under the joint blows of Hitler, Roosevelt and Churchill and under Stalin's leadership, unless the international revolution intervenes in time.[249]

The analysis in the issue devoted to the question of the USSR reached this conclusion not because it was probable, but rather through an absolute 'given' theory, capable even of resisting reality: 'We have nothing in common with those opportunists who, enslaved by events, cannot abstract from them'.

Polemicising against the Comités de la IVe Internationale's pamphlet *Pour sauver l'URSS, il est encore temps*,[250] *La Seule Voie* was scandalised by this statement:

In the countries crushed under the fascist jackboot the struggle must begin with the most pressing national, economic and political demands of the masses oppressed by fascism. All actions by the masses capable of being turned against the system must be encouraged.

La Seule Voie replied:

The last sentence is a monument to their ignorance of the experience of the Bolshevik seizure of power. No: even in revolutionary conditions, when the masses were armed, where the bourgeoisie's power was contested in the streets and the power of the working class was growing, that is to say in a period of dual power in July, the Bolsheviks led by Lenin and Trotsky, far from encouraging the masses' actions, held them back and discouraged it.

Critiquing the 1940 positions of *La Vérité*, *La Seule Voie* argued:

Taking action today amid political confusion and denouncing 'little groups who sneer from the sidelines as they wait-and-see' is not building the Fourth International, but rather means preparing defeat amid the quagmire of national unity.

The task of the period was to theoretically train the brains-trust of a future revolutionary party with which the working class, when the time was right, would find its political lead.

It is not the revolutionary organisation which will create a revolutionary situation: this will inevitably arise from the belligerents' inability to bring an end to the war. This war will not end with a military settlement; Stalin cannot triumph; but ultimately neither can Hitler, nor the Anglo-Americans. Marxist analysis allows us to affirm that only revolution can end the war, and it will begin in Germany, with the United States becoming the last bastion of counter-revolution.

Therefore it was sufficient to wait for revolutionary events, which they knew would lead to a revolution analogous to that of Russia after February 1917. It would be in such a situation of dual power that the theoretically trained cadres would intervene. While making clear that 'historical determinism has nothing to do with abstract schemas', *La Seule Voie* could use it to predict how events would unfold.

Only the Bolshevik-Leninists can, and must – through diligent effort – provide any leadership to the class and, with it, substantially build the party during a situation of dual power. The masses, spontaneously resisting the current order and those who defend it, will instinctively build its organisation, which will be soviets. The Bolshevik-Leninists, few in number, must be among the masses calling on them to build the organs they are starting to create. [...]

It would be mistaken to think that as soon as the party is created, power will immediately fall into the hands of the workers. For October to happen, it was necessary that the masses, all the masses, recognised the leadership of the Bolshevik Party, and that does not just take one week, but rather, several months. The traditional parties will revive and, in the euphoria of victory, the war over, they will again set to their no-less-traditional task of transforming dual power into the power of the bourgeoisie. Here, the task of the Bolshevik-Leninist party will be to win over the majority of the exploited, for the full transfer of power to the 'Committees'.

La Seule Voie added, oh-so modestly: 'Theoretical analysis can go no further: the relations of concrete forces during this period of dual power will determine the tasks of the revolutionary leadership.'[251]

In October 1942, the Revolutionärer Kommunisten Deutschlands proposed to *La Seule Voie* an initiative to build a genuinely communist international, now that repression had wiped out the Comités de la IVe Internationale:

The Fourth International is dead as an organisation, and never existed as an international. One more obstacle to the building of the true Fourth Communist International has been swept aside. Forward, to the building of the proletarian party....[252]

La Seule Voie replied: 'There must be some mistake: you have got the wrong address, comrades'.

Having explained that the group had nothing of the ultra-leftism decried by Lenin, the reply was indignant about the attitude of the RKD:

We are tempted, reading this, to add: 'Long live the police who have taken this obstacle out of our way, thanks to Pétain and Hitler for having created such great police'. It seems you believe the police have fulfilled an 'objectively' progressive role in arresting the Bolshevik-Leninists, or those who call themselves such. Without doubt we are exaggerating, or being sensitive. But what is at issue is more than that. We are not getting worked up about bad phrasing. It is not at all about an accidental misjudgement, as if by chance. We do not know what you think of the repression which has so heavily struck the Stalinist party. We do not want to make out that you are saying you are pleased by it: but without doubt, there too an obstacle to building the Fourth International is removed. So too, the war Hitler is waging against the USSR. Indeed you say, to underline your position, that Hitler's victory would open the way to socialism. That is the same way of looking at things, whether in terms of the police repression against the revolutionary vanguard in France or as regards the war against the USSR.[253]

Nos Combats and Libertés

Entirely different was the orientation of the *Notre Révolution* group. After Meichler's arrest in late 1941[254] the newspaper's name was changed to *Nos Combats* from January 1942: albeit a modest precaution given that the typography remained the same and the new newspaper started with issue 13, following the former newspaper's numbering.

It is impossible to know how *Notre Révolution*, which made no allusion to the USSR in its statement of principle, reacted to the attack against the Soviet Union. But *Nos Combats* was critical of the chauvinist hysteria whipped up by the Anglo-Americans and Moscow. Its first issue was devoted entirely to an explanation that the responsibility for the war 'was not that of one man nor one more or less bellicose people, bur the capitalist system'.

> Anglo-American propaganda, supported by that produced in Moscow, presents Hitler as the cause of the current conflict, while Dr Goebbels' propaganda blames it on the City of London, Wall Street and international Jewry.
>
> The greatest error socialists could make would be to let this idea influence them, letting themselves believe that the war is due to this or that government, dictator or people. War is a social phenomenon, a social crisis whose causes are independent of any human will. The causes of the conflict are inherent to the current system of production.
>
> [...] We can easily understand the basic difference between the socialist point of view and the bourgeois point of view. The goal of the bourgeoisie is to preserve its privileges. To this end it will sacrifice this or that government, or event a country, as long as it can continue to appropriate surplus-value. The goal of socialism, on the contrary, is not

vengeance against this or that man, or this or that people: but rather to abolish the causes of war: which means, the capitalist system.[255]

The article continues with an explanation of the themes of the statement of principle which appeared in the first issue of *Notre Révolution*:

In that the current war plays a revolutionary role, insofar as it disorganises and dissolves the capitalist system, socialists must intervene in the conflict with their programme in order to bring out the full revolutionary meaning of the war… It is precisely to the extent that it actively intervenes in this war, to the extent that it takes the leadership of the fight against fascism into its own hands, that the working class can disrupt the bourgeoisie's calculations and make this war the last humanity shall ever know.

But in March, *Nos Combats* explained with a concrete example how the working class could take the leadership of the war into its own hands. Analysing developments in Britain, the newspaper reported on Churchill's Cabinet reshuffle:

giving an important role to Sir Stafford Crips[256] [sic], a very advanced left-winger, and Major Atlee[257] [sic], also playing a more important role in the British government than ever before.

It concluded:

The British working class now has every opportunity to take the leadership of the war into its own hands. It must kick certain reactionary elements out of the army, industry and finance, and must group around itself all the working classes of the world fighting for their independence. Only after eliminating these elements, particularly in the army, can it realise its desire to take a more active role in the war, creating the second front demanded by the greater part of the public opinion which brought Sir Stafford Crips [sic] to power.[258]

Thus the working-class taking power would be realised by a greater degree of Labour Party participation in the national unity government: as if this would change the class character of that government.

The February issue, entirely devoted to the Montoire accords, was no different from any of the Gaullist newspapers. It included the following leaflet, with the usual nationalist themes:

My lords of Vichy ...
Do not come and pray at our graves
You supplied our chains
You handed over our goods
You handed over our forces
You handed over our lives

> We reject your national day of mourning. France was bereaved on the day of your treason. Your 'collaboration', worse than an alliance, has left our country open to attacks from its former allies.

You did not want the French to die in the fight.
But today, they are falling victim, because of you.

> Marshal Pétain, Admiral Darlan, Mr Pucheu, you are responsible for the blood spilt. The blood of the hostages, the blood of our dead in Le Havre, Brest and Paris, will rain down on you.

Do not come to pray at our graves.[259]

The May 1942 issue appeared under the title *Libertés*, which it would keep until the end of the war. It devoted three pages to 'the situation in May 1942'. It made no allusion to the working-class struggles of France or Europe, nor even the Partisan actions which were starting to take place in the Balkans. The analysis only addresses the relative strengths of the great powers on the military terrain. 'The independent role of the proletariat', on which the first issue of *Notre Révolution* was based, was entirely forgotten. 'The objective: win the war and liberate France'.[260]

The newspaper declared that it 'found widespread sympathy among all sorts of people' and defined the possibilities for action thus:

> Now, each comrade must rally round five other comrades, who have known each other well since before the war; having something in common whether that be through their workplace, place of residence or long-standing friendship; they can meet up easily at any moment; and one of them responsible for the others...
>
> They will meet together, discuss, distribute the newspaper, at the same time as keeping informed about what is going on around them. They will be carefully on the look-out for collaborators and Hitlerites. In each area they will address those around them, and, when conditions are more favourable, nothing will be easier than to provide the necessary cadres and directives, and this even at short notice.[261]

As we see, this was not about organising working-class action. The article does indeed conclude: 'If we know how to rely on ourselves, victory will not be the victory of one imperialism over another. Our struggle is a proletarian struggle, for socialism'.

But that was not the struggle it proposed organising for (being extremely vague on this matter). It was about assisting the Anglo-American victory over the Axis. That is why the newspaper devoted a page to the 'American rearmament effort'.

'L'Insurgé'

In March 1942 another newspaper was launched in Lyon, with a fairly similar orientation: *L'Insurgé*. Behind this was a former PSOP member and long-time socialist activist, Marie-Gabriel Fugère (alias Sauvaget), an electrical fitter.

> The creation of the movement was discussed for a long time, during the last months of 1940 and early months of 1941, in small groups including Fugère, the law student Maurice Zavaro – a former PSOP youth leader – Suzanne Nicolitch, a university lecturer sacked by Vichy and send to Trévoux; the lawyer Pierre Stibbe, who had escaped from a prison camp, and various trade unionists and socialist activists.[262]

Fugère and S. Nicolitch were still in contact with Marceau Pivert, now in Mexico. The *Mémorial de L'Insurgé* recalled Marceau Pivert's letter to De Gaulle, adding 'It is likely that it was Marceau Pivert who first brought the issue and the necessity of decolonisation to General de Gaulle's attention'. It then praises S. Nicolitch's action in handing his 'remarkable' Masonic message to Roosevelt to the US Embassy in February 1941, 'remarkable given the timing, as Stalin still scrupulously adhered to the clauses of the German-Soviet treaty'.[263]

With S. Nicolitch as its leading theorist, the group was from the start even more confused than *Notre Révolution*. However, it was a proletarian group which organised in workplaces and working-class areas:

> A Central Committee was established including two former PSOP activists, Fugère and Poncet, and three former Socialist activists including Barboyon (alias Lacroix). Groups were established in various districts of Lyon (Croix Rousse-Vaise, Lyon-Centre, Left Bank of the Rhône) and in workplaces (the Electro-magnetic Company where Fugère and Foray (alias Duprat) worked; Zénith carburettors; the Rochet-Schneider and Lumière factories; the Grange-Blanche Hospital where Lacroix worked) as well as in the suburbs and in Villefranche-sur-Rhône.

Issue 1 of *L'Insurgé* thus appeared in March 1942, with a thousand two-page copies printed in Villeurbaine. It had two epigraphs, one of which evoked the Great French Revolution 'Liberty, equality, death to tyrants' and the other the revolt of the *canuts* [Lyon silk workers]: 'Live working or die fighting'. It had as a sub-heading 'Organ of working-class and peasant liberation' and explained, a few lines lower down, its desire to create a world 'where happiness would not be a privilege, and poverty would not be a death sentence'.

In this newspaper one could read an unpretentious working-class voice put directly, in a sometimes maladroit but always vigorous language …

L'Insurgé placed itself within the social movement in rejecting any chauvinism: 'We have conceived of the Resistance', Fugère said, 'essentially with the objective of developing the workers' movement and building a socialist Europe'.

The movement then spread further across several parts of the Southern Zone, almost always via former PSOP activists: Trévoux, in Ain, Bourg and Miribel, Montpellier and Languedoc (with Valière), Nîmes, Narbonne, Toulon (with Lucien Vaillant), Sainte-Maxime, then Saint-Etienne, Avignon, Clermont-Ferrand, Grenoble, Annecy, etc.

Politically the movement was eclectic.

The PSOP provided *L'Insurgé* with a number of its former cadre and activists. But from the start they were together with Socialists, libertarians, and even Communists dismayed by their party's attitude to the German-Soviet pact.

All tendencies of the socialist left and French trade unionism were expressed in *L'Insurgé*. Alongside Marxist currents there was a resurgence of the pre-1914 revolutionary syndicalism, strongly imbued with Proudhonist federalism.[264]

This tendency was particularly marked in the Loire, where there were more than a hundred activists involved, most of them revolutionary syndicalists of various tendencies as well as some libertarians.

In issue 7 (September 1942) first appeared the sub-heading 'Socialist organ of proletarian liberation'. Starting with the special issue 9 (October 1942) the Saint-Étienne group introduced the heading 'CGT newspaper for the freedom of France and Europe and the reconstruction of trade unionism worldwide', which in issue 15 (May 1943) became *Le Peuple syndicaliste*, founded by activist members of the CGT.[265]

L'Insurgé proclaimed that it was: 'a proletarian newspaper produced by workers… in service of the great cause of national and social liberation…

one among the handbooks of the revolution.'[266]

Its epigraph quoted Romain Rolland:

It is not a question of fighting nations, but their Duces, their Führers and the like, who blind them, dupe and oppress them. We are companions in the sufferings and the labours of all peoples: we extend them our hand, to constitute a single people of the world to stand up to the New Holy Alliances of reaction. For a worldwide front![267]

It thought it necessary: 'to assert and loudly proclaim the revolutionary positions of the world proletariat, the French people in particular'.[268]

L'Insurgé explained that the war was an imperialist war. But of the two rival imperialist camps, one was tied by tradition to relatively democratic structures; the other albeit 'established thanks to the former camp's indulgence, wherever there was the threat of socialism', was by nature linked to authoritarian power structures. 'Thus it must be understood that fascism is the main enemy of all peoples'.

It added:

Indeed it is the only enemy. The other, liberal capitalism in its decline, is nothing to worry about. Just a push, our desire for it, will be enough to bring it down the day after victory is secured. That is why we revolutionary socialists, disciples of Marx, Lenin, Karl Liebknecht and Rosa Luxemburg, have called the French proletariat to take part in the struggle against fascism as part of the struggle waged by the Allied nations, the USSR in the lead.[269]

L'Insurgé saw sure signs of revolutionary victory in its sister movements around the world, the parties of the Front ouvrier international.

The theory was, clearly, a simplistic one: the 'Allied' imperialisms would take charge of destroying the main enemy, Hitlerism. Following this, 'just a push, our desire for it' would be enough to bring them down, since they represented a moribund system. The immediate task was thus to aid their victory and thus bring about 'the victory', all the while maintaining the proletarian and revolutionary principles which constituted this 'desire'.

L'Insurgé tried to bring about an autonomous working-class force around its newspaper team. The campaign it led against forced labour in Germany, for example, at no time took on a nationalist character. It was similar to that led by *La Vérité*. It popularised news of strikes and tried to organise and generalise them. Indeed these struggles became widespread in the Lyon region. On 14 October 1942 the train drivers at Oullins spontaneously walked out, occupying the depots and, chased by the Garde Mobile, they demonstrated noisily through the streets of the town. The depots and workshops in Vaise, Badan, Saint-Étienne and Valence walked out in turn. On the 15th the strike spread to the main engineering factories (SICMA, SOMUA, Berliet, REP, Maréchal, Brassaira, Câbles de Lyon, etc.). On the 16th the movement ebbed, but other factories went on strike such as Seguin and Lumière. The workers reversed the deportations to Germany.

L'Insurgé thus appealed for 'the creation of factory committees able to coordinate action and even organise violent resistance to the authorities'.[270]

It did not identify its cause with that of the Allies:

The current war has no meaning for the proletariat except to the extent that it is able to achieve social liberation on the back of the fascist defeat. Moreover, a simple military victory followed by a return to the old political establishment will not mark the defeat of fascism. Fascism will never be totally annihilated until the day that the social and economic conditions which favour its emergence are themselves destroyed, meaning, the day when social revolution is achieved

We fight for the establishment of a new republic, which this time must be a social republic, a workers' republic. We have the right to proclaim this because the national interest demands it, because the workers are those who are suffering most in the current situation and they are everywhere on the front line of the struggle against the invader.

'The new French workers' republic will not oppose other peoples, but rather will federate with the other socialist republics being built by workers of other lands. It will be one of the pillars of a true new Europe, a socialist Europe.[271]

But its boundaries with the bourgeois Resistance movements were vague. When the first government of Algiers was established under the leadership of Darlan, *L'Insurgé* attacked the likes of Darlan and Pucheu but then continued:

Furthermore we can only approve of the radio message of the Comité national de la France combattante, refusing any responsibility for the secret negotiations between the Americans and Darlan and committing never to ally with the Vichyists, giving the French people itself centre stage once victory is achieved. We hope that they will stick to this formal commitment ….[272]

Thus *L'Insurgé* appeared to be the left wing of the Resistance. This was apparent in its declarations but all the more clearly in its organisation. For financial reasons the newspaper team was charged with printing and transporting other Resistance newspapers: 'It survived because its initial leader, Fugère, had printed and transported other clandestine newspapers, including *Libération*'.[273]

But this collaboration could not be limited to a mere exchange of services. It had political implications too. The first collaboration with *Combat* led to unity negotiations, which fell apart. But collaboration with *Libération* (Sud), although it did not lead to unification, did lead to a form of osmosis: practically speaking, all the *L'Insurgé* groups participated in distributing *Libération* (and sometimes, *Le Populaire*). Most of the time it led to the integration of their military operations. *L'Insurgé* soon understood (by February 1943) the need for maquis, but in reality it could not constitute its own independent maquis. Its forces were integrated into the mainstream Resistance. Instantly, its proclamations of proletarian class independence became worthless. The *Mémorial de L'Insurgé* is significant in this regard, as in this text the leaders in each region or of each group explain their activity. Very few of them make reference to independent working-class activity or even political positions. Most of them only relate acts of resistance within the framework of the official movement. Even the exceptions (Loire, Clermont-Ferrand) underline their movement's close ties to the official Resistance. M.G. Fugère was himself proud indeed to state that '*L'Insurgé*, copied in London by the Free French, is sent to numerous countries, along with the rest of the French Resistance's press'.[274]

Indeed it was the British Government that facilitated its pact with De Gaulle against Darlan.

Working-class activists organised around *L'Insurgé* sought the road of resistance but were nauseated by the Gaullist press. Jean Duperray, a revolutionary syndicalist from Saint-Étienne, explained this frankly:

> The clandestine newspapers which reached us by various means did not seem very interesting. Most of them were close imitations of the British and Gaullist radio, and, whatever their titles, seemed uniformly based on the most basic patriotism without any of the working-class concerns which we had… We distributed these with no great enthusiasm. All of them seemed to confuse the cause of the most retrograde nationalism with that of freedom, and had no objective other than the extermination of the German people, considered en bloc as the incarnation of fascism; even at the very moment when collaboration by the bourgeoisie and part

of the French population showed how lacking the myth of the 'Boche' was for explaining fascism ....

Even the most left-wing publications disappointed us. They did not demonstrate any social concerns and had no ambition except to organise battalions against the 'Boches' ....

L'Insurgé were quick to praise themselves:

The tone and the concerns of this newspaper appeared to break with the tone and concerns of others. It proclaimed itself not just a socialist organ of liberation, but of proletarian liberation.

Most regions of *L'Insurgé* had relations with *La Vérité* groups. Jean Duperray, for example, was very shaken up by the arrest of 'our comrade Antonia Lafond, Trotskyist activist in the Montbrison region'. Via Cerf and Arnaux, who worked in the Loire, the group was in contact 'with Trotskyist activists distributing *La Vérité*', and Dupperay referred to an activist who regularly carried the paper 'in his Tyrol bag, bulging with vegetables'.[275]

But, he added, 'the doctrinaire complexes of *La Vérité* appeared to us to have little relation with the possibilities of the situation'.

Chapter 5

1943: THE TURNING POINT

The political and military developments of 1943

1943 saw Axis forces retreat on all fronts.

In Africa, the German-Italian troops, fighting in retreat across Tripolitania, withdrew to Tunisia: there they joined with the forces of von Armin, sent to establish a bridgehead. The attack on this bridgehead, which began in March, achieved success by May: 200,000 German and Italian troops were taken prisoner.

In June, the Anglo-Americans occupied the small islands of Pantelleria and Lampedusa. In July they landed in Sicily, which they fully occupied by 16 August, taking another 37,000 German prisoners and 140,000 Italians. In September, they reached continental Italy.

On the Eastern front, the defeats for Hitler were even more devastating. The long battle at Stalingrad ended on 3 February with the capitulation of von Paulus. The Soviets unleashed a far-reaching offensive. Crossing the Donetz, in March they took Kursk, Bielogorod, Vorochilov and Rostov. Von Manstein's counter-attack in the Kharkov sector only delayed their advance. The Wehrmacht offensive in July resulted in disaster. A new Soviet offensive pushed the Germans back to Dniepr. On 25 August they retook Kharkov, and Tanganrog on the 30th. In September they reoccupied Briansk, Novorossiysk, Poltava, Smolensk, and in the south, the Kuban. In December 1943, they reached Kiev and the still-occupied Crimea was cut off.

The Germans paid a heavy price in the USSR: one million dead and 100,000 prisoners. These defeats had considerable political consequences: across Europe a growing segment of the bourgeoisie lost confidence in Hitler and turned to the Allies, at the same time as the wave of working-class and popular revolt grew.

The first major crack was in Italy, where in the North there were strikes from March. In July fascism fell, and the bourgeoisie hurried to support the

Allies to check the movement of the masses.

A popular insurrection forced the Axis troops out of Corsica. The Communist resistance in Albania and Yugoslavia made further advances. The red partisans took advantage of the disarmament of the twelve Italian divisions and by the close of 1943 they had liberated the greater part of the territory.

Forced into relying on the manpower of the occupied countries, and deporting European workers to the Reich like slaves in place of mobilised German workers, Hitler sparked a huge working-class and popular resistance across the whole of Europe. This was clearly the case in France, where the Vichy régime was forced to place itself more and more openly at his service, Darnand organising an auxiliary fascist militia in January 1943. In February Laval introduced compulsory labour, forcing young people to go to work in Germany for two years. They joined the maquis to avoid the STO [Service du travail obligatoire: Compulsory labour service]. Workers resisted slavery with sabotage and strikes.

Europe was a powder-keg. The German bourgeoisie began to distance itself from Hitler: a hundred generals and bourgeois personalities established a Free Germany Committee in Moscow. Suffering privations, ruined by bombings, decimated by heavy losses on all fronts, the German people felt the Nazi defeat was near. The army started to lose discipline: the population no longer had confidence in Hitler.

Thus, there ripened the conditions for a European revolution much more powerful even than that at the end of the First World War.

But in 1943 the protagonists organised to stop this. The demand for unconditional capitulation (at January's Casablanca conference) served to galvanise the German people behind their army. The USSR pursued a policy of national war: it constituted a free German government, but out of bourgeois and conservative forces.

As for the Communist parties, except in a few countries like Yugoslavia, they more and more devotedly participated in the union sacrée along with the social democrats: the dissolution of the Third International in May 1943 gave the imperialist powers a clear sign that they would desist from any revolutionary activity.

The first test cases showed the effectiveness of the counter-revolutionary forces. In Italy, while the workers in the north were crushed by Nazi troops, in the centre and the south the revolutionary movement was run into the ground by reformism. Could the revolution erect its barricades in Germany, and across Europe? Could internationalist revolutionaries – very few in number – impact on the course of events?

The national conference of the Parti ouvrier internationaliste

In early January 1943, as the reversal in the balance of forces was still not yet clear, the Comités de la IVe Internationale held its national conference in Paris: 25 to 30 representatives of the Central Committee and the main branches met for several days in a disguised meeting room in Pétain's youth headquarters, beneath a large portrait of the *Maréchal*. There were fake agendas on the tables. Everything was organised such as to allow the rapid burning of the real documents.

The conference adopted the reports presented by the Central Committee on the international and French situations 'underlining the crisis of world imperialism and the rise of proletarian and revolutionary movements'.

It considered that the politics of the Front national and of terrorism encouraged by the PCF had 'terrible repercussions on the coherence of the working class'[276] but this 'did not manage to drag the great mass of the class into the dead end of chauvinism and individual action'.

It concluded by referring to the need to 'redouble efforts to mobilise the working class in a struggle for its own objectives and to gather behind it the mass of the petty bourgeoisie'.

As against the national front policy, the national council counterposed a workers' front strategy. The real front was not that of the imperialist war but rather that of class struggle. The struggle of the working class had to have as its objective not the victory of the bourgeois state, but socialist revolution. This objective required workers to become conscious of their opposition to capitalist interests and to reactionary chauvinism, as well as their cohesion as a class and international solidarity. The working class would learn of its independent strength in the fight against deportations, on its own terms in the workplace, renewing the spirit of the 1936 strikes, in Paris, Brest, Nantes, Saint-Nazaire, Ambérieu, Limoges, Oullins, Toulouse, Grenoble, Clermont-Ferrand, Chambéry, etc.[277]

To prevent the workers' movement from being side-tracked into nationalist positions and being used by the bourgeoisie, revolutionaries had to try to build working-class unity in action, without party divisions, and build a workers' anti-capitalist front.

Resisting Hitlerite imperialism which sought to deport them as slaves to the Reich, workers naturally put forward the most basic national demand: to work in their own country, not to be separated from their loved ones, not having to be so many head of cattle for the temporarily victorious imperialism. These demands could be used to nationalist ends by the bourgeoisie and its agents. However they could also play a part in the more general working-class struggle.

Revolutionaries could only help such a development if they took their place in the front line of the working class's struggles, including for national and democratic freedoms. Such was the conclusion of the national council which adopted the theses of the provisional secretariat of the Fourth International.

At the same time, the national council reaffirmed its own conception of what the vanguard was. It desired the regroupment of internationalists, but:

> Above all it is important that this regroupment takes place within a party always ready to take its responsibilities in the daily struggles of the working class, experiencing each day's struggle alongside the class and in each case bringing its own slogans, organisational solutions and perspectives. The reconstitution of a workers' front must allow the working class to again find the cohesion which is indispensable in action; the participation of the revolutionary party in each day's struggle, the path to revolution.

The national council lauded the Central Committee's efforts 'on the path to revolutionary regroupment'. It proposed to the *La Seule Voie* group that it should participate in the planning for its June congress; political discussion would go in tandem with joint work which would test in action the possibility of unification. Although recognising its extreme weakness the organisation displayed – by again taking the title 'party' – its desire to play its part in mass action. A minority desired the name Parti communiste révolutionnaire. Marcel Hic advocated the name Parti ouvrier internationaliste, allowing for renewal of the pre-1936 Trotskyist tradition. This was the only issue on which the national council was divided.

The other internationalist groups

In late February Paris also played host to the 'pre-conference' of the *La Seule Voie* group.

Having paid homage to the Bolshevik-Leninists who had fallen victim to repression (notably seven comrades from the group itself, referred to by their initials) the pre-conference declared its faithfulness to the tradition of the pre-war PCI and claimed ownership of its fight against 'official Trotskyism'. It adopted the name Comité communiste internationaliste pour la construction de la IVe Internationale (CCI), a name 'which affirm[ed] the continuity of both our tradition and our movement'. It then embarked on a 'turn':

During the recent period, by force of circumstance the training of our activists took on a preponderantly book-learning character. Our activists progressed as far as they could within the limits of such work. For certain there were dangers with this means of existence and development but we have always paid attention to such dangers. The organisation cannot become a red university, nor even develop red professors as a substitute for vanguard class fighters. it is not enough to be right and voice the correct line. That has no value unless it is used to convince, to win over the vanguard, to create a pole of revolutionary leadership and build the party. We do not defend our politics and our programme by showing it to be impeccable, superb, a marvel; but in attacking all its open and hidden enemies – particularly the latter – in unmasking and denouncing them.[278]

A pre-revolutionary situation had developed: '*La Seule Voie* moreover took stock of the mood of the exploited masses, the struggles of the vanguard and the problems of BL (Bolshevik-Leninist) regroupment.'

The CCI decided to launch an agitational newspaper, *Le Soviet*. The first issue appeared in April 1943, copied recto-verso: following *La Commune* which had 159 issues before the war, it was numbered as 160, lending it the guise of long-standing clandestine activity.

Finally the CCI addressed a letter to the POI Central Committee on the issue of unification: accepting 'with satisfaction' the offer to participate in its congress, it reiterated its request to participate in the European executive committee and proposed the summary of its preconference theses as the points of political agreement.

The 73 theses of its resolution represented a very long document, titled 'Americanisme contre bolchevisme'. This resolution was based on a theoretical schema which can be summarised as:

1. The pre-revolutionary situation was underway. It would inevitably result in the transformation of the war into civil war and revolution. Germany was key to the situation.

2. In the current period the USA represented the main enemy. Its victory would see Europe returned to an agricultural continent of barbarism and dictatorship.

3. The USA's immediate objective was the destruction of the USSR. They would only later take action against Hitler. Thus there would be no second front before the fall of Stalin:

The turn in the balance of forces in the imperialist war, illustrated by the American landings in North Africa, poses the question of ever-greater and determined action against the USSR by Yankee imperialism.

4. Only opportunists could believe that at the present stage Hitlerism represented the main enemy. The need to fight him was only because of the need 'to defend the revolutionary achievements in the USSR'.

5. It was necessary to convince individual advanced workers against 'the main enemy, the USA'. Thus the need for workers' groups 'to raise the consciousness and organisation of the vanguard of the working class with propaganda for our programme'.

6. The moment was ripe for the Fourth International. It would take leadership of the masses at the necessary moment, on condition that the Bolshevik-Leninists were united 'on the Bolshevik-Leninist programme and not amid confusion over opportunist petty-bourgeois and nationalist positions'.

The CCI congratulated itself on the lucidity with which it used Marxist analysis to discern truths key to any revolutionary policy on the war: the impossibility of any alliance, even temporary, between the USA and USSR; the inevitability of Soviet defeat.

> We wrote this at a time when the Red Army was heavily engaged in its winter offensives against the German army. It would have been easier and more 'logical' according to some people's reasoning to predict the military victory of the USSR over Germany, the spread of Stalinism in Europe and other similar hypotheses. This would have been mere short-termism, which is exactly what the POI leadership did, dragging it into the worst nationalist and opportunist mire. This opportunist policy left it completely unable to clearly discern Yankee imperialism's role as the champion of counter-revolution. So, instead of taking the only axis of struggle today imposed on Bolshevik-Leninists – the struggle against Gaullism, nationalism and the super-Wrangel of US imperialism – the POI leadership was always in the shadow of Gaullism, nationalism and Americanophilia.[279]

For POI members it seemed absurd to write history in advance based on prefabricated schemas or on the basis of the experience of the Russian revolution. The CCI's activists sounded like 'a train timetable'. Its dogma (the inevitability of Soviet defeat, the impossibility of a second front) were in their eyes a caricature of Marxist methods of analysis. The imperialist war created favourable conditions for proletarian revolution, but this revolution would not develop unless a conscious vanguard was capable of using the situation, aiding workers' committees to take shape and stand up to the bourgeoisie. This created great disagreement over the nature of the party and its relation to the masses. Indeed the CCI confirmed that this was the fundamental difference:

> The question of the struggle amongst the vanguard for the formation of a Party is precisely the question which divides us from the other Bolshevik-Leninist splinter, the POI. They have thrown themselves into so-called mass work where they put forward slogans which far from helping advanced workers from casting off their illusions (national liberation, national unity, struggle against the occupier),[280] rather, make them all the more attached to them.

According to the POI:

> the revolutionary movement could not win over the working-class vanguard except by sharing in its experiences and in the struggles of the working masses, being ready to take its responsibilities in the daily struggles of the working class, experiencing each day's struggle alongside the class and in each case bringing its own slogans, organisational solutions and perspectives.[281]

In the eyes of the CCI, the masses would recognise the party as their high command at the moment of revolutionary upsurge, because of the quality of its programme. For the POI, the masses would not recognise the party as a leadership except if, fighting alongside it and devoting its efforts to the struggle, it helped them realise their basic aspirations. Concretely this meant understanding the aspirations of the working class and taking these as a starting point. This often meant confused and contradictory efforts. By 1943 POI members felt that they had made no few mistaken statements on, for example, the national question. But they considered it indispensable to fight on the front line against the imperialism which was dominant on the ground and against which workers had to fight to survive.[282]

This conception of the party also meant divergence over the conditions of unity. For the CCI unification demanded agreement over programme – meaning, agreement with *their* programme – and over leadership posts. For the POI programmatic agreement was necessary but insufficient: the viability of a joint party would be tested in joint action. But the conditions of illegality rendered this challenging.

In April 1943 there appeared a new Trotskyist group, the 'groupe Lénine et Trotski'. This was a small group emerging from the Mouvement pour l'abondance.[283] Its leading theorist was Henri Claude (Pouget), who would after the war become the PCF theoretician of political economy. It published a bulletin, *Jeunesse d'Octobre*.[284]

Although it did not subscribe to all the theses of the CCI it was vehemently critical of the politics of the POI. Having characterised this as – 'Today we defend and share in this nationalism of the masses, allowing us to be with the masses when social struggle overcomes the national form' – it comments:

> This tactic is inadmissible. Such politics, with its inevitable concessions to bourgeois nationalism, can only drape in proletarian colours the scourge of nationalism germinating among the proletariat. Indeed it means strengthening the 'national form' to the detriment of social struggle. It is a rejection of the best elements of the class, already now being defined by their detaching themselves from reformist and Stalinist slogans. It destroys the possibilities for an international maturation of the European proletariat. It means reinforcing imperialism![285]

At the same time the group formulated a critique of the 'academicism' of the CCI:

> The best, the most complete, the most hardy of programmes, cannot exercise its vital role except to the extent that it is rooted, combined with the political struggle of a party. And a party, galvanised by its programme, cannot for its part oil the engine of revolutionary war except to the extent that it is linked to the political experience of the masses ....
>
> On this point we must pose the dangers of an excessively academic conception of building the party. This conception has played an effective and progressive role through the first period of regroupment of activists after the Nazi victories of 1940. But already it is some time since the development of events has demanded further, higher stages of organisation. Academicism, when one is unable to pose and resolve the problems of a meaningful Bolshevik orientation, thus risks dragging the Trotskyist vanguard into the worst sterility.

In conclusion the group insisted on Trotskyist unity: 'Fighting for the Fourth International today means fighting for the Bolshevisation of our politics, and, on this basis, the regroupment of Trotskyists.'

The *Lutte de classe* group continued the regular publication of its newspaper (with 17 issues in 1943). In July 1943 it defined its rules of functioning in a report which it published, and which would later inspire the type of organisation embodied by the *Lutte ouvrière* group. It commenced by justifying its independent existence:

> Our independence has always been, and still is, vital to us. We cannot embark upon the development of communist militants (which takes place in the practice of class struggle) amid a petty-bourgeois and opportunist milieu ....

It recognised that:

> among the groups claiming the Fourth International tradition, a degree of factory work has changed little... The experience of the war and the Stalinist about-turns have led certain workers to come together in the POI, in spite of its inability to effectively organise and lead them. The POI has benefited from this current of ideas, in spite of its opportunist politics, in building a numerically stronger organisation. Our task is to demonstrate to these workers the opportunism of the POI leadership and present them with an organisation – and in particular, organisational methods – which inspires confidence.[286]

What did these organisational methods consist of?

> The content of the party's revolutionary action is two-fold: in terms of embodying the socialist goal, the party represents a superior form of human association, including the effective involvement of all in the policies and ideology of the party; in terms of an instrument of struggle against the current capitalist society, the party is adapted to the demands of that struggle, which is not possible without a centralist organisation ....

The party had to be rigorously hierarchical: sympathisers, activists and professional revolutionaries:

> Professionalism implies that each party activist is at the complete disposal of the party, which uses them as it wishes in the best interests of the working class, inside and outside of the workplace.

Only the professional revolutionaries could 'determine the political trajectory of our organisation'.

These characteristics were not particular to the *Lutte de Classe* group. They were imposed on everyone by the conditions of extreme illegality. However, the POI refused to enshrine this as a timeless theory. This was unlike the *Lutte de Classe* group, in whose eyes the situation of endless war and illegality was fated to last until the revolution. This explains why they were determined to continue to act alone.

In January 1943 the Union communiste internationaliste published *Fraternisation prolétarienne*, organ of revolutionary communists in France. This carried the legend 'Neither bourgeois collaboration nor Gaullist or Stalinist chauvinism'. Four issues would appear during the war. The group was based on the politics of the German RKD, who in March and June issued the bulletin *Spartakus*. As we have already seen, it proposed to the *La Seule Voie* group the joint creation of a revolutionary Fourth International.

In 1944 it described itself thus:

Fraternisation prolétarienne places itself at the extreme left of the French workers' movement and its struggles, together with the revolutionary communists of all countries, for revolutionary proletarian fraternisation on all fronts and it all countries. The *Fraternisation prolétarienne* group emerged from the former revolutionary communist opposition to the pre-war Trotskyist bureaucracy. This opposition comprises revolutionary communist groups in France, Belgium, Germany and Switzerland. Comrades Dieter (German RKD), De Lee and Godemaine (Belgian PSR), who died in the course of the war, were leading activists in this movement ....

Fraternisation prolétarienne works against the Americano-Russophile mainstream and tells the truth about exploitation, oppression and triumphant counter-revolution in Russia.

Fraternisation prolétarienne considers all the tendencies who do not tell the whole truth about Russia to be centrists and opportunists, and denounces them as such.[287]

The role of the USSR

On the contrary, if there was one issue where the Trotskyist papers displayed consensus, it was the defence of the USSR. For all of them, the front where the Red Army fought was the front of the European and world proletariat. According to *La Lutte de classe*:

The Soviet advance brings us closer to the socialist revolution in Europe. There is only one way of aiding the USSR, of which all imperialisms are the enemy, including American and British imperialism: extending the proletarian revolution to other countries, and thus to France… Thanks to the strength of the system which emerged from the October 1917 Russian revolution, a new stage is coming in the development of the war, a stage of civil war. Those who Germany conscripts, and who cannot hide, must make Hitler pay by conscious sabotage in close union with the German workers who are fighting to overthrow fascism. Thus they will hasten the defeat of German imperialism, the victory of the USSR, the liberation of prisoners and the collapse of the Vichy régime.[288]

On 28 February *La Lutte de classe* made a rather more guarded assertion: 'The victories of the Red Army will be the victories of socialism if the workers of the capitalist countries of Europe carry out socialist revolution.' Indeed the article explained,

The Soviet bureaucracy, with its secret diplomacy before the war and its policies during the war, has diverted the international proletariat from proletarian revolution in order to defend its untrammelled political rule and privileged economic status within Soviet society. Claiming to defend the so-called 'national' interests of the USSR, it hopes to maintain the status quo of its privileges in a world torn apart by inter-imperialist conflicts.[289]

La Vérité maintained, with similar prudence, that: 'The victories of the Red Army *could* be the successes of the revolutionary vanguard.'

Considering that the Soviet victories were due to the strength of the planned economy, and not Stalin's policy of compromise, it asked:

Thus is posed the question, as in Lenin's phrase repeated by Stalin at the time of the German-Russian pact: will the USSR take the irons out of the fire for imperialism? Why did those who fought at Stalingrad fight until the ultimate sacrifice? … That is the question. Roosevelt is silent because he hopes the USSR will take the irons out of the fire on his behalf. In reality American imperialism is determined to lead the struggle for private property, against revolution and against the USSR when the time comes. The workers and oppressed of Europe, will they be as determined to overthrow capitalism? And what is the Red Army fighting for? Is it defending its borders or 'supporting the coming revolution in Europe'? This, we must answer.[290]

Curiously, this was posed rhetorically, but the question was indeed an essential one. Recent events had started to reveal some of the answers: the dissolution of the soviets spontaneously established in Poland and the Baltic states during the Red Army advance; the return of chauvinism and 'realpolitik'; support for the union sacrée in the Allied countries. Instead of aiding the revolution, surely Stalin would join the Anglo-American efforts to prevent it?

This was not at issue in the eyes of the CCI. The fourteen pages of its resolution concerned the dissolution of the USSR and what this would result in. There could be no collusion with the Anglo-Americans, because the latter simply wanted to destroy the USSR; the fall of Stalin was inevitable. In their counter-revolutionary actions the Stalinists and social democrats could only count on a single source of support: the corrupting influence of the USA.

In the meantime the CCI could not brook any nuance in their affirmation of unconditional defence of the USSR:

> We consider the USSR to be a conquest of the international proletariat. We must defend it unconditionally against all attackers, wherever they come from, just as we would not pose conditions on taking strike action alongside workers.[291] [292]

However, the role of the USSR became clearer through 1943. On 15 May Stalin dissolved the Third International, which had been established as the high command of the revolution. The *La Vérité* editorial commented:

> Does this mean that Stalin has abandoned the Communist Parties as diplomatic pawns, that he has abandoned any idea of pressure on the capitalist governments? Not at all. On the contrary we can be sure that the more he breaks with the communist tradition, the more he will seek to recruit his agents from among the ranks of lawyers in search of payment, writers on the lookout for contracts and bankers who want concessions in the USSR, and among the rotten and treacherous Aragons, Pierre Cots and Hopkinses. But Stalinism will not win their support unless it openly aligns itself with their programme of bourgeois counter-revolution.[293]

In the USSR itself Stalin resuscitated the Holy Synod, replaced the *Internationale* with a nationalist anthem and played at anti-Semitism with the Bund trials.[294]

Octobre asked: 'The Red Army is victorious: but what is left of the gains of October?'

During this period the Nazis succeeded in establishing an anti-Bolshevik legion with former Soviet officers as its cadres.

La Vérité commented:

> Now they have found men to do their dirty work: not former Tsarist officers as one might imagine (there were no White Russians, few in number, except in Cossack units) but rather bureaucrats who rose amid the Stalinist degeneration of the Russian revolution. Vlassov, head of the legion, a Red Army fighter in 1919, is a general who has risen through the ranks; most of the officers collaborating with him are of similar background. They are men from among the social layers who took power in the USSR after Lenin's death. They are the men who supported Stalin against Trotsky and who today have passed into the ranks of counter-revolution.
>
> Thus while the Russian proletariat fights to defend collective property with a dedication which is the awe of the world, the parasitical caste who deny it the gains of the October revolution appear to be mired in a repugnant state of collapse: some of them throw themselves into the arms of Roosevelt, dissolving what was left of the Communist International and preparing further capitulations; while others, in order to continue holding some office, have become Hitler's lackeys fighting against those same workers whose representatives they had claimed to be: 'We want a people's Russia, without communists, Jews and plutocrats', Vlassov said in his rendition of Nazi propaganda slogans.
>
> But the Russian proletariat has perspectives other than living under the thumb of Hitler or Roosevelt. In spite of terrible reprisals, partisan battalions have formed and are fighting in the occupied territories for the defence of the revolution. From Siberia to Soloviev, thousands and men and women have from the outset expressed their fidelity to Bolshevism. It cannot be long until the Soviet proletariat, casting aside the bureaucrats, will resume the path traced by Lenin and Trotsky, that of world revolution.[295]

For the moment, Stalin and the bourgeoisie had the situation firmly in hand. They gave fresh evidence of the role they sought to play. On 12 and 13 July Moscow played host to the establishment of a National Committee for a Free Germany, an analogue of the governments exiled in London. This National Committee was not created by representatives of working-class forces, calling on workers to overthrow Hitler and the capitalist system of which he was the product, but rather composed of over a hundred generals, officers and Catholic and Protestant figures. In terms of the roots of the conflict, it proclaimed, 'Hitler was entirely responsible'. Its programme read:

> We set as our goal the abolition of national and racial hate laws, the abolition of the Hitler régime, a return to free religious thought, free speech, freedom of association and of the press, the right of property over legitimately acquired goods and the return of goods stolen by the Hitlerites to their rightful owners.

La Vérité commented that this meant: 'nothing more than the defence of private property.'[296]

Moreover, according to its manifesto the National Committee for a Free Germany would allow an amnesty 'for partisans of Hitler who break with him and join the Free Germans in good time'.

It concluded:

> German soldiers and officers! You have weapons. Keep hold of them. Following the orders of your current leaders, use your weapons to make your way to the borders of the fatherland.

La Vérité commented:

> Following the orders of your current leaders! Think about this! Do not turn your arms against the bourgeoisie. Your current leaders, the leaders of the soldiers and officers – these fascists, these old-school reactionaries – do not stop them, do not disarm them. Do not make revolution. Moscow now tells you just this.
>
> This is a blatant move against revolution. Hitler is not supported by the whole bourgeoisie. Certain businessman and Reichswehr[297] leaders want to get rid of yesterday's saviour, just as the Italian bourgeoisie pushed out Mussolini. Stalin, having betrayed Leninism at every opportunity and after dissolving the Comintern, is now using the German crisis to support the financiers and generals against Hitler. So how many months does the German bourgeoisie have to break with Hitler? The German proletariat, which from the outset has resisted him, been bloodied, gagged and super-exploited by him, had nothing to do with the war even at the time when the bourgeoisie believed victory possible and sang Hitler's praises. But even if there is no support for the German proletariat from Moscow,

it is coming, and will come, from the rest of the world, from the fighting and revolutionary working class, and in the forefront the nascent Fourth International. 'Prolet aller lander vereingte euch!'

But if Moscow did not support revolution, and on the contrary the USSR and its satellite parties made efforts to head off a revolutionary upsurge, particularly in Germany, surely the balance of forces would be markedly affected, in spite of the internationalists' optimism?

A centrist strategy?

Left-wing socialists hoped to change this balance of forces by using the Allies and putting themselves in the service of the Resistance. They sought to develop their activism on an intermediate course between that of the Trotskyists (doctrinaire and cut off from the masses) and that of the traditional parties (endangering socialism with the union sacrée line). Such was the orientation that the leading such movement, *L'Insurgé* in the Southern Zone, sought to theorise.

Until mid-1943 *L'Insurgé* was barely distinguishable from other Resistance groups, such as *Libération*, with which it had links. The only difference was the lack of 'anti-Boche' slogans and a certain stress on anti-capitalist slogans. For example, issue 17, which like the whole Gaullist press called for demonstrations on 14 July,[298] argued: 'The French working classes are preparing in unison to free themselves from fascism, war and the modern feudalism of capitalism.'

In large characters it proclaimed: 'This 14 July of 1943, many will speak of France, but we will also speak of the Republic.'[299]

This did not mean very much.

In the second half of 1943 and early 1944, *L'Insurgé* became more political and tried to define its line. This development was essentially thanks to the interventions of Gilles Martinet. Taking refuge in Clermont-Ferrand, with Pierre Bernard he edited a copied sheet, *le Bulletin ouvrier*, distributed in the neighbouring *départements*. From September 1943 he actively participated in the publication of *L'Insurgé*, 500-600 copies of which were distributed by the *Bulletin ouvrier* group, the FTP and MOF. Moreover there were constant contacts with the Clermont POI branch.[300]

In terms of general objectives and in terms of analysing the situation, Martinet's theses were reminiscent of Trotskyist positions.

The war was an imperialist war:

1943: THE TURNING POINT 187

> Under imperialism – the ultimate stage of capitalism – this country will never know anything other than foreign domination, rationing and (after a short period of liberty), reactionary dictatorship.

Revolution was possible:

> What was materially possible in an economically backward country isolated from the rest of the world, will be all the more possible in Western Europe, with openings onto all of the seas and supported by the immense Eurasian bloc of the USSR.

This was practically identical to the Trotskyist outlook, except for the fact that Martinet's publication never issued any condemnation of Stalinism or Soviet foreign policy: such polemics would have been a barrier to collaboration with the PCF and the Resistance.

L'Insurgé was in agreement with the Trotskyists over the slogan for a Socialist United States of Europe. It also took issue with the union sacrée and chauvinism:

> The time has come for the workers' movement to turn [patriotism] away from its old ways – narrow-minded chauvinism, 'treacherous Albion' and the 'dirty Boche', the clarion calls of Déroulède, the union sacrée and war every twenty years – it could be a path to glory, rather than nothing but caprice and enslavement.

Of course, we may ask whether patriotism is the best way to find the internationalist path. But the point is that the conclusions were similar.

Moreover, Martinet condemned the class collaboration which, as June 1936 showed, led to the defeat of the working class:

> Of course, the face of the CFLN[301] is not exactly the same as that of the Léon Blum government.
>
> But – and this is the point – in 1943 as in 1936, we find ourselves faced with the same policy: alliance of the working class, the great mass of the peasantry of the middle classes and *part of the bourgeoisie.*
>
> We stress these last few words with good reason, for we cannot understand the defeats of the years 1937-39 if we do not take stock of the fact that finance capital – the infamous 'two hundred families' – were represented in the Popular Front.[302]

Martinet drew the same lessons as the Trotskyists from the failure of the Popular Front:

> Soon after the October revolution Lenin noted that 'the economics of capitalist society are such that only capital, or a proletariat which overthrows it, can be the dominant force'… There was never and never will be a 'shared' state, a 'social' state reconciling the interests of the capitalist and the proletarian, the exploiter and the exploited.

However his conclusions were radically different:

> Does that mean the workers' movement must *today* pose the dilemma 'bourgeois reaction or socialist revolution' and have no interest in anything else? Nothing could be more wrong, more absurd.
> Nothing could be more wrong, because such an attitude, which does not correspond to the concrete problems the masses *currently* face, would leave the working-class vanguard dangerously isolated.
> Nothing could be more absurd, because the democratic revolution whose first signs are already beginning to show, cannot be arbitrarily separated from socialist revolution: only the latter can guarantee (and in certain cases, realise) the principal gains of the former.[303]

Thus the first stage had to be a *democratic* phase: which did indeed mean the shared state, the 'social' state which Martinet had just explained to be impossible – but upon which he relied for the achievement of socialist revolution. From the basis of his argument the only conclusion he drew was that which spoke of an 'uninterrupted battle without major plateaux or long pauses'.

Yet what mattered for now was the first, democratic phase. 'In this struggle, working-class organisations have to, and will have to, make temporary compromises.'

At the same time, the article argued:

> No consideration of a tactical nature should prevent the workers' movement from asserting its own positions – starting from now – and showing without equivocation the only route to salvation.

Thus the idea was thus to protect their freedom of thought and freedom of criticism of the two hundred families' allies.

This perspective allowed for action alongside essentially all of the Gaullist

1943: THE TURNING POINT   189

organisations. Gilles Martinet had shown that this union sacrée policy had been the cause of working-class defeat 1936-39. But the strategy he himself proposed also included a stage of union sacrée, while the driving force of this strategy was the unity and fusion of the two parties who put the policy of union sacrée into practice:

> It is true to say that an immense opportunity – perhaps a unique one – is on offer for the working class. If, benefiting from the powerful tendency towards unity, activists are able to rally their forces and re-establish the dream of trade union unity; if they succeed in building a large mass political organisation, born of the fusion of the Socialist and Communist Parties; if across the whole of France they lead the same campaigns with the same slogans in the workplace and community as well as within their groups: then all popular forces, all the healthy elements of the country – the youth in the lead – will turn towards them, representing a decisive step towards liberation.[304]

What would these slogans be? What kind of liberation? Above, Gilles Martinet did not make this clear. Nor did he explain how the merger of the two parties who prevented revolution in 1936 (and who afterwards travelled further down the road of union sacrée) could guarantee the victory of revolution in the coming period.

On the contrary, he distanced himself from 'leftism', 'workerism', 'revolutionism' and 'abstract socialism': references to Trotskyism.

Proclaiming revolutionary objectives, verbally accepting the lessons of the past and yet in practice not taking account of them – on the contrary justifying by circumstance policies identical to those condemned on principle – and on this basis allying not with revolutionaries but organisations which continued in leading the working class to defeat: such were the politics the Trotskyists labelled 'centrist'.

In reality it was an exaggeration to speak of the politics, or doctrine, of *L'Insurgé*. It was a many-faced movement, varying according to geographical region. More politically defined were the *Bulletin ouvrier* group in Clermont-Ferrand and *Action ouvrière* in Saint-Etienne, whereas in most cases it was simply a Resistance movement like any other.[305] Its activists were, at most, united by a certain working-class sensibility and rejection of the worst chauvinism.

In autumn 1943, the *L'Insurgé* congress met at Villeurbanne – 'a small conference', according to Martinet, and one which underlined the eclecticism of the group. There was only one policy for the participants to discuss, 'the theses of high-technology socialism based on working-class trade unionism and the peasantry' defended by the Loire branch.[306] No general perspectives were adopted.

The *Memorial de L'Insurgé* contents itself with retracing, in an anecdotal manner region-by-region, the very varied activities of activists organised around the newspaper, without ever referring to theory or strategy. In the appendix, as 'doctrinal' documents, it merely reproduces the 1940 appeal of the Front ouvrier international, the exchange of letters between Marceau Pivert and General de Gaulle, the Lyon freemasons' message to Roosevelt of January 1941 and the Manifesto of the fusion between *L'Insurgé* and *Libérer-fédérer* of April 1944.

The orientation defined in Martinet's articles had few practical implications. He devoted himself to proposing a theoretical justification for this eclectic activity, but there was no centrist strategy.

The Allies in North Africa

The Allies' first rehearsal of 'the Liberation' was in North Africa. We must step back in our chronology to trace the consequences of the first landing, Operation Torch of 11-14 November 1942.

This took place amid a regrettable misunderstanding. Vichy representative Admiral Darlan confessed to being poorly informed of the strength of the assailant naval forces. Believing them to be mediocre, he sent the Gaullist conspirators to the High Court and fought a bloody four-day battle which saw a thousand deaths among the French alone.[307] But having realised the real balance of forces he rallied to the Americans. This was a typical example of the two-facedness of Vichy politicians. They welcomed the 'divine intervention' represented by Nazi victory because it allowed them to establish the reactionary régime of their dreams. They were ready to rally behind the Americans if they were stronger, on the condition that their régime should survive: the presence of Admiral Leahy in Vichy seemed to be a sure sign of this.

Indeed the Allies eagerly reaffirmed the authority of Admiral Darlan, a royalist and former leading figure in Pétain's government who had collaborated from the outset. The Admiral furthermore kept General Noguès in his post as Resident-General of Morocco.[308]

In the political sphere, minor concessions were sufficient: he lifted only part of the anti-Jewish laws and freed certain among the political prisoners. Besides this he maintained a colonial régime with Vichyist laws. The government he led was comprised of Vichyists: Peyrouton, Noguès, Boisson and Puchel included. Doriot's party, the Parti Populaire Français, was not banned until eight months later. When Darlan was assassinated on 24 December 1942 by a young Gaullist aristocrat, the Allies appointed as his successor the monarchist General Giraud, who summarised his programme: 'All together with the Marshal [i.e. Pétain], our only passion: duty.' Indeed he left the worst Vichyist representatives in their posts. Later, acting upon American advice, he tried to brush aside his monarchist convictions and the fascist politics of his collaborators with a profession of faith in democracy. But at the same time, as *La Vérité* stressed,[309] he had the Algerian nationalist leader Messali Hadj arrested, demonstrating well enough the reality of his politics.

In November 1942 De Gaulle proclaimed his opposition to the Vichyist régime in Algiers. This was not only a question of personal rivalry. Tied to men who had led France to defeat and to pro-fascist Vichy collaborators, the leadership established by the Americans had no hope of rallying the Resistance in France. It was condemned to be the hostage of the Americans, much as in Vichy it was held hostage by the Germans – incapable of playing the independent role of 'French grandeur' to which De Gaulle aspired. Rather, such a formation would earn the hatred of the masses fighting its homologue in Vichy. They would necessarily seek their own political expression with which to oppose it: opening the way for a revolutionary explosion. The parties (SFIO and PCF) in which they trusted did not ask for any more than to be included in a union sacrée, which could not exist except under the leadership of the 'man of 18 June'.[310]

Despite their doubts, the Americans had to face up to this reality. They constantly attempted to defend the interests of the most reactionary section of the bourgeoisie and the Vichy régime, forcing reconciliation with Giraud onto De Gaulle. They thus hoped to build a widened union sacrée, from pro-fascists to democrats and communists. This was a tall order.

However, the Resistance organisations (from the PCF's Front national to Ceux de la Résistance, via *Libération* and the Centre d'action socialiste) themselves proposed a compromise: 'A government which gives orders and co-ordinates, entrusted to General de Gaulle, with Giraud as commander-in-chief of the army.'

The Americans forced a different compromise: a two-headed leadership.

Thus on 30 May 1943 De Gaulle arrived in Algiers. The PCF officially proclaimed, in a declaration by Fernand Grenier, its 'confidence in De Gaulle, who from the outset has raised the standard of resistance, and in Giraud, commander-in-chief of the armies in Africa'.[311]

On 3 June the Comité français de libération nationale (CFLN) was established, under the dual leadership of De Gaulle and Giraud. The most badly compromised Vichyists were excluded, but so too were the Communists: only André Philip represented the 'workers' parties'. The compromise would last until 1 October 1943, when Giraud agreed to step aside. On 9 November a consultative assembly, substituting for parliament, was convened in Algiers, whereas the CFLN transformed into the 'provisional government of the French Republic'. The Allies did not recognise this government until July 1944.

In *La Vérité*'s eyes, these events were a rehearsal of what the Allies intended to do when they occupied France, and also served as a warning:

> De Gaulle and Giraud seem lighter than a cork in the hands of imperialism. And in the hands of De Gaulle the Parti communiste is lighter still. Only the United States are playing their cards right.

La Vérité drew the conclusion: 'We must organise our liberation ourselves. No more popular front con tricks! For a workers' front.'[312]

In truth *La Vérité*'s analysis was mistaken. Giraud's success could only be an ephemeral one, precisely because he was a hindrance to the union sacrée which was indispensable for the bourgeoisie. In this sense the *Lutte de classes* analysis was more lucid:

> The consolidation of the Comité français de libération nationale and similar bodies which preceded and succeeded it demonstrate, given the compromises made, a first victory for Gaullism. However for this to be completed it must be fulfilled with a Gaullist takeover of the army in North Africa, which is currently the main power base of the Giraudist faction.

As for the sidelined Communists, there was no room for complacency. The 26 Communist MPs 'liberated by the Allies after publicly stating their support for Gaullist dissidence and their backing for the Allies' war aims'[313] made their complaints known. *La Vérité* published these on 12 September under the heading 'Time to understand':

> The 26 have protested against the current régime in North Africa. They have attacked the leading role of 'generals and admirals who were put in place by enemy bayonets to destroy the freedoms of the nation, and continue to do so, believing themselves to be protected by British and American bayonets. In spite of solemn assurances, in Algeria there is neither freedom of the press nor freedom of association nor freedom to hold meetings.'

The 26, *La Vérité* commented,

> thus have their finger on the pulse of the capitalist scheme which has succeeded under the leadership of Giraud and De Gaulle, and which we have denounced from the outset.
>
> But who are they appealing to? To De Gaulle and Giraud, who are themselves the agents of capitalism. To the Allies who are fighting an unremitting imperialist campaign in North Africa to satisfy the interests of British and Yankee big business.
>
> In reality, in tailing Giraud and De Gaulle, the Communist MPs in Algiers have abandoned the politics which would allow a struggle for a full and real democracy, for a government of the people and an army of the people. It is high time to understand this, to attack all the bourgeois schemes against the people, and break with Stalin who gives cover to this.

The removal of Giraud and the establishment of the provisional government were fully exploited by the pro-Nazi occupation press who wanted to spread the idea that Algiers had come under Communist control. *La Vérité* attacked the myth of 'Red Algiers': in the provisional government sat 'just two token Socialist lackeys' (Philip and Le Troquer) who maintained '80 percent of Pétain's laws'.[314]

In spite of the 'Red Algiers' campaign, the democratic wing of the Resistance felt that it had suffered a defeat with the Algiers compromise. This compromise washed away certain illusions, for example those of the *L'Insurgé* group.[315] The POI hoped that this would serve as a lesson and generate broader critical reflection.

The POI and Jean Moulin

Shortly before this point, the POI had established contact with Jean Moulin. It is impossible to pass over this episode in silence, even if the deaths of the only two direct participants makes it difficult to establish the true history. Hostile to the union sacrée, the POI did not entertain any idea of participating in any body regrouping the bourgeois and nationalist Resistance. But it did try and establish links with the progressive wing of the Resistance.[316] To this end, it authorised a small number of its activists to participate in the Vélite-Thermophyles network in Paris. The network's main organiser was a friend of Jean-Paul Sartre, Pierre Kahn, who became secretary of the Conseil national de la résistance (CNR), and whose deputy was an activist close to the POI, Claude Kilian (alias Josse). 'In the CNR', Kilian wrote, 'we were known as 'les trotskos', but this was not a POI network'. Links were made by a Greek militant Vitzoris. It was probably via this intermediary that Marcel Hic made contact with Jean Moulin when the latter arrived in Paris.

It is probable that this 'rallying point' for the Resistance sought to integrate the Trotskyists. But the nature of their relations was made clear from the outset. The political bureau of the POI had mandated Marcel Hic to establish regular contacts with Jean Moulin. The objective was firstly to understand each others' political positions, before establishing practical collaboration and an exchange of information, particularly as to combat the Gestapo.

According to Claude Bourdet, the means available to the Mouvements unis de la Résistance (MUR) in Paris were at first mediocre. The POI agreed to lend a hand in practical matters. An office was fitted out in Rue Daguerre in partnership with the Vélite-Thermophyles network, where the correspondence and memoranda of the CNR were typed out. Two full-timers (René Bleibtreu and Weismaner, alias Delmotte) and a number of typists 'lent' by the POI worked there. The organisation of CNR meetings, and their protection, was entrusted to Kilian and POI members.

For the POI relations with the Resistance served an essential requirement on a different terrain: the supply of arms. The POI understood more and more the urgent need for military organisation, its arming and the arming of the workers. Here its doctrine was defined by Lenin's attitude in 1918: when the Allies offered him arms to repel the German offensive he decided to 'accept Allied imperialism's weapons to combat German imperialism' on the sole condition that this should not be allowed to have any influence on Soviet foreign policy. One could not entirely discount the possibility that in certain circumstances the balance of forces would drive the left wing of the French bourgeoisie to supply arms to workers and the revolutionary party. There were certain echoes of this position in some issues of *La Vérité*, for example the article 'The second front and the workers' front'.[317] 'The Allies will first bring arms: it would be ludicrous for revolutionaries to refuse them: without weapons the struggle against imperialism, whichever imperialism, is impossible.'

Whatever this did mean, it does not imply that a demand for weapons was ever concretely formulated. The arrest of Jean Moulin in June disrupted the relations with the Conseil national de la résistance. The arrest of Marcel Hic in October definitively broke off contacts.

Except at a minor level there were no further relations until 1944: having become aware of a Gestapo threat against Resistance militants, the PCI delegated Henri Molinier to inform the CNR.

The struggle against fascism and famine

1943 saw sharp deterioration in economic and political conditions in Europe and in France. At the same time, fascist violence worsened. The Germans occupied the whole of France. The Laval government's repression reached new heights. Darnand created an auxiliary police force, the Milice. This repression was enforced in all fields: indicative was the death sentence and execution of a woman who had assisted with abortions.[318]

Racism was taught at universities at the same time as raids against Jews took place in the Southern Zone, as they had before in the already-previously occupied areas. *La Vérité* and the young internationalists' newspaper *La Jeune Garde* featured examples of German workers' solidarity with Jewish workers, and students' interventions to boo and chase out racist 'professors'.

Following the orders of the German embassy the fascists of the RNP, the PPF, the Francists and Solidarité français tried to unite their meagre forces. They did manage to reach an accord to establish a series of 'revolutionary committees' (sic).[319] *La Vérité* gave an account of their meeting and published their secret decisions:[320] special courts, auxiliary police 'with the right to search houses, arrest, take suspects to revolutionary tribunals, and ensure the implementation of their sentences', taking hostages and being able to use them in case of disturbances, etc.

In reality the weakness of the fascist groups prevented them from being able to enact their programme on a large scale. They were only capable of acting as auxiliaries to the Gestapo, the 'gestapo française' based at Rue Lauriston in Paris.

La Vérité published 'an enlightening set of minutes' on the role these gangs wanted to play. It was the minutes of a secret meeting attended by 'the representative of von Schleier… the military officials of the RNP, the PPF and the Francists':

> These gentlemen first looked into the role of the Milice: It should not intervene in military affairs: these are the concern of the German army. It task will be to guard its back against any threat of revolutionary uprising.

Putting it a different way, *La Vérité* commented, 'It meant keeping the workers in check while awaiting the replacement of the German sentinels by their American counterparts.

But the meeting became stormy indeed when Doctor Rainsart announced a set of reprisals the Francists planned to carry out in Boulogne, in order to kill 60 Communist workers there. The representatives of the other parties exclaimed in horror: 'The population will tar us all with the same brush!

No, none of us should enter Boulogne'. The German representative also intervened, given the potential consequences, such that the massacre in Boulogne had to be postponed.[321]

La Vérité called for a counter-offensive:

> We must systematically track down all the fascists, kick them out, cut them off from people around them. These hotheads' exhibitionism in the streets cannot be tolerated any longer [...] We will respond, blow for blow. The ground must burn under the fascists' feet.[322]

In spite of their media strength and police support, the fascist bands were less and less able to organise themselves into a political movement. They were increasingly dominated by the thugs of the 'milieu' who put themselves directly at the service of the Gestapo in order to satisfy their urges and organise large-scale robbery. Only the Milice in the Southern Zone represented a serious repressive force.

Bringing reactionaries and fascists together without particular ideology, it rallied adventurers, short-term arrivistes and lumpen-proletarians who saw in it a means of subsistence.

Unlike the fascist groups in the Northern Zone, the Milice was not simply the agent of German imperialism. Its role was to allow French capitalism 'to overcome undamaged the "social troubles" (as they call them) of the post-war period. Pending the intervention of a victorious imperialism to buttress the endangered administration, besieged by strikes and revolts, someone has to guard the safes. Such was the mission of the French SS, which Laval defined as "noble, and essentially French".'

> Hitler has helped them fulfil this task by draining the French working class with removals to Germany. The Gestapo is entrusted with the most advanced workers ....
>
> The workload thus shared, the adventurer Darnand and his thugs are little-worried about the identity of their future bosses. Germans, Americans, what does it matter? In either case the Milice is readying itself to re-establish order by bloodying the workers, whether in the name of National Socialism or of democracy. But this is one big programme for such a small force.

Very much unlike the fascists in the Northern Zone, who were completely isolated, the Milice had a certain base of support among reactionary Pétainist circles. But this base was diminishing.

The main reason for this was clear: the longer the war went on, the worse the poverty became. Shortages threatened to become famine. The effects of economic disorganisation were aggravated by German requisitions and Nazi pillage. This situation exacerbated 'anti-Boche' sentiment. *La Vérité* tried to show that the blame for this situation did not lay with the German people – hardly better off than the conquered peoples – but rather with fascism, war profiteers in all countries, and the capitalist system as a whole.

In early January 1943, *La Vérité* explained why the year began with 'the prospect of European famine'. It illustrated this with a revealing example:

> To get a proper idea of the food situation in Nazi Europe, it suffices to report on Goering's last speech. Goering boasted – as if it were some great success – of managing to maintain the nutrition of the German people. The Reichsmarschall, whose suggestion could serve as a demand on the Hitlerite régime, let it be known that he envisaged distributing to each soldier who crossed the border a ration of 'a kilo of flour, a kilo of bread or beans, a kilo of sugar, a pound of butter and a large, tough sausage'. This gift, which marks the triumph of Nazi idealism over Marxist materialism, is revealing indeed. While across Europe the profiteers of all nationalities regularly stuff themselves and are served the greatest feasts as before the war, it is deemed an exceptional recompense, worthy of 'heroes' on the Eastern Front and elsewhere, to receive these three kilos of the most basic staple foods and this sausage. That shows to what extent German people are truly benefiting from the Nazis' plunder.
>
> In reality, across the whole of Europe, the food situation can only worsen as long as the livelihoods and the bread of the people are in the hands of the capitalist consortiums of Germany and Europe, of which the fat and jolly Marshal Goering is the perfect representative.[323]

Against the famine threat *La Vérité* advanced its demands for popular control of food distribution, which it counterposed to individual attempts at sneaking resources. It popularised those struggles which took place. For instance, the 30 July 1943 edition reported on the struggle by the workers of Oullins for increased rations, the armed peasants in Gourin who forced the mill to grind their corn, and a housewives' demonstration in Kerhoun. This struggle was not only one for the towns: it was also that of 'working peasants', and in places peasants fought back:

In Plounevez and other communes in Finistère they took their pitchforks and forced the miller to grind the corn of their ration. The authorities, alerted, arrived flanked by a German detachment. The peasants demanded the Germans retreat. This demand satistfied, they then demanded a rise in their rations: given their threatening attitude, the sub-prefect was forced to give way.

La Vérité concluded:

In each commune [parish], we must unite all working peasants: farm labourers, tenant farmers, small and medium property-holders – in a Peasant Council which, via its delegates, will set the contribution of the commune and each different farm to the food stock; put on trial and punish black market traffickers; force the commune's rulings on the major property-holders by creating armed cells of a peasant militia; and organise distribution of food to the towns in partnership with delegates from workers' organisations.[324]

Chapter 6

WORKING-CLASS STRUGGLES AND THE ARMED STRUGGLE

Working-class struggles

Poverty was all the more unbearable given that, in spite of spiralling price increases, wages plateaued or even fell. At Chausson in Gennevilliers, for example, management announced the cancellation of the cost-of-living bonus. The workers forced them to keep it by taking strike action.[325] On 10 February the German authorities imposed a generalised pay cut in the building industry. This hit the lowest paid workers particularly hard (1.17% for foremen, 2.81% for builders' mates, 9.62% for labourers, 15.38% for the unskilled and up to 20% off the lowest salaries). 'The Germans' objective is to press more workers to seek employment on the Atlantic coast … where, in spite of the promises, living standards are even worse'.[326]

The same hierarchies were in effect in the engineering industry. An eighteen-year-old earnt twenty percent less than an adult; even a nineteen-year-old received ten percent less. Women only earnt eighty percent as much as their male equivalents, and only seventy percent outside of production.

Given these conditions, strikes were commonplace in spite of the terror. Each issue of the Trotskyist press, whether national or regional, covered these. It is necessary to be aware of the terrible conditions in which these strikes broke out. Two reports (among others) give some idea of this.

La Vérité reported:

Gennevilliers: in Carbonne, workers took strike action to secure a pay increase. The works committee resigned in solidarity with the strike movement. The Gestapo, alerted, surrounded the factory and took 21 hostages, whose fate is still unknown. The employees did not return to work until the Germans threatened to shoot the hostages.[327]

Le Soviet reported on a strike at Gnome et Rhône (Boulevard Kellerman, Paris):

> Management obstinately refused to settle back pay owed from June, so all the workshops walked out together. When the shifts changed over they passed the word on, so the strike held for two days in spite of management pressure to try to sow division. On the evening of the second day, the commissioner of the thirteenth *arrondissement* arrived at the factory accompanied by German soldiers armed with machine guns. They arrested ten workers and forced the others back to work. Triumphant, management continued to refuse to settle the back pay and tried to sow division in deciding to pay the work carried out immediately before and after the strike: as for workers paid by the hour … As the cops took our comrades away, the fascists of the MSR distributed their rag *Moteur* as the police looked on.[328]

La Vérité tried to draw lessons from these struggles in terms of their preparation, how they defined their demands, the tactical use of the trade union as a legal cover and the organisation of the best class fighters:

> 1. The preparation for strikes is almost always insufficient. Everywhere, workers' participation in strikes has been unanimous or near-unanimous; everywhere the most politically advanced workers have been in the vanguard. But, because they have not, in close unity, systematically prepared the demands for strikes, delegations to management, etc., they have been unable to act at the necessary movement with maximum effectiveness.
>
> 2. The trade unions have not been interested – or if they have, only belatedly – in supporting workers' demands and the strikes themselves. However, the trade union is the basis of workers' unity, even in current circumstances, affording the greatest scope for legal activity.
>
> 3. In almost all cases the bosses call on the German authorities. Thus it is not the [Vichyite] Labour Charter and its still-born organisations, but rather the Gestapo, which is the supreme arbiter: it has all the powers it needs, as the bourgeoisie has so long desired.
>
> But, victorious or not, a strike is an achievement, a step forward, if it has allowed for the strengthening of the working class's combativity, cohesion, and organisation. Even if forced to capitulate faced with Nazi machine-guns, a movement is not worthless
>
> – if the workers better understand that unity in a single workers' front

is the best lever of victory;

- if ten, five, or even two revolutionary workers get to know each other in the struggle, and unite in a workers' front group able to intervene as a conscious force in the class struggle. To these workers, the Parti ouvrier internationaliste says: Take courage! Only the workers' front, which has no interest but the long-term interests of the working-class, can transform defeats into fruitful experience and half-successes into decisive victories.[329]

The Trotskyists particularly addressed themselves to women workers, recently recruited into production work to replace men. According to *Lutte de classe*: 'Side by side with men, working women must take action against deportations. The strike weapon must be used in response to the raids.'[330]

La Vérité also addressed itself to women:

The struggle against speed-ups is of importance for the interests of the working class in general and also to women newly brought into industry. Machinery is poorly maintained. No-one should accept working with machines in such a poor state. Regular repairs are necessary – do not be afraid to demand them. It always means times saved, and workers must also concern themselves with their safety. Demand that safety measures are fulfilled.

However, the main effort must be to secure a statutory reduction in production quotas, without affecting wages. It is clear that a working woman cannot tolerate regular pay cuts. There is only one means of struggle: unity, the path of a workers' front. Sweatshop working hours been implemented, in changed working conditions. Without even mentioning the effect of malnutrition on one's physical strength (forgetting this can soon lead to illness), we must unwaveringly demand:

- That working hours for skilled workers are established. This demand can help achieve revised quotas, following modern timing systems. This can only be achieved if all workers are on their guard and do not let foremen, engineers and timekeepers intimidate them. Thus every class-conscious worker must constantly explain that:

- Not putting the brakes on work means prolonging the war, working against the USSR, and prolonging the imprisonment of husbands, sons, brothers and boyfriends;

- That the unity of all workers, a constant solidarity strengthening the workers' front, is the only means by which to struggle effectively.[331]

The Trotskyists incited mass sabotage but were hostile to terrorism which, with its purely military objectives, contrasted with the action of the masses. *Le Soviet* demonstrated this with the example of the Amiot factory:

SECI (Amiot). After bombs were left in the factory, 43 workers were arrested as hostages by the Gestapo as management sounded the alarm.

The so-called 'Communist' party has called on the workers to take strike action to win the freedom of the hostages, 'in the name of France'. With concerted action the workers at Amiot had successfully defeated deportations. But terrorist action causes disruption and prevents the growth of any movement. We are organising solidarity with our imprisoned comrades.[332]

At a basic level there was opposition between the PCF's attitude to working-class struggles and the Trotskyists' position. For the latter, struggles had to help the working class to attain consciousness of its class interests and organise for socialist revolution. In the PCF's eyes strikes and the workers' movement had to be integrated into 'the patriotic struggle'. Typical in this regard was the strike call issued by the PCF in the Southern Zone, in partnership with all of the Gaullist organisations, to commemorate the Battle of Valmy.

La Vérité commented:

Across the whole of the Southern Zone in late September there was intense propagandising to incite the workers to a large strike movement. The intention was to hold strikes as protest actions, as regards … the anniversary of the French victory over the Prussians at Valmy in 1791! … One might have thought there were some rather more 'current' reasons for taking strike action in 1943, for example famine wages, deportations, interminable shifts and the sabotage of civil rights. That is what our comrades tried to explain to the PCF comrades who have raised the idea of a strike. But for the PCF it had to be a 'patriotic' strike.

In reality the strike was almost everywhere a complete fiasco. In Marseille only a few workshops walked out. In Clermont-Ferrand leaflets called on the workers in the Michelin yards to demand, on the anniversary of Valmy, the liberation of two heroes of the patriotic struggle: the trade union rep, arrested as a Communist, and the proprietor Michelin himself, revered for his Gaullism. How surprising then then that not one worker – not even among the Parti communiste members – went on strike with such a slogan: to get the boss released. In Lyon workers refused to walk out in order to satisfy the patriotic appeal. The engineering workers once again showed that they were willing to take action for their own demands or in solidarity, as we saw in the 40,000 strong strike in the region last year. But they could not see either what purpose this strike served or what they would achieve with it. That is why none of them budged.[333]

La Vérité gave the example of the behaviour of the engineering workers at SIGMA in Lyon:

> In some workplaces however, the atmosphere was such that the men walked out. 'We could get them to walk out over anything', one comrade told us. The main factory that walked out was one of the strongest in Lyon, SIGMA. The strike spread from workshop to workshop even without the men knowing what the exact goal was. The situation was serious. Any strike without a precise objective would inevitably end up in fiasco. Defeat and unnecessarily-provoked repression would inevitably result in the exhaustion of workers' combativity. But, rather than letting the strike drape itself in the tricolour, revolutionaries restored its real purposeful character. They proposed to the workers to use as the strikes' demands the demands already presented to management on the occasion of 1 May.
>
> Thus the strike was no longer guided by nationalist motivations and its working-class character – which should never have gone away – was restored. The workers won on several key points, fighting class against class.[334]

This was a good example of the strategy which the Parti ouvrier internationaliste tried to put into effect in workplaces. Its militants would not refuse solidarity to any real workers' action, even if they criticised its objectives. They tried to turn actions away from nationalist objectives and put them back on a class-struggle terrain. Only rarely did they manage to achieve this.

The struggle against deportations of workers

The main driving force behind struggles, apart from wages, food, speed-ups and working hours, was the struggle against deportations. This struggle, immediately political in character, was continuous ever since the first 'draft'.

> 'We are deportees', the workers from Lille wrote on the carriages taking them to Germany. Exactly the right response to two years of terror, repression and propaganda from the press, the radio and the cinema. Still further they raised the slogans 'Down with Hitler! Down with Laval'

and 'We will make the revolution over there!'.

We could cover point-by-point Laval's speech on 20 October and the famous slogan 'The truth is that ...' and show the kind of answer the working class has given to these campaigns of shameful lies.

We have reported on the unanimous strike action in resistance to requisitioning in the factories. Perhaps we did not sufficiently cast the spotlight on the significance of the deportations in the first two-months of the so-called 'replacements', where the workers left with raised fists and singing the *Internationale.*

They can deport us, without rights and without guarantees, like criminals. We are not however defeated, because the hatred of fascism has increased further still, as has the hatred of war and the French exploiters who hand us over to the Nazi war machine. In January, with almost 200,000 more workers taken away, there will be 200,000 more enemies of the Nazis in Germany.[335]

La Vérité reported in each issue on young people's fight against the slavery being imposed on them. For example, in issue 43 (31 March) there was: a demonstration in Brest, on 4 March, of 300 young people singing the *Internationale* and the *Jeune Garde*; in Landerneau, a demonstration of 1,000 young people who forced the liberation of one of their arrested comrades; a demonstration of young peasants in Carnac; and in Sérignac – with a red flag at the head – the armed resistance of young people from the Thouars region ....

But even if there was a common struggle against deportations, even this revealed two different strategic orientations. For the Trotskyists, this fight was part of the struggle for European socialist revolution.

In their eyes, the struggle did not stop at national borders. Workers had to fight not to be taken away, particularly making use of strike action. But if they were indeed forced to leave (since whether directly or indirectly they would be forced to work for Hitler's war machine), they had to continue the struggle in Germany and associate with all European workers taken there, in the first instance the German workers. We have seen how *La Vérité* made an effort to give very precise ideas of how such joint action might be made possible. It continuously gave news on the struggles taking place there. These often resulted in demonstrations of class solidarity. For example, a strike that French workers initiated at the Lokomotiv Fabrik in Vienna on 14 July 1943 with 'patriotic' slogans, resulted in the singing of the *Internationale* by workers from all nations, particularly the Austrians. *Le Soviet*, which does not mention this incident, gave further news on the same factory:

Vienna – Locomotive factory. To protest about the rotten food they had been served, 700 to 800 workers stopped work and persisted in spite of an army intervention which left four wounded. Management was forced to negotiate with delegates chosen by the workers, who achieved a complete satisfaction of the workers' demands. This made a strong impression on the Austrian workers.[336]

La Vérité covered numerous examples of fraternisation. For example in Frankfurt in early September there was a demonstration of Belgian and French workers singing the *Internationale*, and on 15 September a large twenty-four hour strike at the Adler factory, in close collaboration with workers of all nationalities.[337]

Similarly, the regional press published letters from deported comrades. *Octobre* published a letter from Hamburg which concluded:

Many French workers are too inclined to nationalist and jingoist attitudes, while German workers show them the internationalist way. One among many examples: I was working with a German worker and asked him why he worked as little as possible. He replied: 'So that Hitler will not win the war'. Pointing to the workers of various nationalities gathered in the yard, he said, 'It is we who will win it'.[338]

Of course, this worker was not representative of the German working class. But even the Gaullists recognised that there was passive resistance opposed to the régime.

In the *Manuel du déporté en Allemagne*, published by Gaullist Resistance organisations, we read on page 6: 'Throughout the day the German workers will repeat '*Langsam*' (slowly). Seeing French workers working quickly is sickening for them. Deportee, act in solidarity with the German workers'.

La Vérité, quoting this text, commented:

See this from the Gaullists, confirming what we have always said and what comrades returning from Germany tell us.

The proletariat on the other side of the Rhine show no enthusiasm for working for the imperialist war. They sabotage more than a number of French workers, who ask for extra hours. They are against the Nazi régime.

But these democratic teachers tell us that they are waiting for *them* to chase out Hitler. We could retort: what about us? We must add: the German proletariat fears that defeat may mean poverty even worse than that which followed 1918, and the Nazi leaders never forget to dwell on this point in their speeches. Each time there are signs of disarray among the German masses, Goebbels takes to the microphone, and he finds that Churchill and Stalin give the Nazis their best arguments: the utterly reactionary plans for enslavement outlined by the Allies are for Hitler the best, the only, cement for 'morale'.

Under the title 'Nazi confessions', *Libération* of 30 October 1943 quoted extracts from an exposé of the gauleiter Richard Wagner: 'It is almost impossible to imagine what will become of the German people if it loses this war. Our men would be murdered or deported as slaves in their millions'.

These are not only the claims of Nazis, but also Gaullists. Using this title, *Libération* confirms that reducing the German people to slavery is indeed one of the Allied leaders' intentions. It is clear that with such seductive solutions on offer German workers can see no answer other than to continue the hopeless war.[339]

In the Trotskyists' eyes, the task was not to demoralise the German workers but rather to make them conscious of their strength. Indeed, for them the outcome of the European revolution would be decided in Germany: not only in terms of the strategic position of Germany or the traditions of its working class (even if most workers were mobilised), but also because the prodigious concentration of workers of all nationalities made it into a powder-keg.

Yet in reality the immigrant workers did not represent a powder-keg. Firstly because the strategy of the Allies – the USSR included – welded the German people to their state, and in such conditions foreign workers had no power. Secondly because each nationality focused on itself, and each individual too. There was a lack of communist cadre and the propaganda of the Communist Parties was counter to international solidarity.

For the PCF particularly, as with the Gaullist bourgeoisie, the struggle against the deportation of workers was part of the 'patriotic struggle'. 'To leave is to betray', declared the PCF-controlled *La Voix du peuple*. Attacking the Trotskyists, it explained:

A sole means, a sole method: resistance; and not that recommended by cowards and hermits, who claim that workers departing for Hitlerite prison camps can well enough continue the struggle over there by talking with the Germans and aggravating their demoralisation.

La Vérité polemicised in response to *La Voix du peuple*:

> As regards the workers departing for Germany, well, no: they did not *choose* deportation, they were not looking for some pretext. We have told them, and we do still now: resist as far as you can with all your strength! But if you must leave, then do not leave defeated, since there too the struggle against your oppressors continues, since they are also the oppressors of the German people.[340]

The mass of workers seized in the factories could not oppose the raids except through workplace struggle. This hard-fought struggle played – as it does now – an essential role in the growth of consciousness among workers. But, resisting deportations, it could only obtain partial successes. *La Vérité* recognised this:

> Even if the first strikes and first acts of collective resistance did not achieve all that might have been hoped for, it would be wrong to lose heart. This movement, uniting the proletariat in struggle, has won some victories. In many cases, for example, the lists (of deportees) have been cancelled and the deportations called off. In the main, the so-called replacements have considerably slowed down in the recent period. Moreover, the struggle continues in the factories of the Reich … and that is not the worst outcome or the smallest of opportunities.[341]

The limitations of the resistance to deportations to Germany were clear. The large majority of workers had families to care for and they needed their salaries for their kids to survive. When the movement did not achieve the cancellation of deportations orders, they were forced to leave. Only a small minority – largely young people – went underground.

Armed struggle and maquis

With the introduction of STO [Service de travail obligatoire; Compulsory labour service] in February 1943, the struggle against deportations took on a new character. The young people mobilised for STO were much freer in their movements. Draft-resisters fled to the country as agricultural labourers, or the forests as lumberjacks; or they camped or hid themselves at isolated farms. Even if they had not initially intended to get involved in armed struggle, they were quickly compelled to do so, even if just to defend themselves. They were forced to become maquis. The Gaullist and PCF Resistance forces did not have to create maquis so limited themselves to co-ordinating them and supplying them with cadres and weapons. The armed struggle had a mass character. Charles Tillon wrote with good cause:

> Until 1943, Resistance activists, particularly in the cities, lived in secret houses, with the exception of a few partisan groups formed during the 1942 draft. The proliferation of STO draft resisters in the early months of 1943, following the establishment of compulsory labour service, allowed the creation of maquis.[342]

The maquis represented a mass armed force, whose importance was ever-growing. They were the only effective armed response to the armed forces of imperialism, the reactionary government and the fascist and pro-fascist auxiliary forces. But how would they exercise this strength? Would the internationalists be able to make these maquis (or some among them) into a revolutionary force?

Only the 'ultra-left' and the CCI were uninterested in this matter. In neither the (very much reduced) press of the former, nor the literature or theses of the CCI can we find any reference to the maquis and the questions they posed: they did not correspond to their pre-established schemas.

The *Lutte de classe*, on the contrary, posed the question of the arming of the proletariat and the maquis. But it posed it in an abstract way:

> The bourgeoisie will be able to impose whatever it wants on the proletariat as long as it maintains a monopoly of arms. That is why workers, having no trust in the bourgeoisie's slogans, will work for the arming of the proletariat.[343]

The article continued:

> The workers' movement bureaucrats of all stripes who have made a career out of 'defending workers' rights' and who have accommodated themselves well to the domination of the working class, object that the arming of the proletariat could not be realised except in a 'revolutionary' situation. But when the proletariat is armed, the situation will clearly become revolutionary. The fierce, unbreakable desire of the workers to arm themselves as a class flows from the hopeless situation they have been plunged into by capitalist war, representing the only guarantee of their and their loved one's lives.

This was a theoretical approach. The hopeless situation in which young workers found themselves effectively forced them to get armed, and with them, young students, employees and peasants. But it was just them, for the moment. As for the Stalinists and reformists, they did not discourage this desire to take up arms. They encouraged it and tried, successfully, to channel it towards union sacrée with the bourgeoisie. This was the real problem of the maquis.

Lutte de classe could not simply sidestep this:

> The arming of the proletariat and the partisan struggle do not represent one and the same thing: they are even opposed. Partisan struggles are led by a *minority* of the working class mixed up with elements of other classes (and even avowed anti-proletarian forces, pro-British reactionaries and fascists and elements of the old army), they have the objective of military aid to the adversaries of the German army, and are under the control of parties hostile to proletarian revolution.

This meant that the orientation of the maquis was not in their nature (as regroupments of draft resisters) but rather the social weight of the political forces which controlled them. *Lutte de classe* moreover underlined the potential revolutionary strength of the maquis:

> Still, the minority of the working class which participates could provide valuable and experienced cadre for the working class, which devotes all its strength to getting armed, as long as it keeps faith in the historic fate of the proletariat, which must free humanity from capitalism and create socialist society.
>
> If we remember the example of the Paris Commune of 18 March 1871, which was the Paris population's response to the bourgeoisie who tried to disarm them, conscious workers will awaken in the hearts of all workers the ardent desire to become a force by taking up arms, following Blanqui's famous words, 'He who has iron, has bread!'.

The Parti ouvrier internationaliste initially posed the question in a largely similar manner. The editorial of *La Jeune Garde* in March 1943 called for struggle against the STO in a similar manner to the struggle against the draft: sabotaging deportations, organising collective resistance, and, if one had to leave, continuing the struggle in Germany. But at the same time it stressed military questions. The article 'Long live the Red Army of the international working class' focused on the emergence of Red Guards in Russia and their policy of fraternisation with the German troops they were fighting in Ukraine. An article on 'bourgeois armies' stressed the weaknesses which allowed them to be pulled apart. Finally, an article on 'workers' militias' concluded:

> This time [factory] occupations will have to face the fascist gangs of Déat, De Gaulle and Giraud. Waiting until the last minute to organise resistance would mean risking defeat. Starting now, in every workplace and in every district, workers must diligently organise themselves. This must involve drills and exercises in discipline and in the theory and maintenance of weapons in small groups, careful but resolute. These nuclei will tomorrow staff the Red Militia, which will assume a class character. In no way must this militia become the instrument of a party, but rather the organ of the revolutionary proletariat. All revolutionary workers must find a home there, without distinction of political tendency. Officers at all levels will be elected, and subject to replacement if need be. As an expression of the working class and thus needing the total confidence of the masses, the Red Militia, the weapon of the revolutionary workers' front, will defend workplaces and communities against fascist attacks and will organise the proletariat in struggle for the seizure of power.[344]

The same ambiguities as in *Lutte de classe* were apparent. *La Jeune Garde*'s answers were general and theoretical, calling for the proletariat to arm itself and organise in workplaces. But this did not correspond to the time, nor the experience of the working masses, nor even their potential. Workplaces could not put up a working-class armed force to confront fascist forces. Only politicised nuclei of workers could be armed. But they would necessarily intervene from the outside, providing protection: as indeed certain FTP groups did.

The essential question was sidestepped: the draft resisters were arming and organising militarily, so could revolutionaries unite their struggles with those of workers in the towns and countryside and on the basis of socialist objectives?

An abortive effort to build a revolutionary maquis in Haute-Savoie

The Central Committee of the POI tried to respond to this concern. But it faced significant difficulties. The Trotskyist movement's strategy relied on an international perspective (the key to revolution was in Germany) and in all countries was based in the cities. Given this strategy, armed forces based in the countryside and in the mountains could only play an auxiliary role. The second difficulty related to the political balance of forces and above all the fact that the arms and food supplies were essentially supplied by the

Allies: not only were the revolutionaries against the political stream but they could not materially aid the maquis except by signing up to the union sacrée, which they refused to do.

The third difficulty related to the organisation's own weaknesses: it seemed impossible to turn a significant portion of their meagre numbers to the maquis. Moreover, very few among its activists had military experience, particularly directly useful experience such as participation in the Spanish civil war.

However, the Central Committee was aware of the importance of the question. It sent Yvan Craipeau to the Southern Zone to make contact with Youth Hostellers organising draft resisters in Haute-Savoie. The objective was to establish a revolutionary maquis and a school of party military cadres in the Thonon region. Youth Hostel activists were sympathetic to the Fourth International and conscious of the need for a revolutionary perspective. They were all the more keen to collaborate with the POI when the Allies made clear that they refused to support them. Thus an in-principle agreement was concluded.

La Vérité published an editorial elaborating its orientation:[345]

> In Haute-Savoie, some workers have fled the pseudo-draft and have taken refuge in the mountains. A full train which was to leave from Annecy, taking 530 conscripted workers to Germany, remained at the station and only 36 people were deported. Many were later seized from their homes without warning, but a sizeable proportion were able to escape with the aid of locals.
>
> Young people have entered the struggle. In Thonon a third of the recruits who had been conscripted turned up for the medical inspection. Hostility is ever-increasing. Young people have taken to the mountains to escape the raids and defend themselves: the first who received his travel pass alerted others and they all went to a chalet already supplied with food and arms. Contacts were established with other groups: parents, friends and the whole population participate in resistance by sending supplies, keeping totally silent during police investigations, and via solidarity collections.
>
> The Vichy collaborators did not expect this. The police, not enthusiastic about following Nazi orders and affected by the deaths of two too-zealous Milice members, is moreover powerless away from the main roads. Faced with this reality, Laval has tried to make a compromise. Those who have let themselves get taken in by his honeyed words have learnt to their cost that it is costly to believe the promises of a horse-

trader. Many preferred to defend their freedom, knowing that it is up to them to organise resistance and co-ordinate action in all its forms in struggle against the Nazi apparatus, maintaining contact with strikers in the towns and peasants pillaged during the raids.

Meanwhile British imperialism, in suddenly desisting from all propaganda in their favour in the press and on the radio, has also taught them a valuable lesson. If the RAF and its parachutists do nothing when they could be providing them with arms, food and munitions, this is because Churchill and his clique are afraid of bolstering the authentically revolutionary movement in Haute-Savoie (much as they are afraid to land in a country where the proletarian revolution could accompany the defeat of fascism). The movement in Haute-Savoie worries Churchill as well as Laval. This is important. To be victorious the oppressed need rely on nothing but their own forces, discipline and unity.

'What is taking place in Savoie is already being repeated in other areas. We hear, for example, that in Limousin other young people have taken to the maquis and are leading the same struggle as the insurgents in Thonon. The latter have proven that the struggle against deportations must continue.

Taking up arms they have shown that the struggle against deportations is a revolutionary struggle which must conclude with the wiping-out of the oppressors and exploiters of Germany, France and the whole world.

The exceptionally favourable circumstances (mountain terrain, the proximity of the Swiss border, etc.) have at the same time pointed to the limitations of this form of struggle. They have been cut loose by the Anglo-Americans.

They have not been supported by the camp of military revanchism and reactionary Gaullism (the infamous General Cartier sits warming his feet by the fireplace); they cannot count on anyone but themselves, the local population, and the working class who in France and Germany alike are leading the same struggle in different form.

The Gaullists and the maquis

But *La Vérité* was wrong to place so much hope in such a contingent situation: the absence of political and material support for the maquis from London and Algiers. In reality the bourgeoisie understood perfectly how to play its cards. It worked to integrate the draft resisters' struggle into its own political and military strategy.

This was simple. It demanded that the masses renounced any independent initiative and silently let the army assure the substitution of Anglo-American 'order' for Nazi rule. Charles Tillon summarised this objective:

> [...] the political and military high command of the western coalition, for their part, did not want to accord the French any rights except to tolerate – and suffer – everything in the name of the demands of the war.[346]

As they sought to prevent any revolutionary upheaval, their strategy was an exact negative of that of the Trotskyists:

1. Like the Nazis they sought to empty the large population centres. British radio repeated this idea. Tillon commented how 'on 12 May 1944 a representative of the Comité français de la libération nationale called on young people to leave the towns, particularly Paris'.
2. The general application of this demand to all towns in reality had the objective of separating the French Forces of the Interior (FFI) and armed combatants from the civilian population.
3. Recognising the impossibility of preventing the existence of an army of 'irregulars', they sought to place it under the command of the traditional high command. 'What they wanted was to placed the FFI under their command, separate them from the masses and paralyse the popular insurrection.'[347]
4. For these reasons the high command refused arms to the maquis that were outside its control, or did so only sparingly.
5. Finally, they preferred to control large maquis where traditional methods of combat could be employed or high command control exercised directly, regardless of the number of victims.

The Parti communiste, as we will see later,[348] tried to oppose this orientation. But its differences were tactical and it gave guarantees on the basic themes. It wanted to make use of the strength of the forces it controlled, but in no way did it intend to follow the Yugoslav example. The insurrection it planned was a 'patriotic' one which would not question the social order. Even retrospectively Charles Tillon stressed this strongly. In his history of the FTP not one line hints at revolutionary objectives. The ideology projected by the FTP was that of bourgeois chauvinism ('Death to Boches!') and the necessity of union sacrée. Hopes of revolution were not entertained except in a few maquis, such as that of [Georges] Guingouin in Limousin, which were held in suspicion. Contrary to Tito, the PCF was faithful to Stalin's line and the accords he had concluded with the Allies. Far from fighting France's Mikhailovich,[349] De Gaulle, they placed themselves under his leadership.

The Allies were in control of the situation. Thus their hesitations did not last for more than a few weeks. They 'supported' the maquis in their own way, selectively supplying them with arms.

For the revolutionary militants of Haute-Savoie, this material support, even if it was mediocre, counted for more than their political sympathies. The organisation's initiatives for a revolutionary maquis were ultimately unsuccessful. The Haute-Savoie militants joined the FTP, whereas some left in order to maintain links with the POI.

Military measures

Soon after this failure, the Fifth Congress of the POI, which took place in June 1943, was vague on the question of organising draft resisters:

> The workers' front counterposes, as against the mobilisation of the masses under the flag of imperialism and the command of reactionary officers, the slogan of workers' militia and the arming of the proletariat. Starting now it will take the proper technical measures to ensure its achievement.[350]

So what were these 'technical measures?'

Firstly this meant reorganising the military apparatus of the party. Its immediate objective was still to get hold of food ration cards, official papers and the necessary funds – at the expense of the official and fascist organisations. But it was given a second objective: commencing the training of armed groups in towns and workplaces. Subsequently they approved the publication of a monthy newspaper for propaganda and building ties with the maquis and the FTP, *Ohé! partisans*. The first issue appeared in May. It was printed across eight pages and bore the legend 'Better to die on your feet than live on your knees'.

The discussions it developed, based on concrete circumstances, were those as expressed in *La Vérité*'s article: 'Draft-resisters! Your arms must serve the socialist liberation of Europe.'[351]

The POI would work to co-ordinate the activity of revolutionaries within the FTP, notably in Haute-Savoie, in the Paris region, in Brittany, the Loire and the Oise.[352]

Finally, the POI should try to create Red Militia groups in the cities, particularly Paris, in winning over the existing armed groups politically. But this initiative would be in vain. In January 1944, while trying to establish links with one of these groups – whose representatives could not make the rendez-vous because they had just been arrested – Paul Parisot, one of the leaders of the POI, was arrested, while Yvan Craipeau escaped wounded from the French Gestapo.

In early 1944 the Nazis unleashed a general offensive against the maquis. *La Vérité* appealed for solidarity.[353] The article stressed that a struggle between the oppressed and the bourgeois state was underway, and that in this struggle workers could only count on themselves.

> For sure, the maquis will not fall amid the provocations by engaging in pitched battles (contrary to the Algiers high command's strategy). They will adopt the tactic of the partisans: they will disperse before the fascist enemy and appear again behind them.

But the dangers were considerable. The only effective response would be to unleash strike action to force Darnand to 'quickly rein in his guard-dogs in the cities'. But workers had been demobilised by adventurist strikes. *La Vérité* gave advice on how to aid the draft resisters and concluded:

> Where Darnand disperses the maquis draft resisters, they should regroup in and around the factories, the most solid bastions of the working class. It is in the factories that we must begin to arm ourselves, clandestinely. We must give military training to the most combative workers. This is an important task incumbent on workers' groups in workplaces, where workers will have to find arms for their own struggles.
>
> When that happens, they will settle accounts with killers like Darnand, his police and his state … and his commander, the French ruling class.

The European Secretariat's resolution on the 'partisan movement'

In December 1943 the European Secretariat of the Fourth International adopted a position which echoed that of the POI, and which was affirmed by the next European conference.

> Given the character of the partisan movement – part of it spontaneous – as an expression of the inevitable open revolt of wide layers of the working class against German imperialism and against the state established by the indigenous bourgeoisie – in their eyes personifying those guilty for their current poverty and suffering – the Bolshevik-Leninists are obliged to seriously address the masses' desire to resist, and task themselves with directing it towards class-struggle objectives in spite of the various dangers engendered by the nationalist expressions of this struggle.

We might note the expression 'are obliged', which underlines how little initiating role the Bolshevik-Leninists had in the partisan organisations. The resolution goes on to distinguish the mass partisan organisations from 'irregular forces created by nationalist or Stalino-patriotic organisations' in the recent past: it stresses the danger the revolutionary movement saw in the latter. 'But such an attitude [on the part of the Bolshevik-Leninists] has been shown to be absolutely insufficient when the partisan movement takes on a mass character.'

This was, for instance, the case in the Balkans, for geographical, economic and historic reasons, and in the west, starting with the massive deportation of the workforce to Germany.

In this situation, like in Yugoslavia, the partisan movement could offer effective support to the USSR and most importantly allow for the armed masses' entry onto the political stage:

> mobilising a significant section of the active forces of working-class and petty-bourgeois youth; [the participation of the masses] poses the burning question: will these youth foment the revolution or bolster the utterly reactionary forces of imperialism?

Amid the chaos, even 'these small armies' could play a decisive strategic role.

Curiously, the resolution made only a single allusion to the people's armies in Yugoslavia – which by late 1943 were not 'small armies' any more, having disarmed twelve Italian divisions and, to cries of 'Death to fascism! Free the people', liberated most of the territory (Macedonia, southern and western Serbia, Sandjak, Montenegro, most of Bosnia-Herzegovina and part of Slovenia). This was not only a struggle against German and Italian divisions, but also the nationalist and pro-British Chetnicks lead by Mikhailovich. In Yugoslavia, as in Albania and even in Greece, the red partisans started to resolve – militarily – the question of political power.[354]

The resolution answered not the demands of this struggle of the peoples of the Balkans, but rather the more modest struggle of partisans in the west. It stressed that they must:

- play the role of armed detachments in the service of the proletarian revolution and of vanguard of the workers' militias, and not auxiliaries to the imperialist army;
- organise wherever possible in an autonomous manner on a democratic basis, to the exclusion of all bourgeois and reactionary elements;

- organise themselves in the ranks of the military organisations established by the union sacrée... a clandestine faction with its own discipline;

- reject the policy of assassinating German soldiers;

- support workers' struggles... link the partisan struggle to the workplace struggle... support the training of working-class military cadres and the general arming of workers and peasants;

- participate in the class struggle in the countryside... any idea of stealing from the working peasantry must be relentlessly opposed;

- organise propaganda for fraternisation with the occupation troops and open up their ranks to German deserters;

- train working-class activists through the study of Marxism and political discussions.[355]

Taking this belated stance was essentially a theoretical endeavour. Unwilling – or unable – to engage sufficient forces, the Troskyists remained extremely weakly implanted in partisan groups in France and elsewhere.

Moreover, CCI members were more than slightly reticent about this position. Their fusion with the POI in 1944 again put the brakes on its efforts to apply the International's stance. The consequences of this failure were all-important.

L'Insurgé and the maquis

We have stressed the difficulties Trotskyist militants faced in engaging in the maquis' action, given that their general strategy could only incorporate it to a marginal degree.

But the 'centrist' strategy, which on the contrary was based on the Resistance and indeed was deeply embedded in it, reached the same impasse. Activists of the *L'Insurgé* group participated in armed groups and the maquis as individuals, and formed their own maquis in the Annecy area.[356]

In theory, *L'Insurgé* had an understanding of the maquis similar to that espoused by *La Vérité*:

> Indeed the maquis represent a significant revolutionary potential. Here can be found a magnificent youth, ardent and courageous. Above all it depends on the workers' movement, and the politics it decides to follow, to ensure these young people are not the 'veterans' of the future, in the image of those so easily duped in the last war, nor 'reprobates' like the German Freikorps of 1919, but rather the heroic vanguard of the coming revolution.[357]

It stressed that the maquis could only play this role if they were tied to the whole popular movement, 'particularly the actions led by workers'. 'Without this condition – Lenin noted in a September 1906 article devoted to partisan struggles – all forms of struggle within bourgeois society, left to themselves and the spontaneous course of events, get worn down, perverted and sold out.'

Thus the slogan 'Faced with repression: from the countryside to the factory, one sole maquis!'.[358]

As regards putting their politics into action, *L'Insurgé* militants appeared to hold a certain number of trump cards. *L'Insurgé* circulated not only in the Annecy maquis, but also in the ranks of the FTP and other armed groups in the Southern Zone, as almost all the regions covered in *le Mémorial* suggest. However, they nowhere managed to change the course of events. The reports in *le Mémorial* do not mention a single town or a single case where their intervention altered whatever orientation and action the maquis had already pursued, including during the Liberation.

Readers of *L'Insurgé* found in its pages nothing but a variant of Gaullist material. Its activists were the hostages of the bourgeois and Stalinist strategy which made the maquis into an auxiliary wing of the imperialist war effort. In spite of the doubts it expressed regarding participation in the union sacrée – which for the time being was accepted as unavoidable – it was nonetheless its prisoner. After the Liberation they conceded that they had been duped, 'With Liberation our movement was left by the wayside', Marie-Gabriel Fugère bitterly commented.

Their tactics did not allow them to change the balance of forces, which in the last analysis was what mattered most.

The dissolution of the Communist International

On 15 May, as the 'Trident' conference between Roosevelt and Churchill took place in Washington, Soviet radio announced the dissolution of the Third International.

The 24 May *La Lutte de classe* commented on this event in a special issue:

> At a time when the world imperialist war has reached a decisive phase, 'sensational news' spread in the last forty-eight hours by all of the world's press and radio – including those of the USSR – has struck proletarians in all countries with amazement and confusion: Stalin has dissolved the Communist International and recommended that its member parties subordinate their action to the activity of the Allied governments in the struggle against Hitler.

Axis propaganda has pushed the idea that this news is a 'bluff' and 'grotesque manoeuvre'; Allied propaganda has exalted the 'historic significance' of the event.

Stalin has dissolved Lenin's International, thus ceding to the pressure of American and British imperialism. The news of the dissolution of the Comintern was announced immediatedly after a representative of Roosevelt's visit to Stalin and before the conclusion of the Anglo-American political and military conference in Washington....

La Lutte de classe published an 'Appeal to the Communist workers':

In the middle of the imperialist war and under the pressure of the London and Washington capitalists, Stalin – who long ago transformed the Third International from the instrument of world communist revolution into a pawn of diplomatic exchange, has *disavowed the International itself* as an instrument of liberating humanity from war and oppression.

Such are the delights of the 'democratic' imperialist camp which proclaims the bankruptcy of the proletarian International and exalts the 'everlasting' (capitalist) homeland! And Stalin made sure to declare to the Reuters agency in Moscow that the 'dissolution of the International [...] prepares the way for the association of peoples based on equality.'

The pretentions of the 'democratic' imperialists and their bag-carrier Stalin are shameless lies. Where is the worker who does not know that the International was created precisely with the objective of *realising this emancipation*, to realise equality between all nations, as well as the emancipation of the proletariat from the bourgeoisie. Where is the communist militant who does not know that the very foundation of Leninism is the *incompatibility* of modern capitalism (imperialist monopoly capitalism) with the 'association of peoples based on equality?' Have the imperialist war of 1914-18 and the present imperialist war not demonstrated this incompatibility in practice? Can the victory of one imperialist camp over the other (the Allied victory in 1918, Hitler's victory in 1940) mean anything other than reinforced exploitation of the proletariat and the oppression of weaker nations by the bourgeoisie and the stronger imperialist powers? Was not our whole struggle until now intended to demonstrate precisely that only *proletarian internationalism* – whose instrument is the International – can allow for all workers to really have their own country? That the homeland where workers are exploited by capital and could die from hunger is the homeland of capitalism and not their own? That the only basis for the fraternal union of peoples would be the Socialist United States of Europe and the World, and not of isolated and enemy capitalist 'homelands'? In dissolving the so-called Third International to show that 'Bolshevism' will not interfere with each nation's affairs, has not Stalin thus passed into the camp of those who pour calumny on proletarian internationalism?

The imperialist brigands have celebrated their victory too soon. Like in the monarchies of centuries past, in our times internationalism will never die out, because the struggle between classes has not stopped. The dead Third International will be succeeded by the Fourth International.[359]

La Lutte de classe devoted numerous issues to the dissolution of the Communist International and a more theoretical retrospective on 'From the First to the Fourth [International]'.[360]

La Vérité covered similar themes:

On 1st November 1914 Lenin issued his first call for the formation of a Third International. On 15 May 1943, Stalin liquidated the Comintern. Nothing could better illustrate the chasm which divides the two men and their politics [...]

Today, after three years of a second world war, at the very moment when the first waves of a new revolutionary tide are starting to roll around the world, Stalin has broken the organisation supposed to be the instrument of working-class emancipation. Is it not the most terrific display of weakness, the most damning indictment against him, that he should be reduced to such a monstrous 'compromise', renouncing communist propaganda across the world at the same time as he authorises Catholic propaganda in the USSR? American imperialism has gripped the USSR by the throat.[361]

The Communist International justified its dissolution by saying that the Communist Parties, having become significant in themselves, could in any case elaborate their politics without international direction. 'This is, in truth, the most miserable of opportunist sophistry', *La Vérité*'s editorial retorted:

The revolutionary International is not the aggregation of independent national parties: it is a *world* party; it can unite the one and only *world* working class, the proletariat, against *world* imperialism and against finance capital, the *world* master of production and exchange, responsible for the *world* crisis and the *world* war; it struggles for the *world* republic of soviets and the *world* revolution.

Precisely the point, however, is that these were not the objectives of the Communist International. That is why it dissolved, like the Second International in 1914.

Nevertheless, *La Vérité* emphasised that the Soviet bureaucracy had not for a moment ceased to 'use the Communist Parties in its diplomatic games [...] to exert pressure on the capitalist governments'. But these were parties integrated into their own nations' bourgeois community.

La Vérité addressed the allegations in the German press according to which the Fourth International would be Stalin's replacement vehicle, allowing him to pursue his objective of world revolution. 'The Fourth International's time has now come [...] The time has come for it to move from purely theoretical work to everyday struggle, to the leadership of the masses, for the seizure of power.'

In July, *La Vérité* revisited the immediate consequences of the dissolution:

> The Parti socialiste, which is a member of the Socialist International and which has never acted on an international plane, particularly in terms of the struggle against war, 'welcomed the dissolution of the Comintern and saw it as the prelude to the integration of the USSR into the international community; it expressed its wish that the [Parti communiste] should become a loyal part of the national community'. To put it another way: it was eager to forget 'demagogic agitation' and the German-Russian pact, as long as the Parti communiste renounced revolutionary objectives.
>
> However, the Communist workers are not always of the same opinion: there are stormy debates, particularly in the legal parties, such as in Britain and Sweden. In Switzerland the split among the Stalinists and pro-Stalinists is almost a fait accompli: the opportunists around Nicolle approve of the dissolution; there are those around the Zimmerwald organiser Grimm who see it as treachery; Humbert-Droz, a former member of the Communist International executive, left the Swiss [Communist Party] and joined the Socialist Party. The Australian [Communist Party], which in 1939 formed a united front with our comrades, has now disavowed Stalin, as has the Unified Socialist Party of Catalonia (which had been a section of the Third International). These are just the first echoes of the crisis which will soon expose Stalinism as an ideology unrepresentative of the proletariat.[362]

La Lutte de classe and *La Vérité* overestimated the shockwaves the dissolution of the International would have within the Parti communiste.

The news only affected a small minority of old comrades for whom the International meant something. For the large majority, 'proletarian internationalism' was identified with the 'defence of the USSR', meaning, the politics of its leaders. Increasingly, for them this 'defence of the USSR' seemed to be a necessary (and complementary) part of their own 'patriotic' and 'national' struggle. The dissolution of the International, long ineffective, was in line with the nationalist ideology which was more and more their own, given that their party recruited on this basis.[363]

In the prisons and the camps

The POI constantly made attempts to realise unity in action with Communist workers. In July 1943, for example, in a 'Letter to a Communist worker', it addressed the slogan of 'popular committees' raised by the PCF in workplaces and proposed to make this a common endeavour, bringing together workers of all tendencies and the most combative unorganised workers on a class basis.

> If a popular committee in the workplace is nothing but a cell of your party, it loses its purpose and will only respond to the directives set by your own leaders. But the task is to bring together a real popular committee. That means not only opening the doors to representatives of workers' organisations, but further still, staff in the workplace who are not yet organised politically or in the union.
>
> These are problems for the whole working class. The best activists, without party distinction, should meet and discuss. You, ourselves, and others, must discuss together in the popular committees and together find practical solutions for all the problems of everyday struggle.

But the divide opened between the two orientations rendered unity in action practically impossible. Indeed preventing political discussion was among the objectives of the PCF leadership, and it did so by threatening violence in relations with the 'Trotskyists'.

This violence was most sharply felt when one might have expected the greatest degree of solidarity: in the prisons and the concentration camps.[364] Demazière has recounted how an old comrade, at that time the only Trotskyist detainee at the Puy-en-Velay prison, Maurice Ségal (alias Salini), was destroyed:

> From the outside the Stalinists received an order to boycott the Trotskyists. They succeeded in keeping up this discipline. In his dorm

even his oldest comrades, those who he had been sharing his cell with for months, did not say a single word to him. They did not share their rations with him and accepted nothing from him. Under the gaze of the jailers, their imprisoned comrades' watchword was to ignore his presence and tacitly exclude him from the community. On the first day, he asked one of his fellow prisoners, a peasant from Limousin with whom he had previously had good relations, what the reason for this new attitude was. As the old man had expected, they replied only with 'We're following orders', (and would not say anything else to him after). The organisers of their group went to the prison director asking for him to be removed from their dorm,'He is a Trotskyist: he is not a patriot'. That was it: Salini did not want to smile; he did not want to eat; he could not keep himself up; often he felt his mind going haywire: he asked himself what would have come of him if the others had not then arrived.[365]

Indeed, then four other Trotskyist activists from Marseille and Lyon were transferred to the same prison, including Blasco [Pietro Tresso]: 'Blasco had seen many others', Demazière wrote. 'He had saved his skin from the Stalinists almost as many times as from the fascists.'

However the two communities could live side by side by ignoring each other.

Things went a little differently in the concentration camps. It is difficult to tell the number of Trotskyist deportees who were taken there, but without doubt there were over a hundred by late 1943.

The Trotskyists were, moreover, among the first to report on events at the Auschwitz camp. A worker who managed to escape – an extremely rare feat – wrote a forceful, unemotional and concise report published in *La Vérité*, 'There is a crematorium'.[366]

The Communist MP Grenier reproduced large extracts of this on radio transmissions from London (without citing the source, of course) but removed all reference to the presence of Germans in the camp:

> Fernand Grenier has simply expurgated this text of anything which might trouble the poisonous chauvinist propaganda. He has passed over in silence the fact, described by the worker who drew up the text, that there are also Germans in Auschwitz. Grenier does not want it to be said that the German people is also an oppressed people, and that a real revolution can only be brought about by the unity of all the oppressed and exploited.[367]

In the camps, the German communists often worked with the Trotskyists, whose internationalism they appreciated. This was demonstrated in David Rousset's *Les jours de notre mort*, which portrays the activism of a dozen Trotskyist militants, often using their real first names (Roland, Philippe, Marcel, Armand, etc.) The atrocious conditions in which they were held meant the French Stalinists were often unable to carry through their boycott. Moreover, certain among the Trotskyist prisoners, for instance the electrician Roland Filiâtre, held such influence and authority that they were invulnerable to attack.

The Stalinists even conferred roles in the camp political organisation on certain among the Trotskyists, regardless of their affiliations. This was the case with Armand (alias Beaufrère) in Buchenwald. Yet on one occasion Armand alluded to Trotsky's *History of the Russian Revolution*, and even suggested the need for a new International:

> Here at Buchenwald our everyday existence poses the question of internationalism. Our concern is with the whole of Europe. The problem of how it ends – how all this rubbish will end – poses the question of international organisation.
>
> Without doubt, but not necessarily the Fourth International, the Stalinist organiser replies. Now the discussion is curt. Armand is removed from his role.[368]

In the camps, the hostility against Trotskyists was not always limited to ostracism. Where the Stalinists held sway they used it to put their rivals on the transportations lists. Indeed in Buchenwald Trotskyist militants accused a Stalinist of having denounced their comrades to the Gestapo. A later investigation confirmed this suspicion. But in the meantime the Stalinists had managed to get Trotskyists sent to Dora, the salt mines from which few returned. The rivalry was a matter of life and death.

The murder of Blasco and his comrades[369]

They decided that the next step was to resort to murder, pure and simple. Death and apparent fraternity came side-by-side. We have noted that there were five Trotskyist inmates in the Puy-en-Velay prison in summer 1943: Salini (alias Maurice Ségal), Albert Demazière (alias Granet), Jean Reboul, Abraham Sadek (from Lyon) and Pietro Tresso (alias Blasco). Pietro Tresso was one of the founders of the Italian Communist Party, not long ago a friend of Gramsci's, member of its politburo and organiser of clandestine activity in Italy. In 1930 he broke with the Stalinist faction led by Togliatti (alias Ercoli) and joined the Left Opposition. He was a remarkable working-class fighter, as much for his humanism as for his intelligence and courage.

In 1942 he was sentenced to ten years' forced labour by the Vichy courts. By 1943 he was fifty years old. An attempt to break him out of prison had failed.

On the night of 1-2 October 1943, partisans in the region mounted a surprise raid on the Puy prison to liberate the 90 political prisoners there. They also decided to free the Trotskyists (indeed, Demazière indicated in his initial report that one among the maquisards was a Trotskyist). *La Vérité* featured a report welcoming this raid[370]. Demazière's later report read:

One evening they heard a noise. 'Granet', a voice whispered: and he slowly got up and approached the door.[371] Through the crack he saw the face of Chapelle, a rather sympathetic young man who had recently arrived in the prison. 'This evening we're leaving the camp. Get dressed, quietly, one after the other, then get back under the covers. Get your kit together and pack your food. Nothing else. When you hear the clock strike eleven, be ready. When someone knocks on the door, get into single file and wait. Good luck!'.

Granet listened in silence, not asking any questions. If the noise of an escape had reached even them, then perhaps the guards were staging some sort of provocation. Wasn't it true that there had been GMR[372] soldiers in the prison courtyard for the last two months, two posts each staffed by three men armed with machine guns?

One after the other, the men got up, got dressed, rolled up their blankets and lay down again. The last to get up, Salini, the thriftiest of the cellmates, had four rations of sugar left... Nine o'clock ... Ten o'clock ... In the cell, everywhere, silence: hope of freedom had filled the prison. There was neither enthusiasm nor too much anxiety... Reboul kept watch over the courtyard through the bars. He whispered to his companions, 'They are checking their machine guns'; they could hear the metal clinking. Were the GMR on a state of alert? Finally, Granet heard the clock strike eleven. All four rose, and Granet held his ear to the door. First a rustling noise, then the sound of one, two doors opened. Soft steps on the stairs leading to the first floor. Granet counted the seconds in his head. When he reached 700, he again heard the sound of more footsteps, still furtive, but without doubt feet shoed with sandals, the feet of comrades... The latch was pulled and a voice called out: 'Are you ready?' – yes, they were ready!... One after the other, the doors of all the cells opened like at the end of a ballet. The prisoners emerged, pale, bearded, their heads shaved, smiling but silent. The ballet reached its finale as the occupants of one wing saw, facing them, the occupants of the opposite wing. Granet recognised on the bridge above him Sadek, a party comrade who was supervising the operation, machine gun in hand. No-one spoke. Granet assumed that the prison personnel had still not been neutralised. With good reason: arriving with an armed escort, revolvers hanging from their waists, were one, two, three, four guards. The prison director followed. His bald head fuming, he was wearing his uniform jacket over his ridiculous pyjamas. All these gentlemen were now in turn locked up, without anyone feeling the need to comment. Quickly the prisoners found their voice again. The groups which had been standing still in front of the cells now dispersed. Radiant with joy, Granet tightly embraced Blasco, who he had not seen since their transfer to the prison. He shook his hand, many hands which were held out. He learnt that the maquisards had surrounded the prison and were keeping a strong guard over it.

[…] Granet soon saw Marval strangely kitted out: his arms full of various weapons. Taking time to choose, he handed Granet a gendarme's revolver, with the waist belt and everything ….

Finally, they left. One by one the escaped prisoners passed through the gate: a chain of partisans pointed the way out through the darkness towards the road and the trucks. Without even seeing him, Granet could tell Blasco was to his left, and in front he could make out Reboul. Soon enough, the dark convoy of trucks were within reach.

The prisoners were separated out into groups – and among them, the Trotskyist militants. One day, Demazière and two PCF members got lost and could not find their maquis again. Assisted by Resistance-supporting teachers in the Ardèche and subsequently the Resistance in the Drôme, who supplied him with false papers, Demazière crossed the border into the Northern Zone and returned to Paris to resume his responsibilities in the party.

As for the others, they stayed with the maquis in Queyrrière, whose leader was Vial (alias Massat), who was later a member of the PCF Central Committee[373]. An old farmer expressed his astonishment:

I saw the escaped prisoners arrive. They had long beards and bloodied feet, dying of fatigue. I was surprised to see the young people who for some time had been involved in the maquis leading them along, revolver in hand. A funny way to welcome them.[374]

Doctor Schmirer, a Socialist activist in the Resistance, wrote:

> I learnt by pure chance from an FTP partisan returning from the Haute-Loire, as you know, that Tresso was with this maquis along with certain among his former prison cell-mates. He continued to be considered suspect and treated as a prisoner. Thus I begged the comrades, and also an MLN leader, to try and secure his freedom, but I believe they were unable to do so.[375]

Various testimonies suggest that when he was with the maquis, Tresso had problems with his lungs: including that of Marc Bloch, who visited the camps in the region shortly before being shot by the Gestapo. According to an article in the Italian Communist Party magazine *Rinascita*, this was how the French Communists explained Blasco's death to an Italian Communist official.

But the other Trotskyists in the camp – Sadek, Reboul and Salini – also disappeared without trace. Not all these deaths were due to lung problems.

According to all the evidence, the only serious explanation is that advanced in the Puy police commissioner's report of 1945: an account which, moreover, correlates with what locals reported: 'It was to do with their Trotskyism. They were executed as traitors. The Puy police commissioner's report was right'[376].

This was how the Stalinists – without doubt, following orders from their superiors – murdered irreproachable proletarian militants like Blasco. They were not the only revolutionaries who fell victim to the wrath of the Stalinists. But these crimes were unknown to the Trotskyists in 1943.

The fifth congress of the Parti ouvrier internationaliste

In June 1943 the POI congress met, in line with the mandate from the January national conference. Picking up the mantle of the four pre-war POI congresses, this was named the fifth congress.

More than thirty delegates from different regions met in an isolated house in the valley of Grand Morin.[377] Although Marcel Hic and Roland Filiâtre were absent, the national leadership was represented by Craipeau, Gibelin, Rousset and Swann, while the international secretariat was represented by Raptis. Two observers from the CCI attended the debates.

Bearing in mind the conditions of illegality, the POI disposed of not inconsiderable forces. Its propaganda efforts were similarly remarkable. Its two central printshops never rested. *La Vérité* appeared regularly: sixteen issues were published in 1943, from large-format two-pagers to small-format eight-pagers, not to mention numerous duplicated issues. In addition numerous publications, leaflets, pamphlets and a magazine were produced.

Four issues of *La Jeune Garde* had appeared by June 1943. This was the youth propaganda publication – the organisation, for the most part composed of young people, did not have a special youth section. The June issue's title 'We must choose either socialism or barbarism'[378] indicates the tone of this propaganda. Thus read the conclusion of the article 'The path of hope':[379]

> Before you, my comrade, two solutions: barbarism or socialism, that is to say, poverty and war, or else abundance and freedom. It's your choice! 'The youth', Karl Liebknecht wrote, 'is the flame of the revolution'. This flame can never be extinguished. Despite all the defeats and deceptions it burns no less brightly or less clearly. The flame of devotion and sacrifice for the revolution lights the way towards the total liberation of humanity: socialism. The revolution demands all your efforts, your total commitment. With your class brothers, you must fight to realise the international unity of all revolutionary youth, the guarantee of proletarian victory around the world.

We have noted that in May there first appeared *Ohé partisans!*, edited by partisans, whose publication the congress voted through.

There was no less effort on the theoretical plane. *Quatrième Internationale* appeared, very spaced out, printed on ten to twenty pages (two issues in 1943) because it included an anthology of the first four congresses of the Communist International, a vital historical reference after the dissolution of the Comintern.

Also printed were pamphlets, a leaflet for students on the events in Clermont-Ferrand, and from January 1944, *La Lutte des cheminots*.[380]

The rest of the material was duplicated. Fifteen newspapers were produced in different regions, but only three as party organs: *La Lutte ouvrière* (Paris region), *Octobre* (south-west) and *Demain* (Mazamet). The other regions published organs of the Front ouvrier[381] under the title *Front ouvrier de Bretagne*; *de l'Atlantique*; *de Toulouse*; *d'Albi*; *de Pau*; *de Castres*; *de Lyon*; *de Marseille*; *de Clermont*, etc.

Numerous leaflets were produced for workplaces, or on the occasion of particular events. Finally, the POI published two newspapers for German troops: *Der Arbeiter*, duplicated in Brest, and *Arbeiter und Soldat* which was duplicated or printed in Paris.[382] [383]

This brief summary gives some idea of who was represented at the congress. Two major regions were not represented: the North (the POI had no organisation north of Beauvais) and the East (where it had no organisation at all).

La Vérité explored the objectives of the congress:

> On the occasion of the seventh anniversary of the unforgettable movement of June 1936 – also the seventh anniversary of its foundation – the Parti ouvrier internationaliste held its fifth congress in a French town. In spite of the conditions of illegality, a significant number of delegates from all parts of the country attended. Alone amongst the illegal parties, the POI does not prorogue democracy until the future, but practices it in its own ranks in the here and now. This is no accident: it is precisely because it fights for the only government that can be truly democratic, the government of workers' and peasants' councils, and because it is the only party which genuinely fights for the most fundamental aspirations of the masses, that the POI can be a democratic party. Uniting the ranks of the proletariat in the towns and countryside, reinforcing the workers' front in the struggles of today, benefiting from the war-time breakdown of order to resume the interrupted struggle of June 1936, leading it to the triumph of the Socialist United States of the World and building the Fourth International for such an objective, making the POI a revolutionary party capable of leading the decisive struggles now on the horizon: such were the main concerns of the congress. These were summarised in the manifesto which was unanimously agreed at the conclusion of the debates.[384]

This manifesto declared that the Axis forces now faced collapse and that this collapse would open the way for socialism. To this end it was necessary to reinforce a workers' front, which would counterpose 'to the mobilisation of the masses under the command of reactionary officers, the slogans of workers' militia and the arming of the proletariat'.

In the event of Allied landings in France, it called for the mobilisation of the working class, the formation of a common front between the political and trade union organisations freely established by workers, the liberation of the prisons and camps, the election of committees representing the masses, the elaboration of a socialist constitution by a national council of their delegates and the election of a workers' and peasants' government which would declare peace to the proletarians of the world.

The fact that this manifesto was adopted unanimously after five days of debates was first and foremost because it was a synthesis of ideas. Hic had prepared the outline, assuming responsibility for the democratic and national slogans but removing the ambiguities which had marked the previous theses on the national question. It remained general in character on many questions where differences had arisen, for example the importance of the partisan movement.

Not everyone had the same views on the urgency and immediate potential of regroupment with the CCI. Certain people, including Hic, feared that the positions of the CCI would render the party's activity sterile: in their eyes, regroupment demanded prior self-criticism and rallying to the orientation of the Fourth International.

All were in agreement, however, on how to work politically. The congress conveyed in a single fraternal greeting solidarity with POI or Fourth International militants murdered or attacked by the repression, activists in the Dutch RSAP, Parti du Peuple Algérien and 'comrade Pierre Frank, founder of the Ligue communiste, imprisoned by British imperialism on account of his revolutionary record'. With the goal of building the revolutionary party the manifesto made an appeal to those vanguard militants who had 'wished to remain loyal to the flag of Bolshevism-Leninism' for whom it was 'time to resume their place in the revolutionary struggle'. More concretely, plans were made to develops discussions with the CCI and *Octobre* group.

Chapter 7

THE FIRST CRACKS IN EUROPE

The collapse of fascism and the revolution in Italy

The international analysis presented by D. Rousset at the fifth congress of the POI played out in reality the next month: the weakest link in the chain of the Axis, Italian Fascism, broke.

As early as 1 March [1943], *La Vérité* had signalled the crisis of fascism.

> It is as if Mussolini has decided to make a fool of himself. Without doubt he wishes to make his stage exit amidst such mirth that one might feel sorry for him. As Hitler decided to extend full conscription to 16 to 60-year-olds, Mussolini immediately decreed the same mobilisation in Italy, but from ages 14 to 70! However, not all those who could be mobilised are being conscripted, since Italian morale is so bad that generalised conscription would endanger the régime and the Axis.
>
> The Italian cabinet has just been reshuffled. All the ministers have been offloaded. The *Pariser Zeitung* explains that this happens regularly in Italy, or even that this is called a 'changing of the guard' not worthy of attention.
>
> In reality, the removal of Ciano, recently named ambassador to the Vatican, is evidence enough for the character of the operation. The new government in which Mussolini has taken charge of foreign affairs, the secretary of state being a former ambassador to London, is a compromise arrangement. The reshuffle is a concession to Britain. Did it take place with Germany's consent?[385]

La Vérité was mistaken as to the positions of the top fascist dignitaries. In fact, it was the partisans of compromise who were removed: Ciano, Mussolini's son-in-law, who had been the champion of orientation towards the Axis, was now the first to stop relying on the Axis and support the compromise peace demanded by the Italian bourgeoisie. But in the main the analysis was accurate. The reshuffle underlined the extreme crisis of fascism. It proved unable to contain it.

In March, 50,000 workers in Turin went on strike to demand more pay on account of the bombings: their success re-awakened the working class's confidence to take action, and following the dock workers' strike in Trieste, there was a generalised movement in northern Italy against night-time work in regions at risk of bombardment, a movement which in turn was successful. The concessions did not appease the working class: new strikes arose, and everywhere there were demonstrations against the war. The Italian bourgeoisie was frightened. For a long time it had sought to cast aside Mussolini and his policy of alliance with Germany. These events supplied the pretext.[386]

In vain, the new government tried to make concessions, rally the bourgeoisie and soft-pedal the activities of the fascist movement.

On 20 June *La Vérité* heralded the imminent fall of Mussolini:

> As must have been expected, the defeats in Africa did little to strengthen the popularity of fascism in Italy. The soldiers from the peninsula have had enough and the Italian army of 1943 looks little different from the French army of 1940.
>
> Faced with the discontent of the masses, the government proceeds to dismantle the leading role of the Fascist Party: wearing the black shirt, even under one's clothes, is banned on work days.
>
> Scorza, the new party secretary, has issued a decree dissolving the offices responsible for political decision-making and economic controls, replacing each of these with a functionary. In a recent speech he denounced 'the attacks – inspired by Marxism – against the bourgeoisie, the class of the Italian people'. At the same time the *Giornale d'Italia* has defended the Italian bourgeoisie and the role it played in the realisation of national unification. It is not such a long time since fascism demagogically railed against the 'bourgeois mentality'. Today, the proletariat having abandoned it, fascism throws itself into the arms of the bourgeoisie, which alone can be faithful to it: it appeals to the bourgeoisie in the name of opposing the coming revolution [...] This revolution is well underway. The collapse of fascism will at the same time mean the collapse of Italian capitalism and the rise of a socialist republic beyond the Alps. Is that not the reason why the Americans seem none too hasty to land in Italy, and why Churchill, in his last speech of 23 May, explicitly proposed a compromise to the Italian bourgeoisie?[387]

Events moved quickly. On 10 July the American Seventh Army and the British Eighth Army landed in Sicily with 80,000 men and 300 tanks. The Führer and the Duce promptly met in Verona. The German high command had managed to convince Hitler of the need to shorten the front by withdrawing his forces to north of Rome. An emergency meeting of the Fascist Grand Council on 24 July – led by Ciano – refused to concede to the German demands. Mussolini was arrested and imprisoned. The king entrusted power to General Badoglio, who played a double-game in the next six weeks, declaring his loyalty to the German alliance at the same time as negotiating with the Allies.

On 30 July, an article in *La Vérité* written before these events called for solidarity with German and Italian workers:

> Already the strikes and street demonstrations are multiplying. With General Alexander in Sicily protecting the fascists from the fury of the crowd, the Italian revolution will have to march over the bodies of the fascists and their Allied defenders.

At the last minute, the newspaper printed news of the fall of Mussolini:

> The Italian people celebrates with indescribable joy the fall of the Duce. In Milan the crowd invaded the fascist headquarters. In Naples, Turin, across Italy, mass demonstrations have played out to cries of 'Peace! Down with Hitler! Down with Mussolini!'. The Palace at Venice was invaded. Fascist street names are effaced. Fighting between the army and the black shirts.
>
> As the Italian revolution mounts, London is only concerned to know whether Badoglio is capable of 'maintaining order'![388]

At the same time as the issue was printed, on 30 July, a special duplicated issue also appeared with the manifesto of the European secretariat of the Fourth International:

> Workers, peasants, and Italian soldiers!,[389] [...] The Italian bourgeoisie has cast fascism aside in 24 hours, as one might show the door to an untrustworthy or pilfering servant. It has shown itself ready to sign a compromise as long as it can preserve its right to make profits. But as long as the rule of the bourgeoisie survives, whether that means the Montecetini [sic][390] and Anselde [sic],[391] Fiat and the landowners, or the generals and politicians who rule in their name, nothing will change for the Italian people.

The manifesto called on workers to take action to ensure punishment of the fascist leaders, the demobilisation of the army, the immediate liberation of prisoners, freedom of organisation and the freedom of the workers' press and the convention of a national assembly – in sum, democratic freedoms.

It called for action for a general wage increase and in order to secure union rights and the right to strike.

It posed the need for a peace without reparations or annexations.

Finally it suggested that workers should meet in action committees in the towns and in their workplaces to organise struggles and bring together a national leadership of the struggles.

It was necessary to resume the struggle interrupted in 1923.

> Tomorrow, again, Factory Committees must impose workers' control, prepare the expropriation of the capitalists and organise production.
>
> The road of socialist revolution is open to you. Be determined, take it! The revolutionary proletariat of the whole world needs nothing better than your example [to follow].

There was not then any Trotskyist movement in Italy, only a few émigrés returning to their country, such as Fosco. The manifesto was little-distributed in Italy, except it seems in the POI propaganda sheet among a few units of the Italian army.[392]

However, the masses started to move in this direction of their own initiative. *La Lutte de classe* commented:

> It is the working masses who with their powerful strikes in the northern industrial towns, particularly Milan, supported by the whole popular resistance, have precipitated the resignation of Mussolini and the fall of fascism. It is the masses who protested outside the prisons, who forced Badoglio to officially sanction the liberation of the political prisoners, who had in any case freed themselves from jail where government 'action' was lacking. It is the action of the masses which forced the government to arrest the fascist leaders and subject them to the just punishment of the workers. It is the action of the masses which has given real new life to the various political parties, even if all parties are banned by the state. Even if at the moment the draconian measures taken by the government have put a stop to strikes, they cannot but be reinvigorated as the working masses and soldiers work together for their common interests. In Italy, workers and soldiers must solve the fundamental question of peace. Fraternisation between workers and soldiers has already taken place

with troops refusing to fire on strikers. London radio has spoken of the creation of workers' committees, and even soldiers' committees.[393]

However, in reality Badoglio's threats did little to interrupt the strike movement. *La Vérité* reported that they had done little but aggravate the struggles.

> The Italian people wants bread and freedom: bread is scarce but Badoglio insists that the war must continue and has declared a state of siege, banning any meetings and militarising the workforce. But the workers continue with their offensive. There are mass demonstrations in Turin and Bologna and far-reaching strikes by factory and rail workers across northern Italy.[394]

Badoglio tried to divert the movement. He legalised the unions, but given that the situation did not allow for elections, he appointed as their commissioners Socialist, Christian-Democrat and even Communist leaders. The latter – reasonably enough – agreed to take up the union role offered to them ('a function of a strictly trade union character without assuming any political responsibilities') while demanding the release of political prisoners. Meanwhile, workers demanded to be allowed to hold elections for their officials without delay, and continued the movement for immediate peace: in Milan workers stopped work for half-an-hour every day as a protest in favour of world peace.[395]

Moreover, in the workplace they established their own organs of control, organs of the soviet type. In Milan and Turin there were workers' and soldiers' councils.[396]

> A paradoxical, inextricable, situation, [*La Vérité* commented.] Under full-scale German occupation, as Italian troops fight on although decimated by desertion, the liberal and revolutionary parties have spontaneously re-emerged, and are publishing their newspapers and staging meetings. The masses, little-controlled by these traditional organisations, are proving that they have a consciousness and energy which has stunned the old big-wigs and shaken the Badoglio government.
>
> The Italian bourgeoisie has only one concern: damage limitation, compromising with the movement and diverting it with Popular Front-type alliances. For the moment, it has has limited itself to passing the achievements of the masses into law. At the cost of accepting reforms, the Factory Committees created by workers have become legal institutions,

the intention being to empty out their revolutionary content, the soviet form they had already established.

But that does not make for national unity. There is such an atmosphere of distrust that soldiers on leave returning from occupied countries are disarmed at the Italian border.

There is massive agitation in workplaces and in the unions for a general strike. Badoglio takes to the microphone and disavows the movement. Behind him stand the so-called Socialist leaders, who have devoted themselves to servile repetition of his calls for calm and discipline.

Back in 1922 they used to say 'Put down your weapons: do not provoke the black shirts'. Resuming their infamous work in sowing division and servility, they associate themselves with Badoglio's struggle to defend what can still be saved of the capitalist system. We would like to believe that, contrary to the reports of Radio Lausanne, none of the Communists, none of those heroic militants who fought the fascist régime gun in hand until 1928, none of those freed from the prisons and the Aeolian Islands.[397] are mixed up in such alliances.[398]

But the Radio Lausanne reports were indeed accurate. Socialists and Communists used all their prestige – which was immense, in view of their recent struggles – to channel the revolutionary torrent into union sacrée.

But union sacrée was not easy to put into effect. 'Almost immediately the major factories disavowed the signatories [of compromise with Badoglio]'. Badoglio, overcome, left it to the belligerent powers to put down the workers. Fresh theatrical games, whether diplomatic, military or political, intervened to put the brakes on the Italian revolution. The first act in the drama – the armistice – was expected. As early as 15 August *La Vérité* had announced that it was imminent:

> Hitler begs and threatens in vain. The die has been cast. Italy will capitulate. Around the Pope, that great organiser of this type of ceremony, the diplomats will busy themselves, trade over peace, dissect the political and economic conditions and feel the pulse of the new Italian government.

The second act: Hitler sent parachutists to rescue Mussolini from the chateau where he was being held, and made him head of a 'republican fascist government', while the royalist Badoglio government headed for Sicily under Allied protection.

The Italian proletariat is now experiencing a challenging period. Mussolini, 'saved' in a scene perhaps inspired by Hollywood, has returned to power: no government has ever had such insignificant support, its only hope being the Nazi bayonets. Attempted uprisings in Milan, Turin and Rome have been harshly repressed by the German army. In the current situation such initiatives can be nothing more than the effort of a revolutionary minority. The present task is to rally forces for the next mass movement. Beyond that, there is an urgent need to organise fraternisation with German soldiers: indeed, it is clear that as long as the latter continue to follow their officers, their police and their SS, the Italian revolution will face bloody defeats.[399]

However, events unfurled as if the Allies and Nazis had shared out the task of crushing the revolutionaries. The war in Italy became a war of position, reminiscent of the 1914 war. The Allies progressed slowly, while the revolutionary North remained subject to Nazi terror and the factories of Milan and Turin were bombarded by the Allied air forces.

The Italian revolution had significant international echoes: the rapid progress of the Yugoslav partisans, general strikes in Athens, a three-day strike in Bucharest, and a savagely repressed general strike in Portugal. But the first phase of the revolution was over.

What could those who called themselves socialists learn from these first revolutionary movements shaking southern Europe? The news on Italy in the Socialist and Communist press was no different from that in the Gaullist press or the London radio. They were happy to emphasise the consensus of all social classes on getting rid of fascism, the moderation of the Italian Communists and the Soviet Union and, above all, of course, the military significance of Italy's defeat.

For internationalists, the fall of fascism represented the first phase of the social revolution. But they drew different lessons from the Italian events. Let us leave aside the vast polemic in which the CCI tried to justify its 'proletarian schema' that the Americans' objective was not the downfall of Hitler, but rather, that of the USSR, and that there would be no second front before the downfall of Stalin and only then could the revolution begin.[400]

The fundamental differences were over the role of democratic slogans. The CCI chalked up the Italian events in the calendar of Russia in 1917 and qualified them as a 'February' (revolution). But in this group's eyes, the question was not developing these democratic questions to their revolutionary consequences, but rather 'counterposing' working-class struggle to them.

The Italian revolution completely proved the totally counter-revolutionary character of the democratic programme. In spite of the lack of political organisation, the movement of the masses immediately and spontaneously took the character of a struggle which went far beyond democratic demands.[401]

The CCI deduced from this that democratic struggles would not play any role in the rest of Europe.

The POI, the Fourth International and the *Lutte de classe* group considered on the contrary that these democratic demands would arise in revolutionary movements across Europe: the reformists would try and channel them into bourgeois institutions, whereas revolutionaries had to push them to their logical conclusion, socialist democracy.

The liberation of Corsica

A second significant experience began on 9 September: the liberation of Corsica by a popular insurrection. It was rich with lessons in two senses: it demonstrated the potential of a popular uprising faced with an occupation army which was 70,000-strong in this *département* alone; it showed how the policy of union sacrée lead to the appropriation of this victory by the bourgeoisie.

Charles Tillon demonstrated this two-sided character of the struggles in Corsica. However, he was fundamentally interested in the former aspect and did not draw the lessons of the latter.

Let us look at the facts. Corsica was occupied by more than 40,000 Italian soldiers and 12,000 German soldiers – together with around 18,000 German troops arriving from Sardinia.

> From the early months of 1943, the resistance movement took over the whole island. In Bastia on 23 April, 10,000 people, with powerful demonstrations, forced the police prefect Balley to reinstate in full the bread ration which he had just cut.

On the occasion of 1 May the local PCF leaders wrote in their 'Appeal to the people of Corsica':[402] 'We do not separate the struggle for bread from the struggle against the occupier… the Liberation of Corsica will be the work of the Corsican people itself.'

Note the tone of this appeal, very different from the typical chauvinist PCF appeals.

The Front national, led by the PCF, ultimately led as many as 10,000 people. It received weapons from Giraud, whether parachuted in or delivered by the submarine Casabianca.

> The regional leadership of the PCF, correctly understanding the decomposition of the Italian army, the result of the anti-fascist offensive in Italy, envisaged that the signal for insurrection should coincide with Italian capitulation. On 26 August, the leading committee of the Front nationale adopted an audacious line for the liberation of Corsica upon the first signs of armistice, which Badoglio would sign on 3 September but which was kept secret until the 8th. The French high command was informed and numerous telegrams were exchanged between General Giraud, the chief of the military mission in Corsica and the FN leadership. The last telegram signed by Giraud commented 'Please tell the patriots that I am counting on them not to launch operations prematurely…'
>
> On 8 September there was a demonstration in Ajaccio. On the 9th the prefecture was occupied: the *département* committee of the FN, installed in place of the prefecture, dissolved the Vichyist organisations and proclaimed Corsica's adherence to the cause of the Free French. Now the guerrilla movement exploded across Corsica.

His account continued:

> The FN was wise enough to struggle against the tendency towards anti-Italian chauvinism. It showed that it was necessary to concentrate every blow against the Hitlerites and not to divide their forces in attacks on Italian troops, except when they opened fire first.

In Bastia on the 8th, there was a demonstration of young people and a general strike; on the 9th, a patriotic association in one municipality seized the town hall and appealed for armed support. The port of Bastia, occupied by German warships, 'was reconquered with the aid of Italian soldiers'.

The Allied high command refused to support the insurrection. But the insurgents benefited from the auxiliary aid of De Gaulle and Giraud in Algiers. Giraud sent 900 men as reinforcements on 13 September, and a further battalion on the 20th. By 5 October, Corsica was fully liberated.

Charles Tillon's history drew an essentially military lesson: 'The Corsican experience demonstrated the errors of wait-and-see and underestimating the people's capacity to take the initiative'.

However, it implicitly drew a further conclusion:

It must not be forgotten that in Corsica a set of favourable circumstances, including numerous Italian units' refusal to participate in the repression, and even their aid to the Resistance, allowed for a rapid victory.

But it was not a question of favourable circumstances. The Corsican Communists had taken the initiative in challenging anti-Italian chauvinism and supporting fraternisation. Without doubt, they took this initiative for essentially military reasons: it was about distinguishing the secondary Italian enemy from the main enemy, Germany. There was no question of distinguishing class enemies from class allies among the occupation troops. Only such a distinction could have allowed for the generalisation of fraternisation among German soldiers. It is true that they were less sensitive to anti-fascist propaganda than Italian troops, but the national character of struggles did not allow for fraternisation except when the army was in an advanced state of disarray.

The anti-German chauvinist politics of the PCF forbade any fraternisation with Germany soldiers, anywhere in Europe. It prevented the emergence of 'favourable conditions' for a revolutionary movement.

The politics of the 'patriotic union' showed their limitations in Corsica itself. Charles Tillon's history continues:

> The people had at once assumed the control and the responsibilities of state! Sacrilege! Seven months before the opening of the second front, the experience of Corsica increased further the fear big business had as regards the masses organised in the Resistance. De Gaulle, uninterested in the military action once it had finished, sent the prefect Luizet to Ajaccio, charged with defending the sacred relics of state and encouraged to reinstate clan politics.

There is no better evidence of how union sacrée served the bourgeoisie.

Soldat im Westen in 1943

In January 1943, the Front national (which also advanced the slogan 'A chacun son boche' addressed the German soldiers:

> Our struggle is a struggle for justice! The aim of the Allied war effort… is that men should live in peace again, and can work in peace, each man with his own homeland and his own family. It is the task of all nations to build a just future. That means you too!
>
> Most of you have had enough of the war and want to go back to your

families and children. Fight for a return to your homeland, work for this goal and our two peoples will save many victims' lives.

[…] Hand over your weapons, join our ranks […]

He who fights for Hitler shall go down with him!

He who fights against Hitler will win peace![403]

This was meant to be an appeal for fraternisation. But the Front national identified itself with one of the imperialist camps: the common objectives it proposed were the objectives of the Allies, with the intention of having people believe that they were only fighting the war to secure peace. These war aims were the same as Hitler offered them: peace, homeland, family, a just future. Why should German soldiers put their confidence in Churchill rather than Hitler to achieve this?

The Front national, which of course was not working for revolution in France, did not suggest German workers should do so in Germany either.

Soldat im Westen reported a few examples of disobedience and sabotage. But it insisted on the need to 'follow' the officers who were abandoning Hitler. It emphasised the non-revolutionary character of the National Committee for a Free Germany. It championed reactionary personalities, aristocrats and leading officers who joined it:

In Russia, dozens, hundreds of comrades in the prison camps have formed a National Committee for a Free Germany. All these people, whatever their politics, from all classes of the German nation are united: the lieutenant count of Einsiedeln, a grandson of Bismarck… have crossed the lines with their troops in Russia.

We must not bring shame to our children!

Comrades, organise the resistance, join us! (August 1943).

The Italian example was repeatedly used, but not to show the power of the proletariat and its revolutionary will, but rather to celebrate the unity of social classes and all parties, the lack of social transformation, the realism of the USSR in understanding perfectly the colonialist attitudes of the Italian 'anti-fascists' (meaning, the Italian bourgeoisie):

The Italian people have brought down Mussolini in a struggle uniting all classes … now it is organising legally in trade unions and political parties. Strikes and demonstrations are the proof: the fight for peace is underway. A fully just peace plan is thus being drawn up for Italy. *Pravda* in Moscow comments: 'We understand that the Italian anti-fascists want Italy to be able to keep its colonies' (September 1943).

So anti-fascism could perfectly well allow for the continued domination and oppression of the least powerful peoples: but then on what basis could they reproach the Hitlerites for their control over the nations they had conquered?

Above all, it stressed their 'love of Russia':

> 7 November will be the 25th anniversary of the Russian revolution. The French love and admire the Soviet Union, and will express such sentiments on 7 November. This is the same feeling all oppressed people have, boundless hatred for the Third Reich and sincere love for the Soviet Union. For us Germans too, our safety lies in Russia (November 1942).

Safety could be found in Russia, with the Allies, with the well-intentioned officers who handed themselves over to the Russians. Nowhere did *Soldat im Westen* suggest that it could be achieved by the actions of soldiers and workers themselves, still less by their collective and revolutionary efforts.

More accurately speaking, each individual soldier could ensure his own safety by turning himself in. The Allies, the Russians, were just too powerful: only death awaits, unless you turn yourself in. The call for surrender was the leitmotiv of every issue:

> If we march on Russia, we will die!
> If we are POWs, we will live! (May 1943).

Arbeiter und Soldat: Trotskyist propaganda in the German army

In internationalists' eyes, German soldiers were called on to play an essential role in the coming revolutionary events. Their propaganda in the Wehrmacht was of a wholly different character.

Since the CCI began publication of *Le Soviet* in September 1943, the back page was devoted to a German language page titled 'Arbeiter und Soldaten Räte' ['Workers' and Soldiers' Councils]. This was very much generic revolutionary propaganda. The council communists published several issues of *Spartakus*, with which they tried to influence German soldiers.

But the only organisation of German soldiers was that of 'official' Trotskyism. To understand its orientation we need look no further than a single issue of *Arbeiter und Soldat*, printed in April 1944 in advance of May Day. It also focused on the growing understanding that military defeat was inevitable. However, it did not call on soldiers to see surrender as the guarantee of their personal safety:

Today in May 1944 the greater part of the European population is still under the heel of German troops. However domestic as well as international developments show that the end is near. It could happen any day now. But that does not mean that it will just 'happen'. The Nazi clique and its capitalist backers are ready to fight down to the last German worker. As in 1918 only the working class itself can bring an end to the reign of terror and the war. We can only achieve peace with revolution.[404]

Arbeiter und Soldat attacked the counter-revolutionary character of the National Committee for a Free Germany:

They have formed a so-called liberation committee in Moscow, mainly composed of captured Nazi generals. The main task set for this committee is to suffocate the revolution as in 1918, installing a bourgeois government and saving the capitalist system. If they succeed in doing so Anglo-American capital and the Russian bureaucracy will dictate a peace to Germany alongside which Versailles will look charitable. And German capital for its part would dump the entire burden on the workers.

The only ally of the German working class was the international proletariat, but it had to earn its trust and secure this alliance.

In this desperate situation the German proletariat does have an ally; but it will not be able to win it over unless it finally starts fighting for its own interests and fights for them until victory. The emergence of workers' power and the establishment of a government of soviets, whose first task would be to expropriate big business and wealthy landed interests without compensation, is the only solution to the growing barbarism of decaying capitalism. The pioneering struggle of the German working class will set the tone for the proletarian revolution across Europe [...]

1 May 1944 must mark a turn in the fate of the German working class! It must mark the revival of the class front! Our gun barrels and bayonet points must be turned against the real enemy, capital and its agents in our country.

In this vein, we must build secret workers' groups in every workplace and in every army unit! These should bring together the most active militants gifted with the strongest class consciousness. They must follow the latest political developments with the greatest diligence. Everywhere where workers act to resist the apparatus of repression, action groups must go straight to the site of struggle.

They must also prepare for the establishment of soviets when the capitalist war front collapses. That day every unit and every factory must elect a soviet which will be the main organ of struggle as well as the basis for workers' power.

The newspaper concluded:

If it shows itself to be weak and afraid the German working class will fall into long-term poverty and powerlessness: but if it has confidence in its own strength, and untrammeled courage in its convictions, it will take the leading role in the struggle for the liberation of the world working class and humanity as a whole.

But the soldiers' committee and the POI did not limit themselves to propaganda. on 15 October, when it was no longer dangerous to report the facts, *La Vérité* detailed certain examples of fraternisation in the Brest region.

On 27-28 August, there were raids against young people. But the German soldiers stopped the French. A group of young people from the l'Armoricaine work site fled, pursued by an officer: when they came across a unit of German soldiers, they were let through.

Let us explain that the l'Armoricaine guys often spoke on friendly terms with the German workers in uniform … to the extent that eventually the commander of the anti-aircraft artillery unit banned the soldiers from talking to the workers since 'this could harm morale'. Every worker should reflect on that.

La Vérité also featured extracts of a letter which appeared in the duplicated newspaper *Der Arbeiter* produced by German soldiers in occupied France. It already expressed a developed revolutionary politics, even if, almost without exception, its editors were young people who had not been old enough to really know anything except life under Hitler's régime:

We, soldiers, finding ourselves in enemy countries, are in truth nothing but workers, proletarians, who must carry out the orders of the Nazi dictatorship. The situation of our comrades back home is little better, particularly at the moment. We, like them, have to flog our guts out, always for nothing. Will we take the slightest benefit from this? No! So why all this? Will we keep going with this pointless war? No, and once again no. I have always behaved as a good German and obeyed my superiors' orders, but now, enough. Why continue this war which cannot possibly lead to any result?[405]

La Vérité concluded:

Der Arbeiter calls on German soldiers to join the revolutionary struggle. It says: 'Drop your weapons and join the Fourth International'. This slogan is not correct, since the point is not that they should drop their weapons, but rather that they should direct them against their class enemies. However this is just a mistaken turn of phrase, of no consequence. The young soldier who raises his head from the ranks has not yet found the correct 'formula'. If he has dropped his weapon, he will soon enough pick it up again, for the revolution: for his whole outlook is profoundly revolutionary.

The newspaper quoted further from *Der Arbeiter*:

Only a world revolution can bring real peace. Only the socialist republic based on councils can bring freedom and the brotherhood of the proletarians of the whole world. Thus all will be guaranteed jobs and bread. We will put an end to economic crises; we will dispossess the capitalists and create a planned socialist economy, hand in hand with our brothers in all countries. Join our ranks! Workers of the world, unite![406]

However, these young German soldiers had no political experience. *La Vérité* reported on a demonstration by a group of German soldiers, marching through the town of Kerhuon singing the *Internationale*. POI activists there were also young, and too enthusiastic. They were delighted that young workers and German soldiers greeted each other in Brest with clenched fists. Their imprudence would lead to the destruction of the German network in Brest and terrible repression against the whole party.

Repression against the German organisation and the POI

1943 was the high point of the organisation of Trotskyist propaganda in the Germany army. Fourth International soldiers supplied the French militants with arms and documentation. The FTP in Scrignac continued to deal with those who threatened repressive measures. But in October the Gestapo took its revenge.

An Austrian soldier representing Brest on the leadership committee,

Konrad – nephew of the musician Franz Lehar – brought down the entire organisation, possibly having been introduced as a provocateur or possibly having caved in to Gestapo pressure.

A Gestapo detachment raided a meeting which had been staged in Brest without due caution by party activists and German soldiers. Everyone there was arrested. On 6 October 1943 the regional official for fraternisation work, Robert Cruau, was shot along with seventeen German soldiers. Konrad was beaten up for show, but not executed.

This time – like never before – several sections of the illegal organisation cracked. Firstly in Finistère: 18 Breton comrades were arrested on 7 October, including the new regional secretary Marcel Beaufrère and his partner Eliane (a hat-seller), Yves Bodenez (a carpenter), the Kerhuon organiser, and the Berthomé brothers. At about the same time, the Gestapo struck against the Paris group: Filiâtre was arrested and tortured, along with two other members of the leadership, Marcel Hic and David Rousset. So too were others, including Delambre, the electrician Lucien, the photographer André, the typist Anne and the typographer Georges Fournié. Moreover, others such as Yvan Craipeau, escaped pursuit by the Gestapo.[407] In total fifty French militants were arrested after a joint effort of the Gestapo and French police.

Many would never return from the concentration camps, including Marcel Hic, Bodenez and Berthomé. As for the Germans, even if the most 'subtle' escaped, the soldiers' organisation lost fifty of its militants, such as Hans and Willie, tortured to death. It was practically destroyed. The newspaper *Der Arbeiter* disappeared (which is why *La Vérité* was now able to mention it). *Arbeiter und Soldat* would not appear again until 1944.

However, the repression against the party was not over. Arrests continued thus: on 15 February 1943 Jean-René Chauvin was deported to Mauthausen; in June the mechanic Eric Schultz; Mathias Corvin, one of the Paris organisers; and Adeline Raymond, who managed to escape after she had been tortured. In December Marie and the trade union officer Pradalès were arrested. Before, arrests had never had a snowball effect: for good reason, the Chinese-wall tightness of the organisation had never caved in. But this time it did give in, and not only in northern Brittany: from Brittany to Paris, the repression claimed a hundred victims, both French and German. It decapitated the national leadership, which lost three of its five members.

The situation was so grave that on 15 October, breaking with its usual silence, *La Vérité* featured a box with an article to warn the whole party:

As a result of our fraternisation propaganda, the Gestapo is hunting down our militants.

For two weeks the Gestapo has been working overtime. In an attempt to stop the deadly blows our fraternisation propaganda is striking against the Nazi régime, it is hunting down our militants, and is aided in this by reports from the police prefecture. In its blindness the Gestapo is searching out and arresting without discrimination suspected Trotskyists, former activists, sympathetic trade unionists, and those who have abstained from any real activity since the beginning of the war. All those who have approached us, whether close or distant contacts, are being targeted. All of them must be on their guard.

As for us: nothing will stop us, neither the inevitable provocations nor the arrests and torture they promise us.

We know that in extending a hand to the German worker in uniform we are attacking Hitlerism with greater effect than any terrorist assassinations could achieve. That the Gestapo has realised this – even if too late – is just more reason for us to continue.[408]

Of course, the article must not be taken at face value. Where it asserts that the Gestapo was striking blindly, it was attempting to protect some of the arrested comrades. in reality, the Gestapo was relatively well informed. It had at its disposal a complete volume on the activism of the Trotskyists and their organisers, which fortunately was littered with errors:[409] for instance not understanding that several pseudonyms referred to the same person. These mistakes were of some use to the comrades being tortured, like Roland Filiâtre.

La Vérité sought to give militants fresh confidence by showing that the struggle continued. The 15 October issue devoted two pages to various manifestations of fraternisation.

But October's repression had grave consequences on the orientation of the POI. Its leadership was weakened. For a time Yvan Craipeau had to assume the most varied responsibilities (newspaper, military equipment, finances, external relations, etc.). The two surviving members of the leadership co-opted three new comrades: Spoubler (alias Marcoux), Essel (alias Lessart) and Parisot – himself arrested in January 1944 – while Demazière became organiser for the Paris region. The leading articles were now signed Auger-Marcoux in order to reassure activists of the continuity of the leadership.

However, militants had lost confidence in the solidity and strength of the party. They were impatient for regroupment, which they expected to reinforce the structure of the organisation. Even within the new leadership the political balance was somewhat changed.

La Vérité uncovers the negotiations between Vichy and Algiers over the transfer of power

Soon before the arrests, the POI leadership dedicated itself to publishing a series of dossiers demonstrating the collaboration between Algiers and Vichy and between Anglo-American capitalism and German capitalism. The arrest of David Rousset meant the near-collapse of information networks and the loss of original documents: only analyses of these remained. However, *La Vérité* decided nonetheless to make use of these analyses.

The first dossier to be published dealt with the negotiations between Vichy and emissaries of De Gaulle. It was no longer possible to give the full minutes of these conversations, as had been planned, but *La Vérité* knew that all its information was based on irrefutable documentation.

> They cannot deny our charge that everywhere officers of the Armée secrète are working to establish anti-revolutionary groups, formations designed to secure order and serve as police in the event of 'troubles' or an Allied landing. They cannot deny our charge that they will be keen to ensure the continuity of anti-communist repression. They cannot deny our charge that, among certain circles in the Resistance it is often said that only the Gaullist forces can stop the masses from seizing the town halls, attacking private property, and that the Vichy police are clearly unable to fulfil this role.
>
> They cannot deny our charge that contacts between Vichy and Algiers have been continuous. They cannot deny our charge that De Gaulle is trying to obtain – from across the sea – recognition by Vichy and the planning of a seamless takeover, arguing that only he could prevent a new Commune [like the revolutionary Paris Commune of 1871], given that he has the Communist leaders behind him.
>
> They cannot deny our charge that Armée secrète agents are building arms depots for the developing police forces, but refuse these weapons to the deserters who have to face the German attacks bare-handed. In the Centre, in the East, in the Alps, the first victims of this Gaullist conspiracy have already fallen, tragically abandoned. They cannot deny our charge that the leadership of the Parti communiste has itself had to raise protests about this state of affairs, albeit confidentially.[410]

On 10 December *La Vérité* continued its campaign with citations of Vichy's documents. Firstly, Pétain's speech of 12 November:

On 12 November, Pétain made a sensational statement:

'[…] I do not want my departure to lead to any period of disorder which will endanger the unity of France. Thus, the objectives of the constitutional provision which will be proclaimed in tomorrow's *Journal officiel*:

First article: in the event that we die before being able to secure the ratification of the new constitution of l'État français[411] by the Nation, our constituent powers will be returned to the Senate and the Chamber of Deputies, meeting as a National Assembly'.

At the same time, Pétain and his clique issued a decree allowing for the shooting of deserters who take part in the maquis resistance. These two decisions seem contradictory: but this is only in appearance: Vichy is readying to take on the revolutionary movements, and both decisions intend to paralyse them.[412]

Yvan Craipeau can approximate from memory the record of the meetings which took place in September between Pétain, numerous members of his cabinet (including the head of Laval's cabinet) and a neo-Gaullist general[413] – having read the minutes of these discussions:

In betting on German victory we have backed the wrong horse. Allied victory is certain. We must save France's interests. Above all, we must prevent revolutionaries from taking advantage of the collapse of the state and taking power. We face a new Commune ten times worse than that of 1871. We must block their path.

To this end, it is necessary that everywhere the insurgents find the new government they have fought for already put in place. This government – and its police – will be ready to make them understand that they are no longer needed.

To this end, the Marshal [i.e. Pétain] must henceforth ensure the unity of the state, calling in the authority delegated to Laval and entrusting it to Algiers[…] meaning, to De Gaulle. I know that you do not like De Gaulle. You would prefer to delegate power to Giraud. But Giraud has no political capital. A Giraud government would be no better recognised by the population than Vichy. The only man who can ensure order with public support is De Gaulle. Only he can carry out the task of suffocating a communard movement. You must resign yourself to handing power to him.

After listening to this, Pétain held an audience with the general in order to delegate him to Algiers. No question that the speech given and the attempted palace coup to overthrow Laval was just the first stage of the manoeuvre.

We understand that von Nidda, the German representative, having been informed by Laval, immediately set off for the Hotel du Parc to 'maintain direct contact with the head of state'. 'If I am prevented from saying what I want', Pétain declared, 'then I will have to consider myself no longer able to fulfil my mission'.

After the war, the historian Robert Aron confirmed the authenticity of these comments:

The Marshal had to cave in. At the last minute, the radio broadcast, instead of the message the whole of France was waiting for (sic!), a selection of *Dédé* (an operetta popular at the time). Aron emphasised the Marshal's heroic resistance: 'He put off all his official dinners'.[414]

The scandal over oil

At the same time *La Vérité* made public a 'Note addressed to the Allied joint command by the leading bodies of the Armée secrète'.[415]

This note signalled that 'some of the bombardment, particularly the recent bombardment of Nantes, have demonstrated a total lack of precision or else the use of erroneous information, and these errors have created a deep malaise affecting all layers of society', *La Vérité* commented.

After initial bemusement there was anger among the population as tens of thousands of innocents were killed without the slightest military pretext, several kilometres from the port installations supposedly being targeted. Yet targeting the military leadership is a taboo: any worker can bet their wages from now until 1950 that the Berchtesgaden and the places where the fate of the world is decided will remain intact until the end of the war. Thus the Armée secrète's note avows, 'At no moment did Allied planes bomb the Briey basin[416], nor the bauxite mines of the south-east, the major industries from where the enemy draws most of its resources'.

The note continues:

Rock-solid sources have infomed us of the constant arrival of armoured trains full of oil from Spain. Others, still yet to be verified, suggest the delivery of a considerable number of planes to Germany via Lisbon.

These sources confirm our own: *La Vérité* will publish further information on the state of the oil market.

The Armée secrète believe that it is enough to publicise such events in order to put a stop to them. We, on the contrary, are sure that these are normal happenings in a war waged by capitalists and with capitalist methods. Only the people themselves, putting an end to capitalist rule by establishing a United States of the World, can put an end to these grubby arms deals by traders who at the same time claim to be guaranteeing peace.[417]

The following month's issue of *La Vérité* did not disappoint.[418] It had precise details on the exchange of oil, information that came from its own sources; two armoured trains from Port-Bou crossed the border every day, meaning 35,000 wagon-loads per year.

La Vérité asked:

Why do none of the Resistance newspapers protest this fact? Neither *Défense de la France*, which boasts of its frankness; nor *Libération*, which claims to be democratic and anti-capitalist; nor *Le Populaire*, nor *L'Humanité*. In all of them, there is a conspiracy of silence.

La Vérité then provided information on the agreements between American companies and the Nazis to guarantee an oil supply to Hitler… under the pretext of supplying Spain.

In the accords which have resulted in the delivery of two trainloads of oil per day to Germany from Port-Bou, one of the most important issues concerns cinema. Since June 1940, the Germans have gained the film rights for a number of French cinema halls, in the form of shares … They have ceded these rights to American companies in exchange for oil from refineries under American control.

The article concluded:

Every worker must realise the true face of the imperialist belligerents, when their mask is torn off. None of them are crusaders for civilisation and peace, but rather capitalist pirates who want a bloodbath of peoples in search of a redivision of the markets, and who even in the middle of the war itself are continuing their lucrative deals amongst themselves. The workers must understand that their fate, and that of the USSR, will not be decided on the battle-lines between rival imperialisms, but rather on the front of class struggle: the workers' front, where the fate of civilisation and peace will be contested by imperialism and the world proletariat.

The Swiss press, in turn, reproduced this information, followed by the Soviet press. By 17 February *La Vérité* could announce:

> The United States have now announced that, as of 1 February, they will stop sending oil to Spain. Echoes of our story in the Swiss press were a stunning vindication of the information published in *La Vérité* regarding oil trafficking via Spain. But the oil scandal is not an isolated event. We have already spoken of the passage of American planes to Germany via Portugal.
>
> Now we can report on the trafficking of iron ore.
>
> Comrades returning from Germany ask us, 'Why are the major German factories not being bombarded?'
>
> 'If 150 workers, women and children in Hamburg have been reduced to ashes, how come the Lena factories – for example – are still standing?'
>
> We are now able to answer their questions. It is because German chemical products are exchanged for special American minerals which the Reich needs for its war industry. Reliable comrades tell us that this barter takes place in Spain regularly.[419]

This was the last issue published by the POI. After unification [with the CCI] *La Vérité* did not continue with this campaign.

The USA: the main bastion of capitalist order

1943 demonstrated the real character of American intervention in Europe. The supposed plans for an anti-Soviet intervention – which had become an article of faith for the CCI – were simple figments of their imagination. The Anglo-Americans, refusing Rudolf Hess's proposals for a change of allegiances, had made their choice. They judged that, for the moment at least, Germany was the main enemy. Having invaded Italy, they prepared landings in France: indeed it was Roosevelt who insisted on this project (Operation Overlord) as against Churchill who wanted to invade the Balkans to impose control there and put an end to the development of the red partisans.

It is true that the Anglo-Americans had no problem letting the Soviets wear themselves out fighting the Wehrmacht, before reaping the benefits of this themselves. Purely military considerations are not enough to explain the mediocre numbers engaged in Italy and the slow pace of Allied progress. Significant too was the division of war supplies which Roosevelt himself exposed, '40 percent to Britain, 39 percent to the Near East and 24 percent to the Soviet Union [sic[420]], which by far and away bears the heaviest burden of the war', *La Vérité* reported.[421]

At the Casablanca conference the Anglo-Americans were above all preoccupied with the question of how to catch up with the Red Army in Europe quickly. Marcel Hic explained,

> At Casablanca they discussed not the Allies' plans, but rather the joint efforts of the British and Americans – Roosevelt himself made this clear. Thus they discussed not how to assist the USSR, but rather the measures needed to speed up British and American army operations such that they could meet with the Russian forces. Just as in the case of German and Russian allied forces coming to meet each other in Poland, each side seeks to reach its ally as quickly as possible to ensure itself control of positions which could prove decisive when waging war in the future against today's ally.[422]

But for the moment American imperialism's counter-revolutionary effort was not expressed via its military operations. On the contrary, in weakening the Nazi occupier, it risked freeing up revolutionary forces. That is why the 15 January 1943 *La Vérité* commented: 'The Americans are in North Africa. We celebrate the blow struck against German imperialism, which allows us to hope for a more rapid collapse of the Nazi army'.[423]

However, the article continued, since the landings they had demonstrated their true role: 'American imperialism wages its war for objectives which are not, and never could be, the same as our own. Its concern is to struggle for world economic hegemony, not for democracy.'

In November 1943, the conference of the American Socialist Workers' Party addressed this issue:

> The preponderance of American power has everywhere begun to assert itself with increasing force. The industrial, financial and military might of the United States has become the decisive factor in the inter-imperialist struggle for world domination.
>
> Washington's diplomatic dealings and political acts during the past year have served to expose the pretence that this war is being waged to defend democracy against fascism and to extend the 'Four Freedoms' throughout the world. They have disclosed the real reactionary character of Washington's war aims, which are dictated by American Big Business's drive for political and economic mastery of the world. The slogan of 'the

war for democracy' was considerably tarnished from the outset by the inclusion of the Vargas and other despotic governments in the 'United Nations' coalition; by demonstrative friendship for the butcher Franco of Spain and dictator Salazar of Portugal; by the wooing of Pétain, the patronage of Otto of Hapsburg and various European monarchs-in-exile. Today the deals with Darlan and Badoglio outline in precise terms the counter-revolutionary policies and imperialist aims of Anglo-American capitalism.

The deal with Darlan, Vichy's hangman and Hitler's collaborator, served to maintain French imperial relations and to secure the collaboration of the French capitalism colonial governors and military caste. The old system of colonial oppression and super-exploitation remains unchanged under De Gaulle as under Darlan and Giraud; neither the African natives nor the French colonial workers have acquired democracy through Anglo-American occupation.

In Sicily AMGOT [Allied Military Government for Occupied Territories] kept at their posts all but the most notorious and hated fascist officials and police. The people are forbidden to carry on political activities; the press is controlled. 'The fascist label is removed' cables the *N. Y. Times* reporter, 'but the same men carry out the same functions'.[424]

Commenting on the decisions at the Casablanca conference, Marcel Hic concluded:

At Casablanca, Roosevelt and Churchill drew up their plans for counter-revolution. The European proletariat must counter this with a revolutionary strategy, the struggle for the Socialist United States of Europe.

Amazingly, Hic did not mention one of the main decisions of the conference: the demand for the unconditional surrender of the Axis countries. *La Lutte de classe* saw this as a simple piece of propaganda, a cover-up for their real intentions, which were simply to achieve peace. The Gaullist press celebrated it as proof of their commitment to anti-Nazism.

Subsequent historians would question the reasoning behind this vital decision: was it to put a stop to any negotiations that might take place between the Wehrmacht and the Soviets? Or, more likely, to reassure Stalin that the Allies would make no separate peace to his disadvantage?

One could also suggest that its central aim was to prevent any movement in Germany for a negotiated peace, leaving the Germans no option but to fight to the last behind their current leadership. For the Americans it was necessary that Hitler should fall under the weight of their own army's blows, not thanks to an anti-Nazi revolution.[425]

Indeed this was the American policy expressed in American Office of War Information director Elmer Davis's speech, commenting on the Allied victory in Tunisia on the radio on 18 May:

> Germany can expect no pity from us. We will be no weaker on the German people than we were on the German soldiers who came down towards our lines from the mountains, glad to see the war was over for them.

Quoting this statement, *La Vérité* commented:

> This is the triumph of Maurassism[426] in the Allied camp: at the very moment when the German people have begun to revolt against Hitler, they are pushed away, with the reply: you are just despicable Nazis, dirty barbarians against whom we must take up the cudgels.
>
> Not only has this policy reinforced the tottering rule of National Socialism; not only has its oppression prepared the ground for the new Hitlers of tomorrow; but furthermore it opens the way for the triumph of reaction across Europe: Maurassian foreign policy and Maurassian domestic policy. This cannot be the politics of the masses: workers will extend a hand to the German and Italian soldiers, as well as the Anglo-American ones. Together with them they will fight for the Socialist United States of Europe and the World.

La Vérité also suggested the slogans to be written on walls or in leaflets: 'Wir sind nicht Deutschlands Feinde; wir wollen die Vereinigten socialistichen Staaten Europas'.[427]

The policies of the Allies made clear to everyone the plans to dismember Germany, which first emerged in the United States (for example the White Plan, and that suggested in *Fortune* magazine) and in Britain (for example that suggested by Lord Vansittart). In France numerous Gaullist publications picked up on this theme, notably including some of the former SFIO Socialists.

La Vérité attacked these imperialist plans, counter-posing to them the Socialist United States of Europe. All signs were that the Allies were attempting to prevent any uprising in Germany. They could count on Stalin's support to this end. The USSR also had plans for a carve-up in

Germany. The Soviet press published a 'peace plan' by the economist Varga, which proposed war reparations thirteen times greater than those in the Treaty of Versailles, the dismantling and export to the USSR of all German machines, and the deportation of five million German workers to the USSR for forced labour.[428]

La Vérité, characterising this as a 'plan for enslavement', concluded that 'The Stalinist bureaucracy has once again proven itself to be the mortal enemy of the socialist revolution'.

It was not by chance that *Contemporary Review* asserted that even if an alliance had been struck with Stalin, it could never have been so with Trotsky.[429]

Chapter 8

TOWARDS 'LIBERATION'

Military and political events before Liberation

In 1944 the collapse of the Nazi empire accelerated. The Red Army reached Galicia in February; freed Leningrad; crushed ten German and Romanian divisions at Kherson in March; and retook Odessa in April and Sevastopol in May. By early June, it had regained the positions it held at the beginning of the German offensive in 1941. It took the offensive into Poland, crossing the borders of East Prussia, as well as occupying the Baltic States. By 1st September it had taken up positions along the whole of the Vistula.

In the west, the Allies who had long dragged their heels in Italy, finally broke through the German lines at Cassino in May and entered Rome, with the Germans containing them on a line between Pisa and Rimini, beyond which the puppet 'Fascist Republic' under Mussolini lived its last few months.

Finally, on 6 June came the long-awaited landings in Normandy. After a period of fierce fighting during which the Allies occupied Caen and Saint-Lô, they opened up a gap at Avranches, after which the whole German defence collapsed. Significantly helped by Resistance movements, the Allies drove towards Paris. By early September, they had occupied Belgium. At the same time the French First Army and the American Eighth Army landed at Saint-Raphaël (15 August); occupied the Midi, joining with the armies coming from the West; and by mid-September the Allies had reached the Vosges and the Moselle and were approaching Aachen. For the majority of the French people the war became a distant affair, much as it had been during the phoney war.

Would revolution break out in Germany, as the Trotskyists hoped? In July and August, in spite of the fictions of Nazi propaganda (which promised the last-minute intervention of dazzling new weaponry), the defeat of Hitler was a done deal.

Eastern Germany was occupied and almost everywhere the demoralised

German troops were pushed back to their own borders. German workers had little time to take the initiative before Allied and Soviet troops occupied their territory. But it was only a section of the bourgeoisie and the officer caste who tried to rid themselves of Hitler, in a July 1944 attempt to secure a compromise peace. The working class, lacking in leadership or perspectives, did not move. Neither did the soldiers and sailors. The anti-revolutionary precautions taken by the Anglo-American imperialists and the Soviet leadership were effective indeed, reinforcing that of the Nazis: that defeat should not lead to revolution as in 1918.

Indeed, the political outcome of the war in Eastern Europe was determined during these months. The French bourgeoisie was convinced that the collapse of Nazi order would mean the eruption of the revolutionary masses. We have seen how this fear led in late 1943 to General de la Porte du Theil's attempt to get Marshal Pétain to join the Allies. He was arrested in January 1944. Vichy was forced to collaborate ever-more-closely with the Nazis. However, as we shall see, the communications between Vichy and Algiers never ceased. All these people had just one thought: ensure the transition from the Vichy régime to the new bourgeois government at the service of the Allies, in such a way as to avoid any revolutionary upheavals. In July and August, Pétain and even Laval tried to carry out this transition themselves.

But there was no need for this. The Communist Party's collaboration with Algiers (two cabinet seats were given to Communist ministers in April) allowed the Gaullists to cut off this alliance: they did not have to face off a Communist attempt to seize power, and on the contrary could count on the PCF's assistance in preventing any uncontrollable movement.

Would the war transform into a revolutionary civil war led by the European proletariat? Indeed it was France that would prove decisive: whether Liberation led to a popular uprising for social liberation, or if it would be no more than a military victory for Anglo-American imperialism.

August 1944 was thus crucial to the whole historic period. The activity of internationalists took on a different political meaning. In 1939 they held back. In 1940 their opposition was still just 'on principle': the task was to try to get organised. In 1943 the task was to elaborate a strategy for revolution. By 1944, it was a different question: it was time to move to taking decisive action. Not only the capacity of the organisation was tested, or the effectiveness of its implantation and its cadre: but also the reality of its theoretical analyses.

The European conference of the Fourth International

In January 1944, the European conference of the Fourth International met. It took place near Beauvais, in the stables of a castle which Dalmas had converted into a lodgings and halfway house for escaped Russian prisoners. Armed groups of POI members kept watch over the surrounding area. The conference was in session for six days.

The turnout was mediocre. The French delegation was the largest, with Craipeau, Gibelin and Spoulber for the POI, Prager and Grimblat for the CCI, Henri Claude and Maillot for *Octobre*. Beyond that there was a strong delegation from the Belgian PCR (including Léon and Mandel), on or two German delegates (including Widelin), two Greeks (Raptis and Vitzoris) and a representative of the Spanish group.

The conference criticised the positions of both the POI and PCR on the national question, as well as the long-standing aggressiveness of the CCI and its schema-mongering. It set out 'as a basic position for all sections of our International in Europe', a 20,000 word document 'Theses on the end of the second imperialist war and the coming revolution' [430] [431].

These theses rejected the CCI's schemas regarding the USA's supposed priority of waging war on the USSR, and on the impossibility of a second front.

Analysing the Allied diplomatic offensive 'From Franco and Salazar to Ismet Inonu',[432] they asserted that 'the fundamental objective [of the bourgeoisie] is to avoid any discontinuity of bourgeois rule, any rupture in the state apparatus, or any fissure by which the proletarian revolution could overwhelm it and march forward'.

All the delegates were however convinced that 'without doubt, the imperialist war will continue its inexorable transformation into a civil war'. The conference predicted that the collapse of Japan would provoke a crisis 'engulfing the entire Far East', first and foremost in China: but the main centres of revolution would arise, albeit with varying speed, in the advanced capitalist countries, meaning America, Japan and above all 'decadent Europe'. The Italian example appeared to confirm this hypothesis.

> 25 July [1943] was not only the last day of Italian Fascism, it was also the first day of the coming European revolution. Spontaneously and with the emergence of 'communists agitating on the inside', the working masses have laid the groundwork for their own power.

The theses had to admit that the Socialist and Communist Parties which had accepted 'the transformation of these embryonic bodies of workers' power into purely economic commissions' exerted 'significant influence over wide layers of the working class'. But they considered that the road was shut to a renaissance of bourgeois-democratic structures: the Italian revolution would see further progress with the extension of the movement into Europe, firstly in Germany.

For now the struggle of the European masses was dominated by the struggle against Nazi occupation:

> At the moment the re-awakening of the masses and their combativity are largely expressed in resistance to oppression and exploitation by the occupier imperialism... The national sentiment of the masses, extremely confused as it is, above all expresses in reactionary terms their hostility to super-exploitation by German imperialism, their opposition to the reactionary régime installed under the aegis of German bayonets, and their refusal to submit to fascist dictatorship.
>
> This revolt hides, behind its nationalist and reactionary form, a revolutionary core, in spite of the attempts by the different national bourgeoisies and world imperialism to divert this to their advantage.

The conference asserted that 'with the constant exacerbation of social contradictions' the masses' resistance would take on 'a more and more acute class character'. It added that this would confront 'the 'enemy' imperialism in the opposite camp, as well as its own bourgeoisie'.

Unfortunately there was no evidence to back up this optimistic analysis. The conference defined its orientation thus:

> The proletariat supports this struggle [against oppression by German imperialism] to facilitate and accelerate its transformation into a generalised struggle against capitalism. This stance demands the most energetic struggle against attempts to re-establish the capitalist state and capitalist armies. On the contrary, everything must be done to develop the embryos of workers' power (militias, councils etc.) along with the most energetic struggle against all capitalist structures.

In turn it addressed the provisional secretariat's directives regarding the partisan movement. But the partisans' role was understood as auxiliary forces for the revolution; their actions subordinate to the revolutionary movement in urban industrial areas.

It denounced 'the crude and self-defeating slogan for 'national insurrection', in reality sure to mask the transition of the leadership of the military apparatus and the police to another leadership in the same mould'.

In the event of an uprising by the mass of the people within the framework of limited [Allied] landings [in France], or their preparation, the proletariat will work to give this [movement] a strong class character: it will oppose any attempt to rebuild the bourgeois army with a struggle for the arming of the proletariat and a workers' militia.

We can see the limit of such directives. Firstly, the internationalists did not seek to take any initiative in the uprising. Thus they evaded the fact that the uprising would seek first and foremost to tear down the structures of Nazi oppression (whether military or political). That only posed the problem: what new structures? Would power be returned to the prefects in Algiers or the Belgian royal family? Or would the armed people keep power: and how? Revolutionaries could only answer these questions if they themselves took the initiative.

The Fourth International believed that the key to the situation lay elsewhere: the revolutionary crisis in Germany would pull the revolutionary movement across Europe in a proletarian direction. 'The German revolution is the dorsal fin of the European revolution'. The theses analysed the exacerbation of contradictions in Germany. The bourgeoisie would try to take the lead, getting rid of Hitler and negotiating a compromise peace. But the German proletariat, 'much greater in numbers and more [geographically] concentrated' than in 1933, would 'play a decisive role from the outset'.

However, unlike what played out in Italy, there were no signals in January 1944 heralding the collapse of the régime. The theses under-estimated the capacity of the dictatorship, and above all, that of the Allied imperialisms which sought to 'take military, political, intellectual and moral leadership of a nation of eighty million people'. They wanted to impose a purely military outcome, thus preventing any revolutionary upheavals.

Indeed, the Soviet Union pursued this policy with determination. The theses explained:

> The bureaucracy has no answer to imperialism except using the methods of imperialism itself: thus it must ensure strategic border positions, create spheres of influence and seek to take charge of the economic resources which will allow it to rebuild and stabilise its economy.
>
> [...] Essentially this means that while it takes advantage of the uprisings of the mass of the people, it instrumentalises these to serve the interests of the bureaucratic caste, via an alliance with sections of the bourgeoisie and petty-bourgeoisie. This manoeuvre is played out under the flag of

private property and bourgeois democracy. In reality, by its very nature, the bureaucracy is unable to do both at once: the economy of its border states cannot be joined together with the Soviet economy except by recourse to the same structures, meaning the nationalisation of industry, the collectivisation of agriculture and planning. The bureaucracy cannot allow for any democracy. On the contrary, the more the development of the productive forces increases the social weight of the proletariat and allows for real proletarian democracy at all levels of politics and the economy, the more the bureaucracy has to break the real proletarian movement to defend its own privileges. The fate of the Vilnius soviet in 1939[433] is evidence enough of what the Stalinist bureaucracy plans for the revolutionary proletariat in neighbouring countries.

But, instead of taking account of the decisive effect the USSR had on the balance of forces, the conference reassured itself by repeating predictions as to the imminent fall of Stalinism:

The war having aggravated the contradictions of the Russian economy to an intolerable degree, without doubt the time has now come for the dissolution of the Stalinist bureaucracy.

The conference adopted a resolution on a strategic orientation to working-class struggles:

The strategy of the Fourth International is always dominated by one central idea: to encourage the masses to take their struggles into their own hands and exercise power for themselves.[434]

One early step in this direction was the emergence of factory committees in Italy. But a rather more modest experience in Belgium gave another example of this:

In some regions, workers are meeting in factories to discuss the problems of the workplace and elect and recall their delegates. Their victories in numerous economic struggles, often even achieved in conflict with the decisions of the occupying forces [i.e. against deportations], have led workers in other companies and in other areas to follow their example.[435]

Similarly, *La Vérité* quoted extracts from *Travail* – the trade union publication of engineering workers in Liège, which declared its support for a revolutionary struggle – and the Charleroi miners' *Réveil des mineurs*:

We must fulfil the tasks of our class. To this end, in each colliery we should form pit committees, comprising the most class-conscious workers and those most devoted to our cause.

We must engage in agitation and propaganda in order to convince workers in other firms to unite their forces with ours in a real *workers' front*. *Le Réveil des mineurs* ... will fight against patriotic and collaborationist tendencies.[436]

The Fourth International conference declared its support for the Workers' Front policy. First of all this meant regrouping revolutionary workers of all tendencies in 'workers' groups'.

But today's working class struggles have already far exceeded the limits of the workshop and the factory. We have seen major waves of working-class struggle arise (strikes in Liège and Charleroi, by miners in northern France, by engineering workers, strikes against deportations, the 11 November strikes, etc.). It is necessary to organise these movements, break them from the nationalist stranglehold still encouraged by the union sacrée parties, and to bring them together with class struggle objectives. That is why the Fourth International emphasises the need for a Workers' Front as a general slogan for propaganda and organisation.

Apart from immediate objectives, this slogan paved the way for workers' committees, or soviets. The Workers' Front had to seek unity with the middle classes, above all working peasants, with slogans such as workers' and peasants' control of food supply and storage. The Trotskyists worked to prepare 'the arming and military organisation of the working class on a factory-by-factory basis'.

They defined the main themes of their programme as follows:

1. Defence of the immediate interests of workers: a living wage (as far as possible, fight for equal cost of living increases, not percentage increments); equal wages for women, young people and workers from the colonies; an end to speed-ups; opposition to extension of the working day; better food.
This struggle 'must be oriented towards wider demands like the sliding scale of wages and workers' control'.
2. Organisation of collective resistance to conscription of the workforce, deportations to Germany and industrial or military mobilisations. 'Orient this struggle in such a manner as to demonstrate the national

bourgeoisie's collaboration with the occupier imperialism and the solidarity between workers in the occupied and occupying countries.

3. Solidarity with the victims of fascist repression, with activists arrested by the police and the Gestapo, and with the draft resisters hunted down as outlaws [...]

4. Organisation of effective contacts with workers deported to Germany in order to spread the struggle to German factories.

5. Organisation of fraternisation with workers in countries subject to fascist dictatorship, whether in the German factories or through propaganda directed at Axis troops (emphasising the importance of this fraternisation in preventing the repression of strikes and paralysing SS interventions, thanks to the soldiers' attitude: following the Italian example).

6. A systematic offensive for the exercise of working-class freedoms: defending the right to strike by taking strike action; election and selection of workers' delegates who will be the real voice of working-class interests; protection of these delegates, etc.

7. Systematic disruption of German war production with collective action in all its forms (go-slows, passive resistance etc,) up to and including mass sabotage ....

8. Preparation for the insurrectionary struggle of the masses: the [Bolshevik-Leninists] explain that the emancipation of the working class must be the act of the working class itself, and they must work not only to get rid of the apparatus of the German state and its satellites, but also at the same time [the apparatus] of the national bourgeoise which will try to re-establish its authority with the support of Allied bayonets; they dedicate all their strength to the armed struggle for the overthrow of the dictatorship of capitalism and for the establishment of the dictatorship of the proletariat.

Contrary to the theses of the CCI, the conference stressed the imminent prospect of [Allied] landings in occupied Europe. The resolution on the coming revolution and the second front[437] remarked that it was 'more than probable that landings would facilitate revolutionary explosions' and tried to give perspectives to the movement in order to:

bring together separate movements, [...] use the appropriate slogans to allow the revolutionary aspirations of the autonomous movement of the masses to achieve meaningful results, and orient [this movement] resolutely towards the transformation of the imperialist war into a civil war.

The resolutions pointed forward to a general strike, the general arming of the proletariat, fraternisation and the seizure of power. But there was no evaluation of the balance of forces to accompany this. The delegates were counting on the eruption of revolution in Germany to radically alter this balance of forces.

The unification of the French Trotskyists: the Parti communiste internationaliste

The European conference decided that the groups adhering to it should take the title of 'internationalist' communist parties. It elected a European secretariat to co-ordinate their activity. It rationalised their statutes: for the illegal period there would be a distinction between contacts, sympathisers, and candidate members incorporated into a cell, who could become full members after a programme or course in which they would be put to the test (three months long for workers, six months for others).[438]

Finally, the conference decided on the unification of its French section (the POI) with two other groups who accepted the Fourth International's discipline: the *Octobre* group and the CCI. The latter had led an interminable procedural battle for 'parity' with the POI (which was five times larger) in its leadership bodies[439]. Ultimately a Central Committee was formed with three POI members (Craipeau, Gibelin and Spoulber), two from the CCI (Prager and Grimblat), one from *Octobre* (Henri Claude) and a representative of the European secretariat (Pablo) to cast a deciding vote when this was needed. This Central Committee was tasked with preparing 'unity from top to bottom, and in all fields, within a maximum time limit of one month'. In the meantime, each organisation preserved its own internal life. Resolutions planned in detail the mechanics of fusion (faction rights remaining in place until the party congress), the functioning of its commissions (workplaces, young people, cadres) and even the leadership of the Paris branch (two POI, one CCI, one *Octobre* member).

The PCI published *La Vérité* (two POI, one CCI and one *Octobre* member [on the editorial committee]) centrally, as well as *La Jeune Garde,* a *Bulletin intérieur* (equal control), *Le Militant* (for cadre training), and the organs of industrial branches like *La Lutte des cheminots*. All these publications were the same as the POI's, as well as all the regional newspapers, with the exception of the Paris region's, which became *Le Soviet*. The theoretical journal *IVe Internationale* was edited by the European secretariat, whereas, significantly, *Ohé! Partisans* ceased publication.

Only the small *Lutte de classe* group did not participate in the unification of the Trotskyists. It considered that the self-critiques by the CCI – and above all, the POI – were insufficient. It wrote in February 1944 that:

If it is able – in a text expressing an official position – to transform the story of the treason of the Fourth International movement into a myth of Bolshevik insight (save for a few errors) the ideological level of the POI must be low indeed.

It was only the failings of the Trotskyists which had left them isolated during the phoney war, whereas, it judged:

Never was it easier to make contact with the masses (and not only with the working-class), and never had the masses been more ready to welcome revolutionary propaganda.[440]

But the *Lutte de classe* group did not explain its own isolation!

A quarter of a century later, a *Lutte ouvrière* pamphlet justified their refusal to participate in unification by citing the lack of any self-critique by the French section. But then it offered a more plausible explanation:

We knew that given our small numbers, it would not be possible for us to sort out the French section from the inside. It had become an opportunist organisation, and our only hope was to try and demonstrate to the most valuable elements of the PCI the correctness of the political and organisational methods of Bolshevism, occasioning regroupment.[441]

In reality this was the self-justification of a sect: the *Lutte de classe* group would remain a miniscule force, without even local influence.

The January national conference of the POI, which saw representatives of the POI meet, ratified unification inspite of its bureaucratic character, inevitable in a period of illegality. Only the representative of the Lyon region, Marc Paillet, insisted on the need for a political discussion in advance, to defend the party 'against opportunism and ultra-leftism'. Quoting Lenin ('Before uniting we must purge ourselves'), he demanded a more developed self-critique by the POI.[442]

However, at the Paris region conference, differences were expressed. The majority resolution, proposed by Essel and Michèle Mestre, again confirmed a break with the nationalist deviations encapsulated in the 1942 theses on the national question, and was entirely based on the orientation defined in the theses of the European conference.[443]

But Swann presented a minority resolution:

The Congress [...] approves of the main themes of the European secretariat's report on the international situation, but cannot accept the condemnation of the theses on the national question which the Party, meeting in its regular congress in 1943, voted for unanimously [...]

[...] The national bourgeoisie is attempting across Europe to exploit to its advantage [the] national movement of the masses, in imposing its own imperialist goals as [this movement's] objectives. But in spite of this fact, the national movement of the masses remains an anti-imperialist movement, and, fundamentally, in its day-to-day actions is as opposed to traditional imperialist oppression as it is to German imperialist oppression. That is why the Fourth International supports the national movement of the masses in Europe against the traditional imperialist oppressor and the German imperialist oppressor, at the same time as supporting the movements of national minorities.

Concretely speaking, in France, supporting the national movement of the masses entails:

a) Fighting with the masses against all forms of imperialist oppression: the occupation, requisitions of farm produce, deportations and the suppression of democratic and working-class freedoms.

b) Explaining to the mass of the people that a free and independent France cannot be conceived of except as part of a Europe united by socialism.

Only if the Party is able to put itself at the head of the masses in today's essential struggles against imperialist oppression, will proletarian slogans and means of action be the slogans and means of action adopted by the national movement of the masses. The path suggested by the sectarians of the CCI, or the imprecise one advocated by the [Central Committee] meaning the capitulation of our Party, cannot but cut us off from the masses, meaning it will lead to the Party being pulled onto the track towards the defeat of the proletarian revolution in Europe.

The minority claimed the tradition of the Transitional Programme of the Fourth International, which recognised that 'there is something just and progressive in the patriotism in the masses'. They declared their hostility towards 'an adventurist fusion led by sectarians within our own organisation, joining with an adventurist group which had been excluded from the International'.[444]

This 'adventurist group' was the CCI, which did not suffer from any lack of modesty:

> The Party needs a revolutionary leadership... the CCI is this leadership. The POI is a petty-bourgeois tendency with a petty-bourgeois social base. The activity of the party can only take place on the basis of aggravated class struggle.[445]

Formed into a faction, it organised stormy interventions in the cells it controlled and constituted itself as a secret leadership of the party. Those who refused this discipline were expelled from the faction... and the CCI fought to hound them out of the party altogether.

This had already happened to Lambert:[446] [447] leader of a tendency hostile to the 'doctrinal rantings' of the CCI, he was excluded from the CCI for his 'irresponsible attitude towards the tasks entrusted to him'.[448] The POI decided that the main reason for this expulsion was political and refused to exclude him from the party. Having opposed the CCI's factional constitution, the CCI minority in turn joined with the *Octobre* group's militants: this faction published a platform which filled the second issue of the *Bulletin intérieur*, believing itself to be the 'authentic' representation of the new party.[449]

The POI majority refused to set up a third faction. It counted on its own political cohesion, its respect for the theses of the European conference and its own superior role in mass work.

This confidence was soon breached, firstly at a political level. The unification process dragged out: interminable meetings of the Central Committee were devoted to sharing out tasks, with the CCI representatives wanting to occupy all important positions and to block decisions. During this period *La Vérité* continued to appear as the organ of the POI. Under the headline 'The flags of the Red Army will join with our red flags', an editorial by Spoulber (alias Marcoux) commented:

> The USSR's armies will not crush the soviets of Berlin, Budapest and Paris. On the contrary it is these Soviets who will remind the Russian army what a soviet army is... Tomorrow, Europe will be ablaze with the flame of revolution.[450]

This poetic messianism elicited reactions from a number of activists who saw in this, with some concern, the same tendency for rhetoric as the CCI's.

The cohesion of the POI was more seriously challenged by an organisational failure. The POI leadership tried to implant itself in armed groups. In January, as we have seen, Parisot was arrested, while Craipeau was wounded by the Gestapo while attempting to establish contact with a partisan group. In early March a military operation in Paris failed, leading to the arrest of seven militants including a young mechanic from Montrouge, Maurice Laval.

These arrests gave the CCI the opportunity they were waiting for to take control of the party. They demanded a stop to unification in the Paris region – under the pretext of security – the replacement of the Central Committee by a body comprised of three members intended to purge the party (in reality, this meant the POI) and to reorganise it. The European secretariat did not agree to entrust sole leadership to the CCI but it did suspend the Central Committee and the regional committee, deciding to take charge of the reorganisation of the party in the Paris region, with a three-member consultative committee. As military organiser of the POI, Craipeau was suspended awaiting the results of an enquiry. Throughout one decisive month – that of the establishment of the party and its press – CCI leaders assumed most organisational posts, initiating a purge and establishing their faction at many of the levers of control. Their behaviour elicited a stormy reaction by the *Octobre* group, which attacked 'the grave dangers presented to the revolutionary party by the infantile, Stalinist and sectarian conceptions of the CCI leadership comrades.[451]

This was the payback for the *La Commune* group which the International had excluded in 1936 at Trotsky's instigation. This meant the loss of a significant number of members, making its mark on the first steps of the unified party. *La Vérité*, now controlled by the CCI, stressed that it had nothing to do with the sixty-four issue that went before (starting again from issue no. 1). It was mainly devoted to propaganda against the Allies. Moreover there could be found the CCI's theses on the impossibility of any second front: 'The second front is nothing but a cynical manoeuvre. The only front that American and British imperialism are determined to establish, is the front against the working class'.[452]

Finally, on 10 April, three months after the European conference, the regular bodies of the party were re-established. *La Vérité* was now numbered in line with previous issues (issue sixty five, new series issue five...) under the control of Spoulber and Prager. But the party was still constrained by a faction which, even if still very much in a minority, diverted all its policies.

Would the PCI influence the course of events?

Any organisation of professional revolutionaries presents a danger: its militants end up living amongst themselves, separate from the real world, judging the mood of the masses by theoretical schemas which can confirm their selective outlook thanks to a narrow fringe of sympathetic and supportive workers. In a period of extreme illegality, the situation is even more serious for the leadership, whose contacts are reduced to a few organisers, themselves without direct relations with the masses.

The circumstances which separated them from the organisation for some time forced them to examine the reality they faced. That is what enabled Lambert to take stock of the real balance of forces: thus the CCI minority platform attacked the CCI perspectives according to which the revolution was an automatic process which the vanguard would inevitably carry through at the given moment, 'one could not imagine any greater caricature of Marxism'. The party was nothing more than 'the embryo of the revolutionary party'. Its role was to 'foment a movement', 'giving workers clear objectives for their struggle at the same time as associating itself with the best militants in this struggle'. At the present moment the Parti communiste français had total hegemony over struggles, and would assume a leadership role via its worker-activists. The future would depend on the role its militants played:

> The nationalism of the masses is superficial and shatters when struggle breaks out. Every workers' struggle, whether for basic demands or in opposition to German exploitation, brings them into direct confrontation against the bosses and the État français,[453] thus leading to the division of the 'nation' and the national unity alliance the Stalinist party hopes to cement with the French bourgeoisie.
>
> It is starting from this objective situation – appreciation of the conflict between a superficial nationalist ideology and the fundamental class instinct of the workers which will kill this off when they take to action – that the Fourth International will now be able, in joining the movement of the masses, to win the most advanced layers of workers to its banner.[454]

Lambert was counting on a general strike to accentuate the divorce between those Communist militants who 'wished to take the next struggle to the limit' and their leadership who wanted to contain them within the union sacrée framework. It was necessary to 'think of the masses, and no longer in terms of a small nucleus', Lambert wrote. But 'thinking of the masses' required an understanding of the real aspirations of the masses in occupied Europe. In taking on board the illusion that their national aspirations were a veneer artificially imposed by the PCF leadership, there was a risk of creating a new mythology: the sidelining of the PCF by its grassroots and the magical powers of the general strike.

Such were the thoughts, at least, of Y. Craipeau, who now returned to the Central Committee. He had used his forced holiday to re-establish contacts among various working-class and peasant forces. He was able to understand the isolation of the internationalists (generally unknown), and the stunning progress of the Stalinists' propaganda and organisation. He came to understand that the masses aspired, above all, to get rid of the Nazis and their satellites, and that they nurtured deep illusions in liberation by the Allies. He was now convinced that the masses could not gain experience except in the course of the struggle against the fascists, taking a lead, and establishing their own power bases in place of the Vichyist authorities. He thought that they could only understand the counter-revolutionary character of the Allies and their agents in this struggle, which at this decisive moment would ultimately be resolved militarily. The party could not intervene in events or pull the vanguard behind it unless it itself controlled or influenced armed groups.

To make this orientation possible, in addition to participating in the production of *La Vérité* Craipeau now devoted himself to military questions, along with the party's new military specialist Marc Laurent (an alias of Henri Molinier).

But the party was not ready for such a policy. This becomes clear when we see a few examples of the critiques of the July issue put forward by certain (CCIist) cells. *La Vérité* had the title 'How to put an end to fascism and war'.

This is a title which a Stalinist would not disapprove of', cell 62 commented. 'Must we remind the *La Vérité* editorial committee that the Fourth International has always fought to demonstrate to the masses that fascism is the expression of rotten capitalism, and that emerging from fascism means nothing if it means going along with the band of Léon Blum or Marty[455] who counterpose to it their sacrosanct democracy, rather than [following] the [Bolshevik-Leninists]?'. 'Equally', cell 51 wrote, 'the majority with the good old habitats of the POI appeal to the tradition of their anti-fascist past. They should pipe down: it is not to their credit.

In terms of the [Allied] landings, the same cell commented:

The party's role in the event of landings will not be to use its slogans to encourage workers on to the course of revolution, but to arm them against the counter-revolutionary danger posed by the USA. All the problems of revolution will pare down to this one alone, which must be patiently explained.

Cell 62 attacked the call for factory committees: 'Advancing such slogans risks throwing the working class onto an adventurist path... as for the slogan for the liberation of prisoners, it is pure provocation ....'[456]

It is true that on the contrary other militants such as Séverin (alias Schmidt), a former military organiser of the POI, invited the party 'to move forward to actions to allow for the effective participation of workers in clandestine groups' raids on prisons and internment camps, the location and execution of spies and the establishment of arms and munitions stocks'.[457]

But the party did not take any practical action on this score.

The activity of the PCI was usually limited to propaganda and workplace activism. Moreover it had at its disposal numerous local offices. The Paris region's meetings were held in a small theatre, under the camouflage of drama projects.

La Vérité appeared regularly, with three issues in May, two in June and July and three in August, along with *Quatrième Internationale* and the *Bulletin intérieur*. However, there was no trace of *Le Militant*, nor *La Jeune Garde*. Workplace publications increased in number: each cell devoted itself to producing a newspaper. It is difficult to know what echo these regional and workplace publications found. One report which reached us was however significant in this regard, even if undoubtedly optimistic: that of the Nantes region (the fourth branch) in May 1944.

> The newspaper *Front ouvrier* remains the sole clandestine publication in the Nantes region. It is well known and exercises a growing influence over the workers. For example, the workers in the Chantiers de Penhoët had moaned about the terrible management of their canteen. Following an article in *Front ouvrier* these protests begun to take shape, with the men sending their representatives to management. The workers at C., who had been hostile to trade unions, organised en masse following the slogans of *Front ouvrier*. In Batignolles, workers in some buildings had to work on 1 May. *Front ouvrier* launched an appeal for a total stoppage, which was followed to the letter. The regard for the newspaper is such that workers, upon finding a package of copies of *Front ouvrier*, spontaneously distribute it in their workshop or introduce it into factories where we had absolutely no previous links, pushing the envelope as far as slipping it into their workmates' pockets. The bosses think they are dealing with a formidable organisation, to the point of complaining to the Gestapo and the French police, as in the case of the Batignolles and Chantiers de Penhoët management. In a more general sense, supervisors, engineers and directors have changed their attitude to the workers after

their names have been published in *Front ouvrier*. This newspaper contributes substantially to the radicalisation of the working masses and the demoralisation of the boss class.[458]

But the report also insisted on covering 'negative aspects'. There were no workers' groups except in certain major factories. The PCI's militants generally worked in small workplaces, with less demand for newsprint. Moreover they lacked theoretical understanding. Propaganda remained at the level of immediate struggles, to the point that 'many believe that it is the [Parti communiste français] who publish *Front ouvrier*'.

The 'workers' groups' were in fact nothing more than groups of sympathisers, and the 'workers' front' slogan remained a propagandist one.

It was on the occasion of 1 May 1944 that the PCI first ventured to launch a generalised slogan. The government had decided to 'celebrate May Day on Sunday 30 April'. The PCI called on the working class to walk out at 10am on Monday 1 May. But it explained: 'If the CGT or the Stalinist party call for strikes at another time on Monday, the PCI will rally behind their directives. Working-class unity against the bosses'.[459]

But the government feared demonstrations and strikes. It abandoned plans to make people work on 1 May and declared it a bank holiday.

> After having decreed that 1 May would take place this year on 30 April, the Vichy government, fearing demonstrations on Monday 1 May, has now announced that this will be a day off. This decision marks an extraordinary retreat by the government under the pressure of the general discontentment of the working masses and the combativity of the working class.
>
> In spite of their army of cops, militiamen and spies, the bourgeoisie and its government fear letting the workers into the factories on 1 May and do not know what to do to stop working-class anger from exploding. They have suddenly stopped talking about the draft in the press: the police raids have relented, as if by chance, in the lead-up to 1 May, and as well as the solemn speeches, they promise ... an extra pound of sugar and other commodities for the 'labour festival' à la Vichy. These are feeble measures to humour the workers.
>
> If events allow them time, the Vichy slave drivers will continue with mass deportations to Germany to decapitate the working class and prevent any mass movement in the industrial centres. The draft, which has its goal replacing the German workers sent to the bloodbath of war against the USSR, also represents the solidarity of the international capitalist class

against the system which emerged from the October Revolution. There will be no other means for the working class to resist the assault of world imperialism if it does not at once prepare its response, a general strike.[460]

The Communists join the government

In 1936, the French Communists declined the offer made to them by Léon Blum to participate in government. But in 1944, like the Socialists, they took part in the union sacrée government.

The Italian party had already taken this course. Having helped Badoglio to domesticate the workplace committees, the Partito Comunista Italiano agreed to delegate five of its members to the government, including its leader Ercoli (an alias of Togliatti). This ministerial role was all the more paradoxical given that it was a government under the same monarchy which the party denounced; Victor Emmanuel himself had called Mussolini to power and led Italy with him for twenty-two years; and ultimately the head of government was still General Badoglio, a former leading Fascist dignitary. Togliatti justified this extraordinary change of direction:

> Italy today does not need more professors and politicians, but generals and admirals, and the Communists must for the moment put to one side their republican convictions to work for the building of a broad-based popular government.[461]

There was no question of raising their revolutionary convictions.

Of course this orientation corresponded well to that of the USSR, as the ambassador Bogomolov explained to De Gaulle on 28 April 1944:

> Early on in the meeting, Mr. Bogomolov expressed his views on Italy. In his opinion, things were going well there. Badoglio seemed able to hold the situation together. The debate over the monarchy had settled down: indeed, the Soviet government was not opposed to the monarchical system.[462]

As for France, the situation was even less complicated. In 1943, the USSR had recognised the Gaullist Comité National as 'the leadership organ of resistant France, its sole objective being to organise the population and French territories (i.e. continental France and also its colonies) for the war effort'.

The Parti communiste had rallied to the Gaullist Resistance and delegated Fernand Grenier to Algiers, taking allegiance to the General [de Gaulle].

At the same time, De Gaulle recounted: 'André Marty repeatedly went to meet Garreau, our representative in Moscow, to tell him that he was at my disposal'.

Of course, De Gaulle did not trust the Communists:

(On the Conseil National de la Résistance) they managed to ensure that five of the fifteen members were either overt or concealed supporters of their own. This council itself delegated its responsibilities to a bureau of four members, two of whom were Communists who established themselves in positions of military control, a so-called 'action' committee dominated by 'party' men.

There were angry altercations with Giraud, who, taking personal initiative and 'through lack of sound judgement', sent the weapons under his control to the Front national in Corsica, led by the Communist Giovani.

But he knew that he had to keep the Parti communiste in line in order to prevent any questioning of his authority or that of the 'État National' (meaning, the bourgeois state).

And the Communists? The role they played in the Resistance as well as my desire to ensure their forces were integrated into those of the nation, at least for the duration of the war, led me to the decision that I should bring two of them into government.[463]

To put it another way, it was about domesticating them when he needed them, and this had to be done at cut-price: De Gaulle offered them 'the Ministry of Aircraft' (where, at least, there was no risk they could pose any danger) and a 'Commissioner of State' without any definite purpose.

From late August 1943 'the party could expect several of its members to be candidates for ministerial roles, to be chosen by me. But at the moment of execution (what an admirable turn of phrase from De Gaulle!), all sorts of problems prevented those who I had called up to the Comité de la Libération from giving me a positive reply. When the party representatives proposed other choices to me, they also insisted that these should receive certain ministerial portfolios. Soon, indisposed to this strung-out horse-trading, I broke off negotiations'.

De Gaulle interpreted their procrastination thus:

In reality there were two tendencies among their delegation. One was violent (sic), following André Marty's line that the party should not tie itself to anyone else, using the struggle against the enemy as direct preparation for a revolutionary action to seize power. There was also that of the manoeuvrers, who sought to inveigle themselves into the state by collaborating with others, firstly with myself: the inspiration for this tactic was from Maurice Thorez, who was still in Moscow and begged to be allowed to return…

But in March 1944 the Communists made their decision. They allowed Fernand Grenier and François Billoux to take the positions I had offered them: the former becoming the Minister of Aircraft, the latter a Secretary of State.

Not only had the Parti communiste broken with communist principle, but it had accepted the seats it was offered without even being able to choose who occupied them.

La Vérité commented:

The Communists have declared themseves ready to 'serve' – as the new minister Grenier puts it – what is clearly a bourgeois state: it is the programme advanced by all the imperialists, that of the 'victory' (of imperialism) and of 'the total unity of France and its overseas territories', meaning, the continuation of colonial oppression, which these two 'communists' plan to enforce in the name of their party.

It requires all the flippancy of a cynical bureaucrat to today dare to speak in such language to a working class exhausted by five years of imperialist war! Stalin's bureaucracy, which has betrayed the world revolution and pushed the debris of the Communist International into a union sacrée in the 'Allied' countries, now guarantees the international bourgeoisie its intention to oppose revolution and defend capitalism. The new lackeys dressed up as ministers, Billoux and Grenier, agents of French imperialism, represent the interests of a small bureaucracy and not those of the working class. They now work towards complete fusion with the national-liberal politics of imperialism. We are thus heading towards a clean and sharp break between the 'patriotic communists' – the wreckage of the Third International – and the internationalist communists….

The article concluded with a question:

But class-conscious workers, those who filled the jails and camps of French imperialism (before filling out those of the Nazis), those who want to put an end to capitalist barbarism, will they not turn away from this latest treachery in disgust? Will they still remain in the parties of Grenier and Ercoli, in the parties of 'my lord, the minister'?[464]

The answer was not so simple. Why should those who had accepted the union sacrée, participation in the bourgeois Resistance under the leadership of De Gaulle and the turn to anti-Boche chauvinism, not then accept the logical next step, participation in government?

Among the leaders of the PCF there were not differences of principle, but rather of tactics. Some of them had not ruled out the idea that the party could use its predominant role in the national struggle to take power. The others wanted to push as far as possible the logic of their participation in the – bourgeois and colonialist – state, reserving full power to the party for a later date. We would see this conflict emerge – typically in a latent form – during and after Liberation.

The internationalists were feeding off illusions when they hoped to exploit the indignation of Communist members over their leaders' participation in government with a simple reminder of revolutionary principle. Its militants and workers found in the De Gaulle government an echo of the Popular Front. They had not drawn the lessons of the 1936 [general strike], which for them seemed like a happy experience. In their eyes the Popular Front had been betrayed: it had not betrayed them.

Effectively the Algiers government was a variant of the Popular Front. It was a right wing variant in which the Gaullist bourgeoisie replaced the bourgeoisie of the Parti radical, which had sunk without trace in the torment of war. It was a variant in line with the 'French Front' project advocated by Thorez in 1937, with a strong representation of reactionary nationalist forces, fiercely determined to insist on their territorial 'rights' as against those of Italy, something which could easily be married with Stalin's plans to carve up Germany.[465]

De Gaulle's objective was to prevent a revolutionary explosion. He had this in mind when reflecting on what to do within France: 'putting a block on goods, banknotes, wages and prices all at once would be lighting the touchpaper... it would provoke a social earthquake'. His plan foresaw 'A substantial increase in salaries – of the order of 30% – with which we shall avoid social crisis'.[466]

He wanted to anaesthetise the working class, and the PCF lent him its help in this policy. But the bourgeoisie did not trust it.

The bourgeoisie prepares for civil war

The differences between the Communists and the Algiers government's strategists appeared to be essentially tactical, or even technical: 'Should we build mass maquis forces, or masses of maquis forces?'; 'Was it militarily possible to defend the Vercors and Glières plateaux?'[467] Tillon explained, in his history of the FTP:

> In the eyes of De Gaulle's high command and the Anglo-American armies, the tightly centralised maquis forces had the capital advantage of being able to control their armed operatives and prepare a return to classical methods of hierarchy which ensured the soldiers were ready to fight without being concerned by objectives. The woollen uniforms were premature, for certain, but there was also the possibility of imposing uniformity on 'those without uniform' and taking control of them: in a word, 'regularising' these 'irregular' troops.
>
> 'Thus they continued to refuse to supply arms to 'irregular' FFI forces: that was because, of course, they were not being refused to those who were considered to be the regular army in waiting.[468]

But a little later Tillon dotted a few i's:

> The policy of large concentrations [of troops] sought to create forces of order as well as forces for fighting the enemy… surely these forces of a classic military character – cut off from the masses and held as reserves – would be ready to impose their own politics when the Germans retreated, given some of their intentions. Was not this one among the goals of the Aigoual maquis, near the Gard mining basin and not far from Marseille?
>
> And had the same plan not been made for the industrial valley of Isère, half way between Lyon and Marseille, with the Allied armies needing to take control of the Northern Zone of France? Finally, any hopes of an attempted communist insurrection were also haunted by the ambitions of those who sought any negotiation possible with the generals now able to replace Hitler with another government. This was the subject of meditation for the 'psychologists of revolutionary war', who were out of step with today's 'communes'.

The fear of a working-class insurrection – led by the PCF – or more precisely the fear that the working class would establish itself in power at the moment of the État français's collapse, haunted the whole bourgeoisie, from Pétain to De Gaulle. The bourgeoisie prepared to co-ordinate the

Vichyist and Gaullist forces to try and confront this. According to Tillon, this fear became a 'hope' of the bourgeoisie's, and the Versaillais[469] of Vichy and Algiers were getting ready for it. But the Communists of 1944 were not Communards:[470] they would make common cause with the Versaillais until the end.

The PCF was well aware of how to use the armed forces at its disposal: but not to help the workers take power, nor to prepare the prior conditions for this seizure of power. Rather, to exert pressure on the bourgeois state, such that it would give sufficient powers to the Communists in its government and follow a foreign policy in line with the interests of the Soviet Union. This policy demanded that the PCF should present itself as a steadfast ally of the national bourgeoisie and at no time disappoint the – still only relative – confidence that had been placed in it.

Under the tricolour flag of the maquis and the camouflage of the common slogan of 'national liberation', there were in reality three different wars being fought:

1. That of the majority of maquis troops, the youth and a number of Communist militants: for them the 'liberation of France' would also mean social liberation, which would purge the country of exploiters and open the way for socialism, as indeed the programme of the Comité National de la Résistance promised. In the eyes of a number of Communist militants, for example Guinguoin in Limousin,[471] the maquis should take power and not let go.
2. That of the BCRA,[472] the generals and the bourgeoisie. In their eyes the maquis were the embryo of the regular army, not only as a 'national' force but also as a force of intervention against the revolution, including against the revolutionary maquis.
3. That of the Parti communiste: the maquis would play an essential role in the national insurrection which would re-establish the 'national' authorities but also allow the Parti communiste to exert heavy influence on them.

The maquis were thus the crucible of a latent but nonetheless unremitting civil war. But this was confused, because no real force clearly and deliberately expressed revolutionary and proletarian objectives. In practice all of them accepted one common national objective, meaning, the union sacrée.

La Vérité's intervention sought to clarify the divisions:[473]

> Last December *La Vérité* published a series of documents demonstrating the collaboration of all tendencies of the bourgeoisie to organise a civil

war against the working class. We have published, notably, the minutes of a meeting of the fascist Milice's leadership. We have also published a report of a meeting between Pétain and a general delegated from Algiers, who had come to ask him to cede power to De Gaulle as the only means of preventing a proletarian Commune.

Today we can cite new proof to support our claims. These are supplied by *L'Humanité*. The 15 March 1944 issue is devoted to a long article by Duclos on 'the fear of the people and betrayal of our homeland'. Duclos elaborates the following indictment: 'certain elements have let tonnes of arms fall into the hands of the enemy rather than giving them to the FTP. They have attempted to poach Resistance fighters from some organisations in order to enrol them in others. The fear of the people means they have turned their back on national insurrection. We have become aware of organisers who were ready to negotiate the protection of their maquis by Vichy.

And Duclos adds, 'This fear of the people could go as far as encouraging the Comités des Forges to try and use the Resistance to build an army of civil war against the patriots in the name of 'securing order'. There are criminals like Pucheu, who was recently one among the foremost agents able to boast of having 500 automatic machine-guns at his disposal.

'But Parti communiste militants will without doubt ask themselves: why does *L'Humanité* not say *which* 'Resistance' organisations are planning such a civil war against the working class? *L'Humanité* cannot denounce them openly because they are part of the same 'patriotic' circles as the Parti communiste and the Front national. But we Trotskyists have no links with these anti-working-class organisations. *La Vérité* can denounce them openly.

'The most typical of these Gaullist anti-Boche 'Resistance' organisations preparing for civil war against the working class is called L'organisation Civile et Militaire (OCM). Its leader was the Count of Vogüe, a big shot in the world of champagne, who the Germans sentenced to death for espionnage but who, it seems, was pardoned on account of services rendered against the working class. The OCM are not the only ones arming themselves against the workers. It is necessary to cite the Armée secrète itself in a large number of *départements*, particularly in the Paris region. Retired military men, Church types and freemasons, *Progrès social français*[474] men and Cagoulards,[475] who supply its cadre, have stocks of parachuted-in weapons almost everywhere. They want to make use of these to stop the workers taking the factories. Recently, they have organised their maquis with the complicity of Vichy, hunting down revolutionary or Communist draft resisters and preparing to crush a new Commune.

But still, any class-conscious worker will ask, what is there in common between these people and us, the revolutionary workers? How can they say that we are fighting for the same interests and under the folds of the same flag? How can we have one joint leadership?[476]

The patriotic workers' militias

Earlier that year the PCF had decided to establish armed workers' groups in the factories, the 'patriotic workers' militias'. A headline in *Métallo* in January defined their purpose:

Form your militias, embryos of the national army of liberation… At the moment when the formidable Allied air offensive has systematically destroyed Hitler's war arsenal, the engineering workers will not sit on the sidelines of this great fight: proud of their record of struggle, they will bring their own active and effective contribution.

La Vérité of 29 April 1944 attacked this 'nationalist trap': 'The workers do not have to take sides in this war… still less form patriotic militias, embryo of the national army.'

Would the party content itself once again with Platonic denunciations of the Stalinist line? If there was to be an expression of working-class opposition against this policy of class collaboration and counter-revolution, where better than among the vanguard of the working class, among those who had taken the risk to establish their own workers' militias within their workplaces. 'Patriotic' or not, at the decisive moment what could such militias do except protect workers' occupations of factories and bring support to neighbouring factories? If the internationalist communists stayed aloof from these militias, how could they establish contacts with the working-class vanguard (the great majority of which was influenced by the PCF) or hope to influence them in a revolutionary direction? It found that the militias were established slowly – which was understandable, given that in the Parti communiste strategy, based on the maquis, they only had a secondary and auxiliary role. As for the internationalist communists, on the contrary, the factories represented the decisive element in their strategy, because this strategy looked towards proletarian revolution.[477] This delay in the organisation of militias in the factories allowed them to take the initiative in some cases, or at least to play a role in their establishment. That is why, critiquing the April issue, Y. Craipeau proposed a turn: using the

PCF slogan to set up patriotic workers' militias, in order to try and give them a revolutionary purpose.

Such was the turn heralded in the 26 May issue of *La Vérité*. It did not content itself with the conclusion 'faced with the bourgeois offensive, arm the working class'. It called on workers to join the patriotic workers' militias.

> The great offensive against the working class is being prepared excitedly. Pétain is profiting from the gradual slowdown of industry in the Paris region to prepare an immense *razzia* of workers and to disperse them in works for Hitler's war effort. De Gaulle promises to mobilise them immediately, to prevent troubles. Darnand's Milice is arming. The OCM is arming, as are the police. The bourgeois 'Resistance' organisations are arming.
>
> Unless it is to be crushed by the forces of reaction, the working class must also arm itself.
>
> Join the militia in your workplace!
>
> The working class is understanding this necessity more and more clearly. In the factories militias are being constituted. Most of the time this is in response to calls made by the [Parti communiste]. The [Parti communiste] has called for the formation of Patriotic Militias in the factories. We have said what we think of this policy. We do not think that the working class should arm itself in order to aid the work of the Flying Fortresses[478] and serve as cannon fodder for Eisenhower. We think that it must arm in order to defend itself against the fascists and the bourgeoisie of all colours: to ensure the freedom that the counter-revolutionary stranglehold would dissolve; to secure bread in taking control of the factories; and to impose peace in defeating capitalism, the source of war. But we have confidence in the working class, and we know that it would be a hard task to recruit it for a capitalist cause. That is why we say to workers: join the militia in your workplace, whatever its label, and make it into what is effectively a workers' militia.

La Vérité offered the example of one factory – which for obvious security reasons it could not name:

> The main factory in the region has been transformed into a powerful working-class bastion where a third of the workers are armed, and many hundreds are armed with submachine guns and light machine guns. These workers are organised in groups of two hundred and groups of thirty. Disciplined in action, they meet in small clandestine groups

of trustworthy men (still too large, in our view) to discuss organising around their demands and the orientation of military action. They refuse to serve any retired military types. The officers, or in any case the commissars who control them and decide on the action to be taken, must be democratically elected by the men.

What do they want to do with their militia? They tell us in one of their newspapers that the workers' militia has the following objectives: defend workers' demands; free the country; establish socialism.

Only the second point remains equivocal: the 'country' must be freed not only from the Gestapo, the SS, the Milice and the GMR[479] but the whole bourgeois police and the whole capitalist apparatus. We must say clearly: the workers' militia must not be at the service of any of the imperialist camps, it must only serve the cause of the proletariat, its Soviet ally and the socialist revolution.

That is the heartfelt wish of the masses. That is why, for example, the armed workers in the region have refused to play the game of Hitler, Roosevelt and the French bosses in treating the occupation soldiers as the enemy. They fraternise with them and call on them to turn their guns in the same direction as their own: against the bourgeois of all countries. That is the way forward for a real workers' militia.

In your factories, demand everywhere the immediate handing-over of weapons stocks to the workers, the democratic election of leaders, and secret militia meetings to decide on actions.

La Vérité warned against premature actions:

The enemies of the working class, Hitler and Roosevelt alike, seek to draw them into premature adventures where their structure will be broken. That is why in September 1943, fostering hopes of an immediate landing in the Balkans, the Allied High Command threw the Greek partisans and workers into an adventurist uprising. They then sat by as the SS drowned the uprising in blood, much like those in Milan (30,000 dead) and Naples. The workers will not let themselves be drawn into such a trap again. They will not allow themselves to be provoked. They will keep their arms for their own struggle, that of the working class and socialism.

Finally, *La Vérité* called for arming, organisation, and the perfection of military instruction; organising workers' groups in the factories and building links between the factories; building links with working-class communities and living areas; building links with red partisans, with poor peasants, with revolutionary elements in the German army...

The slogans of the Central Committee were explained in a *Bulletin intérieur spécial*.[480] The priority was now militia work: 'With the situation having matured the slogan "Let's form workers' militias" has become the central slogan in our agitation'.

In no example – not even in the exceptional cases where they exerted decisive influence in the factory – did the internationalist communists seek to establish a 'Trotskyist' militia. The militias' mass character had to be protected.

On the ground, the balance of forces obliged the 'Trotskyists' to be doubly clandestine:

> For the first time the BL [Bolshevik-Leninists] will find themselves at the side of workers in organisations surpassing the framework of the traditional parties, in which the masses can begin to gain experience of the divergence between their desires and the plans of the Stalinists. But this does not mean that the workers have already withdrawn their confidence in the Stalinists, nor, above all, that the BL will appear as the Messiah upon a simple presentation of their programme.
>
> Indeed, we must not lose sight for an instant of the fact that we must work clandestinely as regards the Stalinists: this, for a long time. All our work must be dominated by an understanding of the counter-revolutionary role of the [Parti communiste], which will show itself most concretely in their desire to physically eliminate the Trotskyists: and not only those *we* call Trotskyists, but also those who *they* label as such, meaning the revolutionary workers.

It was necessary:
1. 'to take the broadest possible initiatives for the establishment of workers' militias', the document giving some examples and explaining how to operate.
2. 'to lead the greatest possible number of workers to join them', the best structure seemingly groups of four organised according to the structures of the factory.
3. 'to encourage the most far-reaching democratisation of the militia: giving the greatest possible power to initiatives from below'. But it warned against ill-considered proposals which would endanger safety.
4. to work to guarantee a close connection between the militia and all the struggles of the working class.

The document gave specific directives on the manner by which weapons should be procured, transported and stocked; on the tasks at hand; the organisation of the factory as a bastion; on links with partisans; how to engage in fraternisation; and on the role of specialists – including those of the FTP – in perfecting military understanding.

Each region would now have to designate a military organiser.

One strange thing was that this turn by the PCI was unanimously supported, with everyone understanding the need for it. Criticisms focused on the formulations in articles and the texts on how it should be applied. The 'CCIist' cells wanted the workers' militia to establish itself as a soviet-in-embryo and consider its military tasks as secondary. 'Today the wing (of the bourgeoisie) on the march is that of those who support the Algiers committee democrats. We must concentrate the fire of our propaganda against them'.[481]

Essel (alias Lessart) replied in the name of the majority:

The idea that we should see the militia as the single organisation for struggles is straightforwardly determined by the conception ... that the bourgeosie and its agents are in our eyes a single bloc. We must not confuse the fronts of struggle.[482]

In spite of these difference, the Trotskyists engaged in mass work in unison for the first time. The results were remarkable enough: in a certain number of major factories, notably in the western suburbs of Paris, within two months they occupied various organising roles in the workers' militias. But we would see the limits of this success: militants did not have time to transform their personal credit into political credit; and moreover their were isolated in their factories, since the party did not dispose of external military forces to transform the character of the workers' militias' activity. These remained boxed into the role which the [Parti communiste] had planned for them in its strategy, that is to say, a very much secondary role.

Towards the general strike

From 29 April the call for a general strike was increasingly the main slogan of the internationalist communists: along with those of workers' militias and fraternisation.

1 May was seen as a dress rehearsal: a 'May Day of preparation for the general strike against the draft'.[483] It was around a general strike that the working-class could express its response. That was the indication of the advice the PCI gave workers at the time of [Allied] landings:[484] 'first of all, defend your freedom [of action]', not letting themselves be mobilised by

either 'Laval and the German high command to work under the scourge of the war effort' or Eisenhower and De Gaulle; 'open the prisons and the camps' before the SS could murder the prisoners; unleash a general strike.

> Rely on yourselves alone to free you from capitalist oppression. Do not wait for the bosses to get worked up and call on the aid of Eisenhower's bayonets. As the Hitlerite stranglehold weakens, launch a general strike even more unanimous, even more irresistible than that of June 1936: not in order to pave the way for Eisenhower, but to reconquer and extend the gains of June 1936: the 40-hour [working week], paid holidays, a living wage and a sliding scale of wages [increases tied to inflation], working conditions fit for humans, control of hiring and firing by workers' representatives, along with their control of the accounts and management of the factory. If the bosses try and block your control, you will take production directly into your own hands in collaboration with your specialist comrades. Leave the hypocritical rhetoric about socialism to the Hitlerites and the 'democrats': make it happen.

The strike would involve the occupation of factories and mines and the establishment of workplace committees:

> It is in the workplace that you are strong. Remember June '36. Occupy the factories and the mines! Democratically elect your workshop, pit and workplace delegates like in June '36. But this time, it will not be a matter of organising a ball, but rather organising a bitter struggle until the final victory. Your delegates should form enterprise committees, like the Russian workers in 1917 and the Italian workers in 1943. Your workplace council will immediately begin organising defence, food supplies and propaganda. It will control the putting-in-place of the social rights won, hiring and the management of the enterprise. Its members will be recallable at any given moment by the workers' assembly.
>
> It will immediately enter relations with other factories in the area and the region to establish local and regional workers' committees which, allied to district and village councils, will become the organs of workers' power.

The other slogans explained the first: arm the workers' militias; workers' and peasants' control of food supplies; workers' control of housing (indeed many had been left homeless); people's justice:

> It is up to the people to try the fascist executioners, the murderous police,

the killers in Darnand's Milice, the speculators and those responsible for war and famine. The working class has no confidence in Eisenhower's judges. It has no confidence in the bourgeois judges who condemn communist, revolutionary and anti-fascist workers to the death penalty or forced labour in their thousands ....

Fraternise with the German, British and American soldiers. Finally, international solidarity; forward to the Socialist United States of Europe.

On the ground, the workers' movement's main struggle was no longer about deportations. The chaos was such that, their hand forced by circumstance, the Nazis had abandoned recruiting a labour force they could no longer transport for work in Germany. Struggles developed more and more around problems of food supply, with transport problems and the speculation of goods on the black market endangering survival.

It was the lack of bread which provoked the strike in Marseille on 24 May.[485] It rapidly generalised. *La Vérité* reported on it with the following note:

> For many days, the situation was very tense. Registration for bread at the bakeries, which became obligatory on 24 May, triggered the strike. On the 25th, engineering workers and dockers went on strike. There were violent demonstrations, with women at the front. The police and the fire brigade directed fire hose nozzles against the crowd. The PPF bandits opened fire. By Friday (26 May) it was a general strike. The factories, shops and trading centres were all shut. All the traffic was stopped. The trams and trains were on strike. The German officers posted machine guns on the main crossroads of the city, but they held back from intervening.
>
> On Saturday 27th the [Allied] bombing 'liquidated' the situation, luckily for the authorities, in creating a 'serious diversion'. Thus the Americans began breaking strikes even before having occupied the country.

L'Humanité held back from writing that at the time. But from a different viewpoint, Charles Tillon confirmed this picture later on:[486]

> Marseille, which the enemy had thought it had terrorised in January-February 1943 (destroying the Vieux Port district, widespread raids, two thousand deportations) unleashed a general strike on 25 May 1944.
>
> On 20 May the prefect Maljean cut the bread ration sharply and imposed registration in the bakeries. Anger was stirred. On the 24th the Parti communiste, the CGT, the UFF, the FTPF (and many legal unions

controlled by the Resistance) called for a strike for bread. That same evening, walkouts began. On the 25th engineering workers and dockers ceased work. Corteges formed in various districts, marching on the prefecture shouting 'Bread! Bread!'.

On the 25th and 26th Nazi forces patrolled the streets armed with grenades and flamethrowers, fingers on the triggers of their machine guns.

The German general Boïe and the police intendant Mathieu organised the arrest of four hundred known trade unionists on the night of the 26th-27th. The result: by the morning of 27 May the whole city supported the strike and seemed to have 'descended' into the streets. The trains were marooned in the stations… this mass mobilisation, at a spontaneous level, looked to spread, and we can imagine that it would have placed the Germans and Vichyists in a grave situation.

Suddenly, at 10 o'clock, American planes filled the skies and emptied their bombs on the population which was contesting control of the streets with the occupier! The working-class districts were hit first: la Belle de Mai, Saint-Lazare… the result: more than ten thousand homes hit; some five thousand victims under the rubble. No enemy operation suffered even a scratch.

The people of Marseille had nothing left but to clear away the ruins under which their own were suffering. Thus a popular movement, which left the German and French-speaking Hitlerites alike powerless, was broken.

The Marseille strike was rich in lessons. The PCF's militants launched the strike over popular demands (bread), not on the basis of nationalist aims. With this slogan the strike spontaneously developed into a general strike. At this stage the police forces and the occupation army were powerless: the Americans could crush the movement with impunity precisely because they were not occupying the country. On the 27th the masses were confronted with the question of power – as Paris would be in August – but in an entirely different context. The Marseille strike, moreover, gave a warning which the Toulouse region of the PCI (if not that of Marseille) would strive to understand: internationalist communists had played no part in the initiative and remained cut off from the masses.[487]

The strike headed little by little towards generalisation, but in a particular situation – that of economic chaos – sabotage, bombings, false alarms and derailings could progressively paralyse industry. Trains circulated with ever greater difficulty, taking incredible detours. Factories were no longer supplied with basic materials and the machines stopped. Food supplies no longer came through, and major towns were on the verge of famine. Strikes by workers multiplied. *La Vérité* related a hundred such cases between April and July. This was also evidenced by the large number mentioned in regional newspapers.

Demands now focused on food supplies and the payment of hours lost, for example at the Radiotechnique in Suresnes:

> Workers went on strike on Saturday 27 May and refused their pay vouchers in protest against famine wages resulting from alarms and interruptions in the electricity supply. The boss had to cave in after half-an-hour, in spite of the Comité Social's blank refusal. The workers won payment for 75% of time wasted due to alarms, without recovery, and the promise of 75% payment for hours lost.[488]

Even immigrants, those struck hardest by repression, went on strike:

> Marseille. In early June, at the Marzagues camp (with around 1,000 Indochinese workers), the Indochinese workers launched a strike together with a hunger strike to protest the diminution of food rations. The camp commandant, a French colonel named Yung, threatened to call in the German repressive forces to shoot two hundred among the protesters. The Indochinese workers continued their strike and ultimately their demands were satisfied.
>
> Earlier, during the Marseille general strike, the Indochinese men called up by the Organisation Todt[489] participated shoulder-to-shoulder with their French class brothers in the general strike.
>
> 'The French workers must understand that we, colonial workers, have the same enemy as them: the bourgeoisie, which exploits us even worse than them. For we Indochinese workers follow the path traced by our comrade Ta Thu Thau and *La lutte* in Saigon,[490] persecuted because they fight for the liberation of colonial peoples, for communism and the Fourth International.
>
> By a group of Indochinese workers.[491]

In late May a strike began to spread among train drivers, forced to proceed in spite of bombings and sabotage. The internationalist communist train drivers supported the movement and took the initiative in some depots.

On 1 July their organ *La lutte des cheminots* called for the preparation of action:

In the stations and in the depots, there are meetings: we must rapidly form clandestine workers' groups, reinforce and arm the workers' militia. We must establish a workers' front.

But the train drivers' strike underlined the fact that the preparation of a general strike corresponded to three entirely opposed strategies:

a) A purely military strategy: disrupting the German army's transport and the auxiliaries of the Milice and stopping the production the Wehrmacht needed. The slogan for a general strike was adopted by London radio after the landings. But the Algiers government feared concentrations of workers. that is why it from the outset devoted itself to evacuating the towns under the pretext of safety. Tillon wrote:

> From late 1943, General de Jussieu Pontcarral (the main leader of the Northern Zone high command of the FFI) called for the abandonment of Paris by the FFI (a similar proposal to that enacted in Lyon). On 12 May 1944 a representative of the 'Comité Français pour la libération national' called on young people to leave the towns, particularly Paris. The BCRA's order was to retreat far way from the towns in order to regroup in 'mobilised maquis' where volunteers would be trained and armed.
> … What the BCRA wanted, indeed, was to place the FFI under its command, to separate it from the masses and thus to paralyse any popular insurrection.[492]

b) A military-political strategy: on the contrary the PCF sought to tie the popular movement to a military strategy co-ordinated with the Allies. In addition to the military objectives it had been assigned by Algiers and London, the general strike called by the CGT had a consequent political objective: reawakening the working masses and ensuring the predominance of the PCF in the coalition government.
c) A social and revolutionary strategy: allowing workers to make themselves master of the economic apparatus and building the structures of their own power. This perspective was held by a number of workers – including within the PCF – but it was not consciously expressed except by the small internationalist minority. Not only were the internationalists few in number, but the objective conditions did not help them: the workers would be masters of empty factories.

Afterword
WHAT KIND OF LIBERATION?

In early August 1944, German troops were retreating in disarray across the territory of France, under the joint pressure of the Allied armies and the partisans. The Hitlerite occupiers' and Vichy puppets' days were numbered. But what would Liberation mean?

The workers, the majority of the maquis fighters, hoped it would not mean a return to the capitalist society of 1939. They aspired to a society which would put an end to the power of money and give political voice to the people. These were the aspirations expressed in vague terms in the programme of the Comité National de la Résistance which heralded 'the establishment of a real social and economic democracy, implying the eviction of the main economic and financial strangleholds over the control of the economy'.

But, as C. Tillon wrote, 'a programme is worth nothing except the means put in place for its application'. How could 'economic and financial strangleholds' be broken, if in the name of national unity, the PS and PCF followed the banner of De Gaulle, who was of course keen to re-establish the power of the bourgeoisie and its state? The PS-SFIO, arising from the ashes, had no objective other than a bourgeois democracy reviving the Third Republic. For the PCF, socialism meant the nationalisation of the economy, plus the control of government by the 'party of the working class'. But the time was not ripe. The party counted on the pressure of the masses and the maquis to allow it to control as many levers of state as possible, in order to later render it master of the entire state apparatus.

The revolutionary militants who thought Liberation should lead to workers' power were few in number. Given that these people were sparsely spread through the Liberation movements, they were paralysed by their nationalist ideology. Organised in small groups like the PCI, practically without weapons, they continued to swim against the current and place their hopes in an uprising of the popular masses in Germany. What effect would they have on the course of events?

Nationalist ideology led to national unity. National unity led to the re-establishment of the bourgeoisie which, having collaborated with the Nazis, would regain all of its political, social and economic power.

In *La Libération confisquée*, we will see how it made use of its strange bedfellows in different fields, from the Liberation itself up until the moment when, in 1947, it was strong enough to cast them aside.

Indeed, from the end of the occupation, this outcome was predictable. The actors were already in place for the final act of the tragedy of the war, and they could not stray from their allotted role. They would blame fate, like in Sophocles. But the tragedy was not fated. It was a tragedy of men, of workers, when they fail to take charge of their own destiny.

APPENDIX

Arbeiter und Soldat

and

Der Arbeiter

Translation by David Broder

AN INTRODUCTION TO THE TROTSKYIST PRESS FOR GERMAN SOLDIERS, 1943-44

by David Broder

The following pages feature a translation of the surviving issues of *Arbeiter und Soldat* and a fragment of *Der Arbeiter*. These give some idea of the internationalism of the wartime Trotskyists and their insistence on differentiating between the Nazis and the conscripts who fought in the Wehrmacht.

The disappointed revolutionary potential of the late First World War period clearly weighs heavily on the minds of the authors. The invocation of the stifled German revolution expresses not only their aspirations for the end of the second war, but also the need to draw lessons from the experience of 1918-19.

This propaganda moreover demonstrates the Trotskyists' belief in the need to appeal to the German soldiers on a class-struggle basis. This was quite unlike the Stalinist propaganda for the troops, whose aim was simply to sow disillusionment, weakening the German front in order to assist the Allies.

However, *Arbeiter und Soldat* also bears witness to the Trotskyists' difficulties in grappling with the historic role of Stalinism. Trotsky had predicted that the war would spell the end of the Soviet bureaucracy: thus the real struggle was between capitalist counter-revolution on one hand, and on the other a working class who would overthrow the Stalin régime all the better to defend the gains of 1917. Yet these newspapers only began to appear several months after the Red Army's stunning victory at Stalingrad, which had demonstrated the bureaucracy's ability to defend itself and the Soviet state. As such *Arbeiter und Soldat* could not portray Stalin as imperilled, but rather saw him as a threat to the putative German revolution.

The history of these newspapers, produced for soldiers serving in the occupation army, is discussed in some detail in chapter IV. The activist Craipeau refers to as Paul Widelin or 'Victor', whose real name was Martin

Monat, joined the Trotskyist movement in exile in Belgium in 1935 and came to Paris in May 1943 to lead the German émigré organisation. The paper was edited and mimeographed at Clara and Paul Thalmann's Paris home. *Der Arbeiter*, meanwhile, was established by the independent initiative of soldiers in Brittany.

Little survives of *Der Arbeiter*. The substantial break in the publication of *Arbeiter und Soldat* between September 1943 and May 1944 was due to the heavy Gestapo repression of the organisation. In its second run, from spring 1944, the paper appeared as the organ of the German section of the Fourth International. Monat survived the October 1943 raids but was captured by the Gestapo in July 1944. He was executed shortly before the Allied liberation of Paris; the paper did not appear again.

My translation originally appeared as 'Trotskyism in occupied France', *Workers' Liberty* Vol. 3 No. 20, June 2008.

The German Revolution is the World Revolution—K. Liebknecht
ARBEITER UND SOLDAT
For revolutionary proletarian unity
No. 1 July 1943

WHAT DOES ARBEITER UND SOLDAT STAND FOR?

Is proletarian revolution coming?

Once again the spectre of communist revolution haunts the globe. In Germany Goering invites his 'compatriots' to eliminate any German worker who speaks out about the coming proletarian revolution. Goebbels writes that 'this war is synonymous with social revolution'. He uses exorcisms like this and others to try and save himself from the abyss of the now inevitable revolution. In Britain even the Tories, hoping to calm the proletarian tide, are talking of projects to improve the well-being of the masses after the war. In the United States high finance warns 'If Stalin goes over to the Trotskyist theory of world revolution'—or, more precisely, if communist revolution breaks out—'we will crush it with armed force'. In the name of the capitalists of the United States and the rest of the world, Roosevelt demanded that Stalin dissolve the Comintern. In Russia—yes, in Russia!—the Stalinist clique has indeed dissolved the International. The Russian bureaucrats have called for revenge against the German people and they have made great pains to prove to their dear allies their honourable intention to crush any communist revolution in the egg.

This is how these gentlemen view the danger of communist revolution, and this is how they prepare to greet it. But what of the workers, the hundreds of millions of exploited? Most importantly, what of the German proletariat? Are we really on the threshold of communist revolution, or will the ruling class have more to show for itself than the bloodbath of peoples it has organised in its quest for profit?

The question must be posed more sharply still. These gentlemen would have no objection to an uprising against Hitler's clique which ushered in victory for the Anglo-Saxon imperialists. On the contrary, it is with this goal in mind that working-class districts are bombed day and night with the aim of heightening exasperation and thus pushing the desperate masses into revolt. An uprising would have its place in these heroes' programme, as long as it brought some dictator to power or, in the worst case scenario, some sort of 'democratic' régime, which they would simply require to respond to the wishes of Anglo-American capital.

But revolutions are a dangerous thing, and a lot can change. If millions of workers took to action they may well go beyond that and fight for their own objectives, creating a Soviet Republic as the basis for socialist construction. But is there any sign that the leaders in Washington, London and Moscow will not get their way? Didn't the German proletariat let the revolution slip through its fingers once already? Haven't Himmler's terror and Goebbels' brutal propaganda broken the German working class and completely destroyed its faith in its own revolutionary strength? Can anyone really believe that the European revolution will go beyond the tight confines of the Anglo-Saxon imperialists' plans? That is the question posed.

Have we advanced since 1918?

The 1918 [German] Revolution failed because of three main errors. First and second: millions of workers were still full of illusions about the capitalist system and the democratic republic. Third: millions of workers who did want to fight for socialism still trusted the old Social Democrat Party which had been degenerate for many years and whose bureaucrats only had one idea in mind: pass the power they held into the hands of the bourgeoisie, disarm the proletariat and take away the main organs of revolution, the workers' and soldiers' soviets.

That millions of workers could still have expected capitalism to improve their conditions can be explained by the fact that before the First World War the capitalist system was still experiencing growth. This period is now definitively over. After the post-war crisis; inflation; a brief stabilisation which nevertheless saw a million German workers unemployed; the great crisis which saw eight million unemployed; and rearmament under the Nazi régime—the only answer to the crisis but inevitably leading to war—the working class has now been broken from its illusions in the capitalist system.

Much the same goes for its illusions in democracy. The 'democratic republic' was ushered in on the end of bayonets directed at the working class. In place of their guns and workers' councils the workers were given ballot papers, the Reichswehr and prison cells. Whether bribed by the capitalists' money, ministerial offices or big jobs in the unions, the workers' leaders blocked any advance towards proletarian revolution. But when crisis came these gentlemen's 'democracy' itself became an obstacle. It was necessary to force down wages and make rapid preparations for the coming war. Little by little, brick by brick, the democratic edifice was dismantled. The Constitution of the Republic left the way clear for such developments. Handing over power to the fascists, the bourgeoisie dealt the final blow to a democracy no longer useful to it. However, at the same time the German worker was freed from his illusions in the peaceful, democratic path to power and gradual progress towards socialism.

There still exists the danger that the Stalinist party, which calls itself Communist, will deny the German workers their revolution via mass repression and GPU terror, much as the Social Democrats did 25 years ago. During the Spanish Civil War this danger played out in all its glory. But the danger should not be overestimated. The capitalist governments' distrust obliges the Russian bureaucracy to unmask itself more and more in front of the international proletariat. Moreover, the German worker has understood this problem and its origins. The misery of the Russian masses and the high life of the bureaucracy teach him that after the failure of the German revolution, and indeed the European revolution, the victorious but isolated October revolution was bound to—and did—collapse. Besides, this bureaucratic layer which came to power after Lenin's death constituted the centre of the Third International and determined the leadership and policies of its member parties. The Russian bureaucrats thus have no more ability or even desire to lead the masses into struggle than the SPD [Social-Democrat] bureaucrats or the unions.

So it is wrong to believe that the German workers have learnt nothing since 1918. It is wrong to believe that the tragedy is bound to repeat itself. It is superficial to say that after ten years of fascist rule we will have to start all over again. In the years following the First World War the German workers learned very rich, albeit very bitter, lessons. They witnessed the collapse of capitalism to a greater extent than the workers of almost any other country; they saw at close quarters the rottenness of bourgeois democracy; they learned to distrust parties and to be careful in choosing their leaders.

All this recently won experience will only be made clear in the struggle itself. When the rancour against the capitalists responsible for the war sweeps away the layer of slurry laid down by the fascists' lying propaganda, it will not take the workers much time to learn and gain experience in struggle, since it will only be necessary to rediscover memories of the past and teach the knowledge of the older generation to the young. This is a sure thing. Gentlemen of London and Washington, Berlin and Moscow, although it is threatened by many dangers, the proletarian revolution you see in your nightmares is knocking at the door and closer still.

Revolution awaits

It is impossible to predict on what day revolution will come. But it will begin to ripen long before it breaks out. When after its quick victories over the less well-prepared and well-armed peoples the German army first met with serious resistance, the fascist attempt to smother the worldwide class struggle was also shown to be impossible. Fascism did succeed, using massive terror, to banish it from the surface for some time. But it came back again! A process of decomposition began both at the front and in the rear. The drunkenness of victory relapsed, the spirit of combativity was dampened, and the foundering of speed-ups and sabotage in the factories became more and more widespread; only the bloodiest terror was just able to keep the front and the economy afloat.

But for the moment there are few who know what the necessary objective is. The smoke-curtain of fascist propaganda has not yet completely dissipated. For the moment the lessons the German worker in uniform has learnt in Russia bring him more confusion than they do clarity, more doubt than they do hope. Already, however, groups are arising everywhere to answer the questions posed. Old cells which survived the years of terror by keeping themselves to themselves are again putting out feelers. New groups are being organised. Light is being cast on the issues in discussion and in writing, in papers and in leaflets. On the first day of open struggle these groups will unite into a revolutionary communist party.

Arbeiter and Soldat is designed for this process of destroying fascist rule and all bourgeois rule, undermining the capitalist war front, rebuilding the proletarian class front and preparing the communist revolution. These are the goals it has set itself.

ON THE DISSOLUTION OF THE THIRD INTERNATIONAL

The Stalinist bureaucrats have dissolved the Comintern. 'Beware', declares the Axis propaganda, 'this is just a manoeuvre, a chimera, playing dead'. 'Hurrah!' the Anglo-Saxon imperialist press cries with joy, 'our allies are not communists, they are good Russian patriots'. 'Of course, it's just a manoeuvre' is the rationalisation the communist worker still committed to the Third International despite all the defeats uses to reassure himself; they are tricking their capitalist adversaries, folding up the flag only to unfurl it again in the future. Such manoeuvres, he tells himself as he reflects, can and must be made when faced with the class enemy. But he starts to have doubts: is the dissolution of the International really another move to trick the class enemy, or might it be a manoeuvre against the workers of the world?

Might the dissolution of the International be a manoeuvre which impacts on the proletariat's class struggle? 'The struggle for the dictatorship of the proletariat necessitates a single, joint, international organisation of all communist forces fighting for that goal' declares the resolution which founded the Third International. But now the man who dissolved this organisation (even if he only 'appeared' to do so) and only in order to wrong-foot the enemy, is also confusing the workers about the task to be accomplished, which is indeed the struggle for the dictatorship of the proletariat. Today when millions of oppressed people hope that the end of the second imperialist war will bring the end of all oppression and the end of all war, today when society readies itself for violent revolutionary struggles, the dissolution of the International can only serve to paralyse the fighting strength of the proletariat, to discourage it and sow confusion in its ranks. No, such a manoeuvre as this is not directed against the class enemy, but it is an effort to trick the workers and above all the International's adherents themselves. This move is a clear rejection of communist revolution.

It is not the first move of this character made by the Russian bureaucracy. We shall only mention the most recent and the worst. In Spain, the proletariat's struggle against fascism and for the establishment of a Soviet Republic was labelled a 'national liberation struggle': the workers' councils were strangled, revolutionary workers were submitted to GPU terror and the cornerstone of the resistance to Franco was broken. In France in June 1936 it put the brakes on the strike wave and buried the nascent revolutionary movement by trapping it into the Popular Front. In Germany it recommended the creation of a Popular Front wide enough to include the Stahlhelm[493] and set as the objective of the struggle the establishment of a 'national-popular government'.

The dissolution of the proletarian front just before the rise of the new revolutionary wave is not simply abandonment or rejection of revolution. It is above all a declaration of war against the coming proletarian uprising. The sole task of the surviving national sections of the Comintern is to suffocate any revolutionary proletarian struggle, following the Spanish model. The communist revolution is international, but it will be strangled country by country.

None of this is very surprising for the German proletariat. They can see for themselves in the East that the Russia of the Stalinist bureaucracy has replaced the Russia of Lenin's day, the Russia of workers, peasants and their soviets. The bureaucracy has long been characterised by its deep, deep hostility towards mass revolutionary struggles. That is why the bureaucrats have always portrayed themselves as intelligent and terribly 'realistic'. 'We will thank you a thousandfold', said Roosevelt, 'if you will dissolve the International'. A thousand thanks and the confidence of Roosevelt, the bureaucrats say, are worth more than the coming revolution and the confidence of the masses'.

But these days no politics are 'realistic' apart from the politics of revolution.

Through their aversion towards revolution, which they have betrayed and sold out to Anglo-American capitalism, through their dogged chauvinism and their barbarous treatment of their prisoners, the bureaucrats have only succeeded in exasperating the German soldier, masking the possibility of revolution and so throwing him disarmed into the hands of Goebbels and his propaganda: in so doing they have prolonged the war. One German worker, upon receiving revolutionary propaganda from a comrade, said: if these publications were distributed widely it would surely take only a few days before revolution broke out in Germany and the war was over. This worker had a more 'realistic' political outlook than that of the bureaucrats over their corrupt twenty-five year rule.

The German media, which tries to pass off the rapacious war of capitalists like Krupp, Kloeckner, Roechling and Borsig as a crusade against 'Bolshevik chaos' must of course do all in its power to expose this 'manoeuvre'. Thus it argues that the dissolved Third International will just turn into a Fourth International. The first part of this story serves to flatter the Stalinist bureaucracy—the second part is an outrage against the organ of the coming revolution: the Fourth International has indeed been created, but as a rallying point for authentic revolutionary communists. It follows the tradition of Marx and Engels, Lenin and Trotsky, Liebknecht and Luxemburg. The organisation has been created to struggle against the treachery of Stalin and his followers, not as some new version of the Comintern. To the extent that it represents a continuation of the Third International, this is only insofar as it will fight to accomplish the tasks set by Lenin—long betrayed by Stalin—in the coming revolutionary struggles: building a single, joint, international organisation to struggle for the dictatorship of the proletariat.

Revolutionary communists welcome the dissolution of the Comintern. Of course, at first it will serve to discourage the workers and sow confusion among their ranks. However, in the last analysis—against the will of the Stalinist clique—it will facilitate the struggle for the proletariat's goals in the coming revolution. It will expose the treachery of the Russian bureaucrats and their Comintern before the eyes of all proletarians. In the last analysis, it can only help to convince the workers of the need to build a new revolutionary International.

COMRADES!

You want to fight for a proletarian revolution. You are convinced of the need for a new revolutionary communist party. You want to win your work colleagues and your comrades on the front and in the barracks over to these ideas. You are yet to succeed in doing so. Many among them are still Stalinists, others hope to see the SPD resurrected, a third group want to re-live the 'good times' of before 1933 and a fourth group is totally uninterested in any talk of politics. But this must not stop you talking to all of them when resistance arises confronting a boss, a tyrannical foreman, an officer or reprisals by the Nazi clique. On the contrary. You, as revolutionary communists, *must be the first* to prove your courage, energy and prudence. Many who would today be unwinnable even with the best arguments could be won over by your attitude. Many will only find the courage to join us when struggle emerges.

19 JULY 1936

On 19 July seven years ago General Franco rose up against the Spanish Republican government. With an amazing action the Spanish proletariat rose up, crushing the military uprising in Madrid and Barcelona. The Republican government, proving its inability to stop the reactionary putsch, was forced to give in faced with the resolve of the working masses. In Barcelona the old Catalan government was replaced with the Central Committee of the Militias, which exercised de facto governmental power. All political parties were represented in the Committee. The Militia Committee was the Spanish version of a soviet. In Catalonia, Aragon, Valencia and Malaga the movement went way beyond the bounds of bourgeois republicanism: it carried out expropriations, collectivised agricultural property and distributed basic goods between workers' and peasants' co-operatives. The old Catalan government was a shadow of its former self. In the provinces mentioned above the workers and peasants held power.

But it did not go the same way in Madrid. The Popular Front government from the start tried to denude the mass movement of its revolutionary characteristics. Only where absolutely unavoidable did it carry out measures to expropriate the bourgeoisie. It engaged in armed struggle against the workers' and peasants' committees. The Republicans, right-wing Socialists and Communists were the protagonists of this effort. It was inevitable that conflict would break out between the two centres, reformist Madrid and revolutionary Barcelona. The international situation was marked by the weakness of the proletariat. Of course, a powerful factory occupations movement was in motion in France. But even there the mass movement was hijacked by the Popular Front government: the Communists and social-democrats put the brakes on the movement, smothering it with a joint agreement. Furthermore the Great Powers each took a stance on Spain. The so-called 'democratic powers' decided on non-intervention, despite the existence of a struggle against the reactionary generals. From the start the fascist powers sent aid to Franco. As for the Soviet Union, at first it took part in the farce of non-intervention, before taking sides with the bourgeois Republic. But it was certainly not on the side of the mass revolutionary movement. All the USSR's arms shipments to Spain had the sole aim of strengthening the bourgeois republic by crushing the workers' revolution. It only gave weapons to organisations who loyally followed this line.

In the second month of the war the Russians demanded the dissolution of the Central Committee of the Militias and the re-establishment of the former bourgeois government. After a weak show of resistance the anarchists capitulated. The workers', peasants' and militia committees were deprived of their authority and were gradually broken up. The GPU hunted down revolutionary workers' organisations and suppressed them.

The proletarian masses rose up against this anti-working class agenda once again in Catalonia, Aragon and Valencia in May 1937. During their three-day uprising the masses took control of the streets and neutralised the Communist and Republican organisations. Unfortunately, they did not have a workers' party which could have given the masses' struggle direction. The movement was decapitated by the treachery of the anarchist leaders and the uprising was crushed into the ground. The defeat of the revolutionary movement broke the cornerstone of the resistance against Franco. The fascist uprising could not be defeated on the basis of defending the bourgeois Republic.

How can we explain the Communists' behaviour? There is only one possible explanation for such an attitude: the Russian bureaucracy's only fundamental political principle was staying in power and hanging onto its privileges. Any mass revolutionary movement would threaten the power of the bureaucracy. Therefore any revolutionary movement was a mortal enemy. No to revolution! No problem with the imperialist Great Powers! The Russian bureaucracy is the incarnation of counter-revolution. It is not just Stalin. The bureaucracy is a social force, a new generation motivated by stark nationalism, a heartfelt sense of self-entitlement and parasitism. The bureaucracy would sacrifice anything to remain in power, including the social and political gains of the October revolution.

The example of Spain teaches us this: the revolution cannot succeed without a revolutionary party. There was none in Spain and the revolution perished. Moreover, any future revolution will have as its enemy not only the local bourgeoisie but also the Russian bureaucracy. In the coming German and European revolutions we must take account of these two lessons.

THE WORKING CLASS IN THE WAR

The Belgian workers, the majority of wehom saw in advance that the war was fought solely in the interests of the wealthy capitalists, entered the war reluctantly. That was one of the main reasons for Belgium's quick defeat, saving the lives of many of its people. However, the workers' movement suffered a heavy blow from the German victory. A wave of nationalism and enthusiasm for the Royal Air Force swept over the country and had a significant effect over even the working class. The main reason for this was the deterioration of living standards caused by the decline of imports and the export of basic goods and coal to Germany. One of the first German decrees slashed wages, forcing poverty on the working class. The workers and their families tried to make the best of things with Sunday trips to the countryside where basic goods were not so expensive. Those unable to do so could 'freely' travel to Germany. Despite the poverty of the working class, or indeed because of it, the Belgian and German industrialists producing armaments made a roaring trade. Prices went up, but wages did not budge. This was the Belgian proletariat's first experience of national socialism.

During winter 1942 the German authorities started mass deportations of workers to Germany. A protest strike broke out in a large firm of around 10,000 workers in Liège. After a three-day strike the authorities postponed the deportation of the workers until February 1943. The Liège province was the main theatre of a feverish revival of workers' organisations seeking to resist the deportations. New trade unions, weapons of a class-conscious proletariat, were established to replace the old ones which had been broken up. The still weak revolutionary communist party made its first steps in heavy industry.

When another strike resisting the deportations broke out at the end of February—30,000 workers struck in the Liège province alone—we saw the interesting spectacle of the capitalist owners helping the German authorities break the strike. The workers thus saw that all the chatter about national unity was just bluffing, and it only took a few days to collapse when profits and good business were threatened. The workers feared that if there was any trouble or any demonstrations the German soldiers, under the control of the military authorities, would open fire. A leaflet circulated among the workers calling for fraternisation with the German workers in uniform who wanted to go back to their homes just as much as the Belgian workers wanted to stay in theirs. There had not been any fighting or any fraternisation, but the leaflet had a profound impact on the workers. They had realised who the real enemy was and where they could find their real ally. At the start of the fighting the artificial front of national unity was replaced by the class front of the Belgian and German workers against the Belgian and German capitalists and their military backers.

The struggle finished after three days. It proved that the new organisation was still too weak and too inexperienced to unite the masses faced with reprisals by the German repressive apparatus. But at root this struggle was a rehearsal of the coming revolutionary period. The defeat of the workers can therefore only mean a limited period of demoralisation. They will realise their mistakes and resolve to put their experience to use in future struggles. The organisation is growing. There have indeed been other isolated strikes in big factories to prevent fresh attacks on living standards.

WORKERS, SOLDIERS!

Many foreign workers, tricked by the bourgeoisie's lying propaganda, believe that all of you are fascists. They believe that you wanted the war. They reproach you for not having thrown down your guns as they have. They do not understand the cocktail of lies, terror and espionage which have driven you to take up arms. Talk to them, wherever possible! Explain your situation to them! Tell them that you hope for the end of this war no less than they do! Tell them that you are reading yourself for this outcome and the proletariat's settling of scores with the class enemy! In doing so you can guarantee the future proletarian revolution today. In doing so you will help its spread across Europe. In doing so you will be leading a better and more effective foreign policy than no matter what bourgeois minister!

DO YOU REMEMBER?

1) That in July 1917 there was a powerful working-class demonstration in Petrograd? At the time the Bolshevik Party, led by Lenin, was a revolutionary party. The Bolsheviks had understood that the countryside and the front were not yet ripe for the conquest of power by the proletariat and that the movement had gone too far in Petrograd and Moscow. That is why they tried to hold back the action. This showed itself to be a mistake when the leadership of the masses then fell into the hands of anarchists and provocateurs. Realising their error they soon corrected it. The party tried to limit the movement to an armed—but peaceful—demonstration, which was a partial success. Thanks to its thought-through conduct, after the defeat of the action the party won the confidence of the best working-class militants. Despite this there was soon a massive campaign of lies. The Bolsheviks were falsely accused of being agents of Ludendorff[494]. Lenin and Zinoviev were forced into hiding. Trotsky, Lunacharsky and others were thrown into prison. However, three months later, they seized power and the Second Congress of Soviets could take charge.

2) That in July 1932 the von Papen[495] government sacked the Prussian Social-Democrat ministers Braun and Severing? The Social-Democrat bureaucrats held back the workers. Indeed, the Reich government had acted in a perfectly 'legal' fashion, and there would soon be elections. In place of the armed struggle, the ballot paper. The KPD [Communist Party] called a general strike. But no-one listened. Why? Because less than one year previously it had called for workers to vote with the Nazis in a referendum against these same Prussian ministers. Because its policy of splitting the unions (RGO [Revolutionäre Gewerkschafts-Opposition, the Communist-led unions]) had isolated it from the workers in the factories. Because its theory of social-fascism had divided it from Social-Democrat workers who wanted to fight. That was how it prepared the worst of all defeats, defeat without a fight.

ONCE AGAIN, FEED YOUR MOUTH WITH THEIR PROMISES

'Dear compatriots, rations will now be increased further still. The excess in the Ukraine which already this year has... etc., etc.' Thus spoke the party propagandists, Hitler, Goering, Goebbels and others last winter. Long-term continuation of the war and continuing military profits depended on the maintenance of the front. That is what Messrs Krupp, Siemens, Roechling and others, the suppliers in heavy industry, wanted to see.

But promising something and having the means to supply it are not the same thing. Now they have cut the meat ration by 100g a week: not of course without rubbish excuses. Workers are tightening their belts and clenching their fists: with which, when the time is right, they will one happy day feed their mouths.

PEACE! FREEDOM! BREAD!

PEACE: Only world proletarian revolution can bring us peace and the end of all wars. FREEDOM: This is not possible for all the exploited except in the framework of a Socialist Republic of Soviets. BREAD: Only the expropriation of capital and the establishment of a socialist planned economy can guarantee bread for all and an end to economic crises.

The German Revolution is the World Revolution—K. Liebknecht
ARBEITER UND SOLDAT
For revolutionary proletarian unity
No. 2 August 1943

THE AGENDA OF GLOBAL CAPITAL

The beginning of the workers' revolution in Germany comes closer and closer. Already the Italian workers are taking action; in the Balkans, in Portugal and in Spain military régimes and fascist dictatorships are collapsing. How much time can be left before the German workers and soldiers break the chains of fascism and the great struggle between the exploited and the exploiters consumes Europe?

It is high time that the Anglo-American capitalists come to the aid of German and European capital. If the brotherhood of high finance are now determinedly and stubbornly making war with the blood of their respective working classes, they will all the more determinedly and fraternally help each other when they need to defend their sacred rights to private property and capitalist exploitation. The bosses know full well that working-class revolution can be contagious, now more than ever.

But arms alone will not be enough to bat down the European revolution. The people on the ground on the Anglo-Saxon side carrying the weapons are themselves workers and peasants. Of course they have been able to mobilise them to fight against a fascist Germany. But would they let them push them into fighting a proletarian Europe? Didn't the bourgeoisie already have a tough time in 1918-19 when it tried to strangle the victorious workers' and peasants' October revolution in Russia? The mutiny of the French fleet in the Black Sea as well as the strike by British dockers who had to ship arms to Russia may well have left as much trace in the minds of the wealthy capitalists as they have in the memory of the global working class.

What has changed over the last 25 years? The British working class has been radicalised. In 1926, betrayed by the union bureaucrats, the miners held a year-long strike. During the capitalist crisis the American paradise was transformed into a hell for 13 million unemployed workers. Even during the war there has been news of strikes by miners, armaments workers and transport workers in Britain as well as a 600,000-strong strike in America. Will the British and American workers want to fight the revolutionary workers—who will have made clear their interests and their real tasks—after having fraternised them? This problem is not as simple as Messrs. Churchill and Roosevelt would have us imagine. They know that perfectly well themselves, which is why they do not want to confront the revolutionary masses of Europe, above all those of Germany, with tanks and machine guns alone, but with a much more effective weapon: poison.

The poison to which we refer is that which the bourgeoisie used to paralyse the revolutionary struggle of the German working class in 1918. It was the Social-Democrat leaders themselves who disoriented the working class with their lies and false promises, setting one part of the class against another and little by little destroying the gains of the revolution. But this was just the tip of the iceberg for the Social-Democrat bureaucrats. In 1933, after Hitler's seizure of power, they showed the German workers their true colours. This time around, global capital needs someone else to inject poison into the workers' blood in Germany and Europe: it is now the task of the bureaucrats in Moscow, brought to power by the isolation of the victorious October revolution. Despite all the little disputes about where borders should lie, it was in the interests of global finance capital that the Russian bureaucracy recently hurried to inject a dose of poison in the arm of the German revolution.

AN APPEAL FROM MOSCOW

The Moscow transmitter has announced the creation of a 'National Committee for a Free Germany'. This committee is composed of an émigré poet (its chairman), some captured generals, etc. The ex-Communist poet and the ex-fascist generals have published a manifesto, with five particular points of interest for German workers. 1) They claim that the terrible hardship the German workers have suffered is the work of one man, Hitler. 2) All partisans of Hitler who distance themselves from him will be pardoned. 3) The German soldiers on the front should—*under the leadership of their generals* —march on Berlin and overthrow Hitler. 4) A 'strong', 'independent' and 'national' government must be established. 5) Legally acquired property is safeguarded.

German workers and soldiers! Cast your minds back! What happened in 1918? The Kaiser fled, the generals stayed in place. A superficial façade of democracy. We are seeing the same today. In the interests of big business Moscow is offering you a repeat of the tragedy of 1918, with one small difference: this time around the democratic spectacle will soon come to an abrupt end. What will the German workers do? They will put Moscow's poison in an envelope and post it back to Stalin with the note: this time, that is not going to work!

For their part, they will make five proposals: 1) When the scores are settled across the globe, Hitler will certainly not get away. But nor will we forget that he and his clique were acting in the service of big business.

The wealthy barons of industry and the German bankers wanted and led this war just as much, and they will cause a third war if we do not one fine day remove their power to do so. 2) If Goering, another Nazi leader or some Gestapo executioner shits himself and decides to distance himself from his once beloved Führer, that will be no reason for sympathy. 3) We ourselves will decide the way forward for our country, even without our generals. We already let them get away with that in 1918, *which is why again in 1939 they were able to lead us to war far from home*. On the first day of the revolution we will get rid of ranks and we will sack all the officers. We will elect soldiers' committees with the power to give orders and control all our affairs. 4) We do not want an 'independent and national' government! Such a government would not be independent either of the conquering capitalists or our own capitalists, in fact it would be... independent from the control of the workers! On the contrary, we want a *government of the workers themselves*. We can best achieve this with a system of soviets. This time we will not let them take our soviets from us as in 1918. 5) The petty traffickers and wealthy war profiteers in large-scale industry have made their profits in a perfectly 'legal' fashion and have made their giant fortunes in a more or less 'legal' fashion. That is because they made the laws themselves. However, the workers will confiscate their businesses and will furthermore make laws obliging everyone to work and abolishing all exploitation.

WE THE SOLDIERS AND THE EVENTS IN ITALY

German soldiers have received the Nazi press's parsimonious coverage of events in Italy with bewilderment and with anxiety. But through the intermediary of comrades returned from Italy who report on the goings-on there, they know that they have been denied the right to know the truth about the collapse of this most pitiful of fascist régimes in case the parallel which jumps to mind might lead them to more clearly understand the situation in their own country.

Fascism has collapsed because of its inherent weakness, its totally corrupt system of party chieftains which can have no objective other than to exploit the Italian people, above all the Italian workers.

When the British and Americans landed in Italy tens of thousands of Fascist militiamen threw down their weapons and fled. Is this all there is to the Fascist force so often trumpeted by Mussolini?

German soldiers in Sicily have to suffer and spill their blood in the interests of the Nazis who sent them down there and the Fascists who have betrayed them. But what exactly is going on in Italy? Can we hold the Italian workers responsible? As the lamentable failure of the 'Fascist art of governance' and the repugnant corruption of the bloody party bureaucracy became ever more obvious, an ever-stronger resistance grew among the Italian workers. As popular discontent became ever more sharply posed, finally resulting in strikes which gave it its clearest and most determined expression, the army and the King acted to stave off revolution and save what could be saved at the last minute. The strikes were drowned in blood and a state of emergency was declared. But while these measures could for a while postpone the just victory over fascism and imperialisms of all stripes, in the long run this victory is inevitable.

Knowing what happened in Italy, and the speed with which Mussolini's clique broke up, it is easy to understand the sombre discretion of the Nazi press's reports on Italy. German soldiers must not be allowed to draw parallels. They must be bombarded with propaganda, filling his head every day and stopping him from thinking. They know well enough in Berlin that such thoughts can become, and have been proven to become, dangerous for the leading Nazi party dignitaries. Although some of you talk of untrustworthy allies, it is not the Italian people who are to blame. Fascism is at fault. The whole world is today the victim of the folly of the fascist powers and capital's quest for profit. Stalin, who betrayed the proletarian revolution, is the right-hand-man of this imperialist-capitalist clique.

But the current war, in its terrible absurdity, lays the ground for the future workers' revolution in every country. The Fourth International will lead it to victory. *By an infantryman*

Editor's comments:
We wholeheartedly agree with the comrade's letter. But we would go even further. There can be no question of the 'blame' of the Italian people, but only its merit. If in this war—fought not in the interest of the workers but in the interests of capital—the proletariat revolts, whether that be in Britain or America as in Germany, or in Russia as in Italy, there can hardly be any talk of betrayal. We must not talk about the faults of the Italian workers but rather the weakness of the German workers who are still letting themselves go under the butcher's knife in the name of Hitler and in the interests of the Krupps and Borsigs of this world.

All of you who are in contact with our comrades, tell *Arbeiter und Soldat* about your opinions and your experiences.

It is your paper!

TALK OF POLITICS FORBIDDEN!

The closer we come to the end of the war, the quieter are the men up above—

Adolf, Hermann, Joseph and co. But more and more clearly do those down below, the workers and soldiers, raise their voices in protest. Everywhere people are talking about what is going to happen tomorrow when the war is over. The high authorities themselves who, according to Goebbels, know everything, have now remarked on this. They are trying to make use of tried and tested methods, banning soldiers in various units from talking about politics. But the old charm is not working any more. They are talking about politics more and more angrily, now more than ever before. This murmuring and chatter is the distant echo of the coming revolution.

PEACE! FREEDOM! BREAD!

SOVIET GERMANY: HOW WE WANT IT AND HOW WE DON'T

The degeneration of the Russian revolution of 1917 resulted from numerous particularities of the situation in Russia. The fact that it was a backward agricultural country with a politically weak bourgeoisie with shallow roots in society and the existence of a Bolshevik Party of fierce will and unbreakable energy facilitated the working-class seizure of power. Once power was taken these circumstances showed themselves to be obstacles too. The heavy social weight of the huge, ignorant peasant masses made the industrialisation and administration of the country difficult. The postponement of the European revolution, particularly in Germany, added to the difficulties. The Bolshevik Party was torn apart by internal feuding. It gave birth to a bureaucracy which ruled over the masses just as the Tsarist clique used to. What exists in Russia today—the absolute rule of a bureaucracy which appropriates the guise of Bolshevism as a claim to tradition—has nothing in common with socialism.

But the conditions of the German revolution and the construction of a socialist society in Europe are not the same as what existed in Russia. Below we outline how we conceive of this different type of system developing in Germany:

WE WANT a real dictatorship of the proletariat, which means a democracy of all workers. The basis for workers' democracy will be the widespread establishment of workers' and poor peasants' soviets. The soviet is the most important public body. As the most conscious section of the working class, the party must do its work within the framework of the soviets. WE DO NOT WANT the soviets to be the powerless tools of a party which is itself the submissive stage army of a clique. We oppose the substitution of the rule of the state bureaucracy and its party for the rule of the working class. WE WANT the greatest possible democracy for the workers, with no constraints on faith or religion, freedom of the press or freedom of speech, with unlimited rights of association and coalition for all parties who work within the soviet system. WE DO NOT WANT the tyranny of a party. We oppose the repression of any workers' party which stands in favour of a workers' government through the soviet system. WE WANT people's tribunals composed of workers which deliberate and make their judgements publicly. WE DO NOT WANT a GPU which arbitrarily throws people in prison, deports and shoots them in secrecy. We do not want a legal system which does not recognise rights but only brute force. WE WANT workers' control of all public officials, who should be subject to recall at any moment. WE DO NOT WANT the arbitrary rule of a bureaucracy which does not allow the workers any degree of freedom. WE WANT the workers themselves to manage production and distribution. The organisms of the workers' state will carry out the production and distribution plans drawn up by the unions and workers' associations in collaboration with the latter. WE DO NOT WANT dictatorial management of production and distribution by a bureaucratic caste which pockets whatever it pleases. This is, however, what exists in Russia.

HAMBURG: AND NEXT IT'S BERLIN'S TURN

There were fronts in the last war. But now there is another front: back home. That is the bitter experience of the workers in Hamburg. As the British chemicals trusts pocket millions of pounds' worth of profits, the British planes drop thousands of kilos of their explosives on the German workers and their families. But we should have no illusions. Our own exploiters and warmongering hyenas are no better: far from it. If the German High Command had been able to do so it would have done exactly the same to the workers in London. If we want to put a final stop to such horrors we must march alongside the London workers against our common enemy, German and British capital. We have not yet achieved this goal. Down with the Nazi bureaucrats! Down with the war! Down with capitalism!

ONE LESS, BUT ONLY ONE

According to one comrade's report the mayor of Wuppertal has been sacked. He fled to the country in the evening, hearing the alarm, and in the morning returned to the ruins sozzled. That is why the Nazi clique sacrificed him. But how many of those men who escape into the night are so canny as to come back to the town in the morning and still go unnoticed? One of them has been sacked, but how many such men are left? Time to send the whole Nazi clique to hell.

millions of colonial slaves, [illegible], that would still have meant oppression and exploitation for the German worker. Certainly, some people [illegible] would have been able to achieve a 'better' position watching over the slaves or as henchmen of our capitalist masters' police. It was with this goal in mind that the Nazis, certain of victory, created the theory of the superiority of the German race.

Class-conscious workers want nothing to do with that. They struggle for the emancipation of the colonial slaves and for the abolition of all oppressions, not to become whip-holders in the service of the masters of industry. 'A people which oppresses another cannot itself be free' wrote Marx. He who fights for colonial conquest is, in the last instance, fighting for his own oppression. It is this unavoidable truth which obliges us to say openly and unflinchingly: we do not want our own country's capital to emerge victorious from the rapacious imperialist war.

Furthermore, we are not only opposed to the victory of our own country's bandits, we are also opposed to the victory of the brigands on the other side. We want their defeat! It was defeat in reactionary wars which caused the first uprisings of the working class: France in 1871, Russia in 1905 and 1917, and 1918 in Germany. That is why Lenin stressed this one principle for workers of all countries: in a reactionary war, the revolutionary class must wish for the defeat of its own government.

Any prolongation of the imperialist war will mean further sacrifices, above all for the working class, impacting on its strength and on its health, on its supplies and on its lives. That is why we want the soonest possible defeat of our government. But neither desertion, sabotage nor terrorism are the means which could bring about this defeat and a quick end to the imperialist war. Proletarian class struggle is the only means which can lead us to victory. During the 1917 Russian Revolution one soldier said 'sticking your bayonet in the ground still won't get you peace'. To hasten the end of the war we must everywhere create revolutionary proletarian organisations.

Such organisations could allow the widespread extension of the early expressions of working-class anger directed against oppression by big business and the Nazi clique and against their absurd war, causing an abrupt collapse of the system. It is for this reason, among others, that fascism has repressed all independent working-class organisations, helping it to make war for as long as possible and as easily as possible. But it should therefore be clear enough that every new local group and every new cell we build is a brick in the wall we must build. Not only to end this war, but to end all wars. For the revolutionary proletarian party fights in the front rank to lead the revolution to victory, which means replacing the capitalist system with socialism.

DOWN WITH THE WAR! DOWN WITH THE NAZI TYRANNY! FOR A SOVIET STATE!

To achieve this we fight for the defeat of our own capitalism. We know, as revolutionaries, that this will rain down much hatred and many calumnies on our heads. Was Lenin not accused of being an agent of Ludendorff? Did the lying bourgeois press not throw calumnies against Liebknecht and other worthy partisans of the proletarian revolution, having us believe that they had been bribed by the enemy? Knowing that the truth told by the revolutionary class will break through all these pathetic reactionary lies, we raise the standard of the defeat of our own capitalism, the standard of working-class victory.

FOUR YEARS OF WORLD WAR

1. The military balance-sheet: First and second year of the war: victory after victory across Europe. Clear Axis superiority. Third year: first clashes in the East. Retreat in the harsh winter. In summer, however, a significant new offensive. In Africa the advantage shifts between the two camps, before a German advance as far as the Pyramids. Balanced forces.

Explanation of these developments: from 1933 all production, economics, politics and all life in Germany was systematically directed towards war. This gave it a significant advantage.

But the enemies in this imperialist war had much more significant reserves to hand: powerful American industry, vast sources of raw materials across the greater part of the world, and the extent of the huge Russian reserves. Our own were small in comparison. Mr Goebbels placed his hopes in the collapse of the Russians (or at least, acted like he did). It is true that in Russia there is a lack of basic goods. But the Americans send enough goods for them to hold on. The Russians are constantly on the advance. Without doubt the third winter of the war will bring them significant territorial gains, allowing them to threaten eastern Germany.

There is no argument in favour of prolonging the war, except in the eyes of those profiting from it, big business and their military and political servants, the Nazis and the generals.

2. The balance-sheet for the working class. The seventy-hour week, paper-money as wages and empty slogans. Deterioration of food, a lack of clothes and of the most necessary home equipment. Destroyed houses and a lack of accommodation. Families torn apart and family well-being reduced to nothing forever. Limbs mutilated, cut up or frozen. Deformities and diseases. Millions of deaths: burnt, shot, stabbed, suffocated and drowned. Men, women and children. How many families are there left without any

loss to mourn?

3. The balance-sheet for big business. On 1 September, the anniversary of the beginning of the war, the newspaper of the Berlin stock exchange reported its figures on capital and German stocks. Here we add the corresponding figures for 1939. In billions of marks:

Total capital: *1939:* 20.29 *1941:* 24.9 *1942:* 29

Total capital of businesses whose capital is more than [illegible] million marks *1939:* 7.97 *1941:* 11.2 *1942:* 14.1

Percentage of total capital *1939:* 39% *1941:* 45% *1942:* 48.5%

The bottom line is of particular interest for the working class. It shows that big business has grown more quickly than small business has. Even apart from new business, big business has absorbed part of small and medium-sized business.

Capital is getting richer thanks to the blood and sweat of the workers. One thing is missing from this balance-sheet: an account of the revolutionary proletariat.

PEACE! FREEDOM! BREAD!

THE REAL FACE OF THE WAR

The Wehrmacht High Command reports: 'We were stationed around 50 km from Charkow. After a difficult fight we made a forward path for ourselves. One morning we took over the post office. There was a newspaper there, and to our surprise it announced in large type the seizure of Charkow [illegible]. It was only eight days later that we took Charkow.'

From the front: 'My brother had several frozen fingers and similarly his feet were freezing. That didn't stop the bastards sending him back to the East. That is where he is staying…'

Extract from a letter from Hamburg: 'The dead were piled up in a huge mound and burned with flame-throwers. I can only say: don't come back here, you won't recognise the place…'

The birth of children brings joy to the fatherland: 'We had to stay in the line of fire for fourteen days. Then we had eight days' rest. Many were those who stayed back afterwards. Sch. and K. learned the news of the birth of their children just when they had to go back to the front line. Midway, they turned on their heels. I never saw them again: soon after they were shot.'

The family is the cornerstone of the national socialist state: 'My two brothers were killed, one in Russia and the other in Africa. My wife and my son also perished in the last bombardment of Berlin. I knew nothing about the fate of my parents. When I went to the lieutenant to ask for information his only response was: we have more important things to do. Now I know for sure: my father and mother are dead.'

From a soldiers' paper produced by Fourth International comrades we reproduce one comrade's appeal: 'You know, comrades, how Hamburg suffered the most violent of attacks on 23 July 1943. Not only once have these criminals with their incendiaries attacked: no, it has been five times. This is no longer a war: it is no more than murders and more murders. 280,000 women, children and workers lost their lives just because they are German. 'I have lost everything. And for what? Just so that these capitalist bastards can have a better life and bask in their own grease.' 'Dear comrades, we must put an end to this murder and tell people that none of it makes sense. They made us promises which they still haven't fulfilled. Dear comrades, we can't go on like this. So join us. Together we will finally put an end to this war.'

PEACE! FREEDOM! BREAD!

PEACE: Only world proletarian revolution can bring us peace and the end of all wars. FREEDOM: This is not possible for all the exploited except in the framework of a Socialist Republic of Soviets. BREAD: Only the expropriation of capital and the establishment of a socialist planned economy can guarantee bread for all and an end to economic crises.

The German Revolution is the World Revolution—K. Liebknecht
ARBEITER UND SOLDAT
For revolutionary proletarian unity
Organ of the Bundes der Kommunisten-Internationalisten (German section of the Fourth International)
May 1944

1 MAY 1944: THE WAY FORWARD FOR THE REVOLUTION!

A day of significance for the German workers

The SPD leadership's treachery in the First World War left the German working class disarmed. Talk of revolution was smothered by the state of emergency. Therefore it was a liberating act when on 1 May 1916 Karl Liebknecht organised a demonstration in Potsdamer Platz with the support of thousands of workers from Berlin, to remind the workers and particularly the German workers that: *this war is not our war*. It had to be transformed into a proletarian revolution. The enemy was in our own country. Of course, Liebknecht was thrown in jail by the capitalist state's machinery of repression. But his liberatory ideas had already got out.

Revolution came with the Kiel sailors' uprising, putting an end to the war. All of Germany was covered with a network of workers' and soldiers' soviets. The bourgeois order was shaken to the core. German capital had to take action to hold on to power, most importantly using the help of the Social-Democrat bureaucracy. The soviets were dissolved or transformed into a shadow of their former selves as factory councils. In the place of peace, freedom and bread the German workers were given ballot papers, inflation and the Reichswehr.

In the following period there were two 1 May celebrations in Germany: that of the reformists, who for all their treachery still had the confidence of thousands of workers, and that of the young Communist Party, the German section of the Third International, whose task was to win over the majority of the working class to the goal of socialist revolution and lead it to power. Of course, the Third International's centre of gravity was in Russia, where the workers had taken power under the leadership of Lenin and Trotsky's Bolshevik Party. But the Russian workers' and peasants' victorious revolution was left isolated by the failure of the German revolution. Together with the economic backwardness of the country, this situation inevitably led to the bureaucratisation of the workers' state and the Bolshevik Party itself. There was sclerosis at the very heart of the Third International. The German CP, the strongest CP outside Russia, was itself transformed into a wing of the Stalinist bureaucracy without connection to the working masses.

This was made clear on 1 May 1929. In the interests of its domestic policies, the centre in Moscow declared from its ivory tower upon high that a new revolutionary period had begun. This was far from being the case. But to justify its line it had to stage all sorts of 'revolutionary demonstrations'. For this purpose it chose 1 May. The workers in Berlin and many other regions of Germany were called on to build barricades. The police chief Zoergiebel, a Social-Democrat, seized upon this excellent opportunity to send his troops against the isolated Communist workers. Despite putting up heroic resistance they were crushed. The result of this senseless adventure was to demoralise activists and leave the Social-Democrat workers indignant and appalled.

The bureaucrats never learned anything, even from the bloody defeat of their supporters. The errors of the Communist Party increased in number. Disoriented by the theory of social-fascism, its policy of splitting the unions and the tactic of united fronts from below, the revolutionary proletariat was led to defeat after defeat, up until the decisive one: the victory of the Nazi Party without a fight.

The Nazis made 1 May 1933 a national holiday. One more time—and this would be the last—the Social Democrat leaders and the union bureaucrats showed themselves in all their crapulence. Attempting to curry favour with their new masters, these Judases called on their members to participate in the Nazi rally.

It was totally in keeping with the Nazis' methods to keep 1 May as a day of celebration. They use such slogans as 'German socialism', 'the dignity of work' and 'the common interest comes above individual interests' to mask the most shameful of exploitation and the most absolute control. They place a shovel in the hands of the German worker so that he can dig—and lie in—his own grave. That is the meaning of their production of tanks, bombs and warships. War preparations were not enough for the capitalist state to breathe life into the economy, so war itself came.

The period which saw a series of victories—which can be attributed to Germany's weapons advances—is over. We can still not say exactly how many victims the second world imperialist war will have claimed among the German workers. They have been led into the abattoirs in the four corners of Europe, while their families and homes have been pulverised by bombs.

If the war—which had already been lost in advance given the Americans' technical superiority in several fields—does not last ten or fifteen years, as German, British and American capital would have liked, then for this workers across the world will be indebted to the Russian workers who, despite the enormous burden represented by the parasitic rule of the bureaucracy, have repulsed the capitalist aggression against the first workers' state and have thus saved the great conquest of the October revolution, the planned economy.

We must rebuild the class front!

Today, in May 1944, the greater part of the people of Europe is still under the German jackboot. But the course of events, both at home and abroad, show that the final reckoning is imminent. It may arrive one day or the next. *But that does not mean that it will just 'happen'*. The Nazi clique and its capitalist backers are ready to fight down to the last German worker. As in 1918 only the working class itself can bring an end to the reign of terror and the war. *We can only achieve peace with revolution*. But *what kind of peace? And what revolution?*

The old parties, in particular the Stalinist parties, enter the scene hoping to put the brakes on the revolution as soon as possible. They have formed a so-called liberation committee in Moscow, mainly composed of captured Nazi generals. The main task set for this committee is to suffocate the revolution as in 1918, installing a bourgeois government and saving the capitalist system. If they succeed in doing so Anglo-American capital and the Russian bureaucracy will dictate a peace to Germany alongside which Versailles will look charitable. And German capital for its part would dump the entire burden on the workers.

In this desperate situation the German proletariat does have an ally; but it will not be able to win it over *unless it finally starts fighting for its own interests and fights for them until victory*. The *emergence of workers' power and the establishment of a government of soviets, whose first task would be to expropriate big business and wealthy landed interests without compensation, is the only solution to the growing barbarism of decaying capitalism*. The pioneering struggle of the German working class will set the tone for the proletarian revolution across Europe. The revolutionary drive of the German revolution will everywhere overcome the chauvinist and counter-revolutionary influence of the Stalinist clique, first of all in Russia itself. It was the defeats of the German working class in 1923 which had dealt the last blow to the morale of the Russian proletariat and shored up the rule of the bureaucracy.

The German and European workers' struggle for the victory of socialism will give the Russian working masses the courage and strength to overthrow the bureaucracy with a fresh revolution, re-establishing soviet democracy and, in collaboration with the more advanced workers' states, climbing out of their miserable situation.

The union of soviet socialist republics of Europe and the Soviet Union, with its hundreds of millions of collective farms and its carefully planned industry, will be an impregnable communist bastion, a base from which communism will be able to spread across the world.

The Nazi press, totally submitted to the régime's gag, makes great play of mass strikes in Britain and in America. The German workers will not conclude from this—as the propaganda machine oh-so suddenly favourable to strikes would like them to—that the plans of their so-called enemies are bad ones, but rather that they are good.

That is because they now see that Britain and America does not just mean Churchill and Roosevelt, the City and Wall Street, but also the striking workers in Yorkshire and Minnesota. Which of them emerges strongest depends on the actions of the German proletariat in the coming revolutionary period.

In the struggle to lead the revolution to victory the construction of a revolutionary party is indispensable. The Fourth International was established before the dissolution of the Third International, and indeed in a long and unforgiving struggle against it. Its internationalist communist parties fight, whether openly in democratic countries or covertly in fascist countries and occupied territory, for the unity of the revolutionary proletariat. The struggle for the construction of a new internationalist communist party in Germany has also begun. *Arbeiter und Soldat* is one of the means of this struggle.

1 May 1944 must mark a turn in the fate of the German working class! It must start the development of the class front! Our gun barrels and bayonet points must be turned against the real enemy, capital and its agents in our country.

In this vein, we must build secret four-comrade cells in every workplace and in every army unit! These should bring together the most active militants gifted with the strongest class consciousness. They must follow the latest political developments with the greatest diligence. Everywhere where workers act to resist the apparatus of repression, action groups must go straight to the site of struggle.

They must also prepare for the establishment of soviets when the capitalist war front collapses. That day *every unit and every factory must elect* a soviet which will be the main organ of struggle as well as the basis for workers' power!

For a long time the German working class was at the heart of the world proletarian movement. After the defeat of the revolution it lost this central role. But it shall again be at the centre of struggle in the coming period. *The eyes of the class-conscious workers of the world are fixed on Germany.* Weakness and indecision for a long time kept the German working class in poverty and ignorance, but its confidence in its own strength and its courage driven to the limit will make it the vanguard of the world working class and the whole of humanity.

Workers in overalls and in uniform!

On 1 May there will be strikes in the occupied territories and perhaps also working-class demonstrations. The Nazi clique wants to use you as their executioners. Sabotage these actions! Refuse to do this dirty work! Every blow struck against a European worker is a blow struck against the German revolution! Fraternise with the workers in struggle! Their fight is your fight! On 1 May take up the old slogan of joint action: workers of all countries, unite!

GERMAN TRAIN DRIVERS SHOW THE WAY!

A train full of SS returning from Russia derailed. Terrorism, or an accident? That hardly mattered to the SS officer. He needed revenge, so put the French train drivers in charge up against the wall, sent troops to arrest all the men who could be found in the village, and had them shot. What did a few human lives matter to this professional killer, accustomed to mass graves of workers?

But he had not counted on the fact that despite five years of war the German workers haven't lost their good sense and still have some idea of solidarity. The German train drivers helped many Frenchmen to escape, thus saving their lives.

When an inquest later found that the accident was not caused by sabotage but rather the poor condition of rolling stock, revolt took hold of the French and German train drivers. They declared a one hour strike to protest against the murder of innocent workers.

The trains stopped for an hour on this line, with the German train crews supporting the French workers and their protest strike.

With their courageous action the German train drivers showed that workers do not feel national hatred and that their sense of solidarity knows no national boundaries.

When all the workers come to realise this and when they have the courage to act on their convictions, the officers can always shout 'fire!', but the workers, whether or not they are in uniform, will link arms and march together against the common enemy.

THE FOURTH INTERNATIONAL ON THE MARCH!

There has already been a great deal of talk about the news of strikes in Britain, which are said to have broken out against the will of the union bureaucrats and on the instigation of 'dubious' elements. Indeed the minister Bevin, that worthy member of the Second International, has called these shadowy figures by their real name: the Trotskyists, our comrades on the other side of the Channel.

At the same time the police were ordered to make the necessary arrests. Poor Interior Minister! Trying to wipe the coming revolution and the growing revolutionary party off the map with arrests sounds like trying to conjure up a tidal wave with a child's rattle.

The British workers are on strike today because they cannot bear their poverty, the other side of the coin of the capitalists' billions in profits. It is easy to understand why the union bureaucrats are opposed to this. The same goes for the British Stalinist party. The Stalinist bureaucracy has for a long time been selling out workers across the world in the interests of its ally, Anglo-American capital. Only the Trotskyists, the British section of the Fourth International, have taken sides with the British workers' struggle. They must make the British workers aware that their struggle is a rehearsal of the coming revolution, which they must prepare for by uniting their ranks.

The *Völkischer Beobachter*[496] makes fun of Mr. Bevin[497]. It has no right to. It has still not 'observed' that the Trotskyists are playing an active role in workers' struggles in countries occupied by the German Gestapo. It believes that police tyranny and Gestapo terror will succeed in crushing forever the class struggle in Germany and preventing the creation of a revolutionary party. These illusions will not last for long.

THE FINANCE MINISTER'S SPEECH

The German Finance Minister spoke on the radio on 9 April on the question of funding the war. He is called Schwerin-Krosigk, and is a count. Such types were saved by the Republic ruled by Noske and Scheidemann[498], those butchers of workers, and now occupy lucrative public offices, for example the Ministry of Finance. But let him speak for himself: 'In the last world war the Secretary of State Helfferich had to fight against a divided Parliament afraid to take the responsibility of raising desperately needed taxes'. Thank you, Mr Minister! At the time the taxpayer's voice could make itself heard—alas, all too weakly!—in a divided Parliament. But now we have the Gestapo, so... shut it! We now know what tasks, among others, the

Nazi state has been set by big business. Look at what followed: 'Until now we were able to cover around 50% of total war costs through taxation'. So 50% remains not supplied by taxes: he must therefore have made recourse to the tried and tested means of credit. This is indeed the case. But how did he get credit? Let's listen!: 'Unlike in the First World War we have not made a public call for war bonds: we obtained most of the necessary credit from banks and financial institutions (read—savings banks!). We think this to be the means of financing the war with the most discretion. It relies in its greatest part on the savings made by the German people.' So, the money the worker takes to the savings bank is taken by compulsion by the state in exchange for a 'treasury bond' with no value (a bond on a treasury with no money). The state hands the money over to the armaments factory owners so that they can do their great work. All of this has a wonderful name: 'the discreet financing of the war'. But the German worker calls it stealing, and he is right. Pickpockets work 'discreetly' too!

But wait! When the war is over, surely everything will be reimbursed, mark for mark and pfennig for pfennig? Indeed: 'The German saver who does not today spend his money on unnecessary items but takes it to the savings bank is not only helping the war effort but is also acting in the best-advised manner.' Thus following in the vein of the usual promises of paradise the Nazis make... to be fulfilled once they have won the final victory. The count tells us: have faith in the Nazi state and you can become its creditor! And don't worry about that inflation, I already have the solution worked out in my ministerial head. Let us listen closely to the idea he has worked out up there. This is what will really make you laugh: 'The Reich's debts are at root a debt the German people owes itself. Consequently, it can and will be paid off at the end of the war, with part of it made up for by raising taxes on newly flourishing private incomes and the other part consolidated in the long term'. Listen carefully! The money you saved makes you your own creditor. My debts are your debts, jests this ingenious Finance Minister. In order that the state can pay you back its debt it will have to bleed it out of you after the end of the war. Since the birth of capitalism taxes on private incomes have always hit the poor guy hardest. So: this gentleman has taken something off you but in order to pay it back to you he will have to take it off you again. The rest of the debt will be 'consolidated', which means: the payment will be dragged out forever.

Along with His Excellency we have had a brief glimpse of the paradise the Nazi clique and its capitalist backers are diligently preparing for us for after the war. This is reassuring, as we can see that capital will not win out after this final victory. But what does our dear Finance Minister see? Would he like to draw up, as the Berlin stock exchange papers suggest, fresh tax hikes for the distinguished public? Have they not had enough already with an increase of 30% or more? Or would he like to entice the workers with a new 'savings supplement'?

If so he is kidding himself. The workers will not swallow his April Fools, even on the 9th! He should have economised on his wind and used it to cool the burning hot revolutionary soup which the German proletariat will soon serve up for him, his colleagues and his capitalist masters.

THE ENEMY IS IN OUR OWN COUNTRY! (Karl Liebknecht)

The German Revolution is the World Revolution—K. Liebknecht
ARBEITER UND SOLDAT
For revolutionary proletarian unity
Organ of the Bundes der Kommunisten-Internationalisten (German section of the Fourth International)
Special issue June 1944

THE FUTURE IS IN OUR HANDS

Soldiers! Comrades!

A new and decisive phase of the Second World War has begun. Anglo-American capital has launched its troops on the offensive on the European continent. With 4,000 warships, 13,000 planes and half a million soldiers they have begun landings on the French Atlantic coast.

'We are ready for all eventualities' lied the Nazi press, trumpeting itself as ever. They are indeed prepared: for a torrent of military disasters. The German military machine will be forced back, more or less slowly, since American war production alone is much greater than German production. The 'Allies' could have finished off the war long ago had they so wished. But the British and American capitalists—JUST LIKE THE GERMANS—want to drag out the war as much as possible. The more the arms trade rumbles on and the billions in profits stay at a high level, the more they delay the post-war crisis of declining markets. The more Germany and Russia tear chunks out of each other, the better! The more the German and Russian workers spill their blood, the better!

But happy times for the capitalist vultures are coming to an end. The spring offensive has taken the Red Army to the German border. Its next advance may well take it inside Germany itself, causing the collapse of imperialist Germany. Then American and British capital would have to move as quickly as possible to best position themselves for the carve-up.

But the significance of the 'second front' does not stop there.

This front is at the same time THE FRONT OF COUNTER-REVOLUTION! The bridge-head between Le Havre and Cherbourg is the bridge-head against the European revolution! The coming collapse of German imperialism will pose in the most threatening fashion the spectre of proletarian revolution in Germany and across Europe; a revolution much greater than any before.

That is why these gentlemen are showing their hand.

A few weeks ago British radio outlined the programme of these sorry gentlemen. Now they have finally shown their real face. As they preached about the well-being and freedoms they wanted to gift to humanity after the war, they were secretly preparing their usual method of keeping down the revolutionary popular masses in Europe: bashing them over the head. To prevent 'anarchy', by which they mean the emancipation of the working class, and to defend 'order', by which they mean the capitalist system of exploitation, its wars and its crises, they have created an occupation army and a High Command of civil inspectors 'who all know how to make use of a machine-gun'. This plan will be crowned with the establishment of military governments across Europe.

In Germany they want to replace Hitler with Eisenhower, replacing one pest with another.

They know what incredible suffering awaits the masses after the war in destroyed Germany.

They know that the German workers, exploited to the limit, will have to sweat out profits twice over, both for his own exploiters and for foreign capital.

But they also know that the proletariat of Europe will rise up together against the party responsible for its poverty: capital and its lackeys.

They imagine that they will be able to stop this formidable revolution with the same old methods as usual.

That is why they want to replace the Gestapo executioners with a Scotland Yard expeditionary force.

That is why they want to nail our traps shut, tie our hands and impose all the post-war suffering on us.

Comrades! Soldiers!

Faced with this situation Hitlerite propaganda calls on us to hold out and defend ourselves. They have decided to do so themselves.

From Hitler in his headquarters far from the front lines to Goebbels in his bombproof office and Goering in his Marshal's villa, all the party clique and the officer caste have decided to hold out. They will stay as long as possible, gripping on to the butter dish! To postpone for as long as possible defeat and the terrible moment when they are thrown to the mercy of millions of German workers. They are holding out!

The gentlemen of big business also have heavy hearts. The Krupp, Boersig and Kloeckner trusts, oiled with the blood of the German workers, are quietly going on at a fast pace and producing great profit. The German banks' capital has oh-so quietly increased from 21 billion marks in 1939 to 45 billion in 1943. This despite the 100% bluff about 6% dividends and despite the supposed taxes on war profits. With such profits it must be a joy to hold out. German capital does not fear being expropriated by its class brothers on the other side of the water. Wolves do not eat each other. There was no problem in 1918 either. At worst, they will have to share the exploitation of the German workers with their British and American colleagues.

They are holding out!

BUT WHAT OF THE GERMAN SOLDIERS? THE WORKERS IN UNIFORM? THEY DO NOT WANT TO HOLD OUT, AND NOR SHALL THEY!

For almost five years they have been sent into the battlefield or sent abroad, torn away from their families, parents, wives and children and taken from their workplaces. Back home their loved ones have been massacred by bombs, the little property they afforded through their labours has been destroyed and their wives have to do terrible jobs just to get a little to eat and some worthless paper-money. All that for profits for the capitalist hyenas and the empty slogans of their Nazi lackeys.

What is left for the German soldier to defend?

Gestapo terror? The socialism of long journeys on troopships, people's soup kitchens, overtime at work, working on Sundays, wage cuts, speed-ups, the most shameful capitalist exploitation, militarism, great promises and the Second World War?

So why don't Hitler and the Krupps, Goebbels and Siemens defend their paradise themselves? We want to go back home!

But if we do not want to fight this hopeless struggle, does that mean that we want to give the reactionary Eisenhower a free ride to Berlin? Hitler or Eisenhower? Are those the only two choices? There does exist a third: workers' revolution in Germany, Europe and the world, which would kill the capitalist system at its roots and which would put an end to war and crises, and which alone can bring the working masses peace, freedom and bread.

Of course, the British and American bourgeoisie intends to drown this revolution in blood. To do this it will not blush at using the repressive apparatus inherited from German capital, whether that means police, special troops or the old Nazi formations themselves.

But there is a gap in these gentlemen's register! They have not accounted for the British and American workers.

In the first three months of 1943 the British workers had 200,000 strike days. In the same period this year the figure was almost 2,500,000.

Soldiers! Comrades!

Listen to these figures! Understand what they mean! They are a salute from our class comrades on the other side of the Channel, who are shouting to us 'We, British workers, understand each day a little better that the capitalists are not fighting this war to get rid of Hitler and the Gestapo but rather in their own imperialist interests and for profit.'

The British workers have also taken up the struggle against poverty, war and capital. Faced with a proletarian Germany the Churchills and Roosevelts would be keen to unleash the hounds of reaction.

But they would need them to keep down their own workers. The question posed is not: Hitler or Eisenhower, but who will defeat Hitler? EISENHOWER OR THE GERMAN PROLETARIAT?

If the German proletariat defeats Hitler before the final military defeat and occupation and establishes its own power across Germany with workers' and soldiers' councils, the American and British military cliques would then have to openly show before the eyes of the world proletariat who they really are: not liberators from Hitler's dictatorship but the executioners of the European revolution and the champions of Anglo-American imperialist military dictatorship. The American and British workers' march towards revolution would thus make a huge step forward.

THE GERMAN REVOLUTION AS A RESPONSE TO THE ANGLO-AMERICAN INVASION WOULD GIVE THE PROLETARIAT OF GERMANY, EUROPE AND THE WHOLE WORLD A MASSIVE ADVANCE AGAINST WORLD REACTION!

But revolutions do not fall from the sky. They are prepared by innumerable small struggles fought by the revolutionary class. But today there are almost no such struggles in Germany. Struggles over basic demands, for food, for wages, for the most basic rights and freedoms to protest, strike and demonstrate have been crushed by Hitlerite reaction with the bloodiest of terror.

We can only speak one language, the language of weapons

The German workers hold these weapons in their hands already.

But individuals or little units throwing themselves into struggle out of desperation is not very effective. They just make themselves into the disarmed victims of the most brutal of terror. The struggle must be planned and organised, with sufficient size that it can become the signal for revolution across Germany. When the British and Americans invade the revolutionary temperature will reach boiling point. In this situation an uprising by one garrison, in one town or one province, or in one section of the fleet could be the spark which sets off the social explosion.

The day of the Kiel sailors and dockworkers will return!

But this time around the German revolution will be followed by proletarian uprisings *across Europe*!

Therefore the most important slogan now is: ORGANISE TO PREPARE REVOLUTIONARY STRUGGLES!

Form secret cells of three or four people! Bring into these groups all workers who understand the need for revolutionary struggle and want to participate in it! Comrades, you who believe in your unity, form committees for revolutionary struggle!

ON EACH SHIP, IN EACH BARRACKS, IN EACH TRENCH, WE MUST CREATE REVOLUTIONARY CELLS AND COMMITTEES FOR STRUGGLE!

Build links with comrades in other units! Encourage them to form their own cells!

Make contact with the local workers, with the French, Belgian and Dutch workers in the West! Our struggle is a common struggle!

Remain in contact! Do not go into struggle without joint agreement! When struggle breaks out, have the courage to build it as much as possible! Spread news of the struggle by all means to all countries!

Comrades! Soldiers!

As much as we want a repeat of the Kiel days we must not allow the creation of a second Weimar. The workers' and soldiers' soviets which at the time of the revolution spread far and wide at home and on the front must not again be dissolved; on the contrary they must be the foundations of workers' power. But in the struggle for the establishment of workers' power the revolutionary proletarian party is indispensable. The Second International and the former Third International, the reformists and the Stalinists, are planning, on the orders of world capital and the Moscow bureaucracy, to destroy the proletarian revolution from within, as they have in the past. WE MUST FIGHT THIS PROJECT!

The Fourth International, the Trotskyists in America, Britain and the occupied territories of Europe, are holding fast on the side of the working class in its struggles, despite the terror of the Gestapo and Scotland Yard, and preparing the class for its future revolutionary tasks. In Germany too, revolutionary workers are organising themselves under its banner and are building the centre of a new internationalist communist party.

But all the revolutionary cells and committees for struggle must work with all workers—even if today they are still reformists or Stalinists—who sincerely want to fight the current system to the last. The future course of the revolution, and the struggle itself, will attract all these comrades to our ranks!

The German workers' response to the British and American capitalists' invasion must under no circumstances be defence of Hitlerite barbarism! The German workers must respond 'à la russe'—not in the manner of Stalin, but that of Lenin and Trotsky. Their slogans are:

REVOLUTIONARY FRATERNISATION WITH THE BRITISH AND AMERICAN SOLDIERS AGAINST THE GERMAN, BRITISH AND AMERICAN GENERALS AND THEIR CAPITALIST MASTERS!
REVOLUTIONARY FRATERNISATION WITH ALL EUROPEAN WORKERS IN OUR COMMON STRUGGLE!
FOR A WORKERS' REVOLUTION IN GERMANY, EUROPE AND THE WORLD!
Long live the Soviet Socialist Republic of Germany!
Long live the Soviet United States of Europe!
Long live the Soviet Socialist Republic of the World!

The German Revolution is the World Revolution—K. Liebknecht
ARBEITER UND SOLDAT
For revolutionary proletarian unity
Organ of the Bundes der Kommunisten-Internationalisten (German section of the Fourth International)
July 1944

DOWN WITH THE WAR!
FOR IMMEDIATE PEACE!

The attack on Hitler is the last warning of civil war

The Nazi press's propaganda sees the hand of Providence everywhere. Each day they expect the miracle without which victory is now impossible. Even the attack Hitler survived, an attack made by circles of high-up officers and a section of the big bourgeoisie who have realised that Germany's situation is desperate and want to replace the Hitlerite state with another bourgeois state. But the bureaucrats do not want to give up power so quickly; on the contrary, they want to hang on to the butter dish as long as possible. They are defending themselves with the most brutal of terror, Himmler having received carte blanche to exercise it freely; in the big cities of Germany and even in the occupied territories in the West there have been incidents and bloody clashes between the Gestapo and the Wehrmacht. The Hitlerite state is falling apart, which is why they are calling on German soldiers to hold out until the last.

Hitler's fall means revolution in Germany. Only the inhuman terror of the Gestapo, SS and other gendarmes is keeping the German soldiers on the front. All German soldiers and workers have had more than enough of the war and want to go home, above all now that they know that victory is unthinkable. They only have one slogan in their heads: DOWN WITH THE WAR, FOR IMMEDIATE PEACE!

Hitler can rely on the German army less and less. He has to send Waffen SS, parachutists and other shock troops all over the place to stave off collapse.

Signs of discontent in the German army are becoming more numerous and more visible. Everywhere we find fraternisation between German soldiers and French and Belgian workers. Many soldiers have joined the maquis. The courts-martial are in full flow.

Bloody fighting and retreats on all fronts

German troops are being forced back by the formidable strength of the Americans. But the British and American 'liberators' do not want to race ahead, since this would cause the decomposition of the front in Normandy and even the end of the German occupation of France, that is to say, the German revolution, which the American capitalists do not want. These formidable battles are not only happening in France; in Italy too each day more and more significant areas have become battlefields. The Red Army is still progressing: it is in the heart of the Baltic States, it is marching on Warsaw and it has arrived on the borders of East Prussia.

Germany is in an absolutely desperate situation

Hitler, Goering, Goebbels and their lying propaganda put their only hopes of winning the war in some God-given miracle, Providence and secret new weapons. We have already heard such talk once before in the war, from Reynaud, President of the French Council, who said such things a few weeks before the French disaster of June 1940. Like Hitler and German capital today, he was relying on a miracle. But this is hopeless. No miracle is now able to save Hitler and his capitalist backers. Hitler has been pushed back onto his last lines of defence. The domestic situation worsens daily. The more critical Germany's situation becomes, the more the capitalists and the bourgeoisie are divided and turn away from Hitler.

But who will succeed Hitler?

After five years of endless, pointless killing, the soldiers on the front as well as German workers constantly threatened with being sent to the front, unable to voice their discontent and forced to work under constant bombardment, have had more than enough of this war which has taken from them everything they worked so hard to achieve. They can see that they have nothing to gain from this war. German soldiers, workers and peasants want to send the Hitlerite régime to hell, along with the inhuman Gestapo terror which forces them to shoot at the workers and peasants on the other side. Each man is wondering how he can save himself from this hellish war. The Nazi bureaucrats, Goebbels and his henchmen, know that German soldiers no longer want to go and fight abroad. So to get them to hold out for longer the lying propaganda warns of a new, even worse Versailles Treaty in the aftermath of the war in the event that Germany loses.

All the British and American propaganda comes to Goebbels' aid with its unrelenting attacks on the German soldiers, with its plans for a military occupation of Germany of indeterminate length, under American military dictatorship (Eisenhower shall rule over occupied Europe) and even talking of a carve-up of Germany. None of this surprises us. It only proves that the British and American governments are no better than the Nazi clique, that they are doing as they please and that we must rid ourselves of the whole system of capitalist rule, whether that be in Germany or Britain, France or America. That can only be achieved by a victorious workers' revolution in Germany, Europe and the world.

The nationalist policies of the ex-Communist Party aid the reactionary plans of the Americans

But the worst thing is that the British and American capitalists' plans have found solid backing from the nationalist politics of the so-called Communist Party. In Moscow Stalin has created a 'Committee for a Free Germany' composed of barons, counts and captured Hitlerite generals. These gentlemen's goal is to replace Hitler's vacillating régime with a national bourgeois government and so save German capitalism from proletarian revolution. The ex-Communist Party and Stalinist degeneration have cast the Leninist programme of international class struggle and international revolution into the dust. Stalin has dissolved the Comintern, the international leadership of the world revolution, and in every country has introduced a nationalist and chauvinist policy attacking German soldiers. The ex-Communist Parties have replaced the policy of revolutionary fraternisation with fraternisation with their own exploiters, and have united with the reactionary de Gaulle. They would have the workers believe that Churchill and Roosevelt will liberate them. By not calling on the international proletariat to defend the workers' state, instead allying with the capitalist Great Powers and not calling for international fraternisation between workers, Stalin strengthens Hitler's hand, since German soldiers who everywhere meet with hatred and unable to find any solution are ultimately thrown into the arms of Hitler, who tells them that Germany must conquer Europe in order to survive.

Only the transformation of the imperialist war into proletarian revolution can bring peace

Neither Roosevelt-Churchill nor Hitler can bring peace or bring an end to the war. Their peace can only be directed against the international working class.

We must end this war: for immediate peace! Only the will of the exploited working masses can end it, again taking up the struggle against the capitalist rule which caused the war, which is responsible for it, which dragged it out and which will bring more wars if we let it.

Hitler and German capitalism can only be overthrown by the working class. The latter must take its destiny in its own hands and turn the imperialist war into a civil war.

The bourgeois parties have already proven their inability to save Germany from crisis, and all of them have oppressed the working class and thrown it into ever greater poverty. We must not allow the Hitlerite régime to be replaced by another bourgeois government, however 'democratic' it might be, whose main tasks would be to save German capitalism and oppressing the workers and peasants to an even greater extent. For this struggle, hang on to your weapons.

You should hang on to the weapons they have given you to fight for the interests of the Hitlerite clique in order to turn the imperialist war into a war against capitalism, a civil war. The uprising of the German working class, which will create workers' and soldiers' soviets and organise fraternisation with the workers and peasants of Europe, will cast aside any fresh Versailles Treaty and all the rapacious plans of capitalism. The proletarian revolution will overthrow capitalism across Europe and establish in its place the Soviet Socialist United States of Europe. Fraternise with the Russian, American and British soldiers.

Fraternise with the workers of the occupied countries. Do not break their strikes, which signify the struggle against capitalism. On the contrary, show them that you are also exploited workers and peasants, that you are for peace and against Hitler and the war.

Fraternise with the French and Russian prisoners and with the millions of foreign workers in Germany, who are forced to work far from home, far from their wives and children. Invite them back to yours, and try and forge mutual understanding. Together, take home to Germany the struggle for better living standards, against the war and for peace.

Create secret cells of three or four people! In these cells, discuss the situation in Germany. With secretly advertised slogans fight in your units for better living standards and for more leave, and in regard to all issues raised by soldiers. Discuss the illegal papers and circulate them clandestinely among the other soldiers. Explain the situation in Germany and Europe to your comrades.

Comrades, you who believe in your unity, organise yourselves in committees for revolutionary struggle. Wherever you can, help the local workers. Try to build links with them.

Do not think that you are isolated. The proletarian revolution is mounting in every country in Europe, and everywhere the working class is fighting hard, even on the underground, against its own exploiters and against police and fascist terror.

Stay in contact! Do not enter struggle without collective agreement! When struggle breaks out, have the courage to build it as much as possible! Spread news of the struggle by all means and to all countries!

LONG LIVE THE SOVIET SOCIALIST REPUBLIC OF GERMANY! LONG LIVE THE SOVIET UNITED STATES OF EUROPE! LONG LIVE THE SOVIET SOCIALIST REPUBLIC OF THE WORLD! FOLLOW KARL LIEBKNECHT'S EXAMPLE, AGAINST THE IMPERIALIST WAR!

On 1 May 1916 Karl Liebknecht came to Berlin and gave a speech in Potsdamer Platz. He was arrested and put before a military tribunal. To explain his opposition to the imperialist war he wrote a series of texts, one of the most important of which we reproduce here:

'The German government is in its social composition and historical character an instrument for the oppression and exploitation of the working class; at home and abroad it serves the interests of junkerism[499], of capitalism, and of imperialism.

'The slogan 'Down with the government!' is designed to brand this entire policy of the government as fatal for the mass of the population.

'This slogan also indicates that it is the duty of every representative of the interests of the proletariat to wage a most bitter struggle—the class struggle—against the government...

'The present war is neither a war to defend the nation's territorial integrity nor a war to liberate oppressed peoples or assure the well-being of the masses.

'From the standpoint of the proletariat this war only signifies the most extreme concentration and extension of political suppression, of economic exploitation, and a blood bath of the workers in the interests of capitalism and absolutism.

'To all this the workers of all countries can give but one answer: to engage in a bitter struggle, the international class struggle, against the capitalist governments and the ruling classes of all countries for the abolition of all oppression and exploitation by establishing a socialist peace. In this class struggle the socialists, whose only fatherland is the International, fight for all that socialists fight for. The slogan 'Down with the war' signifies that I wholeheartedly condemn the present war and declare myself an enemy of the current war because of its historic nature, because of its general social causes as well as the specific way in which it originated, because of the way it is being carried out and the goals for which it is being waged. That slogan signifies that it is the duty of every socialist and every representative of proletarian interests to participate in the international class struggle in order to end the war.'

CLASS-CONSCIOUS WORKERS AND THE USSR

Soldiers who fought in Russian remain confused about the contradictory character of Soviet life: on the one hand great, undeniable progress in the cities, including new houses, large roads and modern and rich factories, and on the other hand miserable shacks—particularly in the countryside—peasants living in poverty, ignorance and without any comfort. But above all it is the policies of the rulers of the Soviet Union which confuse the German soldiers and workers: their chauvinist policies and their collaboration with the worst representatives of world imperialism, Churchill and Roosevelt. How can we explain it? The Soviet Union is a workers' state, born of the proletarian revolution of 1917 and in which private capitalist property has been expropriated and nationalised.

The USSR, which is a workers' state and not a capitalist state, is defending itself against German imperialism and is fighting a just war.

It is every worker's duty to defend it against imperialism.

But while the USSR is a workers' state, it is at the same time a degenerated workers' state ruled by a parasitic bureaucracy which grew out of the country's backwardness and the postponement of socialist revolution in other countries.

Stalin is the representative of this bureaucracy of party and state functionaries, specialists and army men. Class-conscious workers are for the USSR, for the country which, thanks to its economic system, is closed off from imperialist exploitation and which, because of the nationalisation of private property, can develop its productive forces.

But class-conscious workers are also opposed to Stalin's political régime in the USSR, which hampers the country's economic progress and which leads reactionary policies contrary to the interests of the Soviet people and the international proletariat. The capitalists, whether fascists or democrats, equate the USSR's social system with Stalin's current policies in government. But class-conscious workers, who defend the USSR's economic system against imperialist aggression in this war, also fight against Stalin's political régime. That is to say, class-conscious workers both fight to defend the USSR and criticise Stalin's reactionary policies, encouraging the Soviet masses to overthrow the bureaucratic caste which rules over them.

They do not however allow any let-up in the class struggle in the countries allied to the USSR, declaring the necessity of overthrowing the capitalist régimes of Churchill, Roosevelt and the other 'Allies'.

In Germany they are against Hitler and the German capitalist class who support him, and are for fraternisation with the Red Army, all the while calling on it to take part in a common struggle to overthrow Stalin.

SOLDIERS, HOLD ON TO YOUR WEAPONS (A letter from a soldier)

So comrade, what do you think of the new people who arrived yesterday? Yes, it's the latest reserves: without receiving any training they have been mobilised, given uniforms, wage booklets and identity plaques and been sent to the front, albeit without any weapons. It is as if there were no weapons left in the country. But there are.

But listen for a moment. When I was mobilised four years ago in B., a big industrial town, we too had to wait for our guns, and no artillery arrived until 11 days later, which our instructors bitched about. Mine, a chief-brigadier, a salesman by trade and an SA member, said: 'We have to wait around, but down there they always have the best and newest equipment first'. He was referring to the Waffen SS, who had a brand new barracks not far from our own.

Yes, you know, now he would be able understand why the SS always get the new equipment first, and why the ordinary conscript is sent to the front without any weapons. It is clear that the Hitlerite régime is scraping the bottom of the barrel and that Hitler and his henchmen can only hope for a miracle to allow them to cling on to power. For this reason they must send the SS around the country: on one hand they can keep down the youth with the SS, since they're tough chaps, eh?!, and on the other hand they are the most loyal bedfellows of Hitler, and in the case that the proletariat rose up he could send them in with the Gestapo to crush them. Perhaps you think that they can use their new recruits to do this and so you had better ask them what they think about it? Rubbish, when Hitler's bastards are gone the war will be over! And they say we still have to risk our necks for Hitler and the Nazi bureaucrats, so that they and their backers, the big German capitalists, can continue to rule?!

Do you still believe that they can train up soldiers back home? With weapons? The capitalists and their Nazi lackeys are too afraid to do this. They would prefer to terrorise the masses: that is why the Red Army is already almost at the border, that is why they are already shitting their pants and that is why they are hurrying to dispatch the last workers and agricultural toilers to the abattoir. They think they can cut down the women and children with their Gestapo executioners. As for the soldiers, they will only give them weapons if they can be sure that there is no chance that they will come back, if they are where they have to fire at the enemy and there is no danger that a stray bullet will strike a Nazi bureaucrat, where they can only fire at their opposite numbers, the comrades on the other side. The officers and that reactionary crowd are still in place. Yes, we're forced to do this, what else are you going to do? I know as well as you do that all of us, including the new people, have had more than enough of this senseless carnage, of the great massacre of the international proletariat, but here's the signal that the last hour of the fascist gang has arrived, the moment when Hitler and his bandits will be overthrown by the coming social revolution, the moment when these dogs will pay for the crimes they committed against millions of workers. For that moment, comrade, take care of your weapons! If necessary mend them, and don't let them out of your hands, since you will need them when the time comes for you and us to hunt down the capitalists and the fascist gang of Hitler, Goering, Himmler and their Gestapo executioners. This gang will not give up of its own free will, knowing that doors are closing all around it. It would rather kill the last living thing and destroy the last house before perishing itself! But we will stop this last act of folly by this unruly mob! Comrade! When the last hour sounds, we will all march forward to the socialist revolution with arms linked, carrying the banner of freedom which will bring us peace and bread. We all want to create the free state of all workers, a free socialist Germany of soviets, from which base the socialist revolution would then spread victoriously across the other countries of Europe, until the creation of a free Soviet Socialist European Union! Comrades! Keep your weapon by your side, until you hear the call: arise for the final struggle!

FOR A FREE SOVIET SOCIALIST GERMANY!
FOR A FREE SOVIET SOCIALIST EUROPEAN UNION!
LONG LIVE THE WORLD SOCIALIST REVOLUTION!

DER ARBEITER
NEWS FOR SOLDIERS AND WORKERS IN THE WEST
No. 2, Summer 1943

[Illegible] I came back from leave a few days ago and I was amazed by the situation in Germany. What I saw is not easy to describe.

First off, the town where I grew up has been totally destroyed. Only very few houses are still habitable — you could count them — and only a few have still been spared by bombs. Next, the morale of the population. You can only imagine what has happened. Our women and daughters have been totally morally corrupted by the many workers from abroad [illegible].

And then there are the traffickers, who have set themselves up almost openly in the streets to run their black market, offering their seedy wares with price increases of 500% or 1,000%. So the situation in Germany is catastrophic. It is clear to everyone that morale is sinking day by day.

In brief, the people want an end [illegible] to the war.

Comrades, the Fourth International has shown me the way forward, and you too can participate in it and add your contribution to the effort to bring an end to the war without delay.

Listen to what I say, because things are not getting better for your wives and children back home. Join us, join the Fourth International. We are fighting for peace, freedom and bread.

by a German soldier

Can things go on like this? My wife and children write me letter after letter to complain about the situation, and I can do nothing for them. They can't even console themselves with the idea that the end of the war is near. It breaks my heart when I read that.

That is why I believe that we must put an end to this appalling war. And we soldiers on the front can do something about it. I know a sure means of doing so, which will be good for you too. Alone I can do nothing, but you can co-operate and work with me. Listen carefully and think about what follows.

I am a member of the Fourth International and my top priority is to put an end to the war. We fight against capitalism and for fraternisation the world over. Fighting for this goal we will make it impossible for any state to rule or exercise its dictatorship over Germany, which would result in the partition of the country and massive tax increases.

Comrades, the Fourth International fights so that no-one should have to fear another even worse way of life.

Think of your wives and children.
Imagine a real and [illegible] peace.
Do you not want to fight for that?
Join the Fourth International.
by a comrade

The famished and martyred proletariat of Europe cannot put a rapid end to its distress unless it makes a clear break with world imperialism, avoiding any collaboration with its own bourgeoisie and rejecting Stalin's so-called 'union sacrée'. Destroy fascism by destroying capital.

For the real freedom of the dictatorship of the proletariat.

Only under the banner of the Fourth International will the masses be able to establish the dictatorship of the proletariat across the world, in Germany, Poland, Spain, Belgium, [illegible], Greece and above all [illegible] in Italy and in France [illegible] sections of the Fourth International [illegible] for the building of the struggle for socialism in Europe and proletarian revolution across the world.
by the Fourth International

Comrades!
It is rather difficult to understand all this at a glance, but fundamentally it is quite simple. These are nothing other than the ideas of the Fourth International. Above you will see the little cartoons representing our German capitalists. There are not many of them, but they are some of the biggest ones. There are hundreds of such capitalists whose constant aim is to fill their wallets with our money. The government is under their thumb and produces the propaganda these capitalist dogs need. To prolong the war, for more and better armaments, etc. Do we soldiers want to fight for these people? No.

Think about it. Join the Fourth International.

Fight for peace, freedom and bread.

NOTES

1. The official figure. Other figures given range closer to 5,000: see discussion of the numbers in Robert Mencherini, *Résistance et Occupation (1940-1944) Midi rouge, ombres et lumières 3*, Syllepse, Paris, 2011, p. 587.
2. A regional administrative unit of France. After its territorial gains in the First World War, France had a total of 89 *départements*.
3. Not necessarily meaning 'non-violent', but opposed to war between the rival powerful states.
4. Section Française de l'Internationale Ouvrière, or French section of the Workers' International. It merged into the Parti socialiste in 1969, and it is part of the same international organisation as the Labour Party in Britain and Germany's Social Democrats.
5. Also known as the Third International.
6. Ideally intended to secure full freedom of debate but maximum unity in action, holding leaders accountable to implementing majority decisions. This condition was opposed by most of the SFIO's MPs and councillors, who refused to join the new party.
7. Cachin was a member of the foreign affairs commission of the French parliament, and visited Italy in spring 1915 in a successful effort to secure its entry into the war on the side of the British-French Entente; in February 1917 he made a further official visit to the country – now France's ally – meeting with King Victor Emmanuel III in Rome.
8. With his health failing in 1922, Lenin worked on a *Testament* which he wanted to be read out at the Soviet Communist Party's Twelfth Congress in April 1923. The final draft of this document called for the ousting of Stalin as General Secretary, but it was also critical of other party leaders, and all of them – including Trotsky – colluded in preventing its publication.

   Even after being forced out of his post as People's Commissar for Army and Naval Affairs in January 1925, Trotsky persisted in denying its existence, although only under pressure from the party leadership did he agree to write an article rebutting the American Left Opposition supporter Max Eastman's revelations about the *Testament*'s content. Still loyal to party discipline, Trotsky called on Monatte and Rosmer to desist from publishing the magazine *La Révolution prolétarienne*, saying they should instead address their grievances with the PCF leadership to the Comintern.
9. His speech is reproduced in part at http://www.marxists.org/archive/bordiga/works/1926/comintern.htm
10. The PCF's willingness to distance itself from the French establishment during this period did also therefore express a degree of communist principle. For instance, in response to the 1931 colonial exhibition in Paris – where the French government exhibited human beings from the empire in cages – the PCF staged an alternative event, 'The truth on the colonies', which provided a damning indictment of democratic France's civilising mission in Africa and Indochina.
11. Including organising together to break up Social-Democratic meetings;

344 SWIMMING AGAINST THE TIDE

jointly-called strikes against Social-Democratic authorities such as the 1932 Berlin transport strike; and support for the 1931 Nazi-initiated referendum to overturn the Social-Democratic government of Prussia, a state comprising almost two-thirds of the country.

12 An international collective security organisation and precursor to the United Nations.

13 Pierre Laval, a politician who over his career journeyed rightwards from the SFIO towards prominent service in the war-time pro-Nazi régime based at Vichy. Prime Minister of France 1931-32, 1935-36, 1940 and 1942-1944.

14 The 1919 settlement to the First World War, which imposed harsh terms on Germany.

15 Even the elections staged by the revolutionary Paris Commune on 26 March 1871 had excluded women, although the council thus elected passed a never-realised bill giving women political equality with men. The SFIO's Jules Guesde sponsored a parliamentary motion for equality of civil and political rights in 1920, which was passed by the National Assembly but rejected by the Senate in 1922. Vichy France's constitution promised women the vote, but the régime staged no elections; French women were first actually able to vote at the 1945 municipal and legislative elections.

16 See Jacques Danos and Marcel Gibelin's *June '36: Class Struggle and the Popular Front in France* (Bookmarks: London, 1986).

17 An agreement between Britain, France, Italy and Germany authorising Hitler to annex the German-speaking Sudetenland area of western Czechoslovakia, dated 29 September 1938. This effort to appease the Nazi leader was badly received in Czechoslovakia itself, particularly given that it was in breach of the French alliance with that country; no Czech representative was allowed to attend the Munich conference; and most Czech military installations were situated in the now annexed territory, leaving the country defenceless. Indeed, Hitler betrayed the pact by invading the rest of Czechoslovakia in March 1939.

18 For an English-language collection of some of their writings, see 'From Syndicalism to Trotskyism', *Revolutionary History*, Vol. 7 no. 4.

19 Naville split with the Surrealists in 1929 after a debate amongst their number where he argued that it was necessary to prioritise everyday political struggle above purely Surrealist activity.

20 The term 'Trotskyist' was initially used in a hostile manner. It was coined by Constitutional Democrat leader Pavel Milyukov after the 1905 revolution in the Russian Empire. In the 1920s Stalin used the term in order to imply that his rival was deviating from Marxist and Leninist orthodoxy; the Left Oppositionists referred to themselves as 'Bolshevik-Leninists' to insist on their claim to the revolutionary traditions of 1917. However, the term 'Trotskyist' has now largely lost its pejorative character. French does not share the English-language distinction between the value-neutral 'Trotskyist' and the pejorative 'Trotskyite'.

21 See 'Octobre noir', reproduced pp. 119-137 in Boris Souvarine, *A contre-courant*, Denoël, Paris 1985.

22 Open letter to the editorial committee of *La Vérité*, quoted in Y. Craipeau, *Le*

mouvement trotskyste en France, Éditions Syros, Paris, 1971, p. 37.
23 'The Truth'.
24 Craipeau, *Le mouvement trotskyste en France*, pp. 38-39. In *Contre vents et marées* he describes the 1943 membership of the main Trotskyist organisation, the Parti ouvrier internationaliste, as 'three or four hundred activists, almost all young people between 18 and 25 years old'.
25 The international organisation established by Trotskyists after the Third International had become a mere mouthpiece for Stalin. Its founding conference took place at Alfred Rosmer's house in Périgny on the outskirts of Paris. There were around twenty delegates from 11 countries: most of them were Europeans, since numerous sections further afield were prevented from sending a delegate due to financial and legal obstacles. Only Yvan Craipeau and the two Polish delegates voted against the proclamation of a new international, arguing that this was a premature step.
26 A member of the Union communiste kidnapped and killed by PCF members in September 1944.
27 A former leading member of the Communist Party of Italy (PCd'I), Tresso was forced into exile in France by the Fascist régime in 1929. Near-simultaneously expelled from the PCd'I for his Trotskyism, he became active amongst the French Trotskyists and took part in the founding conference of the Fourth International. In 1944 he was murdered by Stalinist maquisards. Discussed in detail in Chapter VI.
28 Both these faces of the PCF would show themselves again in the war years. First came accommodation to the German invasion of France in the name of opposition to British imperialism, a position in reality motivated by the need to defend the Hitler-Stalin pact. Subsequently Hitler's disavowal of the pact forced Stalin to join the Allied camp, and the PCF thus enthusiastically supported the French Resistance alongside the conservative Charles de Gaulle, advocating crude nationalist slogans and falling silent on French colonialism. The fact that both positions were determined largely by the strategic interests of Moscow confirmed the validity of the Trotskyists' critique of Stalinist 'Socialism in One Country', which prioritised the stability of the Russian state over the need to spread revolution internationally.
29 Leon Trotsky, 'To Build Communist Parties and an International Anew', July 1933. These theses examined the collapse of the Third International as an instrument of revolution, its complete lack of internal democracy and its failure to critically reflect on the policies which had eased Hitler's seizure of power. Although it did not proclaim the establishment of a new international, the text argued that this was a necessary objective.
30 For an exposition of his position see Yvan Craipeau, 'La Quatrième internationale et la Contre-Révolution Russe', *Quatrième internationale*, June 1938, pp. 81-85.
31 Craipeau wrote: 'In 1937 my theses were in the minority in the movement. In the POI they had the support of a third of the organisation, including Maria [Craipeau – his wife], the Filiâtres, Jean-René Chauvin, Essel, Régnier (an alias of Eggenschwiller) and Kunstlinger. The leaders of the party and the

youth almost all remained loyal to the official line' – *Mémoires d'un dinosaure trotskyste*, l'Harmattan, Paris, 1999, p. 148.
32. For Leon Trotsky's reply to Craipeau, see his November 1937 article 'Once Again: The USSR and its Defense', available at www.marxists.org/archive/trotsky/1937/11/ussr.htm
33. Lucien Laurat, an Austrian communist, developed the theory that the Soviet bureaucracy was a historically novel ruling class in his 1931 book *L'économie soviétique: sa dynamique, son mécanisme*. At the time he was a member of the Cercle communiste démocratique, as were Boris Souvarine and the philosopher Simone Weil. In *Mémoires d'un dinosaure trotskyste* Craipeau does not mention whether he was aware of Laurat's work at the time, only commenting (p. 147) that he had not read Otto Bauer's writings on state capitalism in Russia.
34. In *Mémoires d'un dinosaure trotskyste* Craipeau asserts (p. 188) that he now considered that the USSR was state-capitalist in character. However he does not explain when or why he abandoned the bureaucratic collectivist analysis, merely commenting that in 1946 Marcel Pennetier had adopted some of Craipeau's own 1937 arguments in order to argue that the bureaucratically-administered economy was state-capitalist.
35. Initially published in French in 1939: the book was soon banned and few first edition copies survive. A partial English translation, *The Bureaucratisation of the World*, was published by Tavistock, London in 1985: the translator Adam Westoby did not reproduce the latter two-thirds of the book, which most notably include chapters on fascism, Jews and America's New Deal.
36. Craipeau comments in *Mémoires d'un dinosaure trotskyste* (p. 147) that he did not think it was worth refuting Rizzi's arguments, considering 'absurd' Rizzi's belief that Franklin Roosevelt's New Deal, fascism and Stalinism were all evidence of a worldwide trend towards bureaucratic power. For discussion of the debate on the class character of the Soviet Union, see Marcel van der Linden's *Western Marxism and the Soviet Union: A Survey of Critical Theories and Debates Since 1917* (Haymarket Books: Chicago, 2009).
37. The Union communiste (UC), which did not take part in the Trotskyist unification of 1944, is typically referred to by the name of its newspapers: during the war *La Lutte de classe*; subsequently *Voix ouvrière*, and from 1968 *Lutte ouvrière*.
38. See the account by Union communiste member and strike leader Pierre Bois, 'The Renault Strike of April and May 1947', *Revolutionary History*, Vol. 2 No. 1, Spring 1988. This is a translation of a supplement which appeared in *Lutte ouvrière* no. 143, May 1971.
    This was the first major post-war strike movement in France. The Communist ministers had used their influence in the working class to insist on the need to increase production rather than fight management: 'Produire d'abord, revendiquer ensuite'. The strike ultimately provoked the PCF's departure from the *tripartiste* (three-party: Gaullist, Communist, Socialist) national government, at a time of escalating Cold War tensions.
39. 'Sacred union': a union of the whole French population across class and

political divides – DB

40 The second international socialist conference against the First World War, held in April 1916 – DB

41 An August 1939 non-aggression pact between Hitler and Stalin which included provisions for the re-division and annexation of central and eastern Europe by the two powers – DB

42 Apparently a reference to Étienne Fajon's 'Nationalisation et État' (*Cahiers du communisme*, February 1945), discussed in detail in Craipeau's *La Libération Confisquée* (Savelli/Syros, Paris, 1978), pp. 70-72 – DB

43 'Against winds and tides' – DB

44 'The stolen Liberation' – DB

45 The understanding promoted by Stalin that social-democratic parties were just as counter-revolutionary as fascists, if not even more dangerous since their true character was hidden. See footnote 11 – DB

46 Baron Pyotr Nikolayevich Wrangel was a general of the counter-revolutionary White Army forces in Southern Russia during the 1918-21 civil war – DB

47 'The Truth', official newspaper of the Central Committee of the Soviet Communist Party – DB

48 A 1922 treaty normalising diplomatic relations between the Soviet government and the new German parliamentary republic and promising future trade and military co-operation – DB

49 Józef Piłsudski, Poland's authoritarian head of state 1918-22 and 1926-35 – DB

50 This term was part of common parlance and is repeated throughout Craipeau's text. In fact the Soviet GPU (State Political Directorate) had already been incorporated into the NKVD (People's Ministry of Internal Affairs) in 1934 – DB

51 Leon Trotsky: *Sur La Deuxième Guerre mondiale*. Collected by Daniel Guérin (La Taupe-Bruxelles); article 'Après Munich, Staline cherchera un accord avec Hitler'.

52 Same collection, 'La Capitulation de Staline', 11 March 1939.

53 Read for example, Ph. Robrieux: *Maurice Thorez* (Fayard, Paris).

54 Y. Craipeau: *Le Mouvement trotskyste en France* (Syros, Paris); extracts of the recording of a discussion between young anti-Trotskyist socialists and leaders of the Youth Communist International. See the account given by Fred Zeller: *Trois points c'est tout* (R. Laffont).

55 *Syndicats*: organ of the reformist trade unions (under Léon Jouhaux) before the war.

56 Daniel Higou: *Histoire du socialisme en France* (PUF, Paris).

57 The KAPD was founded on 'ultra-left' positions, notably its hostility to trade unions. It collapsed one year later. On this subject see Pierre Broué, *The German Revolution: 1917-1923* (Haymarket Books, Chicago, 2006). Bordiga, founder of the Communist Party of Italy, was hostile to the united front tactic. It was primarily against the KAPD (and its theoretician, the Dutchman Gorter) and against Bordiga that Lenin polemicised in *Left wing communism: an infantile disorder*.

58   J. Rabaut: *Tout est possible* (Denoël-Gonthier, Paris).
59   Engelbert Dollfuss, Chancellor of Austria 1932-34. His Christian Social Party's 'Austrofascism' was modelled on Italian Fascism, and he crushed all other parties including Communists, Social Democrats and Nazis. This led to protracted fighting between the fascists and the Social-Democratic Republikaner Schutzbund during Austria's February 1934 civil war. Dollfuss was assassinated by pro-German Nazis in Vienna on July 25 1934 – DB
60   Leon Trotsky: *Le Mouvement communiste en France*. Collected by Pierre Broué (Minuit, Paris).
61   Leon Trotsky, preface to Fred Zeller's pamphlet *La Voix des socialistes révolutionnaires*, November 1935. See *Le Mouvement communiste en France*.
62   Marceau Pivert's letter published in *Révolution*, organ of the Seine region Jeunesses socialistes, August 1935.
63   On 3 and 4 May 1937, to stop the Civil Guards from disarming them and breaking up their organs of dual power, the workers of Barcelona rose up and took over the Catalan capital. They were supported by the POUM, the Libertarian Youth and the Friends of Durruti. The movement ended on the 6th. See P. Broué and E. Temine: *The Revolution and the Civil War in Spain* (Haymarket Books, Chicago, 2008).
64   Neville Chamberlain, Conservative UK Prime Minister 1937-40. Chamberlain was forced to resign after the May 1940 Allied retreat from Norway, and was replaced by Winston Churchill – DB
65   D. Guérin, *Front populaire, révolution manquée* (Maspéro, Paris).
66   Rigaudias's own name and his pseudonym Rigal are used interchangeably throughout *Contre vents et marées* – DB
67   Permanent Administrative Commission – DB
68   The 'syndicalists' like L. Bardin, a leader of the technicians' federation, and his brother 'Boitel' in the post were hostile to joining the PSOP, as were P. Naville and the majority of the JSR. The minority included a large number of working-class activists, such as those in the western suburbs of Paris, along with Eggens and R. Filiâtre, as well as Yvan Craipeau and activists from the Mantes region, where Trotskyists controlled the majority of the unions. Politically (with the exception of a few leaders like Rous, Claire and Barta), it was similar to the tendency who had the previous year ceased to recognise the USSR as a workers' state.
69   During the war René Lhuillier participated in the left socialist group 'Libertés'. Léon Bardin was manager of the Berliet factories in Lyon after they were seized in 1944.
70   The month of the Munich Conference at which the Britain and France granted Hitler permission to seize the Sudetenland from Czechoslovakia. The British Prime Minister Neville Chamberlain promised that the agreement had sealed 'Peace in our time'. In fact war mobilisation was already underway in the major European states and many still believed war to be inevitable – DB
71   A letter published in *Le Mouvement communiste en France*. D. Guerin described Maxton's attitude in *Front populaire révolution manquée*: 'However, pacifist equivocation continued to blight us. The British ILP was beset by a

scourge: its president and MP James Maxton. The old Scotsman had a safe seat in the Commons and a proletarian fiefdom in Glasgow. In the aftermath of Munich he made a speech in the manner of Giono in which he addressed Neville Chamberlain, "saviour of peace", with enthusiastic congratulations. This unfortunate speech led Trotsky, not without reason, to characterise the ILP as a "miserable pacifist clique" and it furthermore made our sister party vulnerable to Stalinist attacks'. In April 1939 Fenner Brockway and Maxton proposed the convening of a congress in which the Moscow and Amsterdam Internationals were to participate.

72 D. Guérin: *Front populaire*. At the first PSOP conference, André Cerf (alias Carton) proposed a motion on trade union activity which received 32 percent of votes.

73 This initially involved activists from the *La Commune* group like R. Favrier and Grimblat (alias Privas) and after their expulsion (because of their links to R. Molinier), former POI activists like Kunstlinger.

74 G. Valois, initially a monarchist theorist, had almost entirely crossed the political spectrum. In the period leading up to war he edited an irregularly-appearing newspaper of Proudhonist inspiration, *Nouvel âge*, which was influenced by abundancism and always ready to suggest 'plans' to solve every problem. Bergery, a far left activist in the Parti radical and a fellow-traveller of the [Parti communiste], had founded an unusual group, Front commun. He would go on to belong to Pétain's 'brains trust' after the Armistice.

75 Y. Craipeau, 'Charlatans de la paix', April 1939; 'Les pacifistes de M. Bonnet et le parti révolutionnaire', May 1939, in *La Voie de Lénine* issues 1 and 2.

76 *Juin-36*, number 57: here too appear all the other motions submitted to the Saint-Ouen congress.

77 *Cahiers rouges*, the theoretical journal of the PSOP, number 3 (June-July 1939). Michel Collinet, who participated in the activity of the Ligue communiste in its early days, broke with it in 1930 and created the Gauche communiste. Later, he joined the Parti socialiste, and after the war he would for a time become an SFIO theorist.

78 Henrik (H. Kunstlinger): 'Le devoir historique absolu', in *La Voie de Lénine*, number 2.

79 Daniel Guérin: *Front populaire et révolution manqué*. Two years later, Marceau Pivert would himself break with Lovestone and his imperialist corruption.

80 *Réveil syndicaliste*, 2 January 1939.

81 *Réveil syndicaliste*, 10 April 1939.

82 *Réveil syndicaliste*, 31 July 1939.

83 *Le Libertaire*, 3 August 1939.

84 Daniel Lizou: *Histoire du socialisme en France*.

85 Paul Déroulède was a well-known nationalist MP in the late nineteenth century, who took an anti-Semitic stance during the 'Dreyfus affair'. This scandal over the unjust conviction for treason of the Jewish Captain Alfred Dreyfus was a dominant theme of 1890s French politics, creating lasting divisions between 'Dreyfusards' and 'Anti-Dreyfusards'. Its later ramifications included the 1905 law declaring separation between the Church and the state,

and the radicalisation of Zionist leader Theodor Herzl – DB
86 When some important tasks were not carried out, the *La Voie de Lénine* leadership – unsurprisingly – looked for a scapegoat, and expelled Barta: this was not without political fall-out.
87 *Juin-36* (11 November 1939) devoted two columns to warning against the 'Trotskyists'. Under the title 'The JSOP continues on course' Chapelain attacked the JSOP majority which supported the Comités pour la IVe Internationale. It 'forcefully attacks and denounces as saboteurs those who want to divide revolutionary youth forces by organising outside the Party while keeping the same 'JSOP''. Arrested in December 1939 he was later sent to a concentration camp: he would ultimately join the PCF.
88 Paris is divided into twenty numbered districts, known as *arrondissement*s – DB
89 From Maurice Jaquier's report on the activity of the PSOP. Jaquier was at that time the administrative secretary of the PSOP. We shall follow his course through the war.
90 *Juin-36*, 4 December 1939.
91 E. Rouaix denounced 'the snitch D. Haas, who joined the PSOP in Metz after being the Alsace-Lorraine *L'Humanité* editor' (from a letter to D. Guérin).
92 Daniel Guérin: *Front populaire, révolution manquée* (Maspéro, Paris). He goes into more detail in an article in *Sous le drapeau du socialisme*, number 41, September-October 1967.
93 A letter from Daniel Guérin to Marceau Pivert (Amsterdam archives). The other information was supplied by several letters from Daniel Guérin to Yvan Craipeau.
94 Letter to Y. Craipeau (1969).
95 Letter by G. Vereeken, 1969. See *La Guépéou dans le mouvement trotskiste* by G. Vereeken (published by la Pensée universelle, 1976).
96 In fact Walter Held was murdered as he travelled across the Soviet Union, not in Spain. A number of letters on the killing were published in *Revolutionary History*, Vol. 1, No.4, Winter 1988-89 – DB
97 On this point read W. Solano's biography of A. Nin in *Les Mouvements d'émancipation nationale* (Syros, 1975).
98 Trotsky: 'Fighting against the Stream', Fourth International, May 1941.
99 The repressive laws are outlined in Jean-Pierre Besse and Claude Pennetier, *Juin 40: La négociation secrète*, Les Éditions de l'Atelier/Éditions ouvrières, Paris 2006, p. 76:
'On 24 August 1939 the Communist press was suspended.
'On 26 September 1939 the decree announcing the dissolution of the [PCF] and affiliated organisations was promulgated, appearing the next day in the *Journal officiel*.
'On 18 November 1939 a decree was adopted as to the measures to be taken regarding individuals who endangered national defence and public security, which involved administrative internment in police-controlled detention centres.
'On 10 April 1940 the Serol decree declared Communist activity to be treason,

subject to the death penalty.'
The effects of these decrees are detailed on p. 79:
'A full breakdown of the repressive measures 'against Hitlero-Communist agitation' in the Daladier archives, dated 1 March 1940, lists 10,500 warrants and 3,400 arrests, 489 individuals interned under the terms of the 18 November 1939 decree. Curiously historians who have quoted this document have not noted the given figure of 14 death sentences passed by military tribunals (100 in total along with the decrees of 29 July, 26 September and 3 November 1939 for crimes against the external security of the state, with 4 condemned to unlimited forced labour, 29 to limited terms of forced labour, 3 to deportation, 10 to detention and 40 to imprisonment with a fine. In the Seine *département* alone, the police gave the figure of 1,500 arrests' – DB

100 A leading member of the Parti communiste français – DB
101 A. Lecoeur: *Le Parti communiste français et la Résistance* (Plon).
102 *L'Humanité*, 10 April 1940.
103 For this whole period, consult the work of the former Communist A. Rossi: *Les Communistes français pendant la drôle de guerre* (les Iles d'or, 1951). Vehemently hostile to the PCF from a social-patriotic standpoint, it includes a number of original texts.
104 Daniel Lizou: *Histoire du socialisme en France*.
105 Daniel Lizou: *Histoire du socialisme en France*.
106 Daniel Lizou: *Histoire du socialisme en France*.
107 L. Laurat: *Histoire du syndicalisme français*.
108 See *L'Étincelle*, 15 December 1939.
109 According to the Nice-based worker-activist Ciabucci.
110 Led by Maria Craipeau, P. Souzin and M. Gibelin.
111 From the *Lutte de Classe* group's 'Organisational report'.
112 See *L'Étincelle*, 15 November 1939.
113 Leon Trotsky, 'Après la paix imperialiste de Munich' in *Sur la Deuxième Guerre mondiale* (Éditions de la Taupe).
114 Daniel Lizou: *Histoire du socialisme en France*.
115 Daniel Lizou: *Histoire du socialisme en France*.
116 i.e. the government announced that it would not mount any defensive effort in the hope that the Germans would thus not feel the need to bombard Paris – DB
117 *L'Humanité*, 25 April 1940.
118 The meeting took place between Gailledrat and Prager (*La Commune*), Gibelin and Craipeau (*L'Étincelle*).
119 Fred Zeller from Paris had encouraged the Nantes organisation to take up this perspective. It was not long before he shifted to the other extreme.
120 H. Noguères: *Histoire de la Résistance en France* (Robert-Laffont).
121 *L'Humanité* no. 55, 17 June 1940.
122 A. Lecoeur: *le PCF et la Résistance* (Plon).
123 Letter from the PCF to the Propaganda-Staffel, 25 June 1940.
124 *L'Humanité*, 25 June 1940.
125 For a full account of the negotiations over the legal publication of *L'Humanité*,

see Jean-Pierre Besse and Claude Pennetier, *Juin 40: La négociation secrète*, Les Éditions de l'Atelier/Éditions ouvrières, Paris 2006. The Communists also requested the liberation of their militants who had been imprisoned by the French authorities for defeatist propaganda (p. 106) – DB

126 *L'Humanité*, 4 July 1940.

127 Fernand de Brinon, Vichy's representative to the German High Command in Paris from 1940. In 1942 Pétain appointed him Secretary of State, making him the third-ranking official of the Vichy régime and its only official representative in Paris. He was executed for war crimes in 1947 – DB

128 Charles Tillon: *Les FTP* (10/18) The term 'let' is obviously a euphemism. Later, Tillon expressed himself more explicitly:

'The hesitation which followed the German-Soviet pact; the lack of precision of the International's directives which did not push for struggle against the Nazis but suggested accommodating to them and not 'provoking the beast'; as well as not saying what was going on, all added to the disarray of a party which had been forced into clandestinity after September 1939, persecuted and left disorganised. This was the cause of the mistakes made, such as the July 1940 efforts of the Parti communiste leaders to get the Germans to allow the publication of *L'Humanité*: much like the decision that Communist activists should come out of clandestinity, as if there could have been legal status for Communists under a Fascist occupation'.

Interview with *Que faire?*, no. 4, July 1970.

129 *Le Parti communiste dans la Résistance: De la guerre à la Résistance* (Éditions Sociales, Institut Maurice Thorez).

130 Daniel Guérin: *Front populaire...* see also *Mémorial de L'Insurgé* (Imprimerie nouvelle lyonnaise).

131 This appeal had been written in advance, in 1938. But it was not known of in France. Notably, it proclaimed:

'We are your class brothers and we appeal to your working-class consciousness. Since the start of the war our activists in the international workers' front against war have struggled against their own country's imperialism.

'That is why, in the metropolises as well as in the colonies, they have been persecuted, put on trial, imprisoned and even executed by the governments contending for global hegemony.

'Comrades! We want to talk to you like our great dead would have done: like Karl Liebknecht and Rosa Luxemburg, symbols universally admired by the international revolutionary proletariat. At no point has our voice been mixed up with that of the imperialist bandits who started the current war. From the first moment of the war, we have struggled against the London and Paris imperialists just as much as against the bloody dictatorships in Berlin and Moscow.

'We are the Third Camp, the camp of the oppressed in every country, the camp of those who die for nothing, the camp of widows and orphans, the camp of colonial slaves who fight the modern slave-owners, the camp of the hungry and the poor. The camp of the world socialist revolution.

'Your Führer has led you to the hollowest of victories... but for how long?...

Stop the massacre! Overthrow your masters! Hold out the hand of brotherhood to the workers and peasants of the world…'
(Text *in extenso* in *Le Mémorial de L'Insurgé* and *Front Populaire* by Daniel Guérin).
132 Daniel Guérin: *Front populaire…* see also *Mémorial de L'Insurgé* (Imprimerie nouvelle lyonnaise).
133 In fact, by this time there was no longer a PSOP 'leadership'. Suzanne Nicolitch was completely isolated. Only later did she make contacts in the Lyon region, as *Le Mémorial* showed. But, without doubt, Marceau Pivert was unaware of this. So too the Trotskyists exiled in the USA, who devoted many of the issues of *La Vérité* they published in New York to the ghost of 'Pivertist centrism'.
134 Jacques Doriot was a PCF member and mayor of Saint Denis who in the early 1930s advocated alliance with the SFIO against the fascists. He was expelled for this position, but as the PCF itself adopted the Popular Front policy, he swung to the far right, forming the fascistic Parti Populaire Français. This party organised military support for the Wehrmacht, and Doriot fought on the Eastern Front. He was killed in 1945 – DB
135 Daniel Guérin: *Front populaire…* see also *Mémorial de L'Insurgé* (Imprimerie nouvelle lyonnaise).
136 The Workers' Opposition was a short-lived left-wing opposition in the Russian Communist Party. It emerged in 1920 in opposition to the bureaucratisation of the Soviet state – DB
137 The revolutionary left wing of the Italian Socialist Party – DB
138 *La Révolution française*, July 1940.
139 Maurice Jaquier: *A propos du mouvement national révolutionnaire*, notes and documents produced in partnership with J Rous and Fred Zeller (April 1974).
140 See the von Ribbentrop-Molotov declarations of September 1939 or Dimitrov's October 1939 appeal.
141 This theory was supported by a minority in the POI from 1937 onwards. The counter-theses of Yvan Craipeau were published in extract form in the *Quatrième Internationale* of June 1938 as well as Trotsky's response. An analysis of this appears in *In Defence of Marxism*.
142 Maurice Jaquier was arrested in March 1941. Henri Barré, condemned to death by a German military tribunal, saw his sentence commuted to life imprisonment upon the intervention of Cyrille Spinetta. Jean Rous rejoined the Parti socialiste before leaving in 1947 – only to return fifteen years later. Fred Zeller supported the PCI then after the war became a freemason and in 1971 became the Grand Master of the French Grand Orient.
143 The group only consisted of young people who had belatedly joined the PSOP (such as Beaufrère); those who had never been able to follow up their decision to accept the instructions of the Fourth International (like Hic, Parisot and Rousset); and those who were in prison (like Rigaudias and Schmidt).
144 This letter is lost, but M. Beaufrère recalled most of its themes, which can also be found in the later writings of Marcel Hic.
145 Broué: *The German Revolution: 1917-1923*
146 Karl Radek, a Bolshevik active in both the Russian and German Communist

Parties during his life. He was a proponent of the German Communist Party's strong focus on propaganda against the unjust Treaty of Versailles and the 1923 occupation of the Ruhr by France. Radek controversially gave a speech in homage to Leo Schlageter, a Nazi shot dead by French troops. Radek was later murdered by the Soviet secret police in 1939 – DB

147 Secular Youth Hostel Centre – DB
148 One of the first newspapers published in Paris under the control of occupation forces: the occupiers tried to win workers' movement journalists to it, and indeed many Communists and ex-Communists worked there.
149 M Bleibtreu, A Essel and Georgette Gabey took the initiative here.
150 The French word for harvest mite, *aoûtat*, is derived from the word for August, *août* – DB
151 The title of *L'Étincelle* was recycled by activists in the free zone for their regional paper, then by a dissident group opposed to defence of the USSR.
152 Leon Trotsky: 'We do not change our course', 30 June 1940. This text was not known of in occupied Europe during the war – DB
153 Leon Trotsky was wary of the Fourth International's opposition to imperialism being confused with a pacifist opposition to war in general. Indeed in his articles on the American Socialist Workers' Party and the war suggested participation in the American war effort on the basis of workers' control of conscription and training:

'The liberals and democrats say: "We must help the democracies by all means except direct military intervention in Europe." Why this stupid and hypocritical limitation? If democracy is to be defended, we should defend it also on European soil; the more so as this is the best way to defend democracy in America. To help England – to crush Hitler – by all means including military intervention, would signify the best way to defend "American democracy". The purely geographical limitation has neither political nor military sense.

'That which we workers find worth defending, we are ready to defend by military means – in Europe as well as in the United States. It is the only possibility we have of assuring the defence of civil liberties and other good things in America.

But we categorically refuse to defend civil liberties and democracy in the French manner; the workers and farmers to give their flesh and blood while the capitalists concentrate in their hands the command. The Pétain experiment should flow from the centre of our war propaganda. It is important, of course, to explain to the advanced workers that the genuine fight against fascism is the socialist revolution. But it is more urgent, more imperative, to explain to the millions of American workers that the defence of their "democracy" cannot be delivered over to an American Marshal Pétain – and there are many candidates for such a role.' – Leon Trotsky, 'How to Really Defend Democracy', *Fourth International*, Vol. 1, No. 5, October 1940, pp. 126-127.

We should understand that the life of this society, politics, everything, will be based upon war, therefore the revolutionary program must also be based on war. We cannot oppose the fact of the war with wishful thinking; with pious pacifism. We must place ourselves upon the arena created by this society. The arena is terrible – it is war – but inasmuch as we are weak and incapable of taking the fate of society into our hands; inasmuch as the ruling class is strong enough to impose upon us this war, we are obliged to accept this basis for our activity[...]

We must say: "Roosevelt (or Willkie) says it is necessary to defend the country; good! Only it must be *our* country, not that of the 60 families and their Wall Street. The army must be under our own command; we must have our own officers, who will be loyal to us." In this way we can find an approach to the masses that will not push them away from us, and thus to prepare for the second step – a more revolutionary one.'- Leon Trotsky, 'Some Questions on American Problems', *Fourth International*, Vol. 1, No. 5, October 1940, pp. 132-135 – DB

154 Louise and David Korner ('Barta') both hailed from Romania, arriving in Paris in 1936. They were life partners – DB
155 *La Vérité*, issues 2,3 and 4.
156 *La Vérité*, issues 2,3 and 4.
157 *La Vérité*, 15 December 1940.
158 *La Vérité*, 30 August 1940.
159 A major employers' federation based on the iron industry – DB
160 *La Vérité*, issues 2,3 and 4.
161 *La Vérité*, 30 August 1940.
162 *La Vie ouvri*ère, the secret organ of Parti communiste trade unionists in the CGT.
163 Only after the end of the war was it possible to understand what had really happened in 1940. In September 1939 the revolutionary groups went underground. At the time the Stalinist and Trotskyist spheres of influence were geographically delineated: Ho Chi Minh's Communist Party was stronger in Tonkin, while the Trotskyist group La Lutte was dominant in the south (in the election in Saigon its leader Ta Thu Thau beat the government and the Stalinists, winning four-fifths of the vote). It had the best cadres and also had some influence over the Communist Party in the south: under conditions of illegality the Stalinists and Trotskyists were able to form a united front.

In June 1940 Japanese troops invaded southern Vietnam, but the French administration remained in place. The Sixth Congress of the Indochinese [Communist Party], meeting in the south, decided to build an anti-imperialist front against both the Japanese and the French. The discrediting of the French authorities, along with their laxity, allowed the development of a revolutionary movement. On 23 September 1940 the native soldiers of the Bac Son and Binh Gia garrisons rose up, giving the Indochinese [Communist Party] an armed wing. On 23 November deserters were in revolt across large areas of southern Vietnam, including Tan An, Mytho and So Trang. The insurrection was initiated by the Trotskyist organisation La Lutte and those whom it influenced in the Communist Party (its Central Committee supported the action only belatedly, and even then probably only due to the pressure of their peasant rank-and-file).

The insurrection was drowned in blood. The French army's intervention in the

Joncs plain, to the north-west of Saigon, meant that it was crushed within two weeks. A hundred revolutionaries were killed, and six thousand were arrested: the majority of Trotskyist activists were imprisoned. The consequences of this failure were dire: between November 1940 and June 1941 the revolutionary movement was smashed, after which point only a few insignificant actions took place.

When the August 1944 revolution happened, this destruction of revolutionary cadre hurt badly, particularly in the Trotskyist movement. Critically examining this failure, the Communist Party turned to organising the Viet Minh.

164 The February 1941 strike was an early response to anti-Semitism in German-occupied Europe, unique in its scale and timing.

The Netherlands fell to Germany in May 1940, and it was placed under a German civilian administration, unlike both nominally-independent France and Denmark, and Belgium which came under direct military control. The Reichskommissar for the country was Arthur Seyss-Inquart, the Austrian Nazi leader.

Anti-Semitic measures soon followed. In November 1940 Jews were banned from all public functions.

The Dutch were very hostile towards the occupier, not least on account of the June 1940 bombing of Rotterdam (killing 30,000), food shortages and unemployment and deportations of Dutch workers to Germany. School and university students struck in November 1940 in protest at the ousting of Jewish officials and university professors.

After a series of attacks on Jewish businesses over the winter, on 11 February 1941 there was protracted streetfighting between the Dutch fascist Nationaal-Socialistische Beweging and Jewish self-defence organisations, who killed the fascist Hendrik Koot. In response, on 12 February 1941 German soldiers and Dutch police encircled Amsterdam's Jewish Quarter and imposed a series of checkpoints to cordon it off from the rest of the city, demanding that the Jewish leaders 'disarm' their people.

The first stirrings of mass working-class protests came on 17 February when 2,000 shipyard workers went on strike in solidarity with 128 dockers threatened with deportation. The Germans were forced to capitulate.

During the fighting between Dutch fascists and Jews the Koco ice-cream parlour, owned by German Jewish refugees Ernst Cahn and Alfred Kohn, had served as a base for the Jewish self-defence groups. However, their secret vigilante organisation was betrayed and on 19 February German police raided Koco. The café's tenants were prepared for attackers and responded with salvoes from a gas cylinder, forcing the police to scatter. But this resistance only provoked further repression. In a pogrom on the weekend of 22-23 February, 425 Jewish men were rounded up and taken to the Kamp Schoorl army camp, and subsequently the Mauthausen and Buchenwald concentration camps. Only two of the 425 survived the war.

With news of the SS pogrom soon spreading across Amsterdam, an open-air meeting at the Noordermarkt square on Monday 24th called for action against anti-Semitism and deportations. The initiative for the strike was largely from members of the pro-Moscow Communistische Partij Nederland and Henk Sneevliet's anti-Stalinist Marx-Lenin-Luxemburg Front. They spread an appeal for a general strike the next morning, the 25th.

First to come out in solidarity with the Jews were the tram drivers, followed by civil servants, teachers and dockworkers. The strike also spread from the capital to the nearby towns Haarlem and Utrecht. However, the Nazis immediately moved to crush the strike, imposing martial law and bringing in SS machine-gunners to silence the workers. By Wednesday 27th the movement was defeated – DB

165 *La Vérité*, 30 August 1940.
166 Banner headline, *La Vérité* 15 October 1940.
167 *La Vérité*, 30 August 1940.
168 *La Vérité*, 15 September 1940.
169 Otto Abetz, the German ambassador to Vichy France – DB
170 'It is only natural that isolated organisers separated from the centre, without a collective leadership able to discuss and set down a line, had differing interpretations of events and political problems. One must understand these circumstances when considering the different attitudes of PCF members in different regions'. From Charles Tillon's *Les FTP* (published by Livre de Poche).
171 *Que Faire*, number 5, reply to Y. Craipeau.
172 A. Lecoeur: *le PCF et la Résistance* (Plon).
173 A. Lecoeur: *Le PCF et la Résistance*. It was no accident that A. Lecoeur later became leader of a small 'social-democratic party', which was nationalist and vehemently anti-communist.
174 Madeleine Riffaud: *les Carnets de Charles Debarge*, (published by Éditions sociales).
175 Beaufrère, who escaped arrest by a hair's breadth, was sent away from Paris. Rigaudias left for the United States. Souzin was arrested in late 1942. Swann was removed. In October 1943, all five members of the leadership were arrested (including Filiâtre, Hic and Rousset) and so were replaced by Essel, Demazière, Parisot and later Marcoux. The meetings were held either at Rousset's house, Royer's house or, most often, at the house of Lucien Herr on Rue Schoelcher, where a typing service was in place.
176 Jean-René Chauvin describes the social composition of the POI's successor organisation, the Parti communiste internationaliste, as of 15th January 1948: Full members: 457; Candidate members: 69; Youth: 100 (65 of them in Paris) – total, 626; 83 women; 144 blue-collar workers; 11 peasants; 73 white-collar workers; 99 civil servants; 42 students; 83 miscellaneous; 53 trade union officials; 125 ex-PCF; 92 ex-SFIO; 12 ex-Resistance; 147 full members in Paris, 310 outside the capital; 12 full-time organisers, 1 part-timer. – DB

From *Un trotskiste dans l'enfer nazi*, Éditions Syllepse, Paris, 2006, pp. 236-237

177 Sylvain Irkine and other 'Croquefruit' comrades moved to Lyon where, in early 1943, they worked at the regional headquarters of the Mouvement uni de la Résistance (MUR). Arrested by the Milice in August 1944, Sylvain Irkine was tortured and deported to Auschwitz, where he was killed.

178 Jean Rabaut explains: 'As men of the left, the three directors [Jean Rougeul, Sylvain Itkine and Guy d'Hauterive] had implemented a liberal work régime. The fixed pay rate was higher than that of similar enterprises, and the workteams were free to fulfil their work quota at their own pace. The recruitment of workers was a motley affair: denizens of the Left Bank, apolitical Russian émigrés, but also Trotskyists, Pivertists, and communists from the various oppositional currents. However, it so happened that someone troubled the mood of harmony: Abelsen, known as Hardy, decided to try and increase production at the expense of working conditions, meaning the capitalist spirit and discord amongst the employees. Now all the old sectarian quarrels resurfaced. Interminable discussions, hands covered in fruit purée, on the nature of the new régime: what stage of Thermidorian reaction had the terrible Abelsen reached? All this amazed the (only two) real proletarians in the workplace, two workers from Marseille who understood nothing of this revolutionary dialectic...'- *Tout est possible! Les 'gauchistes' français 1929-1944*, Denoël, Paris 1974, p. 347 – DB

179 A short-lived revolutionary government established after France's military defeat by Prussia in their 1870 war and the subsequent armistice in 1871. The Paris Commune sought to establish a new socialist order and continue the war effort, but in May 1871 it was crushed by the bourgeois government based at Versailles, just two months after its establishment – DB

180 Leon Trotsky: *Sur la Deuxième Guerre mondiale* (published by La Taupe).

181 *La lutte contre la Deuxième Guerre impérialiste mondiale*, November 1940 pamphlet.

182 Khrushchev said 'During and after the war, Stalin advanced the idea that the tragedy suffered by our nation in the first part of the war was the result of the Germans' 'unexpected' attack against the Soviet Union. But, comrades, this was completely untrue. When Hitler came to power in Germany he set as his goal the destruction of communism. The fascists said it openly. They did not hide their plans. They made all sorts of pacts and blocs to achieve their aggressive aims, such as the infamous Berlin-Rome-Tokyo Axis. Many events in the pre-war period clearly showed that Hitler was getting ready to start a war against the Soviet Union and that he had massed enormous numbers of troops and armoured units on the Soviet border'.

Khrushchev recalled the warnings Stalin had been given by Churchill on 3 and 18 April 1941 and in the following days; by military attachés in Berlin on 6 and 22 May (telling him the exact date of the invasion); by the Soviet Embassy in London, predicting the exact number of divisions that would engage combat: 147.

'But', Khrushchev said, 'Stalin was not at all worried by these warnings. Indeed, on Stalin's orders no attention at all was paid to such information, with the aim of avoiding provoking military clashes'.

A few days before the invasion, the head of the Kiev special military district informed Stalin that 'German armies are on the River Bug preparing for attack and will probably begin their offensive in the very near future'.

He asked for authorisation to prepare defensive measures.

'Moscow replied to this suggestion by claiming that it would be a provocative step and that no defensive measures should be taken on the borders, since they would give the Germans a pretext for taking military action against us'.
Khrushchev added:
'Even when fascist armies had already invaded Soviet territory and begun military operations, Moscow gave the order not to react to German fire. Why? Because Stalin, despite all the evidence, believed that the war had still not begun, that it was only a provocation on the part of a few undisciplined elements in the German army, and that if we reacted it would give the Germans cause to start the war'.

183 Reported in *La Vérité*, 5 December 1941.
184 Henri Noguères: *Histoire de la Résistance en France* (published by Robert Laffont).
185 Henri Noguères: *Histoire de la Résistance en France* (published by Robert Laffont).
186 De Gaulle: *Mémoires de guerre*.
187 Henri Noguères: *Histoire de la Résistance en France* (published by Robert Laffont).
188 Craipeau uses the English expression in the original text – DB
189 *Loustanau-Lacau: Mémoires d'un Français rebelle* (published by Robert Laffont).
190 Henri Noguères: *Histoire de la Résistance en France* (published by Robert Laffont).
191 Henri Noguères: *Histoire de la Résistance en France* (published by Robert Laffont).
192 Henri Noguères: *Histoire de la Résistance en France* (published by Robert Laffont).
193 Henri Noguères: *Histoire de la Résistance en France* (published by Robert Laffont).
194 Henri Noguères: *Histoire de la Résistance en France* (published by Robert Laffont).
195 C. Pineau: *La Simple Vérité* (published by Julliard). The subsequent quotes are also in this book.
196 Bureau central de renseignements et d'action (Central Bureau of Intelligence and Operations), an intelligence service established by the Free French high command in 1940 – DB
197 Henri Noguères: *Histoire de la Résistance en France* (published by Robert Laffont).
198 Quotes from Charles Tillon's *Les FTP* (published by Juillard, p. 198) in Noguères' work. These comments do not appear in the Livre de Poche edition of *Les FTP*.
199 *Le Populaire*, 15 July 1942.
200 Account quoted by H. Noguères, op. cit.
201 Many Communist activists outside Paris had had policies different to their leadership and had resisted the occupiers long before this turn. But the change of direction was determined by orders from abroad. This can be seen by

the developments in the Indochinese [Communist Party] on the same date, making a turn to the Allies.
202 This wartime Resistance force, initiated by the Parti communiste français, has no connection with the similarly named far-right party founded in 1972 by Jean-Marie Le Pen – DB
203 Henri Noguères: *Histoire de la Résistance en France* (published by Robert Laffont).
204 Account quoted by H. Noguères, op. cit.
205 *Les Cahiers du bolchévisme*, issue 2-3 of 1941.
206 *La Vérité*, December 1941.
207 Debû-Bridel: account quoted by H. Noguères, op. cit.
208 A chaucun son boche – DB
209 A Jewish member of the Communist Party of Czechoslovakia. Deputy minister of foreign affairs from 1948, he was arrested in 1951 as an alleged participant in the 'Rudolf Slánský conspiracy', and imprisoned on charges of Zionism, Titoism and Trotskyism until his 1955 release. 11 other supposed co-conspirators were executed – DB
210 Account quoted by H. Noguères, op. cit.
211 Account quoted by H. Noguères, op. cit.
212 Rémy: *Mémoires d'un agent secret de la France Libre* (published by France-Empire).
213 Account quoted by H. Noguères, op. cit.
214 *La Vérité*, 15 March 1942, article by Y. Craipeau.
215 Account quoted by H. Noguères, op. cit.
216 De Gaulle: *Mémoires*: the word 'openly' was added in the official version.
217 Charles Tillon: *Les FTP* (Livre de Poche).
218 Account quoted by H. Noguères, op. cit.
219 Account quoted by H. Noguères, op. cit.
220 Account quoted by H. Noguères, op. cit.
221 *Soldat im Westen*, November 1942.
222 Testimony recorded by Yvan Craipeau.
223 Laroche was the pseudonym of Szajko Schönberg, a member of the group, but it was also occasionally used by Clara and Paul Thalmann. Indeed, it was the Thalmanns who owned the house on Rue Friant: see *Revolution für die Freiheit*, Hamburg Verlag Association, Hamburg, 1977 – DB
224 'Worker and Soldier' – DB
225 Testimony recorded by Yvan Craipeau.
226 'The Worker' – DB
227 André Calves explains how fraternisation was initiated (p. 75 in *Sans bottes ni médailles*):
'Robert Cruau had the chance to contact a sergeant whose father was a Communist official. This sergeant was already pretty politically aware. He could sometimes access certain official stamps and render certain services to a number of comrades. André Darley contacted another German in the DCA [anti-aircraft artillery] unit.
Very soon there was a small group which edited a sheet we printed a hundred

copies of, [*Der Arbeiter*]. According to Robert, the paper very directly impacted twenty-seven soldiers and sailors.

But we did not guarantee the tightness of the group sufficiently. On one occasion Robert met with ten soldiers at the house of a recently recruited girl who lived on the Route du Vallen. Ten soldiers together! It was madness. No-one said so. We all believed, unthinking, that everything would be fine'.

After the war, the Brest PCI also produced a newspaper for German prisoners of war, *Solidarität* – DB

228 'Our Word' – DB
229 Most of these publications were never recovered. But some extracts were published in the French press.
230 Testimony by Pierre Régnier (who became a PSU industrial organiser). Joint 'grassroots' action involving Communists and Trotskyists did not only take place in the factory. Marcel Bleibtreu recounts, for example, how Trotskyist activists at Paris's Medicine Faculty (particularly R. Gorin and himself) distributed leaflets against a racism class (!) organised at the behest of the Vichyists and the occupiers. The action taken jointly with Front national activists resulted in the abandonment of the course before the second session took place: in the wake of this a Trotskyist circle with a dozen members was established.
231 Raid, pillage – DB
232 Similarly André Calves reports on Brest:

'The German authorities decided to send seven hundred workers from the Arsenal to Hamburg. They were not rounded up by police, but simply conscripted. At that time there was no maquis, and not even the suggestion of mass resistance. The majority of Brest's population listened to the London radio, but that did not mean very much. We produced a leaflet, very vague as to our perspectives: simply a denunciation of the deportation of workers and an appeal for organisation ["Razzia d'esclaves en Europe occupée", 19 October 1942, reprinted in *La Verité* 15 December 1942]. We slipped a thousand leaflets into letter boxes. I suppose we were not the only ones to do so. The crowd at the entrance to the Arsenal was very large that evening. The Germans had their train waiting there, sure that they would have more chance this way than trying to do it at the station.

'The drafted workers arrived via Rue Louis-Pasteur. Almost all of them were with their families. Some had drunk a fair amount and were crying in despair. The crowd was silent.

'Near the gates of the Arsenal, some German sailors were sat on the roof of a shed. The young people started shouting "A mort Laval!" [Death to Laval!]. The German sailors threw them two packets of cigarettes.

'Again, silence.

'We heard the noise of the locomotive. Then, from the train, rose the chant of the *Internationale*. The crowd started shouting "A mort Laval! A mort Laval!". Near me, an old man pressed a cop's hat down onto his ears, calling him a bastard. The cop ran away. Now, thousands of people were running, onto the Cours d'Ajot and down towards the commercial port. The train had already left, but we could still hear the *Internationale*. A German soldier, trapped in his sentry box, fired his gun into the air. He was scared, but no-one hurt him. There was not a trace of the police. Everyone headed towards the castle, splitting into two columns. One pressed on towards Recouvrance, the other to Saint-Martin. There were perhaps five to ten thousand of us heading up the Rue de Siam singing the *Internationale* and *La Jeune Garde*. I did not hear anyone singing *la Marseillaise*. Even a grammar-school student near me, close to the Croix de Feu before the war, was singing the *Internationale.*

'We ascended the Rue Jean-Jaurès up to the tax office, then went back down to the bridge. The Germans did not react. At 11pm there were still a few hundred of us, young people, ready to keep going. We had been marching for more than two hours. The German military police arrived, pointing their revolvers, but they did not shoot. They arrested a few young people, who were released 48 hours later. Clearly, the Germans wanted to limit the damage. Perhaps they feared a general strike in Brest?

'The next day, at the Chantier, the German soldiers explained that they had been under the impression that the workers were volunteers to go and work in Germany. They asked us what "Amolalal" (à mort Laval) meant. A corporal who understood French well translated our explanation to the soldiers. The sergeant arrived and barked at the corporal. Work resumed.

'There was more discussion throughout the day. It was said that the train had still not even reached Rennes, that the workers had broken up and even derailed the wagons.

'One certain fact is that that from that day, no-one responded to the draft. When the Germans wanted workers for the Reich, they had to arrest them first. The understanding that lots of people wanted to resist was born in Brest that evening' – pp. 66-67 in *Sans bottes ni médailles* – DB

233 *Lutte de classe* wrote:

'The working-class response to the Laval-Hitler manoeuvres has begun in many factories, on both sides of the "demarcation line", going as far as open resistance and strikes. But it is clear that in the current situation this cannot go any further, until the proletariat is able to wage the decisive battle. The main working-class resistance has consisted of refusing to commit to the 'voluntary' registration.

The 17,000 "voluntary" signatures were only obtained by the most outrageous blackmail. Although the working class may not be in a position to openly resist, it would be a mistake to say "So what's the point of resistance? They will send us by force and we will lose the benefits we've been promised" The so-called benefits are in reality nothing more than what is strictly necessary for the worker to survive. If the use of force will only bring the two imperialist accomplices Hitler and Laval the same results, why would they want to cause themselves so many problems organising the deportations shenanigans?

... Young workers, in imperialist Germany there is a proletariat like in France, which having moved on from the terrible defeat inflicted by fascism in 1933 is leading a merciless struggle against Hitler. Those who are sent by force leave with the conviction that their struggle, welded to the German workers' struggle against the imperialist war, will deliver the world from capitalist oppression and war. Do not go there defeated, do not let yourselves be isolated: the difference of languages is a barrier that can easily be overcome by a firm desire to get on with your class brothers... Let us make for ourselves, of our own will, part of the sacrifice that imperialism would oblige us to make for its pillage: and the working class shall triumph'.

234 André Calves recalls:
'Believing that the revolution in Germany at the end of the war would be of decisive importance, the CCI decided to send a certain number of its best-trained working-class militants to go and work in Germany. These militants organised cells, made contact with the German workers, but later would have to suffer the accusation "of having gone to work in Germany" from within the unified Trotskyist organisation by people who were more "patriotic" than they were Trotskyist' – *Sans bottes ni médailles*, p. 56 – DB

235 Indicative here was Tillon's polemic against Marchais in 1970, who by then had become general secretary of the PCF. He reproached him for having departed for Germany with his workmates; he defended himself by saying he was forced to; but no-one asked him what activism he carried out in Germany, and he did not mention any.

236 By this time Meichler was a member of the *Notre Révolution* group. He had re-established contact with *La Vérité* soon before his arrest.

237 *Les Trotskistes sous la terreur nazie*, PCI pamphlet, 1945.

238 Mouvement Républicain Populaire, the major Christian-Democrat party in the French Fourth Republic – DB

239 Various sources, particularly Albert Demazière.

240 'Our differences with the Three Theses', *Fourth International*, Vol 3. no. 10, December 1942, pp. 372-74 (Felix Morrow). Misattributed by Craipeau.

241 Ibid.

242 'Report on the Fourth International since the outbreak of war, 1939-48', *Fourth International*, Vol 9. no. 8, December 1948. Some similar impressions were expressed at the February 1944 European conference.

243 The issue contained two articles on Stalinism: 'The Soviet bureaucracy and the Stalinist party' and 'Stalinism and fascism'; an article by Lenin 'Where to begin?' and conclusions on the emergency conference of the Fourth International. At least eight issues of the journal were published during the occupation (photographs reproduced in *Les Trotskyistes sous la terreur nazie*), but it only became regular in 1943-1944.

244 Craipeau is mistaken: the group was called the 'Union des communistes internationalistes' – DB

245 Laroche: testimony recorded by Y. Craipeau, 1969.

246 Craipeau is mistaken: the paper established in 1956 was called *Voix ouvrière* (Workers' Voice), not *Voie ouvrière*, which would mean Workers' Path. Along with a number of other Trotskyist, Maoist and anarchist groups it was banned after the May 1968 general strike, and was thus rechristened *Lutte ouvrière* – DB

247 Buccholz – DB

248 Barta (alias Korner): testimony recorded by Y. Craipeau, 1969.
249 *La Seule Voie*, issue 3, July 1942, article dated December 1941.
250 'There is still time to save the USSR' – DB
251 *La Seule Voie*, issue 3, July 1942, article dated December 1941.
252 *La Seule Voie*, issue 5/6, October-November 1942.
253 *La Seule Voie*, issue 5/6, October-November 1942.
254 *Libertés*: issue 44, September 1944.
255 *Nos Combats*, issue 13, January 1942, 'Le socialisme révolutionnaire devant la crise actuelle'.
256 Sir Stafford Cripps, British Ambassador to the USSR 1940-1942; in 1942 Lord Privy Seal, Leader of the House of Commons and member of the War Cabinet; and subsequently Minister of Aircraft Production. In the post-war Labour government he served as Chancellor of the Exchequer 1947-50 – DB
257 Clement Attlee, leader of the Labour Party, Deputy Prime Minister 1942-45 and then Prime Minister 1945-51 – DB
258 *Nos Combats*, issue 15, March 1942, 'L'évolution du mouvement ouvrier anglais'.
259 *Nos Combats*, issue 14, February 1942. Significant also, the news coverage (issues 14, 15, 16) about Lorraine, Alsace and Nord-Pas-de-Calais where important strikes were underway. *Nos Combats* focuses on analysis of the German decrees which sought to attach these regions to the Reich and limit the French government's authority there.
260 *Nos Combats*, issue 16, 'Comment venger nos camarades assassinés'.
261 *Libertés*, issue 17, May 1942.
262 *Mémorial de L'Insurgé*, presented by Fernand Rude (Imprimerie Nouvelle Lyonnaise) as were the subsequent quotes.
263 The message from the Lyon freemasons appealed to Roosevelt in the name of the Masonic fraternity:
'America, we cannot repeat it enough, will win if she can show the other peoples of the world that she is the inheritor of Destiny, that her intervention in European affairs is no cunning calculation nor an attempt to Balkanise a pitifully weak Europe'.
264 *Mémorial de L'Insurgé*, presented by Fernand Rude (Imprimerie Nouvelle Lyonnaise).
265 *Mémorial de L'Insurgé*, presented by Fernand Rude (Imprimerie Nouvelle Lyonnaise).
266 *L'Insurgé* issue 4, June 1942.
267 *L'Insurgé* issue 4, June 1942.
268 *L'Insurgé* issue 6, August 1942, 'Faire le Point'.
269 *L'Insurgé* issue 6, August 1942, 'Faire le Point'.
270 *L'Insurgé* issue 8, October 1942, special issue 'Comités d'usines'.
271 *L'Insurgé* issue 7, September 1942, 'Aspirations du peuple français'.
272 *L'Insurgé* issue 10, November 1942, 'Le peuple français doit lui-même décider de son sort'.
273 *Mémorial*. JM Fugère explained that the group printed 10,000 copies of *Libé-Sud*, sometimes *Le Populaire*, FUJ and certain *Populaire* leaflets. The paper was

supplied by *Libé-Sud*.
274 C. Pineau: *La Simple Vérité* (published by Julliard).
275 *Mémorial de L'Insurgé*, presented by Fernand Rude (Imprimerie Nouvelle Lyonnaise).
276 *La Vérité*, issue 40, 15 January 1943, so too the subsequent quotes.
277 *La Vérité*, issue 40, 'Contre la misère et la guerre: front ouvrier'.
278 *La Seule Voie*, issue 7, March 1943. The summary covers the terms of the resolution.
279 *La Seule Voie*, issue 7, March 1943.
280 However, the CCI pre-conference did make reference to a 1941 text showing that the masses' struggle would necessarily focus on the imperialism which was presently crushing them, German imperialism:
'Given the passivity and disarray caused by the first shocks of war and the debacles of the countries conquered by Hitler, particularly France, the proletariat, under the pressure of the objective situation, will quickly come to understand that it must change this. It will again find its class consciousness, its clarity, its combativity, all the more once it loses any confidence in the régime. In the first stage workers will *surely* be influenced by nationalist and other bourgeois ideologies. But Gaullism, the anti-Boche nationalism of the workers, much like pacifism, is of a different order to that of social-traitors and the petty-bourgeoisie. Under these masks of bourgeois and reactionary ideology, the working class is in a confused sense expressing its desire to fight the ruling system'.
All the same the CCI did not draw any conclusions from this recognition. As against the concrete struggle against the 'ruling system' it substituted the struggle against 'the main enemy, the USA'. This could be nothing more than ideological struggle: 'winning the vanguard to our programme' thus meant convincing individual advanced activists of the correctness of this programme. This was the meaning of the slogan in favour of 'workers' groups' advanced by the pre-conference.
281 *La Vérité*, issue 40, 15th January 1943.
282 We have already seen that the international secretariat was in agreement with the POI (in Marc Lorris's article in the New York *La Vérité*).
In November 1943 the Socialist Workers' Party USA underlined the importance of national demands even before the US invasion of Europe:
'Europe, today subject to Nazi slavery, will tomorrow be invaded by Anglo-American imperialism, equally rapacious.
'In their efforts to replace the Nazis as masters of Europe the Allied imperialists will themselves have to surmount all the problems of the situation which prevented Hitler from pacifying the continent. The peoples of Europe's hatred for the Nazis will tomorrow turn, with sharper vigour, against Yankee imperialism. The European masses' ardent desire to get rid of the invaders and secure national freedom will necessarily be incorporated into their social struggle against the ruling classes and their Anglo-American masters, giving a powerful impulse to the proletarian revolution'.
A resolution of the American SWP Central Committee, 'European Revolution

and the Tasks of the Revolutionary Party', was published in *Fourth International* in its December 1944 issue. The same issue also featured a quote from Lenin: 'Practically speaking the social-chauvinists are carrying out a bourgeois and anti-working class policy, because practically speaking they are not insisting on "defence of the homeland", in the sense of struggle against a foreign power's oppression, but rather on the right of one or other of the "Great Powers" to pillage the colonies and oppress other peoples' (*Socialism and War*, 1916).

283 The Mouvement pour l'abondance and J. Duboin explained that technological progress conditioned social progress: humanity, which had multiplied by a factor of many thousands the energy which primitive man could have marshalled, was on the brink of passing from the era of scarcity (the era of inequality and all the weaknesses of the market economy) to the era of abundance, when man could be master of his own destiny.

284 *Jeunesse d'Octobre*, copied across four pages with no indication of date or origin.

285 *La Seule Voie*, issue 8, April 1943: discussion article.

286 *Rapport sur l'organisation*, a copied pamphlet.

287 *Fraternisation prolétarienne*. Bulletin printed recto-verso. A small group soon broke away (led by Hirzel) to form the Bordigist *l'Étincelle*.

288 *La Lutte de classe*, issue 7, 20 January 1943.

289 *La Lutte de classe*, issue 10, 28 February 1943.

290 *La Vérité*, 1 January 1943.

291 *La Seule Voie*, issue 8, 'De la Révolution d'Octobre à la révolution mondiale'.

292 'Revolutionary defencism' was advocated by the CCI minority led by H. Molinier. The argument against him was all the more curious given that at the time the CCI ignored the existing strike movements, considering their objectives tainted by nationalism.

293 *La Vérité*, issue 46, 20 June 1943.

294 *La Vérité*, 31 March 1943.

295 *La Vérité*, 20 July 1943, 'De Staline à Vlassov'.

296 *La Vérité*, 15 August 1943, 'Staline tend la main à la bourgeoisie allemande'.

297 The German army of 1921-35 – DB

298 Bastille Day, a public holiday in commemoration of the French Revolution – DB

299 *L'Insurgé*, issue 17, July 1943, special edition.

300 In the *Mémorial de L'Insurgé*, contrary to activists in other regions, Gilles Martinet is silent on his relations with Trotskyists. The articles in *L'Insurgé* often echoed those printed in *La Vérité*, which it demarcated itself from. Gilles Martinet claims that they were the collective work of the *Bulletin ouvrier* group, but for the sake of simplicity here I attribute them to him.

301 CFLN: Comité français de libération nationale: the first name of the provisional government in Algiers – DB

302 *L'Insurgé*, issue 21, last quarter of 1943. 'Est-ce un nouveau front populaire qui s'affirme à Alger?', by G. Martinet.

303 *L'Insurgé*, issue 21, last quarter of 1943. 'Est-ce un nouveau front populaire qui s'affirme à Alger?', by G. Martinet.

304 *L'Insurgé*, issue 20, September 1943. 'Pour le pain et la liberté', by G. Martinet.
305 *L'Insurgé* activists were ready to content themselves with a back-seat role. In late 1943 René Armand was very proud to be accepted onto the clandestine commission of his département: 'We sit as equals alongside representatives of other movements and they take our views seriously'. (*Mémorial*).
306 *Mémorial de L'Insurgé*.
307 In the subsequent footnote Craipeau clarifies that the death toll was in fact 798 – DB
308 General Noguès journeyed an interesting path. Given that he was appointed by Léon Blum he passed for a 'left-wing' general. In June 1940, after a certain hesitation, he turned to Pétain, arrested the MPs arriving from France on the *Massilia* and handed the Resistance partisan G. Mandel over to the authorities. During the German occupation he collaborated with the Germans, facilitating the formation of an auxiliary Moroccan brigade, unbeknownst to the Armistice Commission. The only thing that mattered to him was defending the 'French Empire' in Morocco. On 8 November 1942 his residence was encircled by a colonial infantry regiment. Still in contact with Admiral Michelier, Noguès misunderstood the strength of the Allied naval forces, and having arresting the Gaullist conspirators and sending them to the High Court, he ordered resistance. Four days of bloody battles followed, killing 798 among the French alone. Following this, Noguès rallied behind Darlan. The death toll was swept under the carpet and the general entertained the best of relations with Patton. He was left in his post and became a member of Darlan's imperial council, remaining so until De Gaulle – reconciled with Darlan's successor Giraud – demanded his resignation. He resigned on 4 June 1943 and left for Portugal. Sentenced in absentia to twenty years forced labour after the Liberation, he returned to France in 1954: the High Court deprived him of his citizen status… and immediately freed him from this sentence on account of 'service rendered'. He died in 1971, still a Grand Croix de la Légion d'Honneur.
309 *La Vérité*, 31 March 1943.
310 I.e. De Gaulle's 18 June 1940 appeal on BBC radio for the French to continue fighting in spite of the Armistice – DB
311 Letter by Claude Kilian. The narrative of POI relations with the Resistance can be understood by looking at its contacts with M. Bleibtreu and Cl. Kilian and the recollections of former POI leaders such as M. Beaufrère, Y. Craipeau and D. Rousset.
312 *La Vérité*, 20 July 1943. 'Alger, un avertissement'.
313 De Gaulle: *Mémoires*.
314 *La Vérité*, 17th February 1944. 'La baudruche d'Alger la Rouge'.
315 *La Vérité*, 17th February 1944. 'Alger et nous' (a fraternal discussion with *L'Insurgé*).
316 Shortly before the Liberation of France in 1944, 'Yvan Craipeau made contacts with Albert Bayet, then president of the Fédération nationale de la presse française, to secure the legalisation of *La Vérité*, and together they looked into the possibility of [the Parti communiste internationaliste, successor of the POI] joining the CNR' – Jacqueline Pluet-Despatin, *Les trotskistes et la guerre*

1940-1944, Éditions anthropos, Paris 1940, p. 210.

Because the Trotskyists did not take part in the August 1944 occupations of the Paris printshops, they were not able to seize a Vichyist print press. 72 issues of *La Vérité* appeared under the German occupation, with an average circulation of 4,000. However, Bayet rejected the application to legalise the paper upon the Allied Liberation of France, given that it was not a 'pro-Resistance' newspaper, insofar as it did not support the Free French and the Allies.

Upon his return from Buchenwald concentration camp in June 1945, Jean-René Chauvin wrote a letter to *Sud-Ouest*, *La France* and the PCF's *La Gironde Populaire*, also signed by another five former Mauthausen detainees, calling for freedom of the press. These newspapers all printed the letter but *La Gironde Populaire* replied the next day with an attack on 'Hitlero-Trotskyists who collaborated with the Nazi occupation'. Chauvin successfully sued for libel, but Bayet's decision stood: *La Vérité* was not authorised until April 1946. This only came some 18 months after Liberation, during which time six Trotskyists were arrested for their illegal propaganda. See *Un trotskiste dans l'enfer nazi*, pp. 232-234 – DB

317 'Le second front et le front ouvrier' – DB
318 *La Vérité*, 15 August 1943.
319 *La Vérité*, 30 August 1943. 'Si tu veux la liberté, balaie la vermine fasciste'.
320 *La Vérité*, 15 December 1943.
321 *La Vérité*, 30 August 1943. 'Si tu veux la liberté, balaie la vermine fasciste'.
322 *La Vérité*, 15 December 1943.
323 *La Vérité*, 30 July 1943.
324 *La Vérité*, 15 January 1943. 'Contre la misère et la guerre: front ouvrier'.
325 *La Vérité*, 10 February 1943.
326 *La Vérité*, 20 May 1943.
327 *La Vérité*, 1 March 1943.
328 *Le Soviet*, 14 September 1943.
329 *La Vérité*, 31 March 1943.
330 *La Lutte de classe*, 5 February 1943.
331 *La Vérité*, 1 March 1943, 'Les ouvrières organisent la lutte pour ralentir la production'.
332 *Le Soviet*, 14 September 1943.
333 *La Vérité*, 20 November 1943.
334 *La Vérité*, 20 November 1943.
335 Report by Ciabucci, a building worker and POI member in Nice, deported to Vienna.
336 *Le Soviet*, 14 September 1943. Other news on the same factory in *La Vérité* of 15th January 1944.
337 *La Vérité*, issue 53, 15 October 1943.
338 *Octobre*, organ of the POI in the south-west, 1 October 1943.
339 *La Vérité*, 15 January 1944.
340 *La Vérité*, 31 March 1943: 'Partir est-ce trahir? Pour la révolution européenne'.
341 *La Vérité*, 15 January 1944.
342 *La Vérité*, 20 May 1943.

343 *La Lutte de classe*, issue 11, 27 March 1943: 'Qui a du fer a du pain'.
344 *La Jeune Garde*, March 1943.
345 *La Vérité*, 20 May 1943.
346 'Masse de maquis ou maquis de masse', in *Les FTP*, Charles Tillon.
347 'Masse de maquis ou maquis de masse', in *Les FTP*, Charles Tillon.
348 'Masse de maquis ou maquis de masse', in *Les FTP*, Charles Tillon.
349 I.e. Colonel Drazha Mikhailovich, a royalist Yugoslav nationalist who prioritised fighting Tito's partisans over resistance to German occupation – DB
350 *La Vérité*, July 1943.
351 'Réfractaires! vos armes doivent servir à la liberation socialiste de l'Europe', *La Vérité*, 25 September 1943.
352 *Les Trotskistes sous la terreur nazie*.
353 *La Vérité*, 15 February 1944: 'Au secours des gars du maquis'.
354 See also *IVe Internationale*, issue 3, January 1944.
355 See also *IVe Internationale*, issue 3, January 1944.
356 Cf. *Mémorial*, testimony of M.G. Fugère, p. 28.
L'Insurgé of 14 July 1943 recounted:
'One of our correspondents in Annecy tells us that in June all was not well for the Italian authorities who attempted to uncover the Resistance in the region. 47 on their side were killed... the Resistance suffered two fatalities, who were taken to Annecy. There was a sizeable crowd at their funerals, proving the sympathy the population has for those who fight back, particularly since Annecy was the town best represented in the Legion.'
357 *L'Insurgé*, issue 23, February 1944.
358 *L'Insurgé*, issue 23, February 1944.
359 'Appel aux ouvriers communistes', a supplement to issue 13 of *La Lutte de classe*.
360 *La Lutte de classe*, 13 June 1943.
361 *La Vérité*, issue 46, 20 June 1943: 'Staline dissout la IIIe Internationale... La Quatrième vaincra', p. 1.
362 *La Vérité*, issue 49, 30 July 1943: 'Feue la IIIe Internationale'.
363 In fact, this concession by Stalin was no freak. It was not by chance that Stalin reduced the International to silence for eight years. The Soviet bureaucracy did not renounce the International and proletarian revolution under the pressure of imperialism: it wanted to do so itself. For a long time, in its eyes 'internationalism' had meant subordination to its own nationalist interests, directly exercised by its own political apparatus, and not under the umbrella of the International. It substituted the politics of territorial expansion for those of proletarian revolution. The ghost of the International haunted it as much as it did the Allied powers. This was clearly demonstrated immediately after the war. Strongly reinforced and surrounded by satellite states, the Soviet bureaucracy never resuscitated the International. The Cominform was a mere liaison organisation, only active in the dispute with the Yugoslavs and liquidated after the break with them rendered its superfluous. It was the apparatus of the Soviet state itself, its army and its diplomats, which guaranteed

the subordination of satellite forces to its politics.
364 See *La quarantaine anti-trotskiste au camp de Châteaubriant.*
365 A. Azzaroni, P. Naville, I. Silone: *Blasco* (Azione Comune, published by Polyglotes).
366 *La Vérité*, 13 May 1943, 'Déportation en Haute Silésie'.
367 *La Vérité*, issue 53, 15 October 1943.
368 David Rousset, *Les jours de notre mort*, published by Pavois.
369 See also Pierre Broué and Raymond Vacheron, *Meurtres au Maquis*, Grasset, Paris, 1997 – DB
370 *La Vérité*, 20 November 1943, 'La libération de Puy-en-Velay'.
371 Here Demazière refers to himself in the third person, using the alias 'Granet' – DB
372 Groupes mobiles de réserve, military police units created by the Vichy régime – DB
373 From *Blasco*: Massat was removed from the PCF Central Committee after revelations about the death of Tresso (alias Blasco) in the Italian Communist Party organ *Rinascita* in 1964. This was perhaps not pure coincidence. Demazière refers to the presence in Queyrrière of another PCF organiser, Jean Burles, who had also escaped from Puy and was later a Central Committee member. When Demazière met him twenty-five years later, Burles claimed never to have heard of Blasco.
374 A. Azzaroni, P. Naville, I. Silone: *Blasco* (Azione Comune, published by Polyglotes).
375 A. Azzaroni, P. Naville, I. Silone: *Blasco* (Azione Comune, published by Polyglotes).
376 A. Azzaroni, P. Naville, I. Silone: *Blasco* (Azione Comune, published by Polyglotes).
377 'We managed to squat the offices of who-knows-what Pétainist youth organisation. The congress took place under posters of the Marshal in full dress uniform... Each delegate had a folder with the emblem of the Pétainist organisation, with false minutes inside. Everything was organised such that we could hide the real documents in case of danger.' – Yvan Craipeau, *Mémoires d'un dinosaure trotskyste*, l'Harmattan, Paris, 1999, p. 165 – DB
378 'Socialisme ou barbarie, il faut choisir'- DB
379 'Le Chemin de l'Espoir' – DB
380 'The train drivers' struggle'
381 Workers' front – DB
382 One of the few complete collections is that of *Octobre*. There are only a few extant copies of *Front ouvrier de Bretagne*, which was often quoted in *La Vérité*; only 1944 issues of the Toulouse, Pau, Albi, Castres, and Atlantic region publications; and none of the Marseille, Clermont or Lyon ones (and in 1945, the printed *Front ouvrier* replaced *Front ouvrier de Lyon*). There is no trace of the factory bulletins, only centrally-edited leaflets: as for students, there remain two 'Lettres à un ouvrier communiste' [Letters to a communist worker]; [see footnote below – DB] Quotes from various among these publications appeared here and there in *La Vérité*.

383 In the original footnote Yvan Craipeau comments that '*Der Arbeiter* is lost, and the only extant issues of *Arbeiter und Soldat* are those from 1944'. However, three issues of *Arbeiter und Soldat* from 1943 and three from 1944 are reproduced in *Fac-simile de La Vérité clandestine (1940-1944)*, (Etudes et Documentations Internationales, Paris, 1978), along with a fragment of issue two of *Der Arbeiter* (summer 1943). See English translations of these in the appendix – DB
384 *La Vérité*, issue 47, 5 July 1943. The minutes include certain deliberate errors, designed to mislead police surveillance.
385 *La Vérité*, 1 March 1943, 'Un débarquement italien… en Italie'.
386 *La Vérité*, 25 September 1943, 'La révolution italienne continue'.
387 *La Vérité*, 20 June 1943, 'Chemises noires en solde'.
388 *La Vérité*, 30 July 1943.
389 *La Vérité*, special duplicated issue produced on 30 July 1943: the printed issue written before these events was published on the same day.
390 A reference to Pisa chemicals firm, Montecatini – DB
391 A reference to Genoa-based engineering conglomerate Ansaldo, which was heavily involved in supplying machinery and infrastructure for the war effort – DB
392 According to the testimony of Roland and Yvonne Filiâtre.
393 *La Lutte de classe*, 4 August 1943.
394 *La Vérité*, 15 August 1943.
395 *La Vérité*, 15 August 1943.
396 *La Stampa*, 16 August 1943, cited in the December 1943 CCI news and media bulletin.
397 Also known as the Lipari Islands, these were home to those in forced exile during the war – DB
398 *La Vérité*, 12 September 1943. The revolutionary parties referred to by *La Vérité* were of course essentially the Socialist Party and Communist Party.
399 The 31 July 1943 resolution published in the November edition of *La Seule voie* characterised fascism as a 'Bonapartist mode of government' whose fall 'would necessarily be expressed in the Italian situation by a breakdown in the balance of class forces'. It was the fall of Mussolini which brought about a breakdown in the balance of class forces (as if this was not itself the result of such a rupture!). The intervention of the mass of the population was not taken into account, since it was not foreseen in their 'proletarian schema'.
400 Charles Tillon: *Les FTP*. The previous quote is from a footnote. The main thrust of the text seems to have been inspired by Arthur Giovani, the main PCF leader in Corsica at the time. Having become a member of the Central Committee and then the control commission, he would later espouse oppositionist positions to the left of the party.
401 *La Seule Voie*, November 1943.
402 'Appel au peuple de Corse' – DB
403 *Soldat im Westen*, issues quoted: 16, November 1942 (printed); 21, January 1943; 25, May 1943; 28, August 1943 (printed); 30, September 1943.
404 *Arbeiter und Soldat*, organ of the Bundes der Kommunisten-Internationalisten

(Deutsche Sektion der Vierte Internationale). On the masthead were printed the words 'The German revolution is the world revolution (Karl Liebknecht)', May 1944.
405 *Der Arbeiter*, organ of the German soldiers' committees, quoted in *La Vérité*, 15 October 1943.
406 *Der Arbeiter*, organ of the German soldiers' committees, quoted in *La Vérité*, 15 October 1943.
407 Warned that the Gestapo would arrive the next day, Y. Craipeau stayed overnight in another wing of the school building where he was living. After the Gestapo search he left Taverny, guided by a group of his pupils who scouted for him.
408 *La Vérité*, 15 October 1943, 'Alerte aux agents de la réaction'.
409 This volume of information on the Trotskyists was for the most part based on the police files provided by the Popular Front-era police. In terms of pre-war activism, the documentation supplied by the 'Socialists' against their former comrades was relatively accurate. But the updates since the beginning of the war were littered with errors and the police confused pseudonyms. Roland Filiâtre spoke of how the police tried to pressure him by telling him about the arrest of a comrade… but with his own pseudonym. They had separate searches underway for Francis, Auger and Craipeau, in fact all the same person.
410 *La Vérité*, 15 October 1943.
411 'The French State', official title of the state best-known as 'Vichy France'. This name was used in counterposition to the pre-war title 'La République française', which characterised the state as a 'French Republic'- DB
412 *La Vérité*, 10 December 1943, 'Vichy se prépare à faire peau neuve'.
413 Probably General de la Porte du Theil, arrested by the Nazis on 5 January 1944. A 'private' conversation alluded to in R. Aron's *Histoire de Vichy*, p. 367.
414 R. Aron, *Histoire de Vichy*, volume II (Éditions A. Fayard).
415 'Note adressée par les organes dirigeants de l'Armée secrète au commandement inter-allié' – DB
416 At the time a leading centre of steel production – DB
417 *La Vérité*, 10 December 1943: 'Ceux qui ont rasé Nantes ravitaillent l'Allemagne en essence'.
418 *La Vérité*, 15 January 1944: 'Une guerre de forbans capitalistes: Roosevelt ravitaille Hitler'.
419 *La Vérité*, 17 February 1944, 'Une guerre de forbans capitalistes: après le pétrole, les minerais'.
420 Craipeau misquotes the *La Vérité* piece and thus his figures add up to 103%. In fact the article cites Roosevelt promising that 21% of Lend-Lease aid is destined for the USSR – DB
421 Craipeau mistakenly references *La Vérité*, issue 44-45, 20 May 1943, whereas this information in fact appeared in 'Les États-unis et la guerre', *La Vérité* issue 40, 15 January 1943 – DB
422 *La Vérité*, 1 March 1943: 'De Stalingrad à Casablanca'.
423 This formulation was vehemently attacked by the CCI and *Lutte de classe*, which only quoted it in part. They saw in this the 'pro-Americanism' of

the POI. In fact it was a simple assertion: that the contradictions between imperialisms would weaken the current dominant power and allow the mass of the population to deliver it a fatal blow. Those who refuse to exploit the divisions between their opponents can never expect success: they can only gargle with revolutionist slogans. What the POI should have been criticised for was not their 'celebration' of inter-imperialist divisions and the blows struck against the Nazis, but rather their inability to take advantage of them.

424 'Perspectives and Tasks of the Coming European Revolution', *Fourth International*, volume 4, issue 11, New York, December 1943 – DB

425 Liddell Hart emphasised this point in his own words, even if he only spoke about the terms of surrender:
'All my contacts (Wehrmacht officers) protested the Allied demand for 'unconditional surrender', which, they insist, had prolonged the war. Had another line been chosen, they – and more importantly, their troops – could rapidly have switched allegiances, whether in patches or as a whole.
Illegally listening to Allied radio transmissions was increasingly commonplace, but Allied propaganda never suggested any conditions for peace which could have encouraged Germans to abandon the war effort. Their silence on this point tended to confirm the claims of Nazi propaganda: that a terrible fate awaited them if they surrendered. Thus the Germans continued fighting even long after they would have been willing to give up.'
Les Généraux allemands parlent (Éditions Stock).

426 A French nationalist doctrine, named after Charles Maurras, closely associated with the fascistic Action Française movement – DB

427 *La Vérité*, 15 January 1944: 'La paix made in USA'. The German slogans mean 'We are not Germany's enemies. We want the Socialist United States of Europe'.

428 *La Vérité*, 15 January 1944, 'Un plan esclavagiste'.

429 *La Vérité*, 15 January 1944, 'Les États-Unis et la guerre'.

430 Presented by Raptis, alias Pablo.

431 'Thèses sur la liquidation de la deuxième guerre impérialiste et la montée révolutionnaire' – DB

432 Dictatorial president of Turkey 1938-1950. Pressured by both Axis and Allies to join the war on their side, for most of the war he maintained an official stance of neutrality, similar to that of Franco in Spain and Salazar in Portugal. Ultimately he made a token declaration of war against the Axis powers on 23 February 1945 – DB

433 Capital of Lithuania, occupied by the Red Army in September 1939 after Stalin's pact with Hitler to re-divide eastern Europe – DB

434 A motion advanced by Craipeau (under the alias Francis).

435 From *Quatrième Internationale*, issue 4-5 (February 1944), as are all the quotes from the conference.

436 Quotes reproduced in *La Vérité* of 15 January 1944, earlier published in *La Voie de Lénine*, organ of the Belgian PCR, on 15 November and 15 December 1943.

437 A motion presented by Spoulber (alias Marcoux).

438 *Bulletin intérieur special* (January 1944), 'Principes d'organisation du PCI'.
439 In 1936, in spite of Trotsky's opposition and his diatribes against this supposed 'principle', the official Bolshevik-Leninist organisation had accepted parity on the leadership with the *La Commune* group in order to achieve unification. However, this was tempered by the presence of a delegate from the youth, who thus had the casting vote.
440 *Les problèmes de la construction de la IVe Internationale*, a *Lutte ouvrière* pamphlet (1969). It cited the two preceding quotes without references.
441 *Les problèmes de la construction de la IVe Internationale*, a *Lutte ouvrière* pamphlet (1969).
442 *Bulletin intérieur du POI*, no. 20, quoted in an article by the Lyon branch in the *Bulletin intérieur du PCI*, no. 3.
443 *Bulletin intérieur du POI* and *Bulletin intérieur du PCI*, no. 1. The ideas of the POI minority were developed in a text written in February, 'La Question nationale pierre de touche de la politique révolutionnaire', which was published in the *Bulletin intérieur du PCI* no. 7, October 1944.
444 'La Question nationale pierre de touche de la politique révolutionnaire', published in the *Bulletin intérieur du PCI* no. 7, October 1944.
445 As reported by the minority in *le Bulletin intérieur*, no. 1. In their reply the CCI majority did not deny this.
446 A former activist in the JCR (the *La Commune* group), Lambert worked in the ranks of the CCI throughout the war. He was expelled for his 'irresponsible attitude, paralysing the work of the organisation and tending to disrupt it through his constant attacks on its rules of functioning and the basis on which it was constituted' (*Bulletin intérieur* no. 9). He would go onto be a member of the Central Committee after the first congress [...].
447 Pierre Lambert, real name Pierre Boussel, later became one among the most prominent figures of French Trotskyism. The PCI split in 1952, and Lambert soon became a leading member of another organisation, also called the PCI. This was part of the International Committee of the Fourth International, whose British section until 1971 was Gerry Healy's Socialist Labour League. Lambert's group went through a series of name changes: from 1965 the Organisation communiste internationaliste; from 1981 PCI again; in 1984 it launched a supposedly broader Mouvement pour un Parti des Travailleurs, which became the Parti des Travailleurs in 1991. He died in 2008 – DB
448 *Bulletin intérieur du PCI*, no. 1: 'Mise au point sur la declaration de l'ex-groupe *Octobre*' (a minority in the PCI).
449 *Bulletin intérieur* no. 2, May 1944: 'La revolution mondiale, en France, et les tâches du PCI'.
450 *La Vérité*, issue 58, 10 February 1944.
451 *Bulletin intérieur du PCI*, no. 1.
452 *La Vérité*, new series issue 1, 25 March 1944.
453 I.e. the Vichy régime – DB
454 *Bulletin intérieur*, issue 6, July 1944.
455 André Marty, a PCF leader – DB
456 *Bulletin intérieur*, issue 6, July 1944.

457 *Bulletin intérieur*, issue 3, June 1944.
458 *Bulletin intérieur*, issue 6, July 1944.
459 *La Vérité*, special issue 1 May 1944.
460 *La Vérité*, new series issue 2, 29 April 1944.
461 Quoted in *La Vérité*, issue 2.
462 De Gaulle, *Mémoires de guerre*, volume 2: also the source of the following quotations.
463 Charles Tillon, *Les FTP*.
464 *La Vérité*, new series issue 2, 29 April 1944.
465 Charles Tillon, *Les FTP*.
466 De Gaulle, *Mémoires de guerre*, volume 2.
467 A short-lived 'Free Republic of Vercors' was established by maquis in June 1944, but it was heavily repressed by the Germans – DB
468 Charles Tillon, *Les FTP*.
469 A reference to the bourgeois parliamentary government established at Versailles in 1870 after France's military defeat by Prussia and the subsequent armistice. The Paris Commune was established by the city's population to establish a new socialist order and continue the war effort; in May 1871 the Versaillais forces invaded the capital and crushed the revolution, killing 20,000 people – DB
470 I.e. the revolutionaries of 1871 – DB.
471 Georges Guingouin was a Communist and head of the Limousin maquis, leading the liberation of Limoges and the surrounding region. He was imprisoned 1953-59 after evidence came to light of summary executions and extortion rackets under his watch in the immediate aftermath of Liberation – DB
472 Bureau central de renseignements et d'action (Central Bureau of Intelligence and Operations), an intelligence service established by the Free French high command in 1940 – DB
473 *La Vérité* issue 65, 26 May 1944, 'La bourgeoisie prépare la guerre civile, formons nos milices ouvrières', by Yvan Craipeau.
474 The Parti social français, led by François de la Rocque, was a conservative party which represented the more moderate parliamentary successor organisation to the far-right Croix de Feu paramilitary group. It enjoyed substantial electoral success and by the outbreak of war it had more members than any other party in France, totalling some 700,000 people. In 1940 the party was renamed Progrès social français, but it soon fell into disarray. The party offered cautious support to the Resistance, for instance giving information to the British Secret Intelligence Service. However, de la Rocque did not recognise De Gaulle's authority over France and persisted in trying to persuade his friend Marshal Pétain to break with the Nazis, holding three meetings with him to discuss his proposals in 1943 – DB
475 A conspiratorial far-right group, 'La Cagoule' (the cowl), officially known as the Comité secret d'action révolutionnaire, which split between supporting Vichy and the Resistance – DB
476 On 25 July, at the Assemblée Consultative in Algiers, Marty gave further

details. 'For example, is it not the case that in France, in a certain département in the centre-west, there is a man who describes himself as the military chief of the Comité des Forges? Has this man not for several months declared that his "secret army" – it was indeed l'Armée secrete – had as its essential goal "maintaining order at the moment of Liberation": a fascist order, the order of Pucheu and of Darnan? He even told anyone who would listen about the number of automatic machine-guns that he had at his disposal: these came from the pre-armistice army, and naturally they would not be used against the Germans'. (*Cahiers du Communisme*, May-June 1946).

477 André Calves was forced to leave Brest after the repression of the *Arbeiter und Soldat* group, and joined the FTP. He comments on the debate among the Trotskyists (*Sans bottes ni médailles, un trotskyste breton dans la guerre*, Éditions La Breche, Paris, 1984 p. 85):
'Because of my FTP activity I could no longer be organised in a PCI cell. I was in contact with Craipeau. In my eyes, we needed to insert militants into the Paris FTP. There were several reasons for this. First of all, it was a valuable milieu, almost entirely young workers. Moreover, although its general orientation was chauvinist, "union sacrée", etc., we had to take account of something very important: the need for a very tight clandestinity meant that a group's organiser could politically influence their comrades without having to fear intervention by a [PCF] thug.
'Finally, the test for becoming a group's organiser was not close alignment with the [PCF's] positions, but rather initiative, pluck, likeability, the capacity to earn the FTP's trust. Any PCI militant could compete with a Stalinist on this terrain. It even seemed to me that a stifled bureaucrat would lose out on this score.
'And then? I don't know.
'Craipeau was not at all against it, nor other PCI organisers. They only objected [by referring to] our weakness and the fact that those who could be doing good work in the FTP were already active in the factories. This was true.
'However, I have often thought about this affair since. A better implantation in the FTP would without doubt have facilitated our workplace activism. The FTP held rallies in some workplaces in the [Paris] suburbs. Work stopped and workers gathered round. The more dubious managers were taken out. Without doubt their speeches had a certain influence. If a Trotskyist FTP had done this in a factory where comrades were active, that would have been no small thing' – DB
478 The Boeing B-17 Flying Fortress, an American bomber plane – DB
479 Groupes mobiles de réserve, military police units created by the Vichy régime – DB
480 *Bulletin intérieur special*, July 1944.
481 *Bulletin intérieur*, issue 3, July 1944.
482 *Bulletin intérieur*, issue 3, July 1944.
483 Jacqueline Pluet-Despatin remarks that, whereas in 1942-43 the POI had stressed the importance of French workers going to Germany spreading an internationalist message as 'the representatives of the June 1936 [general

strike]', at the time of the January 1944 draft it instead focused on boycotts and a general strike against deportations. This was also seen as an act of solidarity with the USSR, given that Hitler needed to bring 1 million European workers to Germany to replace conscripts being sent to the Eastern Front. See *Les trotskistes et la guerre 1940-1944*, p. 187 – DB

484 *La Vérité* issue 67, 22 June 1944.
485 The bread ration fell to 150 grams per person per day – DB
486 Charles Tillon, *Les FTP*.
487 *Bulletin intérieur*, July 1944, 'Résolution du Comité régional toulousain'.
488 *La Vérité*, issue 67, 22 June 1944.
489 An engineering contractor under the Third Reich, notorious for its mass use of forced labour. It was founded in 1938 by Fritz Todt, as an amalgamation of administrative bodies and private companies he controlled and the Reich Labour Service. In 1940 Todt became Minister of Armaments and Munitions, and the organisation took charge of building the Atlantic Wall defences as well as concentration camps and other military infrastructure. However, in 1942 Todt died in a plane crash, and was replaced in office by Albert Speer, who expanded the Organisation Todt's activities and merged it into the ministry itself. By late 1944 it employed as many as 1.4 million workers, mostly conscripted labourers from occupied countries. They were treated like slaves and many did not survive the war – DB
490 *La lutte* was the Vietnamese Trotskyist organisation, and Ta Thu Thau its main leader. In 1945 he was murdered by the Stalinist Viet Minh led by Ho Chi Minh, which crushed the short-lived Saigon Commune revolutionary uprising – DB
491 *La Vérité*, issue 68, 1 July 1944, 'Les travailleurs coloniaux en lutte'.
492 Charles Tillon, *Les FTP*.
493 A paramilitary nationalist organisation – DB
494 Erich Ludendorff was leading organiser of the German war effort from August 1916 to October 1918. In April 1917 Bolshevik émigrés resident in Switzerland including Lenin accepted German help in returning to Russia, and furthermore faced hotly-contested accusations of being funded by the German high command to stir revolution in Russia and thus ensure its military collapse – DB
495 Franz von Papen, a conservative Chancellor of Germany June-November 1932. Failing to maintain consistent support in the Reichstag, he agreed to cede power to Hitler and instead assume the role of Vice Chancellor. Warned that Hitler was exploiting him, von Papen replied 'You're wrong – we've hired him', believing he could tame the Nazis by bringing their leader into the heart of government. However, von Papen was himself soon marginalised as Hitler assumed full power, which he did nothing to resist – DB
496 The daily newspaper of the Nazi Party – DB
497 Ernest Bevin, the British trade union leader, wartime Minister of Labour and Foreign Secretary in the 1945 Labour government – DB
498 Gustav Noske (Defence Minister 1919-20) and Philipp Scheidemann (Chancellor, February-June 1919) were Social Democrat leaders in the early

Weimar Republic. They were notorious for having used the far-right Freikorps militia and the army to crush the January 1919 communist uprising: Noske personally authorised the murder of revolutionary leaders Rosa Luxemburg and Karl Liebknecht – DB

499 The Junkers were the conservative and militaristic landed nobility in Prussia and eastern Germany – DB

INDEX

The following protagonists of *Contre vents et marées* are omitted from this index as they are mentioned on most pages: *Hitler, Adolf; Stalin, Joseph; Vichy régime; Parti ouvrier internationaliste (POI); Parti communiste français (PCF)*

Abetz, Otto 102, 357
Algiers government 169, 191-3, 212, 215, 239, 248-49, 258, 261, 275, 277-80, 285, 290, 366
Anarchists 18, 23, 34, 43, 50, 54, 57-59, 62, 91, 132, 303, 305
Anti-Semitism 91, 107, 119, 152, 183, 184, 195, 349, 356
Arbeiter und Soldat 142-43, 228, 242-43, 246, 293-340

Badoglio, Pietro 233-36, 239, 254, 274
Barta *see* Korner, David
Beaufrère, Marcel ('Armand') 64, 75, 90-92, 108-9, 224, 246, 353, 357, 367
Blasco *see* Tresso, Pietro
Bleibtreu, Marcel 20, 108, 354, 361, 367
Blum, Léon 12-13, 17, 32-33, 36-39, 46, 56, 62, 67-71, 73, 78, 89, 119, 121-123, 187, 271, 274, 367
Bodenez, Yves 26, 246
Bordiga, Amadeo 10, 34, 347
Bourhis, Marc 26, 75, 150
Brinon, Fernand de 84, 352
Buchholz, Mathieu 16, 26, 157, 158
Buchenwald 224, 356, 368
Bureaucratic collectivism 19, 89, 116, 346

Cachin, Marcel 9, 56, 71, 343
Cagoulards/*La Cagoule* 120-21, 280, 375
Calves, André 360, 361, 363, 376
Centre d'action socialiste (CSA) 121, 191

Centre d'action syndicale contre la guerre (CASCG) 43
Centre laïque des auberges de la jeunesse (CLAJ) 90-91, 98
Ceux de la Résistance 191
Chauvin, Jean-René 246, 345, 357, 368
Chamberlain, Neville 38, 43, 69, 70, 348-49
Churchill, Winston 7, 80, 118, 141, 160, 164, 206, 212, 218, 232, 241, 252, 254, 307, 322, 330, 335, 338, 348, 358
Claude, Henri 179, 259, 265
Collinet, Michel 45-47, 110, 349
Colonialism 7, 12, 35, 49, 83, 100, 111, 127-28, 131, 152, 166, 241, 254, 263, 273, 276, 277, 289, 313, 315, 343, 345, 352, 366
Combat 120, 128, 129, 170
Comintern (Communist/Third International) 9-11, 16, 28, 34, 44, 71, 79, 113, 152, 173, 183, 185, 218-221, 228, 276, 296, 299-301, 319, 332, 331, 335, 343, 345.
Comité communiste internationaliste (CCI) 19, 20, 152, 155, 179-83, 208, 217, 227, 230, 237, 242, 252, 259, 264, 265, 267-271, 285, 363, 365, 366, 372, 374
Comités pour la quatrième internationale 60, 73, 79, 90, 92, 106, 114, 159, 350
Confédération générale du travail (CGT) 12, 38, 50-52, 72, 73, 79, 82, 99, 121-22, 158, 167, 273, 287, 290

Conscription *and* draft resistance 149, 158, 203, 207-15, 231, 263-64, 273, 281, 285, 354, 361-62, 377
Conseil national de la résistance (CNR) 193, 194, 275, 367
Corsica, liberation of 173, 238-40, 275, 371
Croix de Feu 12, 120, 123, 362, 375
Croquefruit 108, 357
Cruau, Robert 246, 360
Craipeau, Maria 345, 351
Craipeau, Yvan 17-21, 40, 59-60, 76, 90, 92, 125, 155, 211, 215, 227, 246-47, 249, 259, 265, 268-71, 281, 345, 346, 347, 348, 351, 353, 367, 372, 373, 376

Daladier, Edouard 12, 14, 28, 37, 38, 39, 43, 46, 50, 57, 69, 70, 76, 78, 126
Darlan, François 165, 169, 170, 190-91, 254, 367
Darnand, Joseph 173, 195, 196, 215, 282, 287
D Day (Operation Overlord) 135, 252, 253, 257, 261, 264, 271, 285, 327
Déat, Marcel 32, 86, 107, 147, 210
De Gaulle, Charles 7, 85-86, 88, 95, 105, 111, 118, 119-28, 135, 144, 166, 170, 190-93, 210, 213, 239-40, 248-49, 254, 274-78, 280, 282, 286, 291, 335, 345, 367, 375
Demazière, Albert ('Granet') 20, 109, 151-52, 222-26, 247, 357, 370
Deportations 8, 30, 126, 147-51, 169, 173-74, 201-7, 209, 211-12, 216, 223, 246, 256, 262-64, 267, 273, 287, 304, 312, 356, 357, 361, 362, 377
Déroulède, Paul 57, 128, 129, 187, 349
Der Arbeiter 143, 228, 244-46, 294-95, 341-42, 361, 371
Doriot, Jacques 86, 91, 107, 190, 353
Duclos, Jacques 83, 85, 131, 132, 134, 280

Eisenhower, Dwight 282, 286-87, 328-30, 334

Ercoli *see* Togliatti, Palmiro
Essel, André ('Lessart') 247, 266, 285, 345, 354, 357

Factory occupations 13, 169, 210, 281, 286, 302, 368
Filiâtre, Roland 20, 74, 143, 224, 227, 246, 247, 345, 348, 357, 372
First World War 7, 8, 10, 23, 25, 28, 45, 68, 72, 153, 173, 294, 297, 298, 313, 319, 325, 344, 347
Fourth International 19-20, 25, 36, 40, 42, 48, 60, 63, 75, 77, 93-96, 113, 137, 142, 150-57, 160-63, 175, 177, 179-81, 186, 215, 220-21, 224, 229-30, 233, 238, 245, 259-67, 270-71, 289, 295, 301, 310, 318, 322, 324, 331, 341, 342, 345, 353, 354, 363
Francs-tireurs et partisans (FTP) 129-33, 138, 186, 210, 213-14, 218, 227, 245, 278, 280, 285, 376
Frank, Pierre 14, 17, 18, 20, 37, 40, 64, 230
Fraternisation prolétarienne 181, 366
Freemasons 9, 42, 49, 87, 190, 280, 353, 364
Front national (PCF-led partisan force) 126-29, 174, 191, 238-41, 275, 280, 361
Front ouvrier 228, 272-73, 370
Front ouvrier international (FOI) 48, 62, 63, 85, 155, 168, 190
Frossard, Ludovic-Oscar 9-10

Gibelin, Marcel 75, 90, 92, 227, 259, 265, 344, 351
Giraud, Henri 191-93, 210, 239, 249, 254, 275, 367
Goebbels, Joseph 136, 163, 206, 296, 297, 301, 306, 311, 314, 316, 328, 329, 334
Goering, Hermann 197, 296, 306, 309, 328, 334, 340
Granet *see* Demazière, Albert
Grenier, Fernand 128, 191, 223, 274, 276, 277

Gueguen, Pierre 26, 75, 150
Guérin, Daniel 38-39, 42-44, 48, 59-60, 62-63, 85, 157

Heijenoort, Jean van 152, 365
Hic, Marcel 20, 26, 89, 90, 92, 109, 136, 147, 155, 156, 175, 194, 227, 246, 253, 254, 357
Himmler, Heinrich 297, 333, 340

Jaquier, Maurice 59, 61-63, 78, 87, 88, 350, 353
Jeunesse d'Octobre 179, 366
Jouhaux, Léon 46, 52, 73, 99, 121

Kilian, Claude 193, 194, 367
Klement, Rudolf 16, 65, 102
Kommunistische Partei Deutschlands (KPD) 35, 140, 224, 306, 353-54
Korner, David ('Barta') 95-96, 113, 156-59, 348, 350, 355
Kunstlinger, Henri 26, 60, 345, 349

La Commune 17, 27, 40, 64, 80, 155, 159, 176, 269, 349, 351, 374
La Lutte de classe 118, 158, 181-82, 218-21, 234, 254, 346
Lambert, Pierre 268, 270, 374
Laroche 142, 156-57, 360
La Seule Voie 159-62, 175-76, 181
Laval, Pierre 12, 29, 33, 84, 91, 139, 147, 173, 195-96, 203-4, 211-12, 249-50, 258, 286, 344, 361-62
La Voie de Lénine 43, 60, 64, 350
Lenin, Vladimir 9, 11, 23-24, 30, 35, 45, 68, 115, 131, 132, 141, 161-62, 168, 182, 188, 194, 218-20, 266, 298, 300, 301, 305, 313, 315-16, 319, 332, 342, 347, 363, 366, 377
Le Soviet (CCI) 176, 200, 202, 204, 242
Lessart *see* Essel, André
L'Étincelle (Trotskyist group) 75, 76, 89-90, 92-93, 95
L'Humanité 9, 12, 13, 28, 31, 55, 56, 66, 73, 79-80, 82-85, 91-92, 101-105, 112, 126-28, 138, 251, 280, 287, 351-52

Libération 121-23, 151, 170, 186, 191, 206, 251
Libérer-Féderer 190
Libertés 110, 120, 163-65, 348
Liebknecht, Karl 35, 45, 168, 228, 301, 316, 319, 337, 352, 372, 378
Ligue communiste de France 15, 16, 18, 150, 230, 349
L'Insurgé 88, 110, 166-171, 186-190, 193, 217-18, 366, 367
Luxemburg, Rosa 34, 45-47, 60, 168, 301, 352, 378

Main d'oeuvre immigrée (MOI) 131, 132, 138, 140
Maquis 92, 130, 170, 173, 207-18, 225-27, 249, 278-81, 290-91, 333, 345, 361, 375
Marx, Karl 15, 66, 111-12, 130, 131, 168, 301, 315
Marcoux *see* Spoulber, Nicholas
Marseille general strike 7, 287-289
Martinet, Gilles 186-90, 366
Marty, André 67-68, 271, 275, 374, 375
Meichler, Jean ('Meiche') 109, 149-50, 163, 363
Milice 121, 195-96, 211, 280, 282, 283, 287, 290, 357
Molinier, Henri ('Marc Laurent') 26, 194, 271, 366
Molinier, Raymond 14, 17, 18, 37, 40, 49, 64, 349
Molotov-Ribbentrop Pact *see* Nazi-Soviet Pact
Monatte, Pierre 9, 343
Moulin, Jean 121, 193-94
Mouvement national révolutionnaire (MNR) 87-89, 111, 118, 353
Mouvement ouvrier français (MOF) 144, 186
Munich Agreement 14, 29, 31-33, 38, 43, 50, 80, 344, 348, 349
Mussolini, Benito 8, 15, 32, 46, 69, 79, 86, 96, 101, 185, 231-7, 241, 257, 274, 309-10, 371

Naville, Pierre 14, 17, 18, 344, 348
Nazi-Soviet Pact 14, 24, 29, 55-59, 66, 72, 75, 114, 118, 140, 150, 167, 182, 221, 345, 347, 352, 373
Nicolitch, Suzanne 49, 60, 87, 166, 353
Nos combats 110, 163-64, 364
Notre révolution 109-12, 163-66, 363

Octobre group 230, 259, 265, 268-69

Pablo, Michel (Michalis Raptis) 155, 227, 259, 265, 373
Paris Commune (1871) 112, 209, 248, 249, 278, 280, 281, 344, 358, 375
Parisot, Paul 90, 215, 247, 268, 353, 357
Parti communiste internationaliste (1944-52; PCI) 17, 20-21, 108, 194, 265-66, 269, 272, 273, 285, 288, 291, 353, 357, 361, 367, 374, 376
Parti socialiste *see* Section française de l'international ouvrière
Parti socialiste ouvrier et paysan (PSOP) 19-20, 38-50, 59-64, 74, 75, 77, 85-89, 109, 110, 166, 167, 348, 349, 350, 353
Partito comunista italiano (PCI) 10, 224, 227, 237, 274, 370
Pétain, Philippe 7, 32, 78, 80-81, 82, 84, 88, 92, 94, 95, 104, 111, 119, 120, 121, 127, 130, 152, 162, 165, 174, 190, 191, 193, 196, 248-50, 254, 258, 278, 280, 282, 349, 350, 352, 354, 367, 375
Philip, André 122, 125-26, 192, 193,
Pivert, Marceau 19, 35-36, 38-39, 41, 45, 47, 49, 59, 62, 63, 75, 85-86, 88, 166, 190, 349, 353
Popular Front government (1936-38) 13-17, 30-32, 36-40, 64-66, 82, 127, 187-88, 192, 277, 300, 302, 344, 353, 372
Prager, Rodolphe 259, 265, 269, 351
Pucheu, Pierre 119-21, 150, 165, 169, 190, 280, 376

Radek, Karl 90, 353-54
Raptis *see* Pablo, Michel

Reboul, Jean 151, 224-27
Revolutionärer Kommunisten Deutschlands (RKD) 34, 156, 162, 181
Revolutionary defeatism 23, 24, 35, 36, 41, 44-48, 67-69, 314, 366
Reynaud, Paul 78-80, 126, 334
Rigaudias, Louis ('Rigal') 40, 64, 92, 106, 154, 348, 353, 357
Rizzi, Bruno 19, 89, 346
Roosevelt, Franklin Delano 7, 87, 96, 118, 141, 160, 166, 182, 184, 190, 218, 219, 252-54, 283, 296, 300, 307, 322, 330, 335, 338, 346, 355, 364, 372
Rosmer, Alfred 9, 14, 23, 343, 345
Rous, Jean 18, 40, 44, 47, 59, 74, 87, 89, 348, 353
Rousset, David 21, 64, 107, 224, 227, 231, 246, 248, 353, 357, 367

Sadek, Abraham 26, 109, 151, 224-27
Salini, Paul *see* Ségal, Maurice
Sartre, Jean-Paul 21, 193
Sauckel, Fritz 147
Schmidt, Lucien ('Séverin') 40, 64, 98, 272, 353
Section française de l'international ouvrière (SFIO) 9-20, 30, 32, 34-39, 50, 52, 56-57, 63, 70-72, 78, 80, 82, 88, 121-22, 125, 190, 191, 221, 255, 291, 343, 344, 349, 353
Sedov, Leon 16, 65, 102
Ségal, Maurice (Pierre Salini) 152, 222-27
Service du Travail Obligatoire (STO) 124, 147, 173, 207-9,
Sneevliet, Henk 48, 155, 356-57
Social fascism *see* Third Period Stalinism
Socialist Workers' Party (SWP USA) 151, 153, 253, 354, 365
Soldat im Westen 138-39, 240-42
Souvarine, Boris 9, 14-15, 346
Souzin, Henri 26, 90, 92, 100, 148, 151, 351, 357
Spanish Civil War 13-14, 16, 29, 31-33,

37-39, 55, 46, 79-80, 103, 116, 132, 211, 298, 300, 302
Spoulber, Nicolas ('Marcoux') 60, 75, 247, 259, 265, 268, 269, 357, 373
Stève (Isaac Bloushtein) 40, 64,
Swann (Emile Guikovary) 108, 141, 155, 227, 266-67, 357

Terrorism as partisan tactic 131-37, 174, 202, 247, 315, 323
Third International *see* Comintern
Third Period Stalinism 11-12, 27, 30, 306, 320
Thorez, Maurice 10, 12-14, 31, 38, 71, 79, 82, 85, 127, 276-77,
'Three Theses' 152, 363
Tillon, Charles 85, 102, 128-30, 132, 138, 208, 213, 238-40, 278-79, 287, 290, 291, 353, 363, 371
Tito, Josip Broz 116, 137, 173, 213, 216, 237, 360, 369
Todt organisation 289, 377
Togliatti, Palmiro ('Ercoli') 224-25, 274, 277
Treint, Albert 10, 15
Tresso, Pietro ('Blasco') 16, 26, 151-52, 223-27, 345, 370
Trotsky, Leon 9, 11, 15-19, 28, 30, 35-36, 40-42, 45, 47, 49, 65, 69, 74, 75, 77, 93, 101-2, 117, 152, 161, 184, 224, 256, 294, 301, 305, 319, 332, 343-46, 349, 353-55, 372
Trotsky, Nathalia 152

Union communiste 20, 34, 53, 64, 157, 345-46; *see also La lutte de classe*
Union des communistes internationalistes 156, 181, 363
Union sacrée 23-26, 30-35, 39, 41, 43, 46, 49, 52-53, 56-58, 66-70, 72-73, 76, 82, 95, 173, 183, 186-193, 209, 211, 213, 217-18, 236, 238, 240, 263, 270, 274, 276-77, 279, 342, 376

Vietnam 100-1, 109, 154, 289, 343, 355, 360, 377
Voix ouvrière 157, 346, 363

Weitz, Lucien 47, 59-60, 87
Widelin, Paul ('Victor') 142, 143, 155, 259, 294
World War I *see* First World War

Youth Hostels *see* Centre laïque des auberges de la jeunesse

Zeller, Fred 18, 87, 89, 347, 351, 353
Zyromski, Jean 32, 33, 35, 46, 70, 73

x